Build It with Nitrogen

The Fast-Off-the-Block
Erlang Web Framework

Lloyd R. Prentice
&
Jesse Gumm

Praise

This book is exactly what I wish existed when I started with Nitrogen and Erlang for the web. Takes you by the hand and explains Erlang, Nitrogen, databases and much more. Everything comes together to make your own fast dynamic web site. Erlang and the web are a match made in heaven.

Marc Worrell, creator, Zotonic CMS

...love it. "Love it" is probably an understatement.

Francesco Cesarini, Erlang Solutions

Nitrogen simplifies development of web applications, making simple things easy and difficult things manageable. This book does the same. Projects present Nitrogen concepts and features in an iterative workflow that matches the way developers work. Developers will appreciate its many examples, its streamlined presentation, and numerous references to related material.

Steve Vinoski, Yaws maintainer

...a delightful and informative book that delivers the promise of the real-time web, combining colorful examples with battle-tested Erlang technology.

Evan Miller, creator Chicago Boss

An endless stream of real-world code samples on how to develop solid Erlang web applications with the Nitrogen framework. A real pleasure to read.

Frank Müller, Erlang programmer

I felt like the hero in an adventure story joining the characters and facing the challenges as a team. The fact that I learned about Nitrogen and web security was almost an after thought. I even learned how to extend Nitrogen with plugins! Serious learning wrapped in a fresh, fun package that kept me reading to the end.
Alain O'Dea, Infrastructure and Security Manager, Sequence Bio

...goes into great detail about Nitrogen and Erlang/OTP. Examples are simple yet functional with fictional dialogues bringing humor along the way. Nitrogen seems to be good for writing highly interactive Web applications entirely controlled from the server-side.
Loïc Hoguin, creator Cowboy webserver

Very fun book. Too many programming books are dry. Yours is just a joy to read.
Alex Popov Jr.

ISBN: 978-0-9825892-4-3

Cover design: Joseph DePinho, DePinho Graphic Design

Printed in the United States of America.

WRITERS GLEN
PUBLICATIONS

Marshfield, Massachusetts

To Laurie, love of my life.

−Lloyd

To Jackie, my best half,
and to the memory of Paul Soik,
who cultivated me as a young programmer.

−Jesse

To Rusty Klophaus,
the late, great Joe Armstrong,
and other giants of Open Source.

−LRP & JG

Forward

In the name of productivity, programmers will spend hours speeding up a five-minute task.[1]

Nitrogen is no exception. It began as a tool to speed up the development of a web application for a startup I envisioned back in 2008, and I spent a foolish amount of time building it. Happily, my efforts to blur the lines between front-end and back-end web development in Erlang resonated with others, and the framework quickly became more interesting than the startup. Soon, I shifted 100% of my focus to building Nitrogen, unsure of where that would lead.

My efforts proved fruitful. Nitrogen found a place in the toolboxes of other developers, and opened some great personal and professional doors for me, as well as gave me front row seats to the Erlang community during the the beginning of it's renaissance—I was fortunate to attend conferences and have conversations with Erlang heavyweights like Francesco Cesarini, Richard Carlsson, Ulf Wiger, Mickaël Rémond, and the late, great, great, great Joe Armstrong.

On a side note, that experience burned a crucial professional lesson into my head: "follow the traction."

During those early years as Nitrogen took shape, I received feedback and pull requests from countless generous developers, including both Lloyd Prentice in April 2009 and Jesse Gumm in June 2009. The Erlang community is notoriously positive, and each interaction helped push Nitrogen in a better direction.

Eventually, my work on Nitrogen came to an end. In June 2011, I reached out to Jesse asking if he would take over as the Nitrogen project lead. That was my first time handing off ownership of an open source project and, I imagine, Jesse's first time accepting ownership of one. Neither of us had any clue of The Right Way to do what we were doing. But luckily, Jesse agreed to sign up for

---

[1]Case in point: https://xkcd.com/1319/

this adventure. On a side note, Jesse was by then hard at work building his startup BracketPal.com. If you want something done, ask a busy person.

As of September 2019, Jesse has guided the Nitrogen project longer than I have, and has been the model of an open source project leader. He has corralled contributors, issued regular releases to stay current with the latest best practices, and maintained an active user base, all while following the convention of the existing code as much as possible and generously deflecting credit toward wherever it is most deserved, whether that is to me or other contributors.

This book is the next step in Jesse's journey as project lead, and Nitrogen's journey as a web development framework. Jesse and Lloyd have teamed up to put together a real treasure of a guide—something informative, practical, and entertaining.

This book is ambitious. It covers not only Nitrogen and Erlang, but also a bit of OTP, databases, git, web design, and software engineering best practices. And somehow, it does this well by building up from simple concepts in a sort of "Socratic dialogue"—if Socrates had a "California surfer" sense of humor.

Most importantly, the lessons in the book are the result of real experience running Nitrogen in a real production environment. Jesse's startup, BracketPal.com, was built on Nitrogen and was recently acquired by SportsEngine, an NBC company. In that light, the book addresses tech-debt and trade-offs clearly and carefully.

When I began hacking on Nitrogen I hoped for nothing beyond scratching my own development itch. Now I have the joy of reading a book about technology that I helped create, and the pleasure of learning a thing or two in the process. I hope you enjoy reading this book as much as I have, and I hope that learning about Nitrogen sparks in you the desire to build something great.

Rusty Klophaus
Creator of Nitrogen
rusty.io

Authors Note

A big question popped to mind when we decided to write this book. How much can we assume about you?

Here's what we came up with:

- You are comfortable with the Unix/GNU Linux command line.

- You have experience building websites; understand HTML and CSS.

- We don't assume that you know Erlang, but the more you know the better. We'll point the way and suggest learning resources. We have faith that you'll dig in, study hard, and pick up Erlang as you go.

- But we do assume that you have a recent version of Erlang installed on your computer. Check out Chapter 2 if not.

- Our last assumption is that you're passionate about building reliable, scalable web applications using high-productivity tools.

- Note to wizards: No condescension intended if we cover stuff you know.

This is most definitely a learn-by-doing book. You may get the gist by reading at the beach. But to truly master Nitrogen, plop this book down beside your keyboard and work your way through command by command.

LRP & JG

Contents

Contents

Before we begin

- You'll find many code listings throughout this book. Computer display is in normal type; the commands you enter are in **bold**.

- Some URLs and directory paths are too long to fit on one line. In these cases we will break them like this:

  ```
  http://docs.basho.com/riak/1.3.0/tutorials/
  installation/Installing-Erlang/
  ```

  Be sure to rejoin the two lines when you paste them into your browser or use them in code.

- We assume that you are editing code with Vim but, of course, any competent text editor will do the job. That's why we occasionally use ZZ at the end of an editing sequence to signify save and quit.

- You'll create many Nitrogen modules throughout this book. While we haven't done so for space reasons and to avoid annoying repetition, we strongly urge you to start each module with a comment block. Here's an example:

  ```
  %%%-------------------------------------------------
  %%% @author Lloyd R. Prentice and Jesse Gumm
  %%% @copyright 2019 Lloyd R. Prentice and Jesse Gumm
  %%% @doc Associates directory admin page
  %%% @end
  %%%-------------------------------------------------
  ```

  Erlang has a wonderful built-in documentation tool called EDoc that will pick up and pretty print this information and much more.[2]

---

[2]http://erlang.org/doc/apps/edoc/chapter.html

- In the same vein, we've omitted in-line documentation of functions and type-specs.[3] But, when you feel ready to write robust, maintainable, production-quality code, thorough documentation of functions and type-specs should be standard operating procedure.

- CAUTION: In many exercises you will have several windows open on your monitor. These might include one or more UNIX or Linux shells, an editor such as Vim, and an Erlang Shell. We've provided breadcrumbs in the header of each listing to alert you as to which window or terminal you'll be working in or starting in: ($\Rightarrow$ \$) denotes a UNIX shell; ($\Rightarrow$ vim) denotes Vim[4] or other editor[5] of your choice; and ($\Rightarrow$ >) denotes an Erlang shell.

- As you enter project code module by module, function by function, it'll be all too easy to skip a step or introduce typos. The more code you enter without testing, the more likely bugs will compound. The more bugs, the greater the debugging hassle and frustration you'll experience when it comes time to view your work in the browser.

- You'll learn how to compile Erlang modules and view your work in the browser in Chapters 2 and 3. Both steps are dead easy, but make a note of the sequence. You'll save time in the long run if you compile and test frequently.

- After you enter each function, we encourage you to confirm that the module you are working on will compile successfully. Some functions require dependencies. In this case compilation will fail. But the error message will clearly show what's missing and any other bugs you may have inadvertently entered.

---

[3]http://erlang.org/doc/reference_manual/users_guide.html

[4]Vim (https://www.vim.org) is the preferred editor of your authors.

[5]Other common editors are Emacs (https://www.gnu.org/software/emacs/), the most popular editor for Erlang, and Nano (https://www.nano-editor.org/), a simple, and easy-to-use editor.

0.1. New to Erlang?

Welcome!

If Erlang is *terra incognito*, prepare for a rewarding journey. But be advised. Erlang may seem strange at first. Yet, as many explorers before you have discovered, Erlang will significantly expand your programming horizons.

For fast fly-over, take time now to review Appendix A—*Erlang from top down*.

We've listed informative resources in Appendix B. Joe Armstrong's *Programming Erlang*, 2nd edition would be a high-payoff investment.

We point to invaluable web resources thrughout this book.

Here are a few tips to help you kick off on the right foot:

- You can find an overview of Erlang data types here:

  `https://erlang.org/doc/reference_manual/data_types.html`

- Erlang is a functional programming language that uses single-assignment for variables. This means that unlike procedural languages, once a variable is assigned (or "bound," in Erlang parlance), it cannot be re-assigned; e.g. `X = X + 1` is meaningless and would throw a run-time error. But never fear, single assignment has distinct advantages and poses few obstacles to fluent development.

- Variables all start with either an upper-case letter or an underscore.

- Assigned variables that are unused will throw warnings unless they start with `_`.

- `_` is called an "anonymous" variable. It never has a value assigned to it, and but matches everything. It's designed for situations where a variable is required, but its value can be ignored.

- An atom is a literal, that is, a constant with a name. An atom begins with a lower-case letter or, if it contains characters other than alphanumeric characters, underscore (`_`), or @, then it is enclosed in single quotes (`'`). e.g. `undefined`, `node@server2`, `'This is not a string'`, `'$end_of_file'`.

Contents

- Functions within the same module are called with
  `<function name>(Args)`. e.g. `get_value(Arg1, Arg2)`

- Functions from other modules are called with
  `<module name>:<function name>(Args)`. e.g. `lists:member(X, Items)`

- The number of arguments required by a function is called "arity," denoted as `<function name>/N` where `N` is the arity. Two functions with the same name but different arity are entirely different functions.

- Functions are defined in modules. The `-export` attribute exposes functions to other modules; e.g. `-export([start/0])`. The attribute `-compile(export_all)` exports all functions defined in the module.

- Finally, Erlang code is loosely structured like a series of sentences:
  - Individual instructions end with a comma (`,`)
  - Separate clauses end with a semi-colon (`;`)
  - A function ends with a period (`.`)

In our experience the Erlang community is smart, creative, gracious, and helpful. When stumped, reach out:

`https://www.erlang.org/community/mailinglists`

Part I.

Frying Pan to Fire

1. You Want Me to Build What?

BOSSMAN: Welcome to the madhouse! Glad to have you aboard.

As you see, we're a lean-and-mean outfit—more work piling up than we can handle. Clients banging at the door. *Erlingo!* they call us.

Your Friendly Webspinners.

Our language? *Erlang/OTP*.

Preferred web framework? *Nitrogen*.

Don't know either? No worry. We'll get you squared away.

Why Erlang? Our clients demand applications that handle high-traffic loads with nine nines availability.[1]

Hard to learn? Excellent resources in Appendix B. Dig in, persevere, and you'll be productive before you know it.

And why Nitrogen? Nitrogen is one of the most productive ways we've found to build full-functionality web applications. You'll be working hand-in-glove with Rusty and Jesse, our in-house Nitrogen wizards.

Stick with the dynamic duo, kid, and you'll be a wizard in no time.

Chomping at the bit are you?

Marketing needs an interactive welcome board for our corporate lobby. They're clamoring for it.

Deadline—day after tomorrow. Bet-the-company client conference coming up. Think you can deliver?

Here's Jesse, our head developer. He'll give you heads up on how we do things around this place.

---

[1] https://en.wikipedia.org/wiki/High_availability

2. Enter the Lion's Den

JESSE: Whoa! Day after tomorrow? That's harsh. But that's Bossman—no moss under that dude's feet. So we best get crackin'.

These three boxes power our trusted in-house development network. We call them Alice, Bob, and Mallory. Yes, indeed, we take security seriously. Rusty will read you in on our security practices later.

We also have a remote server—hostname Charlie. Plan to lease another—probably call it Dora.

Why all the hardware?

Erlang is explicitly designed to support distributed computing. We use the machines on this network to develop and test distributed applications and databases. Set it up on the cheap.

Alice and Mallory are old Dell Optiplex 745s running Ubuntu 18.04. Dual-core, gig of RAM. Company up the road traded up so Bossman picked these puppies up for 50 bucks apiece. Bossman likes to stay lean-and-mean. Truth—the dude's a cheapskate.

Yes, we could use Kubernetes, the cloud, or some such, instead of physical machines. But Bossman is old school. We're trying to talk him around.

Bob is a custom-built PC running Ubuntu 20.04, a six-core processor, and sixteen gigs of RAM.

I tap into the network with my personal MacBook Pro.

Fact is, you don't need all this kit to develop Nitrogen apps. You can do it on your Windows notebook at Starbucks if you're so inclined. I've heard of folks running Nitrogen on Raspberry Pi.

But we're looking toward bigger things here—reliable, industrial strength, scalable apps.

2.1. The Big Picture

Before we begin, let me paint the big picture.

Developing web applications boils down to managing a jumble of languages and network protocols.

As a web application developer your task is to convince hardware on both server and client sides to do your bidding. Problem is, the stupid machines don't speak your native tongue.

On the client side, the browser responds to HTTP/HTTPS protocols conveying digital bits cunningly structured by HTML, CSS, and JavaScript to convey natural language, sound, and images both still and moving.

The server responds to some babel of computer languages—HTTP/HTTPS, HTML, CSS, and JavaScript—to transcribe natural language, sound, and images into cunningly structured digital bits and marshal them into the web of data pipes called the Internet, where, with luck and brilliant engineering, they can reach the client's browser.

It's almost too much for the feeble human mind to encompass. The nitty gritty tedium of it all is mind numbing.

So this is where Nitrogen comes in.

Nitrogen harnesses the power of Erlang to manage all—well, most all—of the fiddly semantics and syntax of HTTP/HTTPS, HTML, CSS, and JavaScript. This means you have that much less to think about when you craft your awesome web application. In the spell of creative ferment, you can produce way-cool web apps all that much faster.

We're not saying that you don't have to understand the alphabet soup of web technologies. The deeper you understand them the better. We are saying that mastery of Erlang Nitrogen will make you far more fluent and productive.

What's the trick?

Nitrogen deploys Erlang records to structure data, Erlang functions to execute logic and embed JavaScript, and the Erlang development platform to organize and abstract server/web/browser communication.

Enough already. Let's install Nitrogen.

2.2. Install Nitrogen

Take a seat, citizen, and we'll log into Bob, show you how to compile Nitrogen.

Nitrogen is written in Erlang and JavaScript. No, you don't need to know much JavaScript. Nitrogen translates.

Erlang is already installed on Bob, of course, but if you want to install it at home, the simplest solution would be to download the "Standard" binary package from Erlang Solutions here:

`https://www.erlang-solutions.com/resources/download.html`

If you're feeling saucy, you could follow the instructions from the excellent Erlang resource, Adopting Erlang, which is a rather comprehensive guide to building on common platforms:

`https://adoptingerlang.org/docs/development/setup/`

If you really want to get into the nitty-gritty of installation and building Erlang, you can also follow official documentation, but we generally recommend this only for advanced users.

`http://erlang.org/doc/installation_guide/INSTALL.html`

Sometimes installing Erlang from source or via your system's package manager can be problematic (for example, the default `erlang` on Ubuntu is notoriously incomplete). So we recommend either downloading the "Standard" distribution from Erlang Solutions, or following the instructions from AdoptingErlang.org.

Once you have Erlang running on your system, Nitrogen is super easy to compile. Let's clone it from GitHub; make a test project called `testproj`:[1]

Listing 2.1   (⇒ $) Clone and Make

```
...$ git clone git://github.com/nitrogen/nitrogen
...$ cd nitrogen
.../nitrogen$ make rel_inets PROJECT=testproj
```

---

[1]If Git is not already installed, download it here: `https://git-scm.com/downloads`

All that text scrolling up the terminal? That's GNU make and Rebar working hard on our behalf to compile Nitrogen. You'll experience a few pauses while Erlang generates your release, so be patient.

Can you imagine entering all those terminal commands whizzing up your screen by hand? Be at it all week. That's the beauty of make—automates the build process. Indeed, it's worth getting to know your way around make.

https://www.lifewire.com/make-linux-command-unix-command-4097054

Looks like we're done:

Example 2.1 Start Nitrogen

```
...
Generated a self-contained Nitrogen project in ../testproj,
        configured to run on inets.
make[1]: Leaving directory '/home/lloyd/Erl/Eval/nitro/nitrogen'
Jesse@Bob:~/nitrogen\$
```

Note that inets refers to Erlang's built-in webserver. That's one of many things we like about Erlang—batteries included.

OK, one more step:

Listing 2.2 (⇒ $) Start console

```
/nitrogen$ cd ../testproj
/testproj$ bin/nitrogen console
...
Erlang/OTP 19 [erts-8.3.5] [source] [64-bit] [smp:3:3]
[async-threads:5] [hipe] [kernel-poll:true]
...
Eshell V8.3.5  (abort with Ĝ)
...
(testproj@127.0.0.1)1>
```

The 1> prompt tells us that we're in the Erlang shell. Much to explore here, but we'll save it for later.

Now, point your browser:

```
localhost:8000
```

As me Cockney-speaking mates would put it, Bob's your uncle! "WELCOME TO NITROGEN" in your very own browser.

Browse around while I snag us a jolt of Club-Mate.

Haven't tried it? Official drink of the Chaos Computer Club. Our Berlin consultant sent it over special.

2.3. Lay of the Land

OK, I'm baaack!

Let's cruise the directories to see what strikes our eye.

Open a new terminal. This will give us two terminals—an Erlang shell with the > prompt and a Unix shell with the $ prompt. In the Unix shell, cd down to site, and list it:

Listing 2.3 (⇒ $) **Explore site directory**

```
~$ cd testproj/site
~/testproj/site$ ls -l
...
ebin
include
src
static
templates
```

The code in the site directory built the web page displayed in our browser.

Let's look into the templates directory:

Listing 2.4 ($\Rightarrow$ \$) **Explore templates directory**

```
~/testproj/site$ cd templates
~/testproj/site/templates$ ls -l
bare.html
mobile.html
```

A peek in on bare.html will reveal a standard HTML file. We're partial to Vim around here[2], but you can develop Nitrogen applications in whatever code editor you prefer:

Listing 2.5 ($\Rightarrow$ \$) **Review default template**

```
~/testproj/site/templates$ vim bare.html
```

As you see, bare.html is loading a bunch of JavaScript files and style sheets in the head section. You've built websites, so there's nothing here that you haven't seen before.

But, in the body section, we see:

Example 2.2 Snippet of body from template

```
<body>
[[[page:body()]]]
<script> [[[script]]] </script>
</body>
```

And there, my friend, is Nitrogen's secret sauce. We'll unveil the tantalizing mysteries by-and-by.

---

[2] Most of the Erlang community prefers Emacs, but the authors are oddballs and prefer Vim. There are Vim Erlang extensions available emulate Emacs erlang-mode for autoindentation, error detection, etc. See page 17 for how to configure Emacs and Vim to work with Nitrogen source code in a friendly way.

Close out the templates directory, bop into the ebin[3] directory, and list it:

Listing 2.6 (⇒ $) **Review ebin directory**

```
~/testproj/site/templates$ cd ../ebin
~/testproj/site/ebin$ ls -l
index.beam
mobile.beam
nitrogen.app
nitrogen_app.beam
nitrogen_main_handler.beam
nitrogen_sup.beam
```

Note nitrogen.app.

App files are a very big deal in Erlang.[4] The instance in the ebin directory was automatically generated by nitrogen.app.src in the src directory. We'll get to that in a moment.

Next note all the *.beam files.

Say the greybeards, beam stands for Bogdan's Erlang Abstract Machine.[5]

Like Forth and Java, Erlang runs on a virtual machine. Erlang source compiles down to *.beam files and the *.beam files (normally just referred to as beams) execute on the Erlang virtual machine.

If it doesn't already exist, the ebin directory and all in it is created automatically when you compile Erlang source. In principle, you'll never have to look into ebin again—unless you want to confirm that your program has compiled.

With that in mind, look now into the src directory:

---

[3]With the release of Nitrogen 3 (which will use Rebar 3), this directory will actually be located deep in the _build directory. The full path would be something like _build/default/rel/APPNAME/lib/APPNAME-X.Y.Z/ebin

[4]http://erlang.org/doc/man/app.html

[5]https://en.wikipedia.org/wiki/BEAM_(Erlang_virtual_machine)

Listing 2.7 (⇒ $) Review src directory

```
~/testproj/site/ebin$ cd ../src
~/testproj/site/src$ ls -l
actions
elements
index.erl
mobile.erl
nitrogen_app.erl
nitrogen.app.src
nitrogen_main_handler.erl
nitrogen_sup.erl
~/testproj/site/src$
```

Compare the content of `nitrogen.app.src` with `nitrogen.app` in the `ebin` directory. App files provide metadata that tell the Erlang compiler where to find resources that the application needs, such as start and stop functions.

Check out Appendix A. It'll put you way down the road toward understanding how Erlang applications are structured and the secrets behind the widely touted reliability of Erlang.

Note also how the `*.erl` files in the `src` directory have doppelgängers in the `ebin` directory.

Makes sense—`*.erl` source files compile to `*.beam` files, remember?

Explore the `*.erl` files if you wish.

Squint while you eyeball the `*.erl` files. The structure and names of these files follow patterns that you'll see across nearly every Erlang OTP program you'll ever develop. Your understanding of OTP will be wide and deep when you get a handle on why this is so.

Dig in here for details:

`http://erlang.org/doc/design_principles/applications.html`

So what's the point of the `actions` and `elements` directories?

We'll dive into them when we start developing your web app for real.

But for now, look into `index.erl`:

```
~/testproj/site/src$ vim index.erl

    -module(index).
    -compile(export_all).
    ...
```

Hot diggity! Here's the code that produced the Nitrogen home page that's displayed in our browser!

But hey—time to refuel. We'll tackle the Bossman gig after lunch. But real quick before we head out, let's talk about editors.

2.4. Editors

Nitrogen officially supports Emacs and Vim and provides extensions or modules for them. Other editors are sure to work just fine, but you won't benefit from custom Nitrogen extensions.

Why custom extensions for Nitrogen? Nitrogen page modules are just Erlang modules. Good Erlang code doesn't require much nesting, which makes standard Emacs erlang-mode and its variants very useful. Erlang code formatted with erlang-mode might look something like this:

Example 2.3   **Standard Erlang indentation**

```
MyList = [
        some_list_item,
        another_item,
        holy_moly_even_more_items_wow
        ],
```

This is fine until you start writing Nitrogen code. Nitrogen elements often result in several levels of nesting due to the way Erlang records abstract HTML code.

As a result, with standard Erlang-mode, you might end up with something like this:

Example 2.4   Nitrogen with standard Erlang indentation

```
Elements = #panel { body=[
                         #span { text="Hello, World!" }
                    ]},
```

Looks bad. And that's just one level of nesting. Imagine how horrible this code will look with two or three levels of nesting.

Fortunately, we have helper code to help out. Here's how `nitrogen-mode` for Erlang formats the code:

Example 2.5   Nitrogen-recommended Indentation

```
Elements = #panel{body=[
    #span{text="Hello, World!"}
]},
```

2.4.1. Emacs

Nitrogen provides Nitrogen-mode for Emacs. You can find the installation instructions in:

`~/nitrogen/support/nitrogen-mode`.

For Nitrogen-mode to work, your page must have the following line at the top:

Example 2.6   Specifying nitrogen-mode for Emacs

```
%% -*- mode: nitrogen -*-
```

2.4.2. Vim

Vim's support for Nitrogen formatting is simple to configure.

From the base of the Nitrogen directory, run:

Listing 2.9 Installing Vim config for Nitrogen

```
...nitrogen$ make install-vim-script
```

This installs simple Vim rules into your ~./vimrc file. These prevent the auto-indenting of Vim's Erlang extensions from applying to Nitrogen files, but retain syntax highlighting and other goodies.

To apply these rules, add the following to the top of your Nitrogen pages:

Listing 2.10 Specify Vim modeline for Nitrogen

```
%% vim: ft=nitrogen
```

Mixing Erlang and Nitrogen Files

The mode lines for Vim or Emacs will serve you well on your Nitrogen page modules. But there's no need for them on non-Nitrogen Erlang modules. Best to leave them off non-Nitrogen modules.

Part II.

If You Can't Run, Dance!

3. nitroBoard I

JESSE: Specs? From Bossman? You kidding? Typical client—expects developers to be mind-readers. But no worry. We'll brainstorm.

When visitors drop into front office, what do they need to see on the Welcome Board?

Company logo. Check.

VIP welcome line? Hey, that's bodacious. Reads "Welcome!" on days when we don't expect VIP visitors—"Welcome <vip visitor>!" when a client or VIP is expected to drop in.

More than one VIP?

Good point. Matter of layout, I think.

Do we need a visitors' database?

Yeah, we do, but simple simple.

OK, what else?

Hmmm—we'll need an admin page to keep the board up-to-date.

Authentication? Nah—It'll be on a trusted network.

Say again? Boring project? Might surprise you. Certainly more instructive than "Hello World!" wouldn't you say?

Work plan?

Hey—boss is going to love you.

3.1. Kill, Baby, Kill!

Before we dive in, let's kill the Nitrogen instance displayed in your browser.

Why? It's hogging port 8000. We'll need that puppy by and by.

As you'll recall, the command bin/nitrogen console launched an Erlang shell. Turns out, it also started the inets webserver.

So what thinkest thou? Kill the shell, will we also kill Nitrogen? Let's try. Type q() at the Erlang shell prompt:

Listing 3.1 (⇒ >) Kill the server

```
...
Eshell V8.3.5 (abort with ^G)
1> q().
ok
2> jesseBob:~/testproj/site/src$
```

Promising. Now refresh your browser:

Example 3.1 Is it dead yet?

```
Unable to connect
```

Good on ya. The foul deed is done.

The q() command is one of several ways to exit from the Erlang shell. Dig into Erlang docs to discover others. Don't forget that every Erlang shell command must be terminated with a period before the command will execute.

Of course, in the event the Erlang virtual machine or shell becomes non-responsive—like say you accidentally type an infinite loop into the shell—there's always the tried-and-true, kill-it-with-fire method: CTRL+C.

Sooner rather than later you'll need to know your way around the Erlang shell. Why not start now? Make it your best friend.

```
http://www.erlang.org/doc/man/shell.html
```

3.2. Create a New Project

Before we create a new project we need to decide whether to compile a full or slim release and on which webserver. When we first installed the Nitrogen demo, we entered the following command:

```
~/nitrogen$ make rel_inets
```

Result: Erlang created a new project, configured as a full release on inets, Erlang's built-in webserver. The release included the Erlang Runtime System, known affectionately in the Erlang world as ERTS, and all else required to run the demo. Tar up a full release, ship it to another 'ix system, untar it, and it will run without the bother of installing Erlang separately.

Here's bedtime reading for fun and profit:

```
http://erlang.org/doc/man/inets.html
http://www.erlang.org/documentation/doc-5.0.1/pdf/erts-
5.0.1.pdf
```

Turns out, if Erlang is installed on the target system, you won't need to include the full ERTS in your release. In this case you can compile what's called a slim release.

We'll go for slim here.

Added bonus: Nitrogen offers a selection of webservers: Yaws, Cowboy, MochiWeb, Webmachine, and inets.[1] Since we expect nitroBoard to experience very light loads, we'll stick with inets. Also, let's call this project nb[2] for nitroBoard. Thus, we enter:

Listing 3.2 (⇒ $) **Make a new project for nitroBoard**

```
~/testproj/site/src$ cd ../nitrogen
~/nitrogen$ make slim_inets PROJECT=nb
~/nitrogen$ cd ../nb
```

---

[1]http://yaws.hyber.org/
https://github.com/ninenines/cowboy
https://github.com/mochi/mochiweb
https://github.com/Webmachine/webmachine
http://erlang.org/doc/man/inets.html
[2]Full code for nb is here: https://github.com/BuildItWithNitrogen/nitroboard1

From here on we'll morph the nitrogen demo source into nb. Anything can happen, so let's put nb under version control. Git is our version control system.

```
http://git-scm.com/
```

Ask nicely and Rusty will bring you up to speed on our Git workflow in Appendix C. When you've finished your app, you can post it on GitHub:

Listing 3.3 (⇒ $) Initialize Git

```
~/nb$ git init
Initialized empty Git repository in /home/jess/nb/.git
~/nb$ ls -al
...
bin
BuildInfo.txt
do-plugins.escript
etc
slim-release
git
lib
log
Makefile
plugins.config
rebar
rebar.config
releases
site
```

Way cool!

Much to be learned in the nb directory—in particular, the bin and site directories will play big in our life. The bin directory contains useful tools; site is where we'll find all the files we need to run our site.

For present purposes we can ignore the other directories so don't feel overwhelmed. Do note, however, the .git directory, where Git stores version records.

For now, let's bring up the demo source and morph it to our needs.

Double-check that you've closed the Nitrogen instance you were working with earlier and that no other programs are using port 8000.

Now enter:

Listing 3.4 (⇒ >) Start Nitrogen

```
~/nb$ bin/nitrogen console
...
(nb127.0.0.1)1>
```

There's ye olde Erlang shell. It should look familiar. Keep an eye on it. It will come in handy.

Now, open our new instance of Nitrogen in your browser:

`localhost:8000`

And there, in the browser, is our patient, all prepped up for cosmetic surgery.

Now, *in a new terminal*, that is, the Unix shell with the $ prompt, open up the site directory. You now have two terminals open. We'll work in the Unix shell:

Listing 3.5 (⇒ $) **Back to the site directory**

```
~/nb$ cd site
~/nb/site$ ls -l

    ebin
    include
    src
    static
    templates
```

This should also look familiar.

And so, Nurse Ratched, it's time.

Scalpel!

3.3. Prototype Welcome Page

First cut, let's say nb needs two user-facing pages:

- index—lobby display

- visitors_admin—maintain visitor appointments

The Nitrogen demo provides an index page that we can morph into our welcome board. Indeed, you're looking at it in your browser. From your working terminal bop into the src directory and open up index.erl:

Listing 3.6 (⇒ $) **Open index.erl in your editor**

```
%% -+- mode: nitrogen -*-
~/nb/site$ cd src
~/nb/site/src$ vim index.erl
```

The index.erl file is a plain vanilla Erlang module. Cast your eye on the function inner_body/0. We'll make minor changes to it in a moment. But first, shift attention back to the Erlang shell and enter the following:

Listing 3.7 (⇒ >) **Start sync:go/0**

```
(nitrogen127.0.0.1)1> sync:go().
Starting Sync (Automatic Code Compiler / Reloader)
...
ok
(nitrogen127.0.0.1)1>
```

What happened here?

The Erlang function sync:go/0[3] tracks and automatically compiles the changes you make in Erlang source files. It's pretty neat.

Let's change the function inner_body/0 in index.erl. Out of the gate, the first few lines of inner_body/0 look like this:

Example 3.2 (⇒ $) **inner_body/0**

```
inner_body() ->
    [
        #h1 { text="Welcome to Nitrogen" },
        #p{},
        "
        If you can see this page, then your Nitrogen
        server is up and running. Click the button
        below to test postbacks.
        ",
        #p{},
        #button {id=button, text="Click me!",
                postback=click},
        #p{},
        ...
```

[3]Sync is an application for automatically recompiling and loading changes to Erlang code. Originally a part of Nitrogen, it has since been split off into its own application which can be used in any Erlang application. You can find it on Github: https://github.com/rustyio/sync

3. nitroBoard I

Make the following changes:

Listing 3.8 (⇒ vim) Revise index.erl

```
inner_body() ->
    [
        #h1 { text="Welcome to Nitrogen" },
        #p{},
        "
        If you can see this page, then your Nitrogen
        server is up and running.  Click the button
        below to test postbacks.
        ",
        #h1{ text="Erlingo!  WEBSPINNERS" },
        #h1{ text="WELCOME!" },
        #h2{ text="Rusty Klophaus" },
        #h2{ text="Jesse Gumm" },
        #p{},
        #button { id=button, text="Click me!",
                  postback=click},
        #p{},
        "
        Run <b>./bin/dev help</b> to see some useful developer commands.
        ",
        #p{},
        "
        <b>Want to see the ",
        #link{text="Sample Nitrogen jQuery Mobile Page",
              url="/mobile"},"?</b>
        "

    ].
```

Save your changes, cast your eye on the Erlang shell, and behold the helpful handiwork of sync:

Example 3.3 index.erl recompiled

```
=INFO REPORT==== 17-May-2019::14:32:48 ===
/home/jesse/nb/site/src/index.erl:0: Recompiled.
=INFO REPORT==== 17-May-2019::14:32:48 ===
index: Reloaded! (Beam changed.)
```

Refresh your browser and, by gum![4] To the delight of our eyes, your changes have been compiled!

OK, we admit, this screen ain't pretty. But it gives us a canvas to work on. What's going on here?

3.4. Anatomy of a Page

In Nitrogen-speak a page is an Erlang module. It is *not* an HTML page—rather, it provides the source code for building an HTML page.

Let's examine index.erl. The first few lines are plain vanilla Erlang:

---

[4]"by gum," not to be confused with *Gumby*, which is a totally different thing.

Example 3.4   index.erl

```
%% -{*}- mode: nitrogen -*-
%% vim: ft=nitrogen

-module(index).
-compile(export_all).

-include_lib("nitrogen_core/include/wf.hrl").
```

The first two lines are comments. The first comment enables nitrogen-mode for Emacs; the second tells vim that this is a "nitrogen" filetype. Percent symbols at the beginning of the line give it away.

The next three lines are attributes signaled by hyphens at the start of the line. The first attribute, -module, with appropriate argument, is mandatory in every Erlang module. It declares the name of the module. Note that the name of the module is the same as the filename less the .erl extension. This is also mandatory in Erlang. Note also that the module attribute ends with a period, as do all Erlang attributes and functions.

The second attribute declares which functions in the module can be exported. Every function in index.erl is exported so can be called from other modules.

If we wished to export a subset of functions and keep others private, we'd use:

-export([<export1/n1>, <export2/n2>,...]).[5]

The third attribute, -include_lib, imports the wf.hrl file from nitrogen_core. The nitrogen_core library is the engine that powers Nitrogen. It's included as a library of your main application. Usually, *.hrl will import one or

---

[5]It's preferred practice in Erlang to use the attribute -export to clearly identify functions that can be exported. -compile(export_all) is convenient for development and testing, so we'll use it here. But it would be wise to replace it with -export before releasing the module for production. Indeed, using -export explicitly can clue you into dangling functions - functions that are no longer called within a module. A Nitrogen page must export main/0, but most will also export title/0, body/0, event/1, as well as any functions that must be available to postbacks or template callouts.

more record definitions. The `nitrogen_core/include/wf.hrl` file specifically includes all the built-in Nitrogen elements.

Now note that `index.erl` has five functions:

```
main/0
title/0
body/0
inner_body/0
event/1
```

Each function has the form:

```
<function name>(<function arguments>) ->
            <function body>.
```

Again, note the period at the end.

If you glance back and forth between the body of the five functions in index.erl and the copy displayed in the browser, you will gain a fair understanding of each function's purpose. The function `main/0` might trip you up. If you guessed that it's calling the template `bare.html` you'd be right on the button.

What's with this `function/X` thing we keep writing?

In Erlang we sometimes call functions by "arity;" e.g., body/0, sync:go/0, etc. Arity means "the number of arguments passed to a function." So sync:go/0 takes zero arguments. It can also be called as sync:go(). The function lists:map/2 takes two arguments. It can be called as lists:map(SomeFunction, SomeList). You can assign functions to variables with in format:

```
MyFunction = fun my_module:some_fun/3,
MyFunction(A, B, C).
```

The first phrase assigns my_module:some_fun/3 to the variable MyFunction. The second phrase demonstrates how MyFunction can then be invoked in exactly the same way as my_module:some_fun/3.

The purpose of event/1 shouldn't surprise you. It implements an action triggered by a button click, giving us a clue as to how Nitrogen implements interactive functionality.

Take away: an HTML page in Nitrogen is rendered by an HTML template that embeds an Erlang module called a Nitrogen page. Each Nitrogen page should accomplish just one task such as:

- Allow the user to log in: user_login.erl

- Change the user's preferences: user_preferences.erl

- Display a list of items: items_view.erl

- Allow the user to edit an item: items_edit.erl

So how is a Nitrogen page rendered? Here's the simple story for a typical page:

1. User hits a URL.

2. URL is mapped to a module.

3. Nitrogen framework calls module:main().

4. module:main() typically returns a #template{} element.

5. The #template{} is sent to Nitrogen's rendering engine.

6. The template includes raw HTML mixed with callouts back into the page module (in the form of [[[page:some_function()]]]).

7. Those functions return other Nitrogen elements.

8. Those elements are also run through Nitrogen's rendering engine, converting all elements into HTML and Javascript.

9. This process continues until all elements have been converted to HTML and Javascript.

10. Nitrogen sends the rendered output (HTML and Javascript) to the browser.

Woohoo! We're rockin' now.

Brief aside: See if you can find an Erlang list in `inner_body/0`. It will look like [a, b, c, ...]. What do you suppose that's about?

Lists are big business in Erlang. More here:

```
http://www.erlang.org/doc/man/lists.html
```

3.5. Anatomy of a Route

Note step two above. A URL that maps to a module is called a route. Here's how Nitrogen processes routes:

- Root page maps to `index.erl`:

```
http://localhost:8000/ -> index.erl
```

- If there's an extension, assumes a static file:

```
http://localhost:8000/routes/to/a/module
http://localhost:8000/routes/to/a/static/file.html
```

- Nitrogen replaces slashes with underscores:

```
http://localhost:8000/routes/to/a/module ->
        routes_to_a_module.erl
```

- Nitrogen tries the longest matching module:

```
http://localhost:8000/routes/to/a/module/foo/bar ->
        routes_to_a_module.erl
```

- If a module is not found, go to `web_404.erl` if it exists.

- The underlying platform handles static files that aren't found (not yet generalized).

This suggests that nitroBoard will have at least three pages:

```
index.erl
visitors_admin.erl
directory_admin.erl.
```

They will be called as follows:

```
http://localhost:8000/ -> index.erl
http://localhost:8000/visitors/admin -> visitors_admin.erl
http://localhost:8000/directory/admin -> directory_admin.erl
```

3.6. Anatomy of a Template

A template is your grandfather's HTML page with a dash of Nitrogen's secret sauce—one or more callouts. The callout below, for instance, slurps a Nitrogen page into the template:

```
[[[module:body()]]]
```

This callout slips JavaScript into the template:

```
[[[script]]]
```

The callouts look like an Erlang list in a list in a list:

```
[[[module:function(Args)]]]
```

But don't be fooled. They're pure Nitrogen—module:function(Args) is an Erlang function call. It returns a result and plugs into the template. A call to the module page refers to the current page.

3.7. Elements

A Nitrogen element is simply HTML or an Erlang record that renders to HTML. Here's what you need to know about Erlang records:

- When compiled, a record is a plain vanilla Erlang tuple. But the record definition provides the compiler with enough information to enable the programmer to address fields in the tuple by name.

- A tuple is a basic Erlang data structure of the form:

  ```
  {<datum 1>, <datum 2>, <datum 3>}
  ```

- Tuples may be defined with any number of fields, but once defined, the number of fields, that is, length, cannot be increased or decreased. Problem is, if a tuple gets too long, you get confused as to which chunk of data goes into which field.

- An Erlang record is, arguably, a hack to solve this problem. In source, an Erlang record is defined as:

  ```
  #label {name1=<datum 1>, name2=<datum 2>,
        name3=<datum3>}
  ```

More here:

```
http://www.erlang.org/doc/reference_manual/records.html
```

So, back to Nitrogen elements. If our page contains an element of the form:

```
#label { text="Hello World!" }.
```

It will render as:

```
<label class="wfid_tempNNNNN label">Hello World!</label>
```

Each Nitrogen element has a number of basic properties. All of the properties are optional.

- **id** – Set the name of an element.

- **actions** – Add Actions to an element. Actions will be described later.

- **show_if** – Set to true or false to show or hide the element.

- **class** – Set the CSS class of the element.

- **style** – Add CSS styling directly to the element

Look over the Erlang record definitions, er, I mean, Nitrogen elements in:

index:inner_body/0.

Nitrogen sports more than 70 elements for most anything you want to display on the screen. Categories include:

- Layout (templates, page grid, etc.)

- HTML (links, lists, images, etc.)

- Forms (fields, buttons, dropdowns, etc.)

- jQuery Mobile elements

- RESTful Form Elements

- More (drag and drop elements, wizards, spinners, progress bars, etc.)

Check it out:

http://nitrogenproject.com/doc/elements.html

Find examples, including module source, here:

http://nitrogenproject.com/demos/simplecontrols

And more :

http://nitrogenproject.com/demos

Every Nitrogen element can be mapped into:

1. An Erlang tuple

2. HTML

Give it a shot. In your infinite free time, trace through the Nitrogen source code. See if you can map element source code into respective tuples and HTML. You can find source code here:

```
https://github.com/nitrogen/nitrogen_core/tree/master/src/elements
```

If none of the elements provided by Nitrogen suit your needs, you can create your own. See Chapter 14.

3.8. Actions

A Nitrogen action can be either JavaScript or some record that renders into JavaScript. Examples:

- ```
  #button { text="Submit", actions=[
  #event{type=click, actions="alert('hello');"}
  ]}
  ```

- ```
  #button { text="Submit", actions=[
  #event{type=click, actions=#alert { text="Hello" }
  ]}
  ```

Sometimes setting the actions property of an element can lead
to messy code. Another, cleaner way to wire an action is the `wf:wire/N` function:

- ```
  wf:wire(mybutton, #effect{effect=pulsate})
  ```

The above code might not do what you expect. Indeed, as written, it would immediately cause the mybutton element to pulsate, rather than pulsating when you click the button. Instead, you'll want to use the #event{} action to require some kind of user interaction to trigger the action.
Example:

```
wf:wire(mybutton, #event {type=click, actions=[
    #effect {effect=pulsate}
]})
```
```

It's worth noting that a few elements contain helper attributes called `click` (most notably `#link{}` and `#button{}`), so you don't have to use the actions attribute for extremely common cases:

```
#button{text="Submit" click=#alert{text="Hello"}}
```

3.9. Triggers and Targets

All actions have a `target` property. The `target` specifies what element(s) the action affects.

The event action also has a `trigger` property. The `trigger` specifies what element(s) trigger the action.

For example, assuming the following body:

```
[ #label { id=mylabel, text="Make Me Blink!" },
  #button { id=mybutton, text="Submit" } ]
```

Here are two function calls that return identical results. When you click the Submit button in either case, the label will pulsate. Note the differences in syntax:

```
wf:wire(#event{type=click, trigger=mybutton, tar-
get=mylabel,
        actions=#effect { effect=pulsate } }).
wf:wire(mybutton, mylabel, #event{type=click,
        actions=#effect { effect=pulsate } }).
```

As you see, you can specify the `trigger` and `target` directly in `wf:wire/N`. This can take several forms:

- Specify a `trigger` and `target`.

- Use the same element for both `trigger` and `target`.

- Assume the `trigger` and/or `target` is provided in the actions. If not, then wire the `action` directly to the page. (Useful for catching keystrokes.)

Examples:

- `wf:wire(Trigger, Target, Actions)`

- `wf:wire(TriggerAndTarget, Actions)`

- `wf:wire(Actions)`

3.9.1. The big picture

1. Elements make HTML.

2. Actions make JavaScript.

3. An action can be wired using the action's property or wired later with `wf:wire/N`. Both approaches can take a single action or a list of actions.

4. An action looks for trigger and target properties. These can be specified in a few different ways.

5. Everything we have seen so far happens on the client.

Hey, Dude, volleyball time—nerds vs. marketing. Let's wrap this puppy mañana.

3.10. Enough Theory

Mornin', Dude. My, my—scope out those bloodshot eyes. Up all night?

Marketing sent us a corporate logo file. It's called erlingologo.png. I've taken the liberty of storing it in `~/nb/site/static/images`.[6]

---

[6]You can clone the Erlingo! logo here: http://builditwith.com/images/erlingologo.png. Or, you can make your own *.png image and fake it. But be sure to copy the logo image into .../nb/site/static/images.

As you'll recall, we stubbed the logo into our prototype page with the following element:

```
#h1 { text="Erlingo! WEBSPINNERS" }
```

Problem is, we'd like the logo to show up on all user-facing pages. We *could* insert the logo element in every page. But there's a more efficient way—install it in the template. Indeed, that's exactly what templates are for—to save source duplication.

So let's do it.

In your Unix shell, open bare.html:

Listing 3.9 (⇒ $) Edit the template

```
~/nb/site/src$ cd ../templates
~/nb/site/templates$ vim bare.html
```

And, after the opening <body> tag, add the following code:

Listing 3.10 (⇒ vim) Add HTML to the template

```
<body>
    [[[page:body()]]]
    <div class=container_12>
        <div class="grid_8 prefix_2 suffix_2">
            <div class="grid">
              <a href="/">
                <img src="/images/erlingologo.png"
                    style="width:100%" />
              </a>
              [[[page:body()]]]
            </div>
        </div>
    </div>
```

So, good to go?

Not quite. We need to make slight changes to our homepage (index.erl). If, by chance, you closed your Erlang shell, re-open it and enter:

~/nb$ **bin/nitrogen console**

Don't forget to start sync so that we can take advantage of Erlang's sweet auto-code reloading:

(nitrogen@127.0.0.1)1> **sync:go()**.

Now, in the UNIX terminal, open index.erl:

Listing 3.11 (⇒ $) **Edit index.erl yet again**

```
~/nb/site/templates$ cd ../src
~/nb/site/src$ vim index.erl
```

Next, morph `index.erl` for real. Delete `event(...)` and `inner_body()` and revise `body()` to look like this:

Listing 3.12 (⟹ `vim`) **Revise body()**

```
body() ->
    [ #h1 { text="WELCOME!" },
      #h2 { text="Joe Strongman" },
      #h2 { text="Rusty Klophaus" }
    ].
```

Save and call up your browser:

```
localhost:8000
```

And—Bingo!

That was easy. With a touch of CSS we could reposition the welcome line to make it more attractive, but we'll do that later. Let's focus on visitor functionality. This may get tricky.

3.11. Visitors

On some days *Erlingo!* has no VIP visitors. On a busy day, we may have three or four. Miss Moneypenny, Bossman's secretary, books visitors days in advance. This suggests we need a database of visitors. Nothing fancy. Suppose records in this database have the following fields:

```
Date
Time
Name
Company
```

Now, suppose we have a cron task that queries the database on the date field every morning just after midnight to retrieve visitors of the day. The system then sorts and formats the names and displays them on the welcome page. No visitors, it displays nothing.

But for now, let's keep it simple. Miss Moneypenny can simply refresh the browser every morning before she waters the plants.

So onward!

First off, we need to define the visitor record.

Follow closely. We're going to skim over crucial Erlang concepts.

Review the following for nitty gritty details:

```
http://www.erlang.org/doc/reference_manual/records.html
http://www.erlang.org/doc/man/dets.html
```

3.11.1. Visitor record

First we need to drop into ~/nb/site/include

Listing 3.13 (⇒ $) **New include file**

```
~/nb/site/src$ cd ../include
~/nb/site/include$ vim nb.hrl
```

Insert the following line:

Listing 3.14 (⇒ `vim`) **Our very first record**

```
-record(visitor, {date, time, name, company}).
```

Then save the file.

We've just defined a visitor record.

So what's going on here? Our visitor record definition may be used in more than one module. So we've created the file nb.hrl, which can be included in those modules. The include directory is an Erlang OTP convention designed for just this purpose. More here:

> http://stackoverflow.com/questions/2312307/what-is-an-erlang-hrl-file

> http://www.erlang.org/documentation/doc-5.2/doc/extensions/include.html

We have one more crucial step, so be patient. We need to create a set of functions that enables us to create and retrieve visitor records. Let's do this in a new module called visitors_db.erl:

Listing 3.15 (⇒ `$`) **Open visitors_db.erl**

```
~/nb/site/include$ cd ../src
~/nb/site/src$ vim visitors_db.erl
```

Now insert the following:[7]

---

[7]It's good practice to include header comments at the beginning of every module. At minimum, show author, copyright, and a brief note specifying the function of the module. Where we've left them out, it's simply to save you a bit of typing.

Listing 3.16 (⇒ vim) **visitors_db.erl**

```
-module(visitors_db).
-include("nb.hrl").
-compile(export_all).
```

You may be wondering why we didn't include wf.hrl, that is:

```
-include_lib("nitrogen_core/include/wf.hrl"),
```

Well, we're not coding a Nitrogen page. We're coding a normal Erlang module for retrieving items from the database, so no need to include Nitrogen element record definitions—wouldn't hurt if we did, but why bother?

We'll add create and retrieve functions later. But for now, let's open up a UNIX work terminal so we can play:

Listing 3.17 (⇒ $) **Fire up Erlang shell**

```
~/nb/site/src$ cd ../
~/nb/site$ erl -pa ebin
. . .
Running Erlang
Eshell V6.0  (abort with ^G)
1>
```

The erl -pa ebin command opens the Erlang shell and puts ebin in the code path. To work with records in the shell, first read them in:

Listing 3.18 (⇒ >) **Read record definitions into the shell**

```
Eshell V6.0  (abort with ^G)
1> rr(visitors_db).
[visitor]
```

3. nitroBoard I

The `rr` function reads all record definitions included in the `visitors_db.erl` module. Here's how we can examine the definition of visitor:

Listing 3.19 (⇒ >) Examine the definition of a record

```
2> rl(visitor).
-record(visitor,{date,time,name,company}).
ok
```

This raises a question: How should we format date and time?

Erlang has a calendar library that can help. The following sequence of Erlang shell commands points the way:

Listing 3.20 (⇒ >) The calendar library

```
3> {Date, Time} = calendar:local_time().
{{2019,5,20},{16,6,57}}
4> Date.
{2019,5,20}
5> Time.
{16,6,57}
```

The command `{Date, Time} = calendar:local_time()` pattern matches the output of the Erlang function `calendar:local_time()` to capture current date and time in the variables Date and Time. The variable Date is represented as a tuple: {Year, Month, Day}. The variable Time as: {Hour, Minute, Second}.[8]

Moving on, let's create a record:

---

[8]The library module `calendar` is included in the Erlang OTP `stdlib` application. It includes a number of useful date/time functions. More here:
http://www.erlang.org/doc/man/calendar.html

Listing 3.21 (⇒ >) **Instantiate a record in the shell**

```
6> V1 = #visitor{date=Date, time=Time,
     name="Jesse James", company="Erlingo!"}.
#visitor{date = {2019,5,30}, time = {11,25,54},
        name = "Jesse James", company = "Erlingo!"}
```

We can retrieve data from this record in three ways.

By field:

Listing 3.22 (⇒ >) **Retrieve record attribute by field name**

```
7> V1#visitor.name.
"Jesse James"
```

Through pattern matching:

Listing 3.23 (⇒ >) **Use pattern matching to retrieve record attribute**

```
8> #visitor{date=Date1, time=Time1, name=Name,
        company=Company} = V1.
9> Date1.
{2019,5,30}
10> Time1.
{11,25,54}
11> Name.
"Jesse James"
12> Company.
"Erlingo!"
```

Or, with the Erlang BIF element/2[9]

---

[9]Built-in Function—Note that you'll rarely need to retrieve data from a record with element/2.

49

Listing 3.24 (⇒ >) **Use element/2 to retrieve a record attribute**

```
13> Company2 = element(#visitor.company, V1).
"Erlingo!"
```

The BIF element/2 retrieves the Nth element of a tuple. So element(2, {a,b,c}) would return b. Further, the compiler takes #visitor.company and converts it to the integer that denotes which element of #visitor is represented by the company parameter. That integer is passed along with the record V1 to the element(N, Record) function to retrieve the appropriate value from that field. It's not typically done, but every once in a while, you'll find a need for it.

Yippy! We can now create records, stuff 'em with data, and pop the data back out. Extra points if you can explain why we named the variables above Date1 and Time1 rather than Date and Time. Hint:

> https://stackoverflow.com/questions/52713006/what-is-
> the-need-for-immutable-persistent-data-structures-in-
> erlang

But where should we store our records? Erlang delivers just the ticket—Dets.

3.12. Persistence

Dets provides disk-based term storage:

> http://www.erlang.org/doc/man/dets.html

An Erlang term is any data item. So Dets helps us store any Erlang data item to disk.

Let's explore. First let's create a visitors database and specify the key position and table type:

Listing 3.25 (⇒ >) **Open Dets**

```
14> dets:open_file(visitors, [{keypos,#visitor.date},
        {type,bag}]).
{ok,visitors}
```

So what's {type,bag}? Check the Dets man page.
Now we can play:

Listing 3.26 (⇒ >) **Play with Dets**

```
15> dets:insert(visitors, V1).
ok
16> dets:lookup(visitors, Date).
[#visitor{date = {2019,5,30}, time = {11,25,54},
     name = "Jesse James", company = "Erlingo!"}]
17> V2 = #visitor{date=Date,time={12,20,11},
name="Rusty Scupper",company="Erlingo!"}.
18> dets:insert(visitors,V2).
ok
19> V3 = #visitor{date={2019,6,1}, time={14,0,0},
        name="Joe Strongman"}.
#visitor{date = {2019,6,1},
        time = {14,0,0},
        name = "Joe Strongman",
        company = undefined}
```

Excelente!
Let's see who's coming in on May 30, 2019:

Listing 3.27 (⇒ >) **More lookups**

```
20> Visitors = dets:lookup(visitors, Date).
[#visitor{date = {2019,5,30},
        time = {11,25,54},
```

```
         name = "Jesse James",
         company = "Erlingo!"},
 #visitor{date = {2019,5,30},
         time = {12,20,11},
         name = "Rusty Scupper",
         company = "Erlingo!"}]
```

Ah, a list of two visitors, Jesse and Rusty.

Close out the database for now.

Listing 3.28   (⇒ >) Close Dets database

```
21> dets:close(visitors).
```

3.12.1. Format visitor data

It'll pay to think through one thing before we go further: how should we format our data?

The May 30, 2019 query returned two visitors. For each record in the list, we need to extract the data and format it for suitable display. Let's focus first on how to extract data from a single record. Pattern matching serves us well here. Say we have the following record:

Listing 3.29   (⇒ >) Instantiate a record

```
22> V4 = #visitor{date={2019,5,21}, time={14,58,03},
       name="Francesco Cesarini",
       company="Erlang Solutions"}.
```

We don't care about date and time since we're not going to display them—so we can format the name like this:

Listing 3.30   (⇒ >) Format name from our visitor record

```
23> NN = V4#visitor.name.
"Francesco Cesarini"
24> CC = V4#visitor.company.
"Erlang Solutions"
25> [NN," - ",CC].
["Francesco Cesarini"," - ","Erlang Solutions"]
```

Ah, puzzled by what's going on in line 25?

You can see that it's a list that includes a variable, a string, and another variable. So what good does that do us?

A bunch!

It's what's known in Erlang circles as an IO List[10] (or just "iolist").

> https://prog21.dadgum.com/70.html

When Erlang sends an IOList through standard output or a network socket it will conveniently concatenate all the terms, converting them ultimately to a stream of bytes. Saves programming hassle and considerable CPU cycles.

So, now, our database query returns a list of names. What next?

Erlang has a powerful tool for processing elements of a list—the list comprehension:

> http://www.erlang.org/doc/programming_examples/list_
> comprehensions.html

Think about what we need to do:

- extract every item in a list

- format each item as it comes off the list

- push the formatted value onto a new list

---

[10]We talk about IO Lists in detail on page 551

So let's look at how to do this with our list of visitors using an Erlang list comprehension and an anonymous function[11] assigned to the variable FormatVisitor:

Listing 3.31 (⇒ >) **Format Visitors**

```
26> FormatVisitor=fun(V) ->
      [V#visitor.name,"-",V#visitor.company]
    end.
#Fun<erl_eval.6.54118792>
27> FormattedVisitors = [FormatVisitor(V) || V <-
      Visitors].
[["Jesse James"," - ","Erlingo!"],
 ["Rusty Scupper"," - ","Erlingo!"]]
```

Read the list comprehension right-to-left and it should be transparent. Note the result—a list of two IOLists.

3.12.2. Visitors database

Reopen visitors_db.erl in the UNIX terminal:

Listing 3.32 (⇒ $) **Edit visitors_db.erl**

```
~/nb/site/src$ vim visitors_db.erl
```

And now, let's add open_visitors_db/0:

Listing 3.33 (⇒ vim) **Open visitors_db.erl**

```
-include("nb.hrl").
-compile(export_all).
```

---

[11]https://www.tutorialspoint.com/erlang/erlang_funs.htm

```
open_visitors_db() ->
    File = visitors,
    {ok, visitors} = dets:open_file(File,
        [{keypos,#visitor.date}, {type,bag}]).
```

We'll also need to close the database:

Listing 3.34 (⇒ vim) **close visitors_db.erl**

```
    {ok, visitors} = dets:open_file(File,
        [{keypos,#visitor.date}, {type,bag}]).

close_visitors_db() ->
    ok = dets:close(visitors).
```

We'll definitely need put and get functions. Here's put:

Listing 3.35 (⇒ vim) **put function**

```
close_visitors_db() ->
    ok = dets:close(visitors).

put_visitor(Record) ->
    open_visitors_db(),
    ok = dets:insert(visitors, Record),
    close_visitors_db().

%% @doc Enter VIP visiting today and store in db
put_vip(Name, Company) ->
    {Date, Time} = calendar:local_time(),
    Record = #visitor{date=Date, time=Time,
        name=Name, company=Company},
    put_visitor(Record).
```

And here's get:

Listing 3.36 (⇒ vim) **get function**

```
        name=Name, company=Company},
    put_visitor(Record).

get_visitors(Date) ->
    open_visitors_db(),
    List = dets:lookup(visitors, Date),
    close_visitors_db(),
    List1 = lists:sort(List),
    List1.
```

And now let's top it off with utility functions:

Listing 3.37 (⇒ vim) **Utility functions**

```
    List1 = lists:sort(List),
    List1.

%% @doc Dump the db; handy for debugging
dump_visitors() ->
    open_visitors_db(),
    List = dets:match_object(visitors,'_',
    close_visitors_db(),
    List.

%% @doc Pretty print visitor by name, company, or both
format_name(#visitor{name=Name, company=""}) ->
    Name;
format_name(#visitor{name="", company=Company}) ->
    Company;
format_name(#visitor{name=Name, company=Company}) ->
    [Name," - ",Company].
```

Not much new here. Note the @doc comments. The Erlang documentation utility edoc reads @doc comments to create beautiful documentation. To find out how, check out:

http://www.erlang.org/doc/apps/edoc/chapter.html

Also note that the function format_name/1 employs pattern matching to deal with three possible user inputs:

- name only

- company only

- name and comany

Return of the Function

By now, you should have noticed that there is no return keyword as one would expect in a procedural or object oriented programming language. Erlang's functional nature means that the final term evaluated in a function is that function's return value. So that means there is no need for a return keyword.

3.12.3. Visitors admin

We now need a form to enter visitors into our visitors database. Save visitors_db.erl and create a file called visitors_admin.erl:

Listing 3.38 (⇒ $) **Visitors admin**

```
~/nb/site/src$ vim visitors_admin.erl

-module(visitors_admin).
-compile(export_all).
```

```
-include_lib("nitrogen_core/include/wf.hrl").
-include("nb.hrl").
```

The next few functions may look familiar from the earlier work you've done on
index.erl:

Listing 3.39 (⇒ vim) **Nitrogen page functions**

```
-include("nb.hrl").

main() ->
   #template { file="./site/templates/bare.html" }.

title() -> "Visitor Admin".

body() ->
   #panel{id=inner_body, body=inner_body()}.
```

Note that body/0 calls inner_body/0:

Listing 3.40 (⇒ vim) `inner_body/0`

```
body() ->
   #panel{id=inner_body, body=inner_body()}.

inner_body() ->
   %% We use defer here because this could
   %% potentially be during a redraw.  We want to
   %% ensure the validators are attached *after*
   %% the form is drawn
   wf:defer(save, name, #validate{validators=[
      #is_required{text="Name or Company is required",
                  unless_has_value=company}
   ]}),
```

Forms are easy to create with Nitrogen. Note that we've added our first validator and wired it with `wf:defer/3` rather than `wf:wire/3`. In the case of a page refresh or redraw, the `wf:defer` function assures that form is redrawn before the validators are attached.

Another validator:

Listing 3.41 (⇒ `vim`) **Validate date entry**

```
                unless_has_value=company}
]}),
wf:defer(save, date1, #validate{validators=[
    #is_required{text="Date is required"}
]}),
```

And next, a list of Nitrogen elements:

Listing 3.42 (⇒ `vim`) **Nitrogen elements**

```
    #is_required{text="Date is required"}
]}),
[
    #h1{ text="Visitors" },
    #h3{text="Enter appointment"},
    #label{text="Date"},
    #datepicker_textbox{
        id=date1,
        options=[
            {dateFormat, "mm/dd/yy"},
            {showButtonPanel, true}
        ]
    },
    #br{},
    #label {text="Time"},
    time_dropdown(),
    #br{},
    #label {text="Name"},
    #textbox{ id=name, next=company},
```

```
        #br{},
        #label {text="Company"},
        #textbox{ id=company},
        #br{},
        #button{postback=done, text="Done"},
        #button{id=save, postback=save, text="Save"}
    ].
```

A time dropdown function:

Listing 3.43 (⇒ vim) **Time dropdown**

```
#button{id=save, postback=save, text="Save"
    ].

time_dropdown() ->
    Hours = lists:seq(8,17), %% 8am to 5pm
    #dropdown {id=time, options=
        [time_option({H,0,0}) || H <- Hours]}.
```

Helper functions for time_dropdown/0. Note pattern matching:

Listing 3.44 (⇒ vim) **Time dropdown helper functions**

```
    #dropdown {id=time, options=
        [time_option({H,0,0}) || H <- Hours]}.

time_option(T={12,0,0}) ->
    #option{text="12:00 noon",
    value=wf:pickle(T)};

time_option(T={H,0,0}) when H =< 11 ->
    #option{text=wf:to_list(H) ++ ":00 am",
    value=wf:pickle(T)};

time_option(T={H,0,0}) when H > 12 ->
```

```
    #option{text=wf:to_list(H-12) ++ ":00 pm",
    value=wf:pickle(T)}.


parse_date(Date) ->
    [M,D,Y] = re:split(Date, "/", [{return,list}]),
    {wf:to_integer(Y),
    wf:to_integer(M),
    wf:to_integer(D)}.
```

Let's not forget that we need event functions:

Listing 3.45 ($\Rightarrow$ vim) **Vistors admin event function**

```
    wf:to_integer(M),
    wf:to_integer(D)}.

event(done) ->
    wf:wire(#confirm{text="Done?", postback=done_ok});

event(done_ok) ->
    wf:redirect("/");

event(save) ->
    wf:wire(#confirm{text="Save?", postback=confirm_ok});

event(confirm_ok) ->
    save_visitor(),
    wf:wire(#clear_validation{}),
    wf:update(inner_body, inner_body()).
```

And, of course, we need to save visitor data:

Listing 3.46 ($\Rightarrow$ `vim`) **Save function**

```
    wf:wire(#clear_validation{}),
    wf:update(inner_body, inner_body()).

save_visitor() ->
    Time = wf:depickle(wf:q(time)),
    Name = wf:q(name),
    Company = wf:q(company),
    Date = parse_date(wf:q(date1)),
    Record = #visitor{date=Date,
        time=Time, name=Name,
        company=Company},
    visitors_db:put_visitor(Record).
```

The two `wf:defer/3` functions at the top of `inner_body/0` set up form-field validation. More here:

> http://nitrogenproject.com/doc/api.html#sec-4

`wf:defer`?

It's worth mentioning that `wf:defer/N` is considered a sibling to `wf:wire/N`, the other sibling being `wf:eager/N`.

Both functions wire actions to the browser. The difference here is that actions wired with `wf:defer` will execute after actions wired with `wf:wire`. Because our code is destroying and redrawing the form after every save (with the `wf:update` call), we need to rewire the validators.

Note also the function `time_dropdown/0`. Look closely at the list comprehension. What's that about? We leave that to your brilliance.[12]

The function `time_option/1` also demonstrates pattern matching on function parameters. And more, it introduces a new Erlang concept— guard sequences.

---

[12]Hint: http://www.erlang.org/doc/programming_examples/list_comprehensions.html

Guard sequences are quite handy. For details, drop down to section 8.24 in the Erlang Reference Manual User's Guide:

http://erlang.org/doc/reference_manual/expressions.html

While you're checking out guard sequences, study the rest of the *Erlang Reference Manual User's Guide* with great care. You'll learn much.

Note: We'll show you how to create a custom element for picking time in Chapter 14. Stick with us. Should be fun.

There's yet another thing to observe in visitors_admin.erl—event/1. Here's our very first Nitrogen event handler in the wild. You'd be correct to surmise that event/1 is part of the process that validates data entry and posts data back to the server.

Note first that event/1 is pattern matching on two Erlang atoms—save and confirm_ok. How do we know? The first event/1 function is terminated with a semicolon.

Here's more on pattern matching:

http://erlang.org/doc/reference_manual/patterns.html

Glance back up to the two button elements at the end of inner_body/0. These define the Done and Save buttons at the bottom of our form. Done simply redirects the page to index.erl. Save initiates a postback to event(save) which, in turn, brings up a confirmation dialog. More here:

http://nitrogenproject.com/doc/actions/confirm.html

Note the postback in the #confirm element. Now, who is it talking to? Give yourself a gold star if you said event(confirm_ok).

Extra credit: What is event(confirm_ok) doing for us? Check out these links to learn more:

```
http://nitrogenproject.com/doc/api.html#sec-3
http:
//nitrogenproject.com/doc/actions/clear_validation.html
```

We have one more crucial task. We need to display visitors-of-the-day on our welcome page. Save open index.erl and make the following changes to body/0:

Listing 3.47 (⇒ vim) **Revise index.erl**

```
~/nb/site/src$ vim index.erl

body() ->
    Visitors = visitors_db:get_visitors(date()),
    [
        #h1{ text="WELCOME!" },
        #h2 { text="Joe Strongman" },
        #h2 { text="Rusty Klopaus"},
        #list{numbered=false, body=
            format_visitors(Visitors)},
        #br{}
    ].

format_visitors(List) ->
    [format_visitor(X) || X <- List].
format_visitor(Visitor) ->
    Name = visitors_db:format_name(Visitor),
    #listitem{text=Name, class="visitors"}.
```

This might not be a bad time to check our progress. Save and open the browser to:

```
localhost:8000/visitors/admin
```

If all looks good, fill in the appointment form and repoint your browser to:

`localhost:8000`

3.13. Styling

Welcome screen is ugly, you say? Couldn't agree more. Let's tweak CSS to see what we can do to:

Listing 3.48 ($\Rightarrow$ \$) Opening site/static/css/style.css

```
~/nb/site/src$ cd ../static/css
~/nb/site/static/css$ vim style.css
```

Now, change the following in the h1 declaration:

Listing 3.49 ($\Rightarrow$ vim) style.css

```
h1 {
    ...
    font-size: 1.875em 3em;
    line-height: 1.066667em;
    margin-top: 1.6em 0.2em;
    margin-bottom: 1.6em 0.6em;
```

And add the following new declarations:

Listing 3.50 ($\Rightarrow$ vim) style.css

```
    margin-bottom: 0.6em;
}

li.visitors {
    font-size:  2em;
    line-height:  1em;
    margin-top:  0.2em;
    margin-bottom:  0.2em;
}
li.associates {
    font-size:  1em;
    line-height:  1em;
    margin-top:  0.2em;
    margin-bottom:  0.2em;
}
```

Save and refresh your browser:

`http://localhost:8000`

Not too shabby, eh?

3.14. Debugging

If the form fails to show up in the admin page, the problem is most likely in `visitors_admin.erl`. If the entry to the appointment form fails to show up, prepare for a stint of debugging: Check code in `visitors_db.erl` and `visitors_admin.erl` for typos. Also test exported functions in those modules by running them in the Erlang shell. Here's how:

Listing 3.51 (⇒ >) **Test exported functions in the shell**

```
28> l(visitors_db).
```

This loads the module `visitors_db.erl` into the Erlang shell:

Listing 3.52 (⇒ >) What's in our database?

```
29> visitors_db:dump_visitors().
```

You should see a record depicting the appointment you entered. If not, check the functions in `visitors_db.erl` with great care.

Now would be a good time to commit your hard work to Git:

Listing 3.53 (⇒ $) Commiting to Git

```
.../css$ ~/nb
.../nb$ git add .
.../nb$ git commit -m "First commit of nitroBoard I"
```

3.15. What You've Learned

So, compadre, you've employed and seen in action 18 Nitrogen elements. You've created Nitrogen forms, used Nitrogen events, and wired Nitrogen validators. You've created an Erlang Dets database and learned a smattering of Erlang along the way.

Good day's work!

3.16. Think and Do

Deploy and bring up nitroBoard on a local network so Miss Moneypenny can enter VIP visitors from her desk.

4. nitroBoard II

JESSE: No rest for the weary, bro—Miss Moneypenny wants an associates directory under the VIP list[1].

Easy enough, but here's the tricky thing—she wants the listing to show whether the associate is in or out.

So, we need an associates database. Check.

The associate record needs a field to denote in or out. Check.

But who toggles it? When and how?

OK, say we create a module called `iam.erl`. When associates enter `localhost:8000/iam` into the browser address bar, they will:

- choose their own name from a list

- toggle their *in* or *out* status

- redirect back to the welcome page

Makes sense. Let's get to it.

4.1. Plan of Attack

1. Data persistence: associates database

2. Develop admin pages: associates form

3. Update welcome page: display associates

4. Style

5. Test, debug, and revise

---

[1]Code for this chapter can be found at:
    https://github.com/BuildItWithNitrogen/nitroboard2

4.2. Associates

Let's dive into the associates database first. Pretty much same-ol' same-ol'.

4.2.1. Associate record

Drop into ~/nb/site/include, create a new file nb.hrl, and create the associate record:

Listing 4.1 (⇒ $) Revise nb.hrl

```
~/nb/site/src$ cd ../include
~/nb/site/include$ vim nb.hrl

-record(visitor,{date,time,name,company}).
-record(associate, {lname, fname, ext="", in=true}).
```

Then save the file.

4.2.2. Associates database

Now, on to the associates database. Open a new associates_db.erl file and add the familiar module attributes along with a handful of exports:

Listing 4.2 (⇒ $) Create associates_db.erl

```
~/nb/site/include$ cd ../src
~/nb/site/src$ vim associates_db.erl

-module(associates_db).
-export([
    put_associate/1,
    get_associate/1,
    get_associates/0,
    format_name/1,
    format_in_status/1]).
```

```
-include("nb.hrl").
```

A helpful comment along about here might help tune maintenance programmers into the big picture:

Listing 4.3 (⇒ vim) **Add comment to** `associates_db.erl`

```
-include("nb.hrl").
%%---------------------------------
%% Associates:  Exported functions
%%---------------------------------
```

Now program functions to open and close the Dets database:

Listing 4.4 (⇒ vim) **Define associates functions**

```
%% Associates: Exported functions
%%-----------------------------------------------------------------

open_associates_db() ->
    File = associates,
    {ok, associates} = dets:open_file(File,
        [{keypos,#associate.lname}, {type,set}]).

close_associates_db() ->
    ok = dets:close(associates).
```

Handy dandy put and get functions:

Listing 4.5 (⇒ vim) **Define put and get functions**

```
close_associates_db() ->
    ok = dets:close(associates).

put_associate(Record) ->
    open_associates_db(),
    ok = dets:insert(associates, Record),
    close_associates_db().

get_associate(LName) ->
    open_associates_db(),
    [Record] = dets:lookup(associates, LName),
    close_associates_db(),
    Record.
```

How about a function to list all associates? It could be handy when we're developing or testing:

Listing 4.6 (⇒ vim) **List all associates**

```
    close_associates_db(),
    Record.

get_associates() ->
    open_associates_db(),
    List = lists:sort(dets:match_object(associates, '_')),
    close_associates_db(),
    List.
```

And finally, formatting functions:

Listing 4.7 ($\Rightarrow$ vim) **Formatting functions**

```
    close_associates_db(),
    List.

format_name(#associate{lname=LName, fname=FName, ext=Ext}) ->
    format_name(LName, FName, Ext).

format_name(LName, FName, []) ->
    [LName, ", ", FName];
format_name(LName, FName, Ext) ->
    Fullname = [LName, ", ", FName],
    [Fullname, " - ext:  ", Ext].
```

Note that differences between associates_db.erl and visitors_db.erl are minimal. But one important difference: We need to know when an associate is in or out.

So let's modify format_name/1:

Listing 4.8 ($\Rightarrow$ vim) **Revise** format_name/1

```
format_name(#associate{lname=LName, fname=FName, ext=Ext, in=In}) ->
    Status = format_in_status(In),
    format_name(LName, FName, Ext, Status).
```

...and format_name/3:

Listing 4.9 ($\Rightarrow$ vim) **Revise** format_name/3

```
format_name(LName, FName, [], Status) ->
    [Status1, LName, ", ", FName];

format_name(LName, FName, Ext, Status) ->
    Fullname = [LName, ", ", FName],
    [Status1, Fullname, " - ext: ", Ext].
```

While we're at it, add format_in_status/1:

Listing 4.10 (⇒ vim) Add format_in_status/1

```
    Fullname = [LName, ", ", FName],
    [Status1, Fullname, " - ext: ", Ext].

format_in_status(true) -> "IN: ";
format_in_status(false) -> "OUT: ".
```

4.2.3. Associates admin

Now, following the example of visitors, create an associates admin page. Let's start it as usual:

Listing 4.11 (⇒ $) Create associates_admin.erl

```
~/nb/site/src$ vim associates_admin.erl

-module(associates_admin).
-compile(export_all).
-include_lib("nitrogen_core/include/wf.hrl").
-include("nb.hrl").
```

Let's not forget main/0 and title/0:

Listing 4.12 (⇒ vim) Define main/0 and title/0

```
main() -> #template { file="./site/templates/bare.html" }.

title() -> "Associates Admin".
```

Nor body/0:

Listing 4.13 (⇒ vim) **Define** body/0

```
title() -> "Associates Admin".

body() ->
    wf:wire(save, lname, #validate{validators=
        #is_required{text="Last Name Required"}}),
    [
        #h1{ text="Associates Directory" },
        #h3{text="Enter directory listing"},
        #flash{},
        #label {text="Last Name"},
        #textbox{ id=lname, next=fname},
        #br{},
        #label {text="First Name"},
        #textbox{ id=fname, next=ext},
        #br{},
        #label {text="Extension"},
        #textbox{ id=ext},
        #br{},
        #button{id=save, postback=save, text="Save"},
        #link{url="/", text=" Cancel"}
    ].
```

We need a function to clear the form:

Listing 4.14 (⇒ vim) **Clear form**

```
        #link{url="/", text="  Cancel"}
    ].

clear_form() ->
    wf:set(lname, ""),
    wf:set(fname, ""),
    wf:set(ext, "").
```

And our event functions:

Listing 4.15 ($\Rightarrow$ vim) **Define event/1**

```
    wf:set(ext, "").

event(save) ->
    wf:wire(#confirm{text="Save?", postback=confirm_ok});

event(confirm_ok) ->
    [LName, FName, Extension] = wf:mq([lname, fname, ext]),
    Record = #associate{lname=LName, fname=FName, ext=Extension},
    associates_db:put_associate(Record),
    clear_form(),
    wf:flash("Saved").
```

Save and take a look at what we've achieved:

localhost:8000/associates/admin

Enter a few associate names, click "Save", then when you're done adding, click "Cancel" to head back to the homepage.

Look closely to see if you can identify one new element and three new Nitrogen API functions in `associates_admin.erl`.

You've got it:

- `#flash{}`
- `wf:set/2`
- `wf:mq/3`
- `wf:flash/1`

The `#flash{}` element defines a placeholder for flash messages created by the `wf:flash/1` command.

> http://nitrogenproject.com/doc/elements/flash.html

The API function `wf:set/2` should be obvious, but `wf:mq/3`, `wf:q/1`, `wf:qs/1`, `wf:mqs/1`, `wf:q_pl/1`, and `wf:qs_pl/1` are equally important since they enable you to retrieve data posted from the client-side forms back to the server.

> http://nitrogenproject.com/demos/postback2

4.2.4. Display associates

So what's missing?

We still need to display associates on the welcome board. We bring up index.erl and modify `body()` as follows:

Listing 4.16 (⇒ $) Revise `index.erl`

```
~/nb/site/src$ vim index.erl
...
body() ->
    Visitors = visitors_db:get_visitors(date()),
    Associates = associates_db:get_associates(),
```

```
    [
      #h1{ text="WELCOME!" },
      #list{numbered=false,
        body=format_visitors(Visitors)},
        #br{}
        #hr{},
        #h4{text="Associates Directory"},
        #hr{},
        #list{numbered=false, body=format_associates(Associates)}
    ].

format_associates(List) ->
  [format_associate(X) || X <- List].
format_associate(Associate) ->
  Name = associates_db:format_name(Associate),
  #listitem{text=Name, class="associates"}.

format_visitors(Visitors) ->
  ...
```

Save. Now let's take a look at our new handywork. If all is well, you should see the associates listed on the welcome board:

4.3. I am in/I am out

Our associates need to toggle their in/out status. We *could* do this by adding a function to associates_admin.erl. But putting the in/out status update function in a separate module gives us a more elegant, easier-to-remember, URL.

So let's create the module. We'll call it iam.erl. You know the drill:

Listing 4.17 (⇒ vim) **Define** iam.erl

```
~/nb/site/src$ vim iam.erl

-module(iam).
-compile(export_all).
-include_lib("nitrogen_core/include/wf.hrl").
-include("nb.hrl").
```

main/0, title/0, and body/0:

Listing 4.18 (⇒ vim) **Define** main/0, title/0, body/0

```
-include_lib("nitrogen_core/include/wf.hrl").
-include("nb.hrl").

main() ->
    #template{file="./site/templates/bare.html"}.

title() ->
    "I am...".

body() ->
    #panel{id=inner_body, body=inner_body()}.
```

inner_body/0:

4. *nitroBoard II*

```
body() ->
    #panel{id=inner_body, body=inner_body()}.

inner_body() ->
    [
        #h1{ text="I am..." },
        associate_dropdown(),
        #button{id=toggle, postback=toggle, text="Toggle"}
    ].
```

Format functions:

```
        #button{id=toggle, postback=toggle, text="Toggle"\}
    ].

format_iam(List) ->
    [format_name(X) || X <- List].

format_name(Associate) ->
    #associate{lname=LName, fname=FName, in=In} = Associate,
    Status = associates_db:format_in_status(In),
    Name = [Status, " ", LName, ",", FName],
    #option { text=Name, value=LName }.
```

A drop-down:

```
    Name = [Status, " ", LName, ",", FName],
    #option { text=Name, value=LName }.

associate_dropdown() ->
```

```
        Associates = associates_db:get_associates(),
        #dropdown{
            id=associate,
            value="",
            options=format_iam(Associates)
        }.
```

The event function:

Listing 4.22 (⇒ vim) **Define event/1**

```
        options=format_iam(Associates)
    }.

event(toggle) ->
    Associate = wf:q(associate),
    Record = associates_db:get_associate(Associate),
    wf:info("~w~n",[Record]),
    Record1 = toggle_status(Record),
    wf:info("~w~n", [Record1]),
    associates_db:put_associate(Record1),
    wf:redirect("/").
```

Note that we've introduced a new Nitrogen function, wf:info/2. This is just
a shortcut to the Erlang function error_logger:info_msg/2; it is, however,
customizable with a custom log handler.[2] wf:info/2 is merely for debugging.
It'll print the variables Record and Record1 to the Erlang shell.

A function to toggle status should bring us home:

---

[2]Custom handlers are an advanced topic in Nitrogen and are covered in the official documentation at http://nitrogenproject.com/doc/handlers.html.

Listing 4.23 (⇒ vim) Define `toggle_status/1`

```
    associates_db:put_associate(Record1),
    wf:redirect("/").

toggle_status(Rec = #associate{in=Status}) ->
    Rec#associate{in = not(Status)}.
```

Save, and let's have a look at our new page:

`localhost:8000/iam`

Perfect!

All mysteries here are in `format_name/1`, but easy enough to tease out. First we pattern match on the `associate` record to extract name and `status` variables. Next we toggle the `status` flag and, finally, concatenate the variables to form a dropdown option string.

Traditionally Erlang represented strings as memory-hogging lists. This meant that the full fire-power of the list library could be brought to bear.

`https://en.wikibooks.org/wiki/Erlang_Programming/Terms`

Since we're not concerned about memory, we use the list representation for option strings in `format_name/1`.

Erlang also offers `binaries`, which are more compact internally. We could use binaries anywhere we use strings.

```
http://www.erlang.org/doc/efficiency_guide/
binaryhandling.html
```

Fact is, it's easy to convert between the two representations using the BIFs list_to_binary/1 and binary_to_list/1.

```
http:
//www.erlang.org/doc/man/erlang.html#binary_to_list-1
http:
//www.erlang.org/doc/man/erlang.html#list_to_binary-1
```

Nitrogen also offers wf:to_list/1 and wf:to_binary/1. Benefit: more flexible than Erlang's BIFs list_to_binary/1 and binary_to_list/1. Nitrogen also offers Unicode-aware conversions with wf:to_unicode_list/1 and wf:to_unicode_binary/1.

4.4. Styling

Let's tweak styling by adding the following declarations to remove the dots next to each list item.

Listing 4.24 (⇒ $) Revise style.css

```
~/nb/site/src$ cd ../static/css
~/nb/site/static/css$ vim style.css
...

li.visitors, li.associates {
    list-style-type:  none;
}
```

Save and refresh your browser:

```
localhost:8000
```

Not too shabby, eh?

4.5. What You've Learned

So what think you, Dude? May have been a "boring" project, but nitroBoard had much to teach, wouldn't you say?

- introduction to Nitrogen elements and actions

- how to build Nitrogen pages

- how to build forms

- form-field validation

- postbacks

- simple data storage and retieval

- a taste of Erlang

4.6. Think and Do

Suppose a VIP visitor wants to leave a message for an associate who is out. How would you modify nitroBoard to cover that case?

5. Nitrogen Functions

LLOYD: All these woof woof functions—How do you keep them straight?

RUSTY: Woof woof?

LLOYD: You know, wf, as in wf:defer/1.

RUSTY: Take a seat, lad, and prepare for enlightenment.

Nitrogen provides more than 100 web development support functions.

You can see every standard API function provided by Nitrogen by viewing the wf.erl file in the nitrogen_core application.[1] They are usually short and mostly straightforward, but to make it easier, let's run through some of the more commonly used functions in rough order of how frequently you're likely to use them.[2]

Get to know these functions intimately. They will be your milk and cookies in the heat of Nitrogen development.

Trust me: you'll want milk and cookies.

5.1. Wire Actions to the Browser

You'll spend most of your Nitrogen development time constructing actions on the server to be executed on the client. The following three functions will likely be scattered liberally throughout your codebase.

---

[1]https://github.com/nitrogen/nitrogen_core/blob/master/src/wf.erl
[2]http://nitrogenproject.com/doc/api.html

5.1.1. `wf:wire/[1-3]`

`wf:wire` executes a specified action as JavaScript on the client. Your applications will likely call `wf:wire` more frequently than any other function. There are several ways to use it:

`wf:wire(Javascript)`: Send the provided JavaScript string, binary or IOList to the client and execute it as written:[3]

```
wf:wire("alert('Hello there')").
```

`wf:wire(Actions)`: Process the provided actions, convert Nitrogen action elements to their respective JavaScript, and execute them on the client. Actions can be a single Nitrogen action, multiple actions, or an intermixing of JavaScript and actions. From here on out, "actions" will imply Nitrogen action elements, JavaScript, or any combination thereof:

```
wf:wire([#alert{text="Hello There"},
        "$('div.some').hide()"
        ]).
```

`wf:wire(Target, Actions)`: Execute targeted actions on the client. Say you have an element on your page with id=selection_list. The following would hide that element:

```
wf:wire(selection_list, #hide{}).
```

`wf:wire(Trigger, Target, Actions)`: Execute actions on the client where an action is triggered by Trigger, but actually performed on Target. The most common usage is for wiring validators:

```
wf:wire(some_button, some_field,
        #validate{validators=#is_required{}})
```

This function can be used for more than just validators. You could, for instance, do this:

---

[3]https://riptutorial.com/erlang/topic/5677/iolists

```
wf:wire(some_button, some_element, #toggle{})
```

Clicking some_button will toggle the element with id=some_element.

wf:wire(TriggerPath, TargetPath, Actions): The variables TriggerPath and/or TargetPath can be CSS/JQuery selectors. Clicking my_button in the following example will make all elements of the CSS other_class bounce.

```
wf:wire(my_button, "other_class",
        #effect{effect=bounce}).
```

5.1.2. wf:defer/[1-3]

wf:defer[1-3] works the same as wf:wire, except actions wired by wf:defer will be sent to the browser and for execution *after* wf:wire calls. This simplifies wiring actions to newly created elements. The following example shows why the priority wiring system was created. It will seem to work, but then fail. Priority wiring is the broader term to refer to the alternatives to wf:wire, wf:eager, and wf:defer:

Example 5.1 **wf:defer example**

```
body() ->
  #panel{form_wrapper, body=form()}

form() ->
  wf:wire(save_button, lastname, #validate{validators=[
      #is_required{}
  ]}),
  [
      #label{text="Enter Last Name"},
      #textbox{id=lastname},
      #br{},
      #button{id=save_button, text="Save", postback=save}
  ].

event(save) ->
```

```
Lastname = wf:q(lastname),
wf:info("Saving ~p", [Lastname]),
wf:update(form_wrapper, form()).
```

The first time the page loads, everything will work exactly as expected—the validator will be bound and the lastname field will be required. But after entering a last name and clicking "Save," the code will redraw the entire form, attempting to wire the validator and the validator will no longer work. Why is this? If you go through the order of evaluation, you'll see exactly what happens:

The call to wf:update is dependent on the evaluation of form(), so form() must be called and evaluated first.

The first call in form() is wf:wire to wire validators to the lastname field and save_button.

The function event(save):

- gets the value entered by the user in the lastname field

- saves the value in the variable Lastname

- displays Lastname in a "Saving..." message

- updates the form_wrapper panel with the new user-entered lastname value validators attached to the form elements.

This suggests why wf:defer is so convenient. Replacing wf:wire with wf:defer ensures that all validators get wired after wf:update replaces form content.

In short, if you're trying to wire actions to dynamically created elements and wiring keeps failing, you're probably using wf:wire where you should be using wf:defer.

5.1.3. wf:eager/[1-3]

wf:eager does the opposite of wf:defer. Actions wired with wf:eager will execute before actions wired with wf:wire. This would commonly be used to force some element or code to load before, say, rendering a custom action or JavaScript. While you won't need to do this as frequently as wf:defer, it's worth knowing.

5.2. Retrieve Information Submitted by the User

`wf` functions are minimally named, mostly abbreviations. Mnemonics can help you remember them.

5.2.1. `wf:q/1`

`wf:q/1` retrieves values submitted by the user. Mnemonic: "Query."

Call `wf:q` or one of its siblings when you need to return information entered by a user in a form field. Say the user enters "Hello there" into a textbox defined as #textbox{id=greeting} and a postback is executed. You can access the value of greeting inside the event/1 function (or any function called inside that function) by calling `wf:q(greeting)`.

`wf:q` can also be used to retrieve query string information: that is, any parts of the URL after a question mark, e.g., ?.

For instance, assume the requested URL is:

http://mydomain.com/my/page?greeting=hello

Calling `wf:q(greeting)` will return the string "Hello".

Example 5.2 `wf:q` example

```
#textbox{id=greeting}
. . .

event(save) ->
    Greeting = wf:q(greeting),
    %% returns whatever is entered
    %% into the textbox. e.g.: "Hello"
```

If there is more than one element with id=greeting, calling `wf:q(greeting)` will crash with the error too_many_matches. This is because `wf:q` expects a single matching field. To accept more than one field with the same name, you need `wf:qs/1`.

5.2.2. `wf:qs/1`

Retrieve several duplicate fields from the user. Mnemonic: "Query Several."

As noted, `wf:qs/1` should be used when you expect more than one submitted field with the same name. Example: Using `wf:qs/1` to retrieve the complete list of checked fields from a list of check boxes, all with the same id.

Example 5.3   `wf:qs` example

```
#checkbox{id=food, value="pizza", text="Pizza"},
#checkbox{id=food, value="bananas", text="Bananas"},
#checkbox{id=food, value="burgers", text="Burgers"},
...

event(save) ->
    FavoriteFoods = wf:qs(food).
    %% Depending on which boxes are
    %% checked, returns a list like:
    %% ["pizza", "bananas", "burgers"]
```

This also works with lists of form elements #textbox{}, #dropdown{}, etc.), as long as they have the same id.

History of `wf:q` and `wf:qs`

The Nitrogen 1.0 version of `wf:q` returned the same result as `wf:qs` does now. The function `wf:q` used to return a list of all values submitted by the queried ID. But given how common it is for each element to have a unique ID, Nitrogen creator Rusty Klophaus changed the meaning of `wf:q` in Nitrogen 2.0 to "query a single item and crash if there are more than one," and added `wf:qs` to "query all items with the same ID."

The revised semantics is one of the biggest backward incompatible changes from Nitrogen 1,0 to Nitrogen 2.0 But the benefit is cleaner, easier to read code. Further, the error message `too_many_matches` is more descriptive than the alternative error message: `badmatch`.

5.2.3. `wf:mq/1`

Retrieve multiple unique fields from user input. Mnemonic: "Multiple Queries."

`wf:mq/1` takes a list of element ids and returns a list of corresponding values. With `wf:mq/1` you don't have to execute `wf:q` for every data value or execute maps/list-comprehensions. For instance:

Example 5.4   Multiple `wf:q/1` calls

```
FirstName = wf:q(first_name),
LastName = wf:q(last_name),
Address = wf:q(address).
```

... is identical to:

Example 5.5   Call `wf:mq/1` instead

```
[FirstName, LastName, Address] = wf:mq([first_name, last_name, address]).
```

5.2.4. `wf:mqs/1`

Retrieve multiple duplicate fields. Mnemonic "Multiple Query Several."

`wf:q/1` is to `wf:qs/1` as `wf:mq/1` is to `wf:mqs/1`. That is, `wf:mqs/1` will return a list of lists containing values:

Example 5.6   Multiple `wf:qs/1` calls

```
Interests = wf:qs(interest),
Foods = wf:qs(food),
MovieGenres = wf:qs(genre).
```

... is identical to:

Example 5.7 `wf:mqs/1` **instead**

```
[Interests, Foods, MovieGenres] = wf:mqs([interest, food, genre]).
```

5.2.5. `wf:q_pl/1`

Retrieve a list of unique fields and return a proplist. Mnemonic: "Query into PropList"

Rather than returning a list of elements, `wf:q_pl/1` returns an Erlang proplist A proplist is a list of key-value tuples—a useful data structure found throughout Erlang source.[4]

You can use `wf:q_pl/1` the same as you'd use `wf:mq/1`, but you'll get a proplist with ID keys as the return value:

Example 5.8 `wf:q_pl/1`

```
Person = wf:q_pl([first_name, last_name, address]).
%% `Person` will end up being:
%% [{first_name, "Steve"},
%%  {last_name, "Vinoski"},
%%  {address, "Some where deep in Massachusetts"}].
```

5.2.6. `wf:qs_pl/1`

Retrieve a list of duplicated fields and return a proplist. Menomic: "Query Several into PropList"

The function `wf:qs_pl/1` is similar to `wf:qs/1` and `wf:mqs/1`. Using our "Interest, Food, and Movie Genre" example, here's how we'd use it:

---

[4]Maps, introduced in Erlang 17, have replaced proplists to some extent, but proplists won't go away soon.

Example 5.9 `wf:qs_pl` **example**

```
AboutUser = wf:qs_pl([interest, food, genre]).
%% AboutUser will hold the following list:
%% [{interest, ["Bowhunting", "Nunchucks", "Hacking"]},
%%  {food, ["Quesadillas", "Nachos"]},
%%  {genre, ["Dance Movies"]}].
```

5.3. Change Elements on the Page

When we execute a Nitrogen page we wire actions to the client, the client displays or executes our actions, and the server updates the page. Nitrogen provides a comprehensive set of functions to update the page.

If you have no need to dynamically create elements during the initial page-load, you would call these functions inside the page's event/1 function.

5.3.1. `wf:set/[2-3]`

Change the value of a form element, the source of an image, or set the value of a progress bar:

Example 5.10 `wf:set` **with a textbox**

```
#textbox{id=superhero, text="Batman"},
. . .

wf:set(superhero, "Wolverine").
```

Check or uncheck a checkbox or radio box:

Example 5.11 `wf:set` with a checkbox

```
#checkbox{id=agree, text="Do you agree to the terms?"},
 . . .
wf:set(agree, true).
```

Change the path of an image:

Example 5.12 `wf:set` to change the path of an image

```
#image{id=profile, image="/images/no-profile.png"},
 . . .
wf:set(profile, "/images/users/user-profile-5332.png").
```

Way back when I was hosting my Super Awesome Homepage on the now defunct GeoCities, the most cutting-edge thing I could do was to change an image source on the fly, usually by hovering over it. I would search Yahoo or Altavista for how to "change an image on a homepage when moving the mouse over it." I would find a chunk of JavaScript that I could copy-and-paste into my page and replace the image paths with my own images.

Thankfully those days are behind us. Changing images is now super simple. On hover, you might just use the :hover selector in CSS, or bind something with jQuery to the onmouseover action.

And more, with `wf:set` you can change an image dynamically; live-update a status image on a dashboard, say, from green, representing "good," to yellow, representing "high load," or red, representing "serious issues."

Bottom line: Changing the source of an image with Nitrogen is trivial.

5.3.2. `wf:update/[2-3]`

Update the contents of an existing element.

`wf:update` replaces the content of a container element such as #panel, #span, or #tablecell{} with new content. You'll use it frequently:

Example 5.13 `wf:update`

```
#panel{id=my_content, body=[
    #span{text="I am inside an awesome panel."},
    #em{text="Hey! So am I!"}
]},
. . .

NewBody = #span{text="I have replaced a span and an em."}
wf:update(my_content, NewBody).
```

In the listing above, the span labeled "I have replaced a span and an em" will replace the #span{} and #em{} elements, but will still be enclosed in #panel{id=my_contents}.

The result:

Example 5.14 **Result**

```
}
#panel{id=my_contents, body=[
    #span{text="I have replaced a span and an em."}
]},
```

5.3.3. `wf:replace/[2-3]`

Replace an element with new elements.

`wf:replace` is similar to `wf:update` with one significant difference: instead of replacing the content of an element, it replaces the named element itself. If we had used `wf:replace` insead of `wf:update` in Listing 5.12, the #span would completely replace the #panel in the DOM.

5.3.4. `wf:remove/[2-3]`

Remove an element from the page.

`wf:remove` will (surprise, surprise!) remove the named element from the page altogether. Say we have:

Example 5.15 Elements we plan to remove

```
#panel{id=foo, body=[
  #span{id=bar, text="Some span"},
  #link{id=erlang, url="http://erlang.org", text="Erlang"}
]}.
```

If we call:

Example 5.16 `wf:remove`

```
wf:remove(erlang).
```

We see:

Example 5.17 Results of `wf:remove`

```
#panel{id=foo, body=[
  #span{id=bar, text="Some span"}
]}.
```

TADA! The named element is...gone!

Note that the change is to HTML. But we *model* the pages as if they are records. Since we are programming in Nitrogen, it's good to think in terms of Nitrogen elements.

5.3.5. `wf:insert_before`

We can also insert elements into the page relative to a specified element. Nitrogen provides four variations on this concept;

```
wf:insert_before/[2-3]
wf:insert_after/[2-3]
wf:insert_top/[2-3]
wf:insert_bottom/[2-3]
```

To illustrate, say we define the following panel:

Example 5.18   Panel

```
#panel{id=wrapper, body=[
  #panel{id=first_element, text="Foo"},
  #panel{id=second_element, text="Bar"}
]}.
```

Now, a call to:

Example 5.19   Call to `wf:insert_before`

```
wf:insert_before(second_element, #panel{text="Inserted"}).
```

yields:

Example 5.20   Result of call to `wf:insert_before`

```
#panel{id=wrapper, body=[
    #panel{id=first_element, text="Foo"},
    #panel{text="Inserted"},
    #panel{id=second_element, text="Bar"}
]}.
```

5.3.6. `wf:insert_after`

If we want to insert elements after the named element in the DOM, a call to `wf:insert_after` will do the trick:

Example 5.21 Call to `wf:insert_after`

```
wf:insert_after(second_element, #panel{text="Inserted"}).
```

yields:

Example 5.22 Result of wf:insert_after

```
#panel{id=wrapper, body=[
   #panel{id=first_element, text="Foo"},
   #panel{id=second_element, text="Bar"},
   #panel{text="Inserted"}
]}.
```

5.3.7. `wf:insert_top`

`wf:insert_top` inserts elements inside the named element before all child elements.

So a call to:

Example 5.23 Call to `wf:insert_before`

```
wf:insert_before(wrapper, #panel{text="Inserted"}).
```

yields:

Example 5.24   Result of `wf:insert_before`

```
#panel{id=wrapper, body=[
  #panel{text="Inserted"},
  #panel{id=first_element, text="Foo"},
  #panel{id=second\_element, text="Bar"}
]}.
```

5.3.8. `wf:insert_bottom`

`wf:insert_bottom` inserts elements inside the named element at the bottom, that is, after all child elements.

A call to:

Example 5.25   Call to `wf:insert_before`

```
wf:insert_before(wrapper, #panel{text="Inserted"}).
```

yields:

Example 5.26   Results of `wf:insert_before`

```
#panel{id=wrapper, body=[
    #panel{id=first_element, text="Foo"},
    #panel{id=second_element, text="Bar"},
    #panel{text="Inserted"}
]}.
```

A "special" element in the Nitrogen routing enables you to add elements relative to the page body itself. Simply specify the atom page as the target element.

For instance:

Example 5.27   Specify target with the atom page

```
wf:insert_top(page, #span{text="My great element"}).
```

...adds the specified span at the very beginning of the page as "the first element within the HTML <body> tag."

The function wf:insert_bottom will do the same at the bottom of the page.

5.3.9. wf:enable/[1-2], wf:disable/[1-2]

In HTML the disabled attribute will disable, that is, "grey out," a form element. You can dynamically enable or disable a form element in Nitrogen with wf:enable or wf:disable:

Example 5.28   wf:disable

```
wf:disable(my_button).
```

Disabling an element doesn't remove it from the DOM. Rather, it removes it from postbacks or form submissions.

5.3.10. Priority Wiring and Updating Functions

Many of the functions we have presented have both arity 2 and arity 3 versions. That is, they require either two or three parameters. The arity 3 versions enable you toset the priority of execution. For instance:

Example 5.29   Priority Wiring

```
wf:update(defer, my_element, "Everything is awesome"),
wf:update(normal, my_element, "Everything is terrible").
```

Even though the last call changes the content of `my_element` to "Everything is terrible," the end result would actually be "Everything is awesome" because the "Everything is awesome" call is deferred.

Why would I use priority wiring?

By far the most common use case for priority wiring is to deal with elements that have validators or actions wired to them.

Consider this:

Example 5.30 Without priority wiring

```
body() ->
    [#button{id=worker, text="Replace me with a form", postback=update}].

form() ->
    wf:wire(my_button, my_name, #validate{validators=[
        #is_required{text="Required"}
    ]}),
    [#textbox{id=my_name, placaeholder="Enter your Name"},
    #button{id=my_button, text="Say Hi!"}
    ].

event(update) ->
    wf:replace(worker, form());
event(submit) ->
    Msg = ["Hi ",wf:q(my_name)],
    wf:wire(#alert{text=Msg}).
```

If you follow the user behavior without priority wiring, the initial page will display a button that says "Replace me with a form." If you click that button, it triggers the update postback, which replaces the button with the content of `form()`, which also wires a validator to the `my_name` and `my_button` elements. But you'll notice that the validator doesn't actually work. When you click the "Say Hi!" button, the alert will popup even if you leave the content of `my_name` blank.

Why is this?

It's an order of operations thing. When the update postback evaluates, it does so in this order:

1. In order for `wf:replace` to actually execute, it needs to first evaluate the `form()` function.

2. The `form()` function first wires a `#validate{}` to a textbox and button.

3. Then the `form()` function creates and returns a textbox and button.

4. Finally, `wf:replace` executes, wiring to the page the action of replacing the worker element with the content of the now-evaluated return value of `form()`.

See the problem above?

Problem is that the `#validate{}` action is wired to the page before the new form elements themselves are submitted to the page. The effect is trying to wire actions to elements that don't yet exist.

The simple fix is to use `wf:defer` instead of `wf:wire` with the `#validate{}`:

Example 5.31 `wf:defer`

```
form() ->
    wf:defer(my_button, my_name, #validate{validators=[
        #is_required{text="Required"}
    ]}),
    [
        . . .
```

By using `wf:defer` the wiring of the validator is deferred until after the form is written to the page with `wf:replace`. The function `wf:replace` is a shortcut to a `wf:wire` call.

5.4. Conversion Functions

5.4.1. `wf:to_list/1`

Erlang strings do not have a similar internal representation as strings in most other languages. Rather, they are lists of integers. Erlang provides conversion functions from other types to lists including `integer_to_list`, `binary_to_list`, and `atom_to_list`. Nitrogen optimizes this `something_to_list` concept for web development. So Nitrogen assumes that converting a value to a list means convert to a "string." Nitrogen's `wf:to_list/1` function is type-aware and also flattens string lists into a flat string.

Here are examples to play with in your Erlang shell:

Example 5.32 Conversion functions

```
1> wf:to_list(some_atom).
"some_atom"
2> wf:to_list(<<"some binary">>).
"some binary"
3> wf:to_list(123).
"123"
4> wf:to_list(123.5).
"123.5"
5> wf:to_list([some_atom, 56, "Some string"]).
"some_atom56Some string"
6> wf:to_list([56, 56]).
"88"
7> wf:to_list([["some list", "of things"], 1000, <<"a binary">>]).
"some listof things1000a binary"
```

`wf:to_list/1` converts a list of Erlang terms into a string-type list. That said, there are oddities worth noting. Line 5, you'll note, converts the integer 56 into the text "56," while on line 6, it converts [56, 56] into "88." Why is this?

It's due to ambiguity and optimization. Instead of inspecting the whole list, which can take precious time, Nitrogen examines the first element of a list. If it's an integer, Nitrogen assumes that the list is a string. If you look at an ASCII table, you'll note that 56 is the ASCII character for the printable character "8."

It's a hairy situation given the nature of Erlang's odd system for representing strings.

5.4.2. `wf:to_unicode_list/1`

`wf:to_unicode_list/1` works the same as `wf:to_list/1`, except it runs its sublists through Erlang's `unicode:characters_to_list/1` function.

5.4.3. `wf:to_binary/1`

Erlang binaries are awesome things. Effectively, they are just blocks of memory: a set of bytes. And compared with Erlang's list-of-integer strings, Erlang's binaries are more like strings in other languages. Optimizations within the Erlang VM make the shuffling around of binaries very efficient. The only real drawback of binaries is their rather cumbersome syntax. While a string is identified by double-quotes (e.g., `"The cheese is old and moldy,"`) binaries are identified by double-angle-brackets (e.g., `<<"The cheese is old and moldy">>`).

Most sites can get away with using strings most of the time. But if you need to eke that extra bit of performance, you might find binaries worth the syntactical burden. And if you are working with large strings, you absolutely will want to use binaries.

Nitrogen provides a convenient `wf:to_binary/1` function that mostly mirrors `wf:to_list/1`, except, surprise, it returns a binary.

Note: The BIF `iolist_to_binary/1` will not convert an iolist to a binary in the same way. It interprets integers in the same way as `wf:to_list/1`.

5.4.4. `wf:to_unicode_binary/1`

Like `wf:to_unicode_list/1`, `wf:to_unicode_binary/1` returns a binary that has been run through `unicode:characters_to_binary/1`.

5.4.5. `wf:to_atom/1`

`wf:to_atom/1` converts a string, binary, integer, or float to an atom. Be very careful when using this (see 12.1.5 on page 458).

5.4.6. `wf:to_integer/1`

Like `wf:to_atom`, `wf:to_integer` will safely convert a list, binary, atom, or float to an integer. For the conversion from float to integer, it performs `erlang:round/1`.

5.5. Encoding, Decoding, and Escaping

For sake of internet security, it's essential that user-submitted data not display raw HTML. Instead, it must be properly encoded. The characters < and >, for instance, must be encoded to the strings < and >.

5.5.1. `wf:html_encode/1`, `wf:html_decode/1`

`wf:html_encode/1` will properly encode user-submitted data for safe display on the browser:

Example 5.33 Example of `wf:html_encode`

```
1> wf:html_encode("<>&").
"&lt;&gt;&amp;"
```

`wf:html_decode/1` will decode strings encoded by `wf:html_encode/1` with limitation. Currently, `wf:html_encode/1` will only encode troublesome HTML characters: &'"<> and a non-breaking space (HTML's).

The text attribute in many Nitrogen elements automatically HTML-encodes the assigned strings.

5.5.2. `wf:url_encode/1`, `wf:url_decode/1`

You often need to pass values to another website or to another page in your site through the URL. But URLs have special characters. For instance, a pound sign/hash symbol/octothorpe # is interpreted as an anchor. Anything after that will not be passed to the server but is handled client-side.

Values encoded by `wf:url_encode/1` are URL-safe:

Example 5.34   Encoding and decoding

```
1> Enc = wf:url_encode("A bit of this & that.  #winning").
"A+bit+of+this+%26+that.+%23winning"
2> wf:url_decode(Enc).
"A bit of this & that. #winning"
```

5.5.3. `wf:to_qs/1`

Piggybacking on `wf:url_encode/1`, `wf:to_qs/1` will convert an Erlang proplist into a standard URL-encoded query string:

Example 5.35   `wf:to_qs`

```
1> QS = wf:to_qs([{day, "Wednesday"}, {age, 34}]).
["day","=","Wednesday","&","age","=","34"]
2> lists:flatten(QS).
"day=Wednesday&age=34"
```

As you can see, `wf:to_qs/1` returns a proplist. But to see it in a "friendly" way, you'll need to "flatten" the list with `lists:flatten/1`.

5.5.4. `wf:js_escape/1`

You can make explicit JavaScript calls with the `wf:wire` functions. But if your JavaScript code has terminating characters like apostrophes (') or quotes ("), you'll need to sanitize it so it doesn't break JavaScript on the page.

If you called:

Example 5.36 Beware: `wf:js_escape`

```
wf:wire(wf:f("alert(\"You deleted the file called ~s\")", [Name]).
```

... most of the time, you'll be just fine.

But if Name is the string: `"Nick "The Muscle" Beckett"`, you're going to have a problem. It will be rendered client-side as:

Example 5.37 How that alert is rendered

```
alert("You deleted the file called Nick "The Muscle" Beckett").
```

So what's the problem here? The first quote in `"The Muscle"` ends the string, resulting in a syntax error.

This is easily solved by using `wf:js_escape/1` as follows:

Example 5.38 `wf:js_escape`

```
EscapedName = wf:js_escape(Name),
wf:wire(wf:f("alert(\"You deleted the file called ~s\")", [EscapedName])).
```

Now the string will be rendered on the client as desired:

Example 5.39 How `wf:js_escape` is rendered

```
alert("You deleted the file called Nick 'The Muscle' Beckett").
```

The user, of course, will see:

```
You deleted the file called Nick "The Muscle" Becket.
```

5.5.5. `wf:json_encode/1`, `wf:json_decode/1`

JSON has become a popular file format for building web-based APIs, largely replacing XML. Indeed, while the X in AJAX originally stood for XML, most asynchronous requests these days actually use JSON.

Nitrogen uses a modified version of Mochiweb's JSON to encode Erlang terms and decode JSON back to Erlang:

Example 5.40 `wf:json_encode`

```
1> Term = [{fruits, [<<"Apple">>, <<"Banana">>]},
          {numbers, [1,2,3,4]}].
[{fruits,[<<"Apple">>,<<"Banana">>]},
 {numbers,[1,2,3,4]}]
2> Encoded = wf:json_encode(Term).
[123,
 [34,"fruits",34],
 58,
 [91,
  [34,<<"Apple">>,34],
  44,
  [34,<<"Banana">>,34],
  93],
 44,
 [34,"numbers",34],
 58,
 [91,"1",44,"2",44,"3",44,"4",93],
 125]
```

Now, you may be thinking: "What the heck is that? It doesn't look a thing like JSON."

Turns out Nitrogen optimizes the conversion for I/O. Squint your eyes when you look at the return of `wf:json_encode/1` in the previous listing and you'll see what's called an IOList. To make it readable, run it through `iolist_to_binary/1`:

Example 5.41 `iolist_to_binary/1`

```
3> Bin = iolist_to_binary(Encoded).
<<"{\"fruits\":[\"Apple\",\"Banana\"],\"numbers\":[1,2,3,4]}">>
```

You can convert the JSON string back into the proplist format. Indeed, you can convert it to either an IO List or a binary. The result would be the same:

Example 5.42   **Decode JSON from Binary**

```
4> wf:json_decode(Bin).
[{<<"fruits">>,[<<"Apple">>,<<"Banana">>]},
 {<<"numbers">>,[1,2,3,4]}]
```

And you'll see it decodes the same way even if it's an IOList:

Example 5.43   **Decode JSON From IOList**

```
5> wf:json_decode(Encoded).
[{<<"fruits">>,[<<"Apple">>,<<"Banana">>]},
 {<<"numbers">>,[1,2,3,4]}]
```

In the examples above, you may have noticed that the proplist keys originally represented atoms that get converted to binaries. There are two reasons for this. First, JavaScript doesn't have the concept of atoms. But also, using atoms as keys would present a second problem—Erlang has an atom table that isn't garbage collected[5] This means that a runaway script or malicious user could bring down the VM by creating JSON with dynamically created keys. As the JSON Decoder converted those keys to atoms, it could fill up the atom table and cause the VM itself to crash.

---

[5]See page 458 for more about the atom table limit.

Erlang provides a function called `list_to_existing_atom/1` to help mitigate this. But the best policy is to use `wf:json_decode/1`. It will always convert JSON keys to binaries.

One final consideration when dealing with JSON in Erlang is this: As we've noted, Erlang "strings" are just lists of integers. As a consequence, Erlang has no way of knowing if a list of integers in the ASCII range (1-255) is meant to be a string or an actual list. `wf:json_encode/1` will convert all Erlang lists to JavaScript lists and Erlang binaries to JavaScript strings.

5.5.6. `wf:hex_encode/1`, `wf:hex_decode/1`

It's a piece of cake to encode a string or binary into hexadecimal:

Example 5.44 `wf:hex_encode` and `wf:hex_decode`

```
6> wf:hex_encode("This is my string").
{ok,<<"54686973206973206D7920737472696E67">>}

7> wf:hex_decode(<<"54686973206973206D7920737472696E67">>).
{ok,<<"This is my string">>}
```

Keep in mind that the return of both `wf:hex_encode/1` and `wf:hex_decode/1` are both `{ok, Binary}`.

6. nindex

LLOYD: Busy knocking out this database app.

RUSTY: Yeah?

LLOYD: Need to organize those Erlang and Nitrogen weblinks you guys keep thowing at me.

RUSTY: Way cool! Can I fork your code?

LLOYD: For?

RUSTY: I'm coaching the computer club at the high school.

LLOYD: Sure. But give me ten to wrap up the user side.

6.1. Oh CRUD

So here's Rusty Nail at the high school, trying to look like one of the cool kids.

RUSTY: My colleague, Lloyd London, wrote this searchable database to store weblinks. Excellent example of a CRUD application.

OLEG: CRUD—Sounds like something my dog stepped in.

MARSHA: Create Read Update Delete, am I right Mr. Nail?

RUSTY: Exactly. Basic database operations. How did you happen to know that?

MARSHA: Reading up on Dets.

OLEG: Waste of time. Dets is like—training wheels. I want to learn Mnesia.

RUSTY: Don't diss Dets. Dets has it's place.

MARSHA: My big brother says PostgreSQL is wicked cool.

STEVIE: Want wicked cool—look at Riak. It's distributed.

OLEG: Mnesia is distributed, Doofus. But why does it have such a wierd name?

RUSTY: Hey, Dets, Mnesia, Riak, PostgreSQL—these are all fine databases. Depends on your requirements. And the good news—Nitrogen doesn't care which one you use.

STEVIE: Yeah, but it's all so confusing—which one should we use when?

6.2. So Many DBs—So Little Time

RUSTY: Excellent question. Let me read words of wisdom from Joe Armstrong, one of the founding fathers of Erlang:[1]

> For many systems—I use one file per user. The file contains `term_to_binary(X)`, where X is whatever I feel like, to represent the user data.
>
> (Or you can use text files—then you can run amazing things like grep and `find` on them :-)
>
> The OS caches file access and I can easily analyse/dump the files.
>
> I've *never* got to the point where I need to change the file system for a database (but then again I've not built a really big system—and this works fine for several thousand files/users).
>
> If and when the design problems are solved you can change representations *if it is necessary*—choosing a database right at the start is 'premature optimisation'—if you ever get to this point then the choice of representation should be dictated by measurement and not guesswork.

---

[1] http://erlang.org/pipermail/erlang-questions/2014-November/081701.html

Garrett Smith, another Erlang heavyweight, chimed in:[2]

> There are like 100 amazing options!... When I'm starting on something new, I just don't know enough about anything to make the right decision—so I deliberately make the right wrong-decision—that is, the decision that will let me move forward quickly and get to the real problems. I might throw it away later, or I might keep it. But in any case, I'm sure as hell not going to spend a lot of time on it. Not until I'm facing real, hard, visible problems that I can use to inform my next steps.

How you persist data, in other words, depends on the requirements and constraints of your application. First cut, keep it simple. If you need a heavy-duty solution for sake of performance, availability, or scale:

- Align your schema with your real needs

- Research your options

- Test and measure before you make your final choice

'Nuf said. But let me ask, why do we need databases anyway?

MARSHA: Duh—to save data?

RUSTY: Not sure it's so obvious. Sometimes we can recompute data when we need it.

OLEG: Yes, but suppose the computation is really time-consuming? In fact, many times, it's not even possible.

RUSTY: Granted, but it always pays to ask. It also pays to ask who's going to use the data, when, and how will you keep the data up-to-date? Do you need to save out-of-date data for, say, forensic purposes? And more, how are you going to protect valuable data from hardware failure, malware, net splits, and technical obsolescence? Many people have valuable data on media they can't read because data storage technology has passed them by.

---

[2]http://erlang.org/pipermail/erlang-questions/2014-November/081700.html

STEVIE: My head hurts—

RUSTY: Indeed. But, I agree, we often *do* need to save data for future access. So what are our options? *Information Age* ran an overview piece called *The definitive guide to the modern database*—a bit dated, but no doubt you can find it on the web.[3]

As Erlang programmers we're lucky duckies. Erlang has three built-in database systems that will serve many needs:

ets Consider when speed is a high priority since all data is stored in RAM, like a cache system. Reject when you can't afford to lose data or data needs to be replicated across a cluster. Since ETS works entirely in RAM, it isn't really a database, but it's still handy when you need to temporarily store or cache data.[4]

dets Consider when speed is not a priority since all requests immediately go to and come from disk. Reject when speed is essential or you need replication.[5]

mnesia Consider when you want built-in clustering/replication or you need to store Erlang records and terms natively. Mnesia also provides ACID[6] transaction support. The cool thing about Mnesia is that it's built into the Erlang system (no dependencies needed). Reject when you don't want to mess around with records or QLC. Under the hood, Mnesia actually uses a combination of ETS and Dets for storage and caching.[7]

MARSHA: What about PostgreSQL?

RUSTY: Yeah, PostgreSQL works with Nitrogen. Great choice when we need a relational database and it's very popular.

---

[3]The definitive guide to the modern database, http://www.information-age.com/industry/software/123458063/definitive-guide-modern-database

[4]http://www.erlang.org/doc/man/ets.html

[5]http://erlang.org/doc/man/dets.html

[6]https://en.wikipedia.org/wiki/ACID

[7]http://www.erlang.org/doc/man/mnesia.html

If one database or another fits your needs, go for it. But keep in mind that you may have to translate the way you represent data as you move it between your Erlang application and your database.

OLEG: Well, I'm bored. Show me the code.

6.3. Lloyd London's Weblink Application

RUSTY: Righto. So, we agree then. For our next project we'll concentrate on Lloyd London's weblink application.[8]

OLEG: Sounds cool. I could use something like that for my Erlang links.

STEVIE: I've been collecting weblinks for my history class. Have so many I can't find anything.

OLEG: Can we start with Mnesia?

RUSTY: Do you one better. We'll separate the application from the database with a facade.[9] That way we can install any database we choose. Our application will be database agnostic.

OLEG: Facade?

RUSTY: API.

MARSHA: Way cool!

RUSTY: So, Stevie, how are you storing your weblinks now?

STEVIE: In files, like this:

---

[8]Code for this project can be found at: https://github.com/BuildItWithNitrogen/nindex
[9]https://en.wikipedia.org/wiki/Facade_pattern

Example 6.1   How Stevie is storing weblinks

```
HEAD
Topic
Text
Url
...
Text
Url
```

RUSTY: What's in the text field?

STEVIE: I just copy and paste the main headline from the web page.

OLEG: Why not use grep to find what you're looking for?

STEVIE: Yeah, but—

MARSHA: Duh—shell programming class meets on Tuesdays.

RUSTY: Be nice, kiddies. If we have a facade that allows us to plug in any database we want, why not pick up on Joe Armstrong's suggestion and store data in the file system until we decide what we really want?

OLEG: Like, build a fake database?

RUSTY: Well, I wouldn't exactly call it fake. Indeed, I propose that we call our awesome new db JoeDB.

Let's fire up a new project called nindex to illustrate. I suggest a slim release to save time and space:

Listing 6.1   (⇒ $) Make a new project

```
~/nitrogen$ make slim_cowboy PROJECT=nindex
```

STEVIE: So why Cowboy ?

OLEG: Don't you remember what Rusty told us last week? Cowboy is lean and mean; provides high throughput.[10]

RUSTY: Yeah, but we could just as well have specified Yaws,[11] Inets,[12] Mochi-Web,[13] or Webmachine.[14]

They're all fine webservers—each with its advantages.

MARSHA: Shouldn't we initialize git?

RUSY: Excellent idea! And while we're at it, let's open an Erlang console and fire up sync so we can correct code entries as we go.

OLEG: Beware of port conflicts!

MARSHA: Yes! Yes! On it... Kill any other services running on port 8000 or change the nindex port in `../nindex/etc/simple_bridge.config`.

OLEG: Know it all!

Listing 6.2 (⇒ $) Initialize git for nindex

```
~/nitrogen$ cd ../nindex
...
~/nindex$ git init
Initialized empty Git repository in /home/jess/nindex/.git

~/nindex$ bin/nitrogen console
...1> sync:go()
```

---

[10]https://github.com/ninenines/cowboy
[11]http://yaws.hyber.org/
[12]http://erlang.org/doc/apps/inets/http_server.html
[13]https://github.com/mochi/mochiweb
[14]https://github.com/Webmachine/webmachine

6.4. JoeDB

RUSTY: We need a new module for our knock-'em-dead database JoeDB. So,

> cd ../nindex

...and make a new file at site/src/ni_joedb.erl:

Listing 6.3 (⇒ $) `ni_joedb` **boilerplate**

```
.../nindex$ cd site/src
.../nindex$ vim ni_joedb.erl

-module(ni_joedb).

%% Expected API exports
-export([ init_db/0,
          get_all/0
        ]).

%%----------------------
%% @doc joeDB
%%----------------------
```

RUSTY: We need to move on. So, homework assignment: For sake of main-tainers, and a good way to review, flesh out documentation at the top of the page.

For testing purposes, we can initialize our database with a few links:

Listing 6.4 (⇒ vim) **Initialize joeDB** (`joe_db.erl`)

```
%%----------------------

seed() ->
```

```
[[{id, create_id()},
  {topic,"Erlang"},
  {descriptor,"Erlang Programming Language"},
  {url,"http://wwww.erlang.org"}],
 [{id, create_id()},
  {topic,"Nitrogen"},
  {descriptor,"Nitrogen Home Page"},
  {url,"http://nitrogenproject.com/"}]].
```

STEVIE: Hold up! What's that `create_id()` function call in there? Every ID, should be unique, right?

RUSTY: Indeed! Many databases will take care of ID generation on their own. For instance, Riak, PostgreSQL, and MySQL all do this, but others may rely on you to make your own.

Since ID generation is part of the database layer and JoeDB doesn't have a built-in generator, let's add one:

Listing 6.5 (⇒ vim) **A *totally* awesome unique ID generator (`joe_db.erl`)**

```
    {descriptor,"Nitrogen Home Page"},
    {url,"http://nitrogenproject.com/"}]].

create_id() ->
    rand:uniform(999999999999).
```

OLEG: Woah—that's dubious—

RUSTY: It is. As written, I'd never use this particular implementation of create_id/0 in production. I'd go for stronger guarantees against id duplication by adding more 9s—like 30–40 of 'em—or check for prior existence[15].

---

[15]Which can certainly help prevent duplicate creation. But unless it is done as an atomic operation it's still not *guaranteed* to be unique.

But you must admit, with chances of nearly one in a trillion, the probability of
`create_id/0` generating duplicates is pretty low—at least for the low-traffic app
we're building. If you want to be safe, add a few more 9s and you'll be good.

IDs, randomness, and large numbers in Erlang

One of the pleasant features of Erlang is the way it handles large integers.
Erlang doesn't have integer overflow. Instead, it can handle any size of
integer. So you could go to approximately 160 bits (like sha160), and
for all practical purposes eliminate the possibility of a duplicate by just
doing something as simple as

```
rand:uniform(999999999999999999999999999999999999999999999999).
```

(That's 48 nines.)

The liklihood of an ID collision after creating 10^{20} IDs is on the order of
1 in a billion.[a]

Alternatively, you could use third-party UUID generators:[b]

---

[a]http://j.mp/idduplication
[b]https://github.com/avtobiff/erlang-uuid
https://github.com/okeuday/uuid
https://github.com/travis/erlang-uuid

MARSHA: Still, you're cheating—

RUSTY: Guilty as charged. Now, back to `ni_joedb.erl`.

OLEG: Okayyy—

RUSTY: Have faith.

Listing 6.6 (⇒ vim) **Flesh out joeDB(**`joe_db.erl`**)**

```
create_id() ->
    rand:uniform(999999999999).

get_all() ->
    {ok, Bin} = file:read_file("joedb"),
    binary_to_term(Bin).

put_all(Data) ->
    Bin = term_to_binary(Data),
    file:write_file("joedb", Bin).

init_db() ->
    put_all(seed()).
```

OLEG: Oh, way cool! I expected something gnarly. But all we're talking about is a list of records stored in a file called joedb.

RUSTY: Before we proceed, let's seed our nifty new database. Sync should be running, so save the file and let's directly call `ni_joedb:init_db()` in the Erlang shell:

Listing 6.7 (⇒ >) **In the Erlang shell**

```
...2> ni_joedb:init_db().
ok
```

6.4.1. APIs with proplists

RUSTY: Now is a good time to talk about abstraction. We've selected proplists for internally representing records in our database. But we want to give the user a simpler interface—an API.

MARSHA: Erlang has a proplists module. Isn't that simple enough?

RUSTY: Erlang does and we certainly can use it. But suppose we decide later that we want to change the implementation from proplists to records or dicts.

MARSHA: Code dependent on the proplist structure would break.

RUSTY: It would—hard! Instead, we want functions for working with "objects" that hide the implementation of data access. Note that I'm *not* using "objects" in the OOP sense. There is no concept of privatizing data in Erlang. Nevertheless, we want our data to be completely opaque to modules outside of ni_joedb.

STEVIE: And we can do that how?

RUSTY: Fairly simple, actually. First, create a constructor called new/3:

Listing 6.8 (⇒ vim) **Add our API to joeDB (joe_db.erl)**

```
init_db() ->
    put_all(seed()).

%% API functions
new(Topic, Descriptor, Url) ->
    [{topic,Topic},
     {descriptor,Descriptor},
     {url,Url}].
```

RUSTY: Now we need functions to set and get values.

MARSHA: Wait! I'm looking at the proplist module. I see the function named proplists:get_value/2 to retrieve values. But I don't see one to set them.

RUSTY: Unfortunately, there isn't one. To set a value, you delete it first, then prepend it with [{Key, Value}|Proplist], or replace inline with lists:map/2. It's wonky, but truthfully, if I have a proplist-heavy app, I use a third-party module called sigma_proplist,[16] since it does way more than just the proplists module.

Since the release of the maps feature in Erlang 17, however, I opt for maps whenever possible. But we'll talk about that later.

OLEG: You're tangentializing again, Rusty!

RUSTY: My bad. So Stevie, let's see your happy hands work their magic! Show us how to pull values from a weblink.

STEVIE: Here goes nothing:

Listing 6.9 (⇒ vim) **Getters** (joe_db.erl)

```
    {descriptor,Descriptor},
    {url,Url}].

id(Weblink) ->
    proplists:get_value(id, Weblink).

topic(Weblink) ->
    proplists:get_value(topic, Weblink).

descriptor(Weblink) ->
    proplists:get_value(descriptor, Weblink).

url(Weblink) ->
    proplists:get_value(url, Weblink).
```

RUSTY: Way to go!

---

[16]https://github.com/choptastic/sigma_proplist

OLEG: Yeah, but he cheated. Looked at the Erlang docs.

RUSTY: Ah, so you can do better? How about showing us how to set values in a weblink?

OLEG: Oh man! Always picking on me.

RUSTY: We just discussed it.

OLEG: Righto:

Listing 6.10 (⇒ vim) **Setters (joe_db.erl)**

```erlang
url(Weblink) ->
    proplists:get_value(url, Weblink).

id(Weblink, ID) ->
    Weblink2 = proplists:delete(id),
    [{id, ID} | Weblink2].

topic(Weblink, Topic) ->
    Weblink2 = proplists:delete(topic),
    [{topic, Topic} | Weblink2].

descriptor(Weblink, Descriptor) ->
    Weblink2 = proplists:delete(descriptor),
    [{descriptor, Descriptor} | Weblink2].

url(Weblink, Url) ->
    Weblink2 = proplists:delete(url),
    [{url, Url} | Weblink2].
```

MARSHA: Looks like a lot of copy-and-paste.

OLEG: Ah, great minds run on similar tracks. I was thinking exactly the same thing. But I can fix it:

Listing 6.11 (⇒ vim) **Fix the Setters** (joe_db.erl)

```
url(Weblink) ->
    proplists:get_value(url, Weblink).

set_value(Weblink, Key, Value) ->
    Weblink2 = proplists:delete(Key, Weblink),
    [{Key, Value} | Weblink2].

id(Weblink, ID) ->
    Weblink2 = proplists:delete(id),
    [{id, ID} | Weblink2].
    set_value(Weblink, id, ID).

topic(Weblink, Topic) ->
    Weblink2 = proplists:delete(topic),
    [{topic, Topic} | Weblink2].
    set_value(Weblink, topic, Topic).

descriptor(Weblink, Descriptor) ->
    Weblink2 = proplists:delete(descriptor),
    [{descriptor, Descriptor} | Weblink2].
    set_value(Weblink, descriptor, Descriptor).

url(Weblink, Url) ->
    Weblink2 = proplists:delete(url),
    [{url, Url} | Weblink2].
    set_value(Weblink, url, Url).
```

RUSTY: Take a bow, Oleg! You *were* listening all along. But you're forgetting one thing—

OLEG: No way!

MARSHA: We need to export these new functions.

OLEG: Oh, that:

Listing 6.12 ($\Rightarrow$ vim) **Update -export** (`joe_db.erl`)

```erlang
-module(ni_joedb).

%% Expected API exports

-export([ init_db/0,
          get_all/0,
          new/3,
          id/1, id/2,
          topic/1, topic/2,
          descriptor/1, descriptor/2,
          url/1, url/2
        ]).
```

RUSTY: Okay, now we have a fine little API for working with data from the outside world. Let's expand our database interface.

6.4.2. Saving individual items

RUSTY: So, given what we have so far, how can we retrieve a link?

MARSHA: I can do it!

RUSTY: Show us.

Listing 6.13 ($\Rightarrow$ vim) **Get a link from the database** (`joe_db.erl`)

```erlang
          url/1, url/2
        ]).

get_link(ID) ->
  Data = get_all(),
  [Rec || Rec <- Data, id(Rec)=:=ID].
```

RUSTY: You're *almost* home free. But that will return a *list* of proplists, even if it's just a list with a single item. We want a *single item,* or rather a *single proplist.*

MARSHA: Ah:

Listing 6.14 (⇒ $) **Fix** `get_link/1` (`joe_db.erl`)

```erlang
get_link(ID) ->
  Data = get_all(),
  case [Rec || Rec <- Data, id(Rec)=:=ID] of
    [] -> new;
    [Weblink|_] -> Weblink
  end.
```

RUSTY: Like it! I particularly like how you returned new if an item isn't found. So, Stevie, how would you save a single weblink?

STEVIE: Hmmm—How about...this:

Listing 6.15 (⇒ vim) **Save a weblink** (`joe_db.erl`)

```erlang
    [Weblink|_] -> Weblink
  end.

save_link(Weblink) ->
  Data = get_all(),
  Data1 = [Weblink|Data],
  put_all(Data1).
```

OLEG: Wait! What happens if a user tries to update a record instead of add a new one?

RUSTY: Good question. As implemented, it'll just add to the list without removing the previous record.[17] So we have a design decision to make. We could choose to make our `save_link/1` function smart, and automatically update if an item exists, or we could tell programmers using our API that they need to keep track of that themselves.

What do you guys want to do?

MARSHA: The latter sounds easier.

OLEG: It does, but how hard can it be to make our function smarter?

RUSTY: Indeed, not that hard. Also, consider: real-world database products will fail if they don't deal with issues like this.

STEVIE: Then let's make it smarter.

MARSHA: Agreed.

RUSTY: So, problem: How do we edit existing values?

MARSHA: Suppose we just delete the old one and insert the new one like we did with the `set_value/3` function?

RUSTY: That works. Do we want to create a condition that signals to our database adapter that we want to create a new proplist as opposed to saving an existing one?

OLEG: What if we treat an item as new if it doesn't yet have an ID?

RUSTY: That should work. Let's do it. We can check the record for an ID. If it's not set, or set to undefined, we know that we have to insert and generate a new ID. Who wants to take it on?

STEVIE: Well, since I made the `save_link` function—

---

[17]Since we're prepending the new items onto each list, our implementation of `save_link/1` and `get_link/1` will always return the newest link to the given ID. Technically this will work. But it wastes space. And more, the system has to iterate over more items, thus, take longer.

RUSTY: You're on!

Listing 6.16 (⇨ vim) **Add** `save_link` (`joe_db.erl`)

```
save_link(Weblink) ->
   Data = get_all(),
   Data1 = case id(Weblink) of
      undefined -> insert_link(Weblink, Data);
      _ -> update_link(Weblink, Data)
   end,
   Data1 = [Weblink|Data],
   put_all(Data1).
```

RUSTY: Looking good!

STEVIE: Thanks. `insert_link/2` is dead-simple:

Listing 6.17 (⇨ vim) **Add** `insert_link/2` (`joe_db.erl`)

```
   put_all(Data1).

insert_link(Weblink, Data) ->
   Weblink2 = id(Weblink, create_id()),
   [Weblink2|Data].
```

OLEG: What's the point of making a separate function for something as simple as "give something an ID and stick it in front of a list"?

STEVIE: Giving a function an explicit name like `insert_link` makes it self-documenting.

RUSTY: Exactly! When a function is well-named there's less need to add a comment to explain what it does. Plus, it makes life easier for code maintainers. Case expressions already impose enough visual clutter. Adding more operators, symbols, and function calls contributes to cognitive stress.

Believe me, code maintainers are burdened with enough cognitive load without us adding more.

Moving on, what should the update_link/2 link look like?

STEVIE: Hmmm—not sure I know how to do that.

6.4.3. Introducing lists:map

RUSTY: Best way would be to use lists:map. Don't be confused. We're not talking about the map data structure here. Think "function." A map function in Erlang iterates over every item in a list, doing something to each item as it goes. A map function in Erlang is similar to a for loop in other languages. Consider, for instance, the following Java-like pseudocode for iterating over the list my_list:

Example 6.2 Iteration in imperative langauges

```
array my_list2 = new array();
for(i=0,i < my_list.length(); i++) {
   if(my_list[i].id==the_id)
      my_list2[i] = do_something_to(my_list[i]);
   else
      my_list2[i] = my_list[i];
}
```

RUSTY: Here's the Erlang way:

Example 6.3   Iteration with Erlang's map

```
lists:map(fun(SomeItem) ->
   case id(SomeItem)==TheID of
     true -> do_something_to(SomeItem);
     false-> SomeItem
   end
end, MyList).
```

STEVIE: I'm still struggling to grok this.

MARSHA: Same.

RUSTY: That's fair. It takes time to wrap your brain around thinking in maps instead of `for` and `while` loops. Truth is, after working in functional programming exclusively for awhile, I struggle with the context shift back to procedural languages. I keep wanting to reach for `lists:map` and list comprehensions. I forget how to think with `for` and `while` loops.

Anyway, here's how `update_link` should look with a map:

Listing 6.18   (⇒ vim) Build `update_link/2` (`joe_db.erl`)

```
   Weblink2 = id(Weblink, create_id()),
   [Weblink2|Data].

update_link(NewWeblink, Data) ->
  lists:map(fun(Weblink) ->
    case id(Weblink)==id(NewWeblink) of
      true -> NewWeblink;
      false -> Weblink
    end
  end, Data).
```

MARSHA: Interesting. You completely discard the old web link if it has a matching ID and replace it with the new one.

RUSTY: Exactly. This function will certainly have performance issues, like...

MARSHA: ... recalculating `id(NewWeblink)` in each iteration.

RUSTY: Indeed. That's the most glaring issue. It's also the easiest to fix. The other issue is that for every update operation, it has to iterate through the whole list when, truthfully, it should be able to stop when it finds the target weblink. A better solution would be to change our entire data from a list of data objects to a structure better suited to finding things quickly.

MARSHA: For instance?

RUSTY: Oh, a `dict` with an ID as the key might be worth consideration. But let's not get to premature optimization and over-engineering. This is just a stand-in database until we code something better.

6.4.4. Deleting things

RUSTY: Finally, how can we delete data items?

MARSHA: We could search for an ID then remove that item from the list—with `lists:map` maybe?

RUSTY: Good guess, but wouldn't work. The resultant list from `lists:map` will always be the same length as the original. How about a list comprehension?

MARSHA: Ah! Can I give it a shot?

RUSTY: Be my guest.

Listing 6.19 **Add** `delete_link/1` `(joe_db.erl)`

```
    end
  end, Data).

delete_link(ID) ->
    Data = get_all(),
    Data1 = [WL || WL <- Data, id(WL)=/=ID],
    put_all(Data1).
```

RUSTY: Awesome. Nailed it first try. Could also have used `lists:filtermap/2` instead of the list comprehension, but I do like the way you did it.

STEVIE: Don't forget exports.

MARSHA: Right, right.

Listing 6.20 ($\Rightarrow$ `vim`) **Export our new functions**

```
-export([ init_db/0,
          get_all/0,
          get_link/1,
          save_link/1,
          update_link/2,
          delete_link/1,
          new/3,
          . . .
```

RUSTY: Save `ni_joedb.erl` and we're good to go.

MARSHA: This is fun. What's next?

RUSTY: How about hiding our database behind a facade?

OLEG: Yeah... What's with that?

RUSTY: We want to make our database choice *pluggable.* If we decide to switch to a different data store, in other words, we only need to change a line or two of code.

6.5. Facade

RUSTY: Let's start with a new module called `ni_links.erl`.

Listing 6.21 (⇒ $) **Set up new `ni_links` module**

```
../site/src$ vim ni_links.erl

-module(ni_links).
-export([ init_db/0,
          get_all/0,
          get_link/1,
          save_link/1,
          update_link/2,
          delete_link/1,
          new/3,
          id/1,id/2,
          topic/1,topic/2,
          descriptor/1,descriptor/2,
          url/1,url/2
        ]).
```

RUSTY: Now in an amazing feat of Erlang sleight-of-hand—we define a macro as an alias for our backend:

```
        url/1,url/2
    ]).

-define(DB, ni_joedb).
```

RUSTY: Now, taking init_db() as an example, we define our functions to look like this:

```
-define(DB, ni_joedb).

init_db() ->
    ?DB:init_db().
```

MARSHA: Whoa, ?DB? That's a new syntax.

RUSTY: Yep. That's a macro term. The compiler will replace the term ?DB with the definition we declared in the -define term, that is, the atom ni_joedb. You can think of Erlang macros as find-and-replace.

OLEG: Wait—I get it! The facade simply shadows the database functions. We could change the -define(DB, ni_joedb) line to, say, -define(DB, ni_mnesia), and our application would work as advertised!

RUSTY: Clever dude. So, Marsha, can you wrap this up?

Listing 6.24 (⇒ vim) **Wrap up our** *facade*

```
    ?DB:init_db().

get_all() ->
    ?DB:get_all().

get_link(ID) ->
    ?DB:get_link(ID).

save_link(Weblink) ->
    ?DB:save_link(Weblink).

update_link(NewWebLink, Data) ->
    ?DB:update_link(NewWebLink, Data).

delete_link(ID) ->
    ?DB:delete_link(ID).
```

RUSTY: Hold up! Oleg, what's missing?

OLEG: The new/3 function. Oh, and the "getters..."

Listing 6.25 (⇒ vim) **The getters**

```
delete_link(ID) ->
    ?DB:delete_link(ID).

new(Topic, Descriptor, Url) ->
    ?DB:new(Topic, Descriptor, Url).

id(Weblink) ->
    ?DB:id(Weblink).

topic(Weblink) ->
    ?DB:topic(Weblink).
```

```
descriptor(Weblink) ->
  ?DB:descriptor(Weblink).

url(Weblink) ->
  ?DB:url(Weblink).
```

STEVIE: Don't forget the "setters:'

Listing 6.26 (⇒ vim) **The setters**

```
url(Weblink) ->
  ?DB:url(Weblink).

id(Weblink, ID) ->
  ?DB:id(Weblink, ID).

topic(Weblink, Topic) ->
  ?DB:topic(Weblink, Topic).

descriptor(Weblink, Desc) ->
  ?DB:descriptor(Weblink, Desc).

url(Weblink, Url) ->
  ?DB:url(Weblink, Url).
```

RUSTY: Outstanding! So, now, we can access our database without worry about the implementation of ni_joedb.

OLEG: Yeah, but what about search? Say I want to find all links related to Thomas Jefferson. We haven't thought about that.

RUSTY: So, let's see what we can do.

6.6. Search

RUSTY: Let's think it through. We want to return all items that, in some sense, match words or terms in a user-defined search string. Here, I'll sketch it out in a new module called `ni_search.erl`.

Listing 6.27 (⇒ $) **Create a search module**

```
../site/src$ vim ni_search.erl

-module(ni_search).
-export([search/1]).

search(SearchString) ->
    Weblinks = ni_links:get_all(),
    [Link || Link <- Weblinks, filter(SearchString, Link)].
```

RUSTY: The heart of the matter here is `filter/2`. Any suggestions as to what it might look like?

MARSHA: I suppose we could split up `SearchString` into a list of words, then for each web link, do the same with the `Topic` and `Descriptor` and look for matching words.

STEVIE: We can split up `SearchString`, `Topic`, and `Descriptor` by using `string:lexemes/2`[18] from the Erlang string library.[19]

RUSTY: That'll work.

MARSHA: So—how does this look?

---

[18]If you happen to be using Erlang 19 or lower, you'll want to use `string:tokens` instead of `string:lexemes`.
[19]http://erlang.org/doc/man/string.html

> **Listing 6.28** (⇒ vim) **Create a filter function**
>
> ```
> Weblinks = ni_links:get_all(),
> [Link || Link <- Weblinks, filter(SearchString, Link)].
>
> filter(SearchString, Weblink) ->
>    Topic = ni_links:topic(Weblink),
>    Descriptor = ni_links:descriptor(Weblink),
>    SearchWords = unique_words(SearchString),
>    WeblinkWords = unique_words(Topic ++ " " ++ Descriptor),
>    SharedWords = shared(SearchWords, WeblinkWords),
>    length(SharedWords) > 0.
> ```

RUSTY: Promising.

STEVIE: Wait! What's that `length(List) > 0` bit?

MARSHA: We only want to return web links that contain one or more search
terms, so we return *true* if the number of found items is greater than zero.

STEVIE: Got it.

RUSTY: So how would you implement `unique_words`?

OLEG: How is this?

> **Listing 6.29** (⇒ vim) **Make `unique_words/1`**
>
> ```
>    length(SharedWords) > 0.
>
> unique_words(String) ->
>    string:lexemes(String, " ").
> ```

MARSHA: But depending upon `String`, that could create duplicates, right?

141

RUSTY: It could. But here's a nifty trick to delete duplicate items from a list: Recall that a set is a collection of elements with no duplicate elements.[20] Thus, we can deduplicate the list by converting the list of tokens into a set, and returning the set:

Listing 6.30 (⇒ `vim`) **Delete duplicate words — `unique_words/1`**

```
unique_words(String) ->
   Tokens = string:lexemes(String, " "),
   sets:from_list(Tokens).
```

OLEG: Way cool!

RUSTY: We can also use sets to implement the shared/2 function referenced in search/1. In this case we want to return the final list of tokens that are shared between both the search string and the web link:

Listing 6.31 (⇒ `vim`) **Create the `shared/2` helper function**

```
   Tokens = string:lexemes(String, " "),
   sets:from_list(Tokens).

shared(S1, S2) ->
   SharedSet = sets:intersection(S1, S2),
   sets:to_list(SharedSet).
```

STEVIE: Awesome!

OLEG: Wait! We're returning a list converted from a set, and then running length(Words) in search/1. Couldn't we just return the SharedSet from shared/1 and use a function from the sets module to check the length?

---

[20] http://www.erlang.org/doc/man/sets.html

RUSTY: Great catch! Exactly right. The pertinent function is `sets:size(Set)`. Want to take a crack at it?

OLEG: Sure! First, I'd update shared/2 to look like this:

Listing 6.32 (⇒ vim) **Update** `shared/2`

```
shared(S1, S2) ->
    SharedSet = sets:intersection(S1, S2),
    sets:to_list(SharedSet).
    sets:intersection(S1, S2).
```

OLEG: Then, the last line of the filter function would look like this:

Listing 6.33 (⇒ vim) **Rework** `filter/2`

```
filter(SearchString, Weblink) ->
    Topic = ni_links:topic(Weblink),
    Descriptor = ni_links:descriptor(Weblink),
    SearchWords = unique_words(SearchString),
    WeblinkWords = unique_words(Topic ++ " " ++ Descriptor),
    SharedWords = shared(SearchWords, WeblinkWords),
    length(SharedWords) > 0.
    sets:size(SharedWords) > 0.
```

RUSTY: Way to go! You removed an unnecessary conversion and eliminated one line of code.

STEVIE: Sheer genius.

OLEG: Don't I know it.

RUSTY: So, now we have a database. Save it so we can move on to the user interface.

STEVIE: Thought it would never happen.

6.7. Enter the State Machine

RUSTY: CRUD applications can be modeled as state machines.[21]

OLEG: State machines?

RUSTY: What's the first thing we want to see when we enter our weblink database application?

MARSHA: Search for a link?

STEVIE: Yeah, but—we need to enter a link before we can search.

RUSTY: We can give the user a choice—enter a new link or search for an existing link. Let's call this is our initial state. The initial state offers our user two choices: click a button that transitions to an add-new-web-link form or enter search words to initiate a search. Say our user clicks Add new web link, what happens next?

OLEG: Wait, let me try to capture this in a module. First, let's build our code. Then we can fire up our new Nitrogen instance:

Listing 6.34 (⇒ $) Start Nitrogen (should be second nature by now)

```
~/nindex$ bin/nitrogen console
...
(nitrogen@127.0.0.1)1> sync:go().
```

---

[21]Ming, Mike Su, *Using Abstract State Machines to Model a Graphical User Interface System*, http://citeseerx.ist.psu.edu/viewdoc/download?doi=10.1.1.158.8557&rep=rep1&type=pdf

6.8. State One: The first thing anyone sees

OLEG: Dataman is cruisin' now! Fires off the browser. . . .

> localhost:8000

OLEG: . . . and, *voila*, the default Nitrogen index page.

MARSHA: And?

OLEG: Open a new terminal and bring up index.erl:

Listing 6.35 (⇒ $) index.erl

```
~/nindex$ cd site/src
~/nindex/site/src$ vim index.erl
```

STEVIE: Boy's on a roll—

OLEG: Change the page title:

Listing 6.36 (⇒ vim) Change page title in index

```
-module (index).
-compile(export_all).
-include_lib("nitrogen_core/include/wf.hrl").

main() -> #template { file="./site/templates/bare.html" }.

title() -> "My Web Links".
```

OLEG: And—wait, should I delete everything after title/0?

RUSTY: Your call. eb

OLEG: Deleted. Now, we were saying about the initial state—

MARSHA: We were saying that the user has two choices—either click a button that transitions to an "add new" form or enter search words and initiate a search.

RUSTY: For now, just comment in where state changes are introduced in the code.

OLEG: Okay, something like this?

Listing 6.37 (⇒ `vim`) **Add comments**

```
title() -> "My Web Links".

%% ********************************************
%% Initial State
%% User choice:  transition to "add new" form
%% or enter search words and initiate a search
%% ********************************************
```

RUSTY: Just wondering, should we include the add new form in this module?

STEVIE: Might clutter up the module.

RUSTY: My instinct as well.

OLEG: Okay, saving `index.erl`. New module coming up—

MARSHA: Look at those fingers fly!

6.9. State Two: Saving a New Weblink

Listing 6.38 ($\Rightarrow$ $) New module to save a new weblink

```
~/nindex/site/src$ vim new.erl

-module(new).
-compile(export_all).
-include_lib("nitrogen_core/include/wf.hrl").

main() -> #template{file="./site/templates/bare.html"}.

title() -> "New Web Link".
```

RUSTY: Hold it. Voice of experience here. With minor addition we could make the "add new" form do double duty as an "edit" form.

OLEG: Now he tells me. Let me change the name of the module. Let me save this quick first, then I can rename the file:

Listing 6.39 ($\Rightarrow$ $) Rename the module to add_edit

```
~/nindex/site/src$ mv new.erl add_edit.erl
~/nindex/site/src$ vim add_edit.erl

-module(new add_edit).
...
title() -> "Add New/Edit Weblink".
```

OLEG: Better?

RUSTY: Better.

OLEG: So what next?

MARSHA: User sees a form—enters a new record.

RUSTY: Let's call this state two—User creates a new weblink record and saves it to our database.

Listing 6.40 (⇒ `vim`) **Add State 2**

```
title() -> "Add New/Edit Weblink".

%% ********************************************
%% State 2:
%% User enters new link info;
%% clicks Save
%% ********************************************
```

RUSTY: Bravo. What happens when the user clicks Save?

OLEG: Ah, system saves data—state machine returns to the initial state:

Listing 6.41 (⇒ `vim`) **Add more notes for us to use later**

```
. . .
%% clicks save
%% System saves new link info;
%% transistions back to initial state
%% ********************************************
```

OLEG: And in a feat of amazing derring-do Dataman closes out `add_edit.erl` and hyperloops back to `index.erl`:

Listing 6.42 (⇒ $) **Edit** `index.erl` **again**

`~/nindex/site/src$ vim index.erl`

STEVIE: Oleg, you're certifiable—

OLEG: Don't I know it!

RUSTY: So what happens if the user clicks Search?

6.10. State Three: Search

OLEG: Well, assuming the user entered search parameters in the initial state, the system retrieves and returns matching records.

RUSTY: Got it. This then is state three—a set of matching records. But where should we display them?

STEVIE: Looks like the UI in the initial state is pretty minimal. Suppose we put the search results under the enter search words form—maybe put a horizontal rule or something to separate them.

OLEG: Something like this?

Listing 6.43 (⇒ vim) **Add state 3 notes**

```
%% or enter search words and initiate a search
%% ********************************************

%% ********************************************
%% State 3
%% System displays search results
%% ********************************************
```

STEVIE: Yeah, cool. Each result could be a link so when we click on it. . . .

MARSHA: . . . the system displays the record and asks the user what she wants to do next!

6.11. State Four: Display a Record

RUSTY: Let's call this state four. The system displays the record.

STEVIE: Well, if the record is a weblink, we view the web page.

OLEG: Or we might want to edit the link.

MARSHA: Or delete it.

RUSTY: So, once in state four, our user has three choices—view, edit, delete. Each choice leads to a new state:

Listing 6.44 (⇒ `vim`) **Add notes for state 4: display search results**

```
%% *******************************************
%% State 3
%% System displays search results
%% *******************************************

%% *******************************************
%% State 4
%% System displays record
%% User selects view, edit, or delete
%% If view, display web page
%% If edit, transition to edit_add.erl state 6
%% If delete, delete record; transition to
%% State 1
%% *******************************************
```

MARSHA: Hey, this is fun. View leads to state five, edit leads to state six, and delete leads to state seven.

OLEG: And each one of those states leads back to the initial state.

RUSTY: Sharp cookies! It's helpful to draw a diagram:

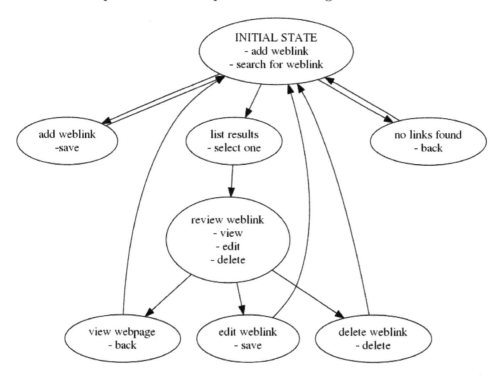

6.12. Page grid

RUSTY: Before we get carried away, let's open a new terminal and check out our template, bare.html:

Listing 6.45 ($\Rightarrow$ $) **Edit `bare.html`**

```
~site/src$ cd ../templates
~/nindex/site/templates$ vim bare.html
```

RUSTY: Look for these lines:

Example 6.4 ($\Rightarrow$ `vim`) **Callout in `bare.html`**

```
. . .
<body>
[[[page:body()]]]
<script>
. . .
```

RUSTY: Templates make it possible to create reuasable page grids.

STEVIE: Page grids?

RUSTY: The abstract composition of content on the webpage. Each box in the grid holds a different unit of content—a place for everything and everything in its place.

MARSHA: Lead on, o guru.

RUSTY: Without going into detail, here's a hint on how to create a template to define a page grid. In this case, our grid will be a single box:

Listing 6.46 (⇒ vim) **Add grid around** page:body **callout**
(bare.html)

```
 . . .
<body>
<div class="container_12">
   <div class="grid_8 prefix_1 alpha">
      [[[page:body()]]]
   </div>
</div>
<script>
 . . .
```

STEVIE: Ah, so I can create a page grid, whatever that is, by defining a set of divs in the template, each div corresponding to an empty box in my page layout.

OLEG: What's that [[[page:body()]]] business?

STEVIE: Don't you remember? It refers to a function, in this case body/0, that plugs content into the div. Any page that calls the template bare.html needs to provide a function called body/0.

OLEG: Ah, I get it! Each module that calls bare.html has a function called body/0. In a template, the module page is converted to the current module. So [[[page:body()]]] in the add_edit module, would be the equivalent of add_edit:body().

STEVIE: That's what I said, Doofus!

RUSTY: Smart cookies! This grid only has one box, but you get the idea.

6.13. State One

RUSTY: Now, close out bare.html and open index.erl. Let's add a body() function with two buttons:

Listing 6.47 (⇒ $) **Add buttons for state one (`index.erl`)**

```
../site/templates$ cd ../src
../site/src$ vim index.erl

%% ********************************************
%% Initial State
%% User choice: transition to "add new" form
%% or enter search words and initiate a search
%% ********************************************

body() ->
  [
    #p{text = "State 1:  Add new weblink or search for existing links"},
    #button{text="Add New", click=#redirect{url="/add_edit/new"}},
    #br{},
    #textbox {id=search_words, class=standard},
    #button {id=retrieve, text="Search", postback=search},
    #button {text="Show All", postback=show_all},
    #hr {},
%% ********************************************
%% State 3: Search results displayed here
%% ********************************************
    #panel {id=search_results}
  ].
```

STEVIE: Why did you add a Show All button?

RUSTY: It'll help us during the testing phase.

MARSHA: Wait! Doesn't the search results panel need text or something?

RUSTY: Due course. But note how the Add New Weblink button transitions off to a page that presents the Add New form, that is, state two. The Search button, however, requires an event function. We'll add this in a moment, but for now let's save and see how it looks in the browser.

MARSA: On it!

154

```
localhost:8000
```

OLEG: Ha! She didn't even check etc/simple_bridge.config for port conflicts. Watch it crash!

MARSHA: Been there. Done that. Read it and weep:

6.14. State Two: Add/Edit

RUSTY: So, Dataman, close out index.erl and take us back to add_edit.erl.

Cool, Now, here's a trick: We want our form to do double duty—add new link and edit existing link. I'll give it a shot:

Listing 6.48 (⇒ $) **A trick** (add_edit.erl)

```
site/src$ vim add_edit.erl

title() -> "Add New/Edit Web Link".

get_linkid() ->
   case wf:path_info() of
        "new" -> new;
        ID -> wf:to_integer(ID)
   end.
```

OLEG: Whaaa?

RUSTY: Recall that the redirect we attached to the The Nitrogen function `wf:path_info/0` strips off everything after the page name. In this case, our page name is `add_edit`, so `wf:path_info/0` returns `"new"`. Also, since `wf:path_info/0` returns a string and the IDs in our database are integers, we need to convert ID to an integer.

STEVIE: I get it!

If we select "edit" anywhere in our state machine, it will redirect to the `add_edit` page with an `id` rather than `new`!

RUSTY: Give the boy a high five! So now, let's flesh it out:

Listing 6.49 ($\Rightarrow$ vim) **Flesh out body/0 (add_edit.erl)**

```
        ID -> wf:to_integer(ID)
    end.

body() ->
    LinkID = get_linkid(),
    Weblink = ni_links:get_link(LinkID),
    form(Weblink).
```

RUSTY: And here's our form:

Listing 6.50 ($\Rightarrow$ vim) **Enter new link (add_edit.erl)**

```
%% ***********************************
%% State 2: Enter new link
%% ***********************************

form(new) ->
```

```
    form(new, "", "", "");
form(Weblink) ->
    ID = ni_links:id(Weblink),
    Topic = ni_links:topic(Weblink),
    Desc = ni_links:descriptor(Weblink),
    Url = ni_links:url(Weblink),
    form(ID, Topic, Desc, Url).
```

RUSTY: Now we need to program `form/4`:

Listing 6.51 (⇒ `vim`) **Define** `form/4` (`add_edit.erl`)

```
    form(ID, Topic, Desc, Url).

form(ID, Topic, Desc, Url) ->
    wf:defer(save_link, topic,
        #validate{validators=[
                #is_required{text="Topic required"}]}),
    wf:defer(save_link, descriptor,
        #validate{validators=[
                #is_required{text="Descriptive text required"}]}),
    wf:defer(save_link, url,
        #validate{validators=[
            #is_required{text="URL required"}]}),
```

STEVIE: Hold up! What does `wf:defer/1`[22] do again?

RUSTY: In this case, `wf:defer/1` tells the system to execute the user input validation functions AFTER all other wired actions. So this will ensure that the deferred validator will wire after the form is rendered and placed on the page. Make sense?

---

[22]http://nitrogenproject.com/doc/api.html

STEVIE: Think so. But go on—

Listing 6.52 (⇒ vim) form/4 continues (add_edit.erl)

```
        #is_required{text="URL required"}]}),
    [
    #h3 {text="Create or Edit Web Link"},
    #label{text="Topic"},
    #textbox{id=topic, text=Topic},
    #label{text="Descriptive Text"},
    #textbox{id=descriptor, text=Desc},
    #label{text="URL"},
    #textbox{id=url, text=Url},
    #br{},
    #button {
        id=save_link,
        text="Save",
        postback={save, ID}
    },
    #link{style="margin-left:10px", text="Cancel", url="/"}
    ].
```

MARSHA: We need an event function for the Save button.

RUSTY: Right you are.

Listing 6.53 (⇒ vim) Define save event (add_edit.erl)

```
        #link{style="margin-left:10px", text="Cancel", url="/"}
    ].

event({save, Linkid}) ->
    save(Linkid).
```

OLEG: Ah, never ends. Now we need the save/1 function.

RUSTY: Let's break up save/1 into two clauses: One for new links and one for existing links.

Here's how we can save new links:

Listing 6.54 (⇒ vim) **Define save/1 (add_edit.erl)**

```
save(Linkid).

save(new) ->
    [Topic, Desc, Url] = wf:mq([topic, descriptor, url]),
    Weblink = ni_links:new(Topic, Desc, Url),
    save_and_redirect(Weblink);
```

RUSTY: Now to update existing links:

Listing 6.55 (⇒ vim) **Define save/1 continues (add_edit.erl)**

```
    Weblink = ni_links:new(Topic, Desc, Url),
    save_and_redirect(Weblink);

save(Linkid) ->
    [Topic, Desc, Url] = wf:mq([topic, descriptor, url]),
    Weblink = ni_links:get_link(Linkid),
    Weblink2 = ni_links:topic(Weblink, Topic),
    Weblink3 = ni_links:descriptor(Weblink2, Desc),
    Weblink4 = ni_links:url(Weblink3, Url),
    save_and_redirect(Weblink4).
```

RUSTY: And, finally, we have the save_and_redirect/1 function:

Listing 6.56 ($\Rightarrow$ vim) **Define** save_and_redirect/1 (add_edit.erl)

```
    save_and_redirect(Weblink4).

  save_and_redirect(Weblink) ->
    ni_links:save_link(Weblink),
    wf:redirect("/").
```

STEVIE: Save and look:

`localhost:8000/add_edit/new`

6.15. State Three

RUSTY: Awesome! Now, open up index.erl so we can activate the search button. We need an event to handle the postback. For sake of clarity, we'll factor the search result into its own function: return_search_results/1:

Listing 6.57   (⇒ $) **Define** search **event (**`add_edit.erl`**)**

```
    #panel {id=search_results}
  ].

event(search) ->
  return_search_results().

return_results() ->
  SearchString = wf:q(search_words),
  Links = ni_search:search(SearchString),
  SearchResultBody = draw_links(Links),
  wf:update(search_results, SearchResultBody).
```

RUSTY: First— draw_links/1:

Listing 6.58   (⇒ vim) **Define** draw_links/1 **(**`add_edit.erl`**)**

```
  SearchResultBody = draw_links(Links),
  wf:update(search_results, SearchResultBody).

draw_links(Links) ->
  #panel{id=show_links, body=[
    #p{text="State 3: Return search results"},
    [draw_link(Link) || Link <- Links]
  ]}.
```

RUSTY: ...and now— draw_link/1:

Listing 6.59 (⇒ vim) **Define** `draw_link/1` (`add_edit.erl`)

```
            [draw_link(Link) || Link <- Links]
      ]}.

draw_link(Weblink) ->
   LinkID = ni_links:id(Weblink),
   Text = ni_links:descriptor(Weblink),
   Url = ni_links:url(Weblink),
   #link{
      text=Text,
      postback={show, LinkID, Text, Url}
   }.
```

OLEG: Wait! Won't that display links next to each other?

RUSTY: Yes, let's fix that with a nifty little trick.

We can use Erlang's `lists:join/2` function to insert a #br{} between each link:

Listing 6.60 (⇒ vim) **A trick:** `lists:join/2` (`add_edit.erl`)

```
draw_links(Links) ->
  #panel{id=show_links, body=[
    #p{text="State 3: Return search results"},
    lists:join(#br{}, [draw_link(Link) || Link <- Links])
  ]}.
```

MARSHA: Interesting. It's like the `string:join/2` function. But without strings.

RUSTY: Indeed! Except it takes a list of anything, and can take anything as a separator. `string:join/2` chokes on anything that isn't a string.[23]

OLEG: So we can search, right?

---

[23]There is also `wf:join/2`, which was included in Nitrogen before `lists:join/2` existed. It will be kept around for backward compatibility.

RUSTY: Save. Then search for "Erlang"!

localhost:8000

State1: Add new web link to db or search for existing links

Add New

Erlang   Search   ShowAll

State 3: Return search results

Erlang Programming Language

OLEG: *That*'s what I'm talking about! Wonder if Show All works?

6.16. Show all

MARSHA: Wait—we don't have an event function for Show All.

RUSTY: Easily fixed:

Listing 6.61 (⇒ vim) **Define show_all event (add_edit.erl)**

```
event(show_all) ->
    show_all().
```

RUSTY: And here's show_all/0:

Listing 6.62 (⇒ `vim`) Define `show_all/0` (`add_edit.erl`)

```
event(show_all) ->
    show_all().

show_all() ->
    Links = ni_links:get_all(),
    AllBody = draw_links(Links),
    wf:update(search_results, AllBody).
```

RUSTY: Now you can take Show All for a spin.

OLEG: Your wish is my command, sir:

`localhost:8000`

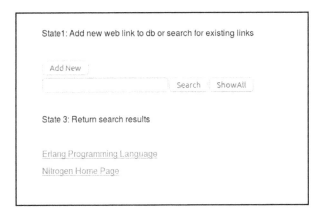

STEVIE: Way to go!

RUSTY: What next?

STEVIE: The app crashes when I click on a link.

MARSHA: Not good!

6.17. Show Selected Link

RUSTY: So, let's think about what we want to show when the clicks on a link. Suppose an inline menu pops up. What do you think?

MARSHA: As my grandma says, sounds groovy.

RUSTY: Okay. The easy approach is to have a menu under each link, but hidden from view.

OLEG: Like it.

RUSTY: The drawback is that we're sending more stuff to the page than we need. If this were a high-traffic site or a large page with many, many links, this approach would not be optimal. But for this, and most, situations, it's fine.

MARSHA: So we need to modify the draw_link function in index.erl—

RUSTY: Yes. Give it a shot:

Listing 6.63 (⇒ $) Modify `draw_link/1` (`index.erl`)

```
draw_link(Weblink) ->
    LinkID = ni_links:id(Weblink),
    Text = ni_links:descriptor(Weblink),
    Url = ni_links:url(Weblink),
    EditUrl = "add_edit " ++ wf:to_list(LinkID),
    [
        #link {
            text=Text,
            postback={show, LinkID, Text, Url}
        },
        #br {},
        #link {text="view", url=Url},
        " | ",
        #link {text="edit", url=EditUrl},
        " | ",
```

165

```
    #link {text="delete", postback={delete, LinkID}}
  ].
```

MARSHA: Something like that, maybe?

RUSTY: Click Show All. See what happens.

MARSH: Should I reload the page?

RUSTY: No need.

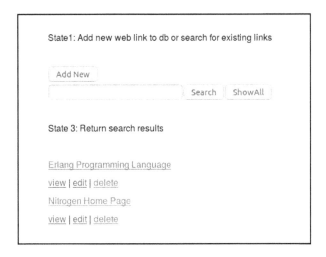

MARSHA: Oh, it's showing all the menus. We don't want that! How can we hide them?

RUSTY: Here's one way—add the attribute `style="display:none"`:

Listing 6.64 (⇒ vim) **Add a style attribute** (`index.erl`)

```
draw_link(WebLink) ->
...

    #link {
        text=Text,
        postback={show, LinkID, Text, Url}
    },
    #br{},
    #panel {style="display:none", body = [
        #link {text="view", url=Url},
        " | "
        #link {text="edit", url=EditUrl},
        " | ",
        #link {text="delete", postback={delete, LinkID}}
    ]}
    ].
```

RUSTY: Note that I wrapped the menu elements in a panel. When you hide the panel, you hide everything in the panel.

MARSHA: Since #panel{} is a <div>, do we need the #br{} any longer? I mean, since a <div> will start on its own line?

RUSTY: Good point. Let's check it out:

State1: Add new web link to db or search for existing links

Add New

Search   ShowAll

State 3: Return search results

Erlang Programming Language

Nitrogen Home Page

STEVIE: Looks like it did before we added the menu.

RUSTY: Right. We only want the menu to show if we click an item. Try it. See what happens.

MARSHA: It crashes!

STEVIE: We forgot to handle the show postback!

RUSTY: We did. But check—we have an interesting option here. We can show and hide things without asking the server to do it for us. We've used Nitrogen actions fairly lightly so far, but we haven't seen how to speed up an app and cut down on code.

Observe:

Listing 6.65 (⇒ vim) **Speed up app; cut down code (`index.erl`)**

```
draw_link(Weblink) ->
   LinkID = ni_links:id(Weblink),
   Text = ni_links:descriptor(Weblink),
   Url = ni_links:url(Weblink),
   EditUrl = "add_edit" ++ wf:to_list(LinkID),
   Menuid = wf:temp_id(),
```

```
[
  #link {
    text=Text,
    postback={show, LinkID, Text, Url}
    click=#toggle{target=Menuid}
  },
  #panel{id=Menuid, style="display:none", body=[
    #link {text="view", url=Url},
    " | ",
    #link {text="edit", url=EditUrl},
    " | "
    #link {text="delete", postback={delete, LinkID}}
  ]}
].
```

STEVIE: What's the point of wf:temp_id()?

RUSTY: It generates a random ID which can be assigned to elements.

MARSHA: Why don't we just name the panel something like menu_panel?

RUSTY: Great question! So what happens when we have more than one such element on the page?

MARSHA: Ah, there'll be multiple menu_panel elements on the page.

RUSTY: Exactly.

MARSHA: Couldn't we create a unique ID by using the ID of record?

RUSTY: We could. And sometimes that's actually what we'd do. But in this case we have no reason to refer to this panel except within this single function. So, to keep it simple, we make a throwaway element ID which we know will be unique rather than messing about with some other kind of ID. Internally, Nitrogen uses these temporary IDs quite frequently.

MARSHA: I get it.

OLEG: And you deleted the postback, so we don't need to handle it.

STEVIE: And that #toggle{} element inside the click attribute? That's intriguing.

RUSTY: Nitrogen has several actions that can be used this way. Click Show All, then click one of the links:

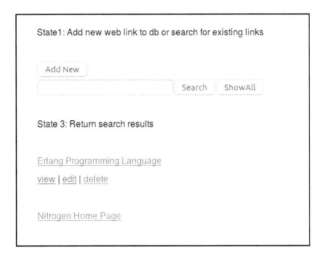

MARSHA: Awesome! The menu pops up. If we click it again, it goes away.

OLEG: Hey! Hey! Let's hear it for #toggle{}!

RUSTY: What happens when we click one of the menu links?

STEVIE: View redirects to the URL, edit redirects to the add_edit page, which is blank, and delete crashes.

RUSTY: We need to handle the delete postback:

Listing 6.66 (⇒ `vim`) **Delete postback** (`index.erl`)

```
event(show_all)->
   show_all();

event({delete, LinkID}) ->
   delete(LinkID).

delete(LinkID) ->
   ni_links:delete_link(LinkID),
   wf:wire(#alert {text = "DELETED"}),
   wf:redirect("/").
```

MARSHA: I don't know— redirecting to the index page after the deletion feels a bit like smashing a fly with a sledgehammer.

RUSTY: What do you suggest?

MARSHA: Maybe we should simply remove that one link from the page.

RUSTY: Good thought. Let's make this change:

Listing 6.67 (⇒ `vim`) **Modify** `draw_link/1` (`index.erl`)

```
draw_link(Weblink) ->
   LinkID = ni_links:id(Weblink),
   ...
   Menuid = wf:temp_id(),
   Linkwrapperid = wf:temp_id(),
   #panel{id=Linkwrapperid, body=[
      #link {
         text=Text,
         click=#toggle{target=Menuid}
      },
      #panel {id=Menuid, style="display:none", body=[
         #link {text="view", url=Url},
```

```
        " | ",
        #link {text="edit", url=EditUrl},
        " | ",
        #link {text="delete", postback={delete, LinkID, Linkwrapperid}}
    ]}
]}.
```

RUSTY: Then, modify the event and delete functions:

Listing 6.68 (⇒ vim) **Modify event/1 and delete/1 (index.erl)**

```
event({delete, LinkID, Linkwrapperid}) ->
    delete(LinkID, Linkwrapperid).

delete(LinkID, Linkwrapperid) ->
    ni_links:delete_link(LinkID),
    wf:remove(Linkwrapperid).
    wf:wire(#alert {text = "DELETED"}),
    wf:redirect("/").
```

RUSTY: Click delete on one of the links now.

STEVIE: Ah, hate to bear bad news. But it still crashes.

RUSTY: Oh, of course. It's still showing the links—trying to call an invalid postback. Click Show All again, then open a link and click delete.

OLEG: It works!

RUSTY: There is one last aesthetic change we can make. Since we've wrapped links in a #panel element, we can remove the lists:join/2 call we did with the #br{}.

OLEG: Why's that?

RUSTY: We wrapped our links in a #panel{} so they will be displayed on the next line without need of #br{}:

Listing 6.69 (⇒ `vim`) **Remove the unnecessary join (`index.erl`)**

```
draw_links(Links) ->
  #panel{id=show_links, body=[
    #p{text="State 3: Return search results"},
    lists:join(#br{}, [draw_link(Link) || Link <- Links])
  ]}.
```

STEVIE: If I'm not mistaken, we're ready add to the add/edit form.

RUSTY: That's, what, state two in our mock state machine?

RUSTY: Hate to say it kiddies, but we're out of time. But let me stress—the state machine we've been toying with provides a conceptual framework for nearly every CRUD application that comes your way.

Data, input forms, and queries change from application to application. But for the most part, CRUD apps all follow this quasi-state-machine logic.

STEVIE: Rock on!

OLEG: Nitrogen rules!

6.18. Exercises

1. Replace the working heads in `index:body/0` and `index:draw_links/1` with more user-friendly text.

2. Buff up styling with CSS. Hint: `nindex/site/static/css/style.css`.

3. As implemented, `ni_search` is case sensitive. That means searching for *erlang* when a search result might contain *Erlang* will not return all results we might want. Make `ni_search` case-insensitive. Hint: `string:to_lower/1` should help you out.[24]

---

[24]`http://erlang.org/doc/man/string.html`

4. Use a custom validator to assure that the URL entered is a properly formed URL (that is, it starts with `http://` or `https://`). Refer to the documentation for the `#custom{}` validator.

   Docs: `http://nitrogenproject.com/doc/validators/custom.html`

   Demo: `http://nitrogenproject.com/demos/validation`

7. nindex on Dets

RUSTY: Okay, troopers, now that you've had the week to play with our weblink application, what should we tackle next?

MARSHA: JoeDB is a hack, right? Would Dets work better?

RUSTY: Well, it's tried and true. Let's see how it compares. We've done a fair amount of Dets so far, so reworking the backend to use Dets should feel familiar. Let's see if we can't crank this out quickly. We'll need the same exports as joedb.erl:

Listing 7.1 (⇒ vim) **Create module:** `ni_dets.erl`

```
site/src$ vim ni_dets.erl

-module(ni_dets).
-export([init_db/0,
         get_all/0,
         get_link/1,
         save_link/1,
         delete_link/1,
         new/3,
         id/1, id/2,
         topic/1, topic/2,
         descriptor/1, descriptor/2,
         url/1, url/2
]).
```

RUSTY: Note that Dets is optimized for working with Erlang records. Since JoeDB is built using proplists, we will need to change the internal data implementation to work with Dets

So, first off, let's define our record:

Listing 7.2 (⇒ vim) **Define weblink record (ni_dets.erl)**

```
        url/1, url/2
    ]).
-record(weblink, {id, topic, descriptor, url}).
```

RUSTY: Since we have an interface for storing and adding new data, we don't need to seed the database. We just need to open and close it. A modification to init_db will do the trick:

Listing 7.3 (⇒ vim) **Define init_db/0 (ni_dets.erl)**

```
-record(weblink, {id, topic, descriptor, url}).

init_db() ->
    open_db(),
    close_db().
open_db() ->
    DB = dets_nindex,
    Opts = [{type, set}, {keypos, #weblink.id}],
    {ok, DB} = dets:open_file(DB, Opts).

close_db() ->
    dets:close(dets_nindex).
```

RUSTY: So far so good. Now, let's modify get_all():

Listing 7.4 (⇒ vim) **Define get_all/0 (ni_dets.erl)**

```
close_db() ->
    dets:close(dets_nindex).

get_all() ->
    open_db(),
    Links = dets:match_object(dets_nindex, '_'),
    close_db(),
    Links.
```

RUSTY: This should look familiar from our work on nitroBoard.[1] Now add get_link():

Listing 7.5 (⇒ vim) **Define get_link/1 (ni_dets.erl)**

```
    close_db(),
    Links.

get_link(ID) ->
    open_db(),
    Link = case dets:lookup(dets_nindex, ID) of
        [L] -> L;
        [] -> new
    end,
    close_db(),
    Link.
```

STEVIE: Refresh me. Why are you using that [L] match instead of just binding the return of dets:lookup to Link?

RUSTY: Because dets:lookup/2 returns a list of items. In this case, we assume there is only one record with the requested ID in the database, so we use

---

[1]See 4.2.2 on page 70.

177

pattern matching to bind Link. If dets:lookup/2 returns a list with one item in it, we return the item. If dets:lookup/2 returns an empty list, we return the atom new[2]. If an error tuple or a list with more than one item is returned, something is wrong with our system and we'll crash—and that's okay!

STEVIE: Got it. I get the feeling that pattern matching is a powerful tool in the Erlang toolkit.

RUSTY: It is. It'll change the way you approach programming. You'll really miss it when you find yourself working in languages that don't support it.

OLEG: So how do we implement the save-link function?

RUSTY: We can use another pattern matching trick. If the id field is undefined, we generate a new record. Otherwise, we insert the record:

Listing 7.6 (⇒ vim) **Define save_link/1 (ni_dets.erl)**

```
    close_db(),
    Link.

save_link(Link = #weblink{id=undefined}) ->
    save_link(Link#weblink{id=create_id()});
save_link(Link) ->
    open_db(),
    ok = dets:insert(dets_nindex, Link),
    close_db().
```

MARSHA: Can we reuse the create_id() function we programmed for JoeDB?

RUSTY: Sure. Copy it over:

---

[2]Just as we did in JoeDB on page 129

Listing 7.7 (⇒ vim) Define create_id/0 (ni_dets.erl)

```
    ok = dets:insert(dets_nindex, Link),
    close_db().

create_id() ->
    rand:uniform(9999999999999999999999).
```

OLEG: Hey, can I take a crack at `delete_link/1`?

RUSTY: Go for it:

Listing 7.8 (⇒ vim) Define delete_link/1 (ni_dets.erl)

```
    rand:uniform(9999999999999999999999).

delete_link(ID) ->
    open_db(),
    dets:delete(dets_nindex, ID),
    close_db().
```

RUSTY: Way to go!

So that's our interface to the Dets database. Simpler than our `term_to_binary`-based database, no?

MARSHA: But we still need to add the API functions for interfacing with `dets_index`, correct?

RUSTY: Indeed! Can't slip one past you. First, we need the new/3 function:

Listing 7.9 (⇒ vim) **Define new/3 (ni_dets.erl)**

```
    dets:delete(dets_nindex, ID),
    close_db().

new(Topic, Descriptor, Url) ->
    #weblink{
        topic=Topic,
        descriptor=Descriptor,
        url=Url
    }.
```

RUSTY: Behold while I demonstrate tricks with records and pattern matching:

Listing 7.10 (⇒ vim) **Define id, descriptor, topic, url functions (ni_dets.erl)**

```
        url=Url
    }.
id(#weblink{id=ID}) -> ID.
id(W, ID) -> W#weblink{id=ID}.
descriptor(#weblink{descriptor=Desc}) -> Desc.
descriptor(W, Desc) -> W#weblink{descriptor=Desc}.
topic(#weblink{topic=Topic}) -> Topic.
topic(W, Topic) -> W#weblink{topic=Topic}.
url(#weblink{url=Url}) -> Url.
url(W, Url) -> W#weblink{url=Url}.
```

RUSTY: That pretty much wraps up our Dets database. But we need to make one last change. We need to tell our application to use our Dets database as the backend. So we edit the ni_links.erl file and change the DB from ni_joedb to ni_dets:

Listing 7.11 (⇒ vim) Update ni_links.erl

```
-define(DB, ni_joedb ni_dets).
```

RUSTY: So, Dataman my good fellow, kill the Erlang console, recompile everything, fire up Nitrogen again, and let's test:

Listing 7.12 (⇒ $) Recompile and test

```
$ cd ../../
$ make
...
$ bin/nitrogen console
...
1> sync:go().
ok
2> ni_links:init_db().
ok
3> ni_links:get_all().
[]
4> New = ni_links:new("Erlang", "Erl",
        "http://erlang.org/doc/man/erl.html").
{weblink,undefined,"Erlang","Erl",
   "http://erlang.org/doc/man/erl.html"}
5> ni_links:get_all().
[{weblink,755151283795099242759,"Erlang","Erl",
"http://erlang.org/doc/man/erl.html"}]
...
```

7.1. Dets Again...No Wait, OTP. Yeah, OTP!

> **Know OTP?**
> If you're an OTP ninja/guru/rockstar and know all about gen_servers and supervisors, feel free to skip this section and jump to 7.2 on page 206.

Rusty Nail was totally unprepared for the response when he ran the nindex program by Jesse James.

JESSE: You're doing it all wrong!

RUSTY: Whoa! What are you talking about?

JESSE: A Dets table is a single file. When you open and close the database with each request—as you have been doing—you're playing with fire. While it works for your use-case, that is, a single-user application, you run into concurrency issues as soon as multiple users pile on.

RUSTY: Tell me, my guru—

JESSE: Best practice would be to build a wrapper around your module to ensure that reads and writes are atomic. Writes most especially.

RUSTY: Ah, you're talking about gen_server. I thought about it, but that means introducing the young folks to OTP. Not sure we have the time.

JESSE: It's essential! Erlang wouldn't be Erlang without it. Here, take this handout I did last year. Might help.

7.1.1. Let's talk OTP

Read the name OTP, "Open Telecom Platform," and you think, "Ah, that's for telecom. We're building web applications. I'm out of here."[3]

---

[3]Garrett Smith has a great video discussing the OTP name and a proposal for a new, hipper, edgier name that would be far more appealing to the masses: https://youtu.be/rRbY3TMUcgQ

Now *that* would be a mistake.

Turns out that Erlang OTP is an outstanding environment for web application development.

But you can't fault Erlang for the less-than-inclusive nomenclature. Erlang was, after all, built for running telecom in an environment where downtime beyond a few seconds a year was penalized with hefty fines. And, indeed, Erlang still powers much of the telecom world. So the name was descriptive, *good* even, for the problem the language was built to solve.

And, face it, at the time, Tim Berners-Lee was off in Geneva dreaming up the web—too far away for brainstorming nominclature over the water cooler.

We consider this fortunate.

Somehow the name OWATP, "Open Web Application and Telecom Platform," just doesn't roll off the tongue.

7.1.2. Why is OTP amazing?

Naming aside, OTP is ultimately what makes Erlang so amazing for web application development. Easy-to-learn syntax, immutable variables, and the simplicity of message passing contribute to the case.[4] But what really makes OTP amazing is built-in "process management and monitoring." If a server crashes, a supervisor automatically restarts it.

Any reasonably complex system will consist of multiple services doing various things. Sans supervision, if one service fails, the whole system dies an ugly death.

Not so with Erlang OTP. When a bug bites, and sooner or later one will, OTP supervisors save your ah—reputation—by bringing the system back to a known state. Supervisors give you the glorious nines of uptime Erlang is known for.

7.1.3. So what is OTP?

OTP is a set of libraries included as part of the standard Erlang system for managing Erlang applications. It consists of servers, supervisors, applications, start-up scripts, logging, behaviours[5] and other goodies.

---

[4]Flame suppressant: Erlang syntax is easy to learn if you don't try to superimpose conventions from other languages.

[5]British spelling intentional.

7.1.4. What is `gen_server`?

A good way to get your feet wet with message passing is by building a server. You can build a server in Erlang from scratch—a useful exercise. Among other things, you'll learn how to process messages and maintain application state. But building a server from scratch risks sneaky hazards and crashes due to pesky edge cases.

`gen_server` abstracts the essential tricks needed to build a rock-solid server capable of responding to requests, updating state, shutting down, and even gracefully upgrading state when a hot-code-upgrade happens.

Don't believe me?

7.1.5. Let's build a non-OTP server

Here we're going to build a simple server *without* using OTP—a typical exercise for tyro Erlang programmers.

So let's build a simple cache server completely unrelated to Nitrogen, just a straight up non-OTP Erlang server. We'll call this server `dict_cache`, as we're going to use an Erlang `dict` to store the values.

Kick off

First, create a new project (not in our nindex directory):

Listing 7.13 (⇒ $) Create `dict_cache`

```
~$ mkdir dict_cache
~$ cd dict_cache
dict_cache$ vim dict_cache.erl

-module(dict_cache).

-export([start/0, get_value/1, set_value/2]).
```

To keep things simple, we'll create three functions: start/0, get_value/1, and set_value/2.

Start with start

First, initialize an empty dict to store values.[6] Then, launch the server:

Listing 7.14 (⇒ vim) **Add start function (dict_cache.erl)**

```
-export([start/0, get_value/1, set_value/2]).

start() ->
   Data = dict:new(),
   Pid = spawn(fun() -> server_loop(Data) end),
   erlang:register(dict_cache, Pid).
```

The function start/1 spawns a new process and registers it under the name Pid.

Erlang processes are lightweight—even more so than threads. But, like OS processes, they're isolated. That is, they do not share data with other processes. Rather, they communicate via messages.

Note spawn/1. The function spawn/1 calls server_loop/1 and passes in the empty KeyValue store Data. The variable Pid captures the process ID of the newly spawned process. The process ID looks like this: <0.30.0>.

We register the process id under the name Pid so we can send messages to the process by name rather than reference, that is <0.30.0>

Loop de loop

The function server_loop/1 is the body of the server. It must do three things: respond to queries, update with new data, and loop forever. We start with the definition:

---

[6]http://erlang.org/doc/man/dict.html

> **Listing 7.15** (⇒ `vim`) Define `server_loop` function
> (`dict_cache.erl`)

```
      erlang:register(dict_cache, Pid).

server_loop(Data) ->
    receive
        {set_value, FromPid, Key, Value} ->
            NewData = dict:store(Key, Value, Data),
            FromPid ! ok,
            server_loop(NewData)
    end.
```

Erlang processes retrieve messages via a `receive block` implemented by the function `receive`. A receive block accepts a message coming into the process and matches it against a set of match clauses. The receive block is similar to a case statement:

- If the incoming message finds a match, which it will if it has the signature {set_value, FromPid, Key, Value}, the matching clause body executes.[7] If the message fails to match, server_loop/1 simply pauses until it receives the next message.

- When a match occurs, the match clause binds its unbound FromPid, Key, and Value variables to the values passed in the message.

- The Key and Value variables update the dict, which in turn is bound to the variable NewData.

- Next, the message ok is sent back to the sending process, FromPid, via a "naked bang."

- Finally, the receive block recurses to server_loop/1 with NewData replacing the old Data.

In our case there is only one match clause—{set_value, FromPid, Key, Value}. The receive block has simply told our server to wait until it receives a

---

[7]http://erlang.org/doc/reference_manual/functions.html

set_value message, then store the new value and send the atom ok as confirmation that the setting was successful.

dict_cache:set_value/2

We now have a function to start the server and a main loop to store new values. We're ready to build the API.

To set and store values we need to send a message to the server that carries both the Key and the Value:

Listing 7.16 (⇒ vim) **API: Define** set_value/2 (dict_cache.erl)

```
            server_loop(NewData)
      end.

  set_value(Key, Value) ->
    dict_cache ! {set_value, self(), Key, Value},
    receive
      ok -> ok
    end.
```

Note that self() is a stand-in for FromPid. It returns the process ID of the calling process. This tells the server: "Hey, go set this value and send a response back to me." This is necessary because a process's mailbox does not record where messages come from.

Also note that we're sending the message to an atom called dict_cache. This works because we assigned a name to our pid and registered it with Erlang via erlang:register(dict_cache, Pid), in start/1.

Think of how we use domain names on the internet to avoid memorizing IP addresses.

Once we've sent a message to the server, we need to wait for a response. When the server returns ok, we know that the value was properly stored.

get_value

To retrieve values we need to modify the server to support a get_value operation. We'll do this by adding a get_value clause to the receive block in server_loop/1:

Listing 7.17 ($\Rightarrow$ **vim**) **Add get_value to server_loop/1 (dict_cache.erl)**

```
server_loop(Data) ->
  receive
    {get_value, FromPid, Key} ->
      Value = dict:fetch(Key, Data),
      FromPid ! {ok, Value},
      server_loop(Data);
    {set_value, FromPid, Key, Value} ->
      NewData = dict:store(Key, Value, Data),
      FromPid ! ok,
      server_loop(NewData)
  end.
```

The get_value clause is like the set_value clause, except it doesn't match a Value. Based on the set_value clause, it should be fairly obvious how it works.

dict_cache:get_value/1

Now we can add get_value/1 to our API:

Listing 7.18 ($\Rightarrow$ **vim**) **API: Define get_value/1 (dict_cache.erl)**

```
      server_loop(NewData)
  end.

get_value(Key) ->
  dict_cache ! {get_value, self(), Key},
  receive
   {ok, Value} -> Value
  end.
```

Let's test. Start an Erlang shell, compile, and then start the server:

Listing 7.19 (⇛ $) Compile and start `dict_cache` (`dict_cache.erl`)

```
dict_cache$ erl
...
1> c(dict_cache).
{ok,dict_cache}
2> dict_cache:start().
true
```

The server starts. Let's set and get values:

Listing 7.20 (⇛ >) Test set and get functions (`dict_cache.erl`)

```
3> dict_cache:set_value(favorite_fruit, pineapple).
ok
4> dict_cache:get_value(favorite_fruit).
pineapple
```

Hot diggity!

A few things to consider

While our non-OTP `dict_cache` server works, there are issues. What happens if a bug crashes the server? It just dies. Moreover, expanding it with more features will require more naked bangs and receive statements. This can quickly get out of hand, ending with an Erlang equivalent of callback hell[8] and spaghetti code.[9]

---

[8]http://j.mp/callbackhell
[9]https://en.wikipedia.org/wiki/Spaghetti_code

7.1.6. So now, let's build a `gen_server`!

We'll use the gen_server behaviour from OTP.[10] Think of a behaviour as a spec for creating a module that follows a particular pattern. A behaviour tells you which callback functions a module will need to define, including the number of arguments and, in more recent versions of Erlang, the types of the arguments and return value.

We start by defining module called `dict_cache2` and its exports:

> **Listing 7.21** (⇒ $) **Create `dict_cache2` `gen_server` module (`dict_cache2.erl`)**

```
dict_cache$ vim dict_cache2.erl

-module(dict_cache2).

-behaviour(gen_server).
-export([start/0, get_value/1, set_value/2]).
```

Note the `-behaviour(gen_server)` attribute. This tells the compiler to check for existence of certain functions, including, among others:[11]

> **Listing 7.22** (⇒ vim) **Define `dict_cache2` exports (`dict_cache2.erl`)**

```
-export([init/1, handle_call/3]).
```

It's a start

Erlang processes are dynamic critters. They start. They run. They die. A gen_server is an Erlang process. So, clearly, we need a way to start it:

---

[10] Erlang has adopted the British spelling of "behaviour," but the American spelling "behavior" also works.

[11] http://erlang.org/doc/design_principles/gen_server_concepts.html

---

Listing 7.23 (⇒ vim) **Start** `gen_server` (`dict_cache2.erl`)

```
-export([init/1, handle_call/3]).

start() ->
  gen_server:start({local, ?MODULE}, ?MODULE, [], []).
```

Okay—What is ?MODULE and why did we pass it to gen_server:start/1 twice?

?MODULE is a a macro that evaluates to the name of the current module. So, in our case, it's converted by the compiler to dict_cache2.

gen_server:start/4 takes four arguments:

- **{local, ?MODULE}**: The argument {local, ?MODULE} registers the gen_server on the local node. The arument {global, ?MODULE} would register the server globally, that is with all connected nodes in an Erlang cluster.

- **Callback** (?MODULE): The second argument specifies that dict_cache2 will be the handler for the server. With more elaborate setups you may want to separate the API from the server itself, in which case, you might use a different module.

- **Args** ([]): We have no arguments to pass in, so we'll use the empty list.

- **Options** ([]): Nor do we have options to pass in, but we could use this list to define default timeouts, debugging options, and similar support functions.

gen_server:start/4 will call init/1 in the Callback module, which we specified via the macro ?MODULE as dict_cache2. Here's init/1:

Listing 7.24 (⇒ vim) **Define** `init/1` (`dict_cache2.erl`)

```
  gen_server:start({local, ?MODULE}, ?MODULE, [], []).
init([]) ->
  {ok, dict:new()}.
```

A gen_server:init/1 function is expected to return the tuple {ok, Server-State}. Since the only thing we care about for now is maintaining the dict, we return an empty dict.

We did something similar when we initialized start/0 function in our non-OTP version.

And now for a loop we don't have to loop

While the non-OTP server had to explicitly define the loop, the gen_server loop is implicit. And, just as the init/1 function didn't actually directly call a loop, the gen_server system took the return value of init/1 and initialized the loop with that initial state.

Next, we define handle_call/3. Each clause of handle_call/3 is analogous to a clause in the receive statement of dict_cache:server_loop/1.

Here's how we set a value:

Listing 7.25 (⇒ vim) **Define handle_call/3 (dict_cache2.erl)**

```
    {ok, dict:new()}.

handle_call({set_value, Key, Value}, _From, Data) ->
    NewData = dict:store(Key, Value, Data),
    {reply, ok, NewData};
```

The first argument, {set_value, Key, Value}, is the message we need to send.

The second argument identifies the sending process. But unlike our non-OTP version, we don't actually have to track it— gen_server tracks it for us. Thus, we bind it with the leading underscore _From. Normally, the Erlang compiler will warn us if a variable is unspecified. But prefixing the variable with an underscore tells the compiler that we don't actually care about the variable.

The third argument is the server's state, which as we defined in init/1 as our dict.

So, what did you expect? Something long, hairy, and complicated?

But no, we simply updated the dict with new values in Key and Value, then returned a tuple of the form {reply, ReplyValue, NewState}. This tuple

192

tells the gen_server to send a reply to the sender with the message ok, then to update the state of the server with NewState.

NewState, of course, is the newly updated dict.

Note that we ended the function with a semicolon. We'll be pattern matching on a handle_call get_value function by and by.

Also note the absence of a loop. gen_server takes care of that for us, automatically looping with the value of NewData.

dict_cache2:set_value/1

Let's not forget our API's set_value function:

> **Listing 7.26** (⇒ vim) **Define set_value/2 (dict_cache2.erl)**

```
    NewData = dict:store(Key, Value, Data),
    {reply, ok, NewData};

  set_value(Key, Value) ->
    gen_server:call(?MODULE, {set_value, Key, Value}).
```

That's it! Hey, you know that server we called ?MODULE? Yeah, that one. Send it a message that looks like {set_value, Key, Value}, wait for a response, then return it.

So our API function set_value/2 fires off the message, which gets handled in gen_server's handle_call function which, in turn, "does stuff," then returns the value ok.

Bottom line: No more sending message directly, writing receive statements, or keeping track of who sent what to whom.

But what about get_value/1?

We go through much the same drill to add a get_value clause to our behind-the-curtains, under-the-hood gen_server loop:

Listing 7.27 (⇒ vim) **Add `handle_call/3` (`dict_cache2.erl`)**

```
handle_call({set_value, Key, Value}, _From, Data) ->
  NewData = dict:store(Key, Value, Data),
  {reply, ok, NewData};

handle_call({get_value, Key}, _From, Data) ->
  Value = dict:fetch(Key, Data),
  {reply, Value, Data}.
```

`dict_cache2:get_value/1`

This should be old hat by now:

Listing 7.28 (⇒ vim) **API: `get_value/1` (`dict_cache2.erl`)**

```
set_value(Key, Value) ->
  gen_server:call(?MODULE, {set_value, Key, Value}).

get_value(Key) ->
  gen_server:call(?MODULE, {get_value, Key}).
```

Time to save and test.

Testing our `gen_server`

Listing 7.29 (⇒ $) `dict_cache2`: **Test**

```
$ erl

1> c(dict_cache2).
dict_cache2.erl:2: Warning: undefined callback function
code_change/3 (behaviour 'gen_server') dict_cache2.erl:2:
Warning: undefined callback function handle_cast/2
(behaviour 'gen_server') dict_cache2.erl:2: Warning:
undefined callback function handle_info/2 (behaviour
```

```
'gen_server') dict_cache2.erl:2: Warning: undefined
callback function terminate/2 (behaviour 'gen_server')
{ok,dict_cache2}
```

Whoa! *What* are those warnings?

When we declare a behaviour, the Erlang compiler expects that all defined functions exist.

In this case, we didn't define the code_change/3, handle_cast/2, handle_info/2, or terminate/2 functions. So the compiler is duty bound to remind us.

But, for this particular example, we don't care about those functions. So, for now, just ignore the warnings. The return value {ok, dict_cache2} tells us that our gen_server actually compiled.

Now we can try it out:

Listing 7.30 (⇒ >) dict_cache2: **Start**

```
2> dict_cache2:start().
{ok,<0.41.0>}
```

Yippee! Server started.

Now set and get values:

Listing 7.31 (⇒ >) dict_cache2: **Set and get value**

```
3> dict_cache2:set_value(favorite_movie, "Aliens").
ok
4> dict_cache2:set_value(favorite_game, "Quake").
ok
5> dict_cache2:get_value(favorite_movie).
"Aliens"
6> dict_cache2:get_value(favorite_game).
"Quake"
```

Awesome!

7.1.7. But let's crash this party!

So far we've been pretending we're living in Rainbow Chocolate Land where it rains candy and the rivers are liquid cheesecake. That is, a bug-free never never land. But it's time to return to the real world.

Both of our servers have a glaring, catastrophic bug.

If you haven't done so already, fire up your Erlang VM, and load dict_cache server, that is, the original non-OTP version:

Listing 7.32 (⇒ $) Prepare to crash

```
$ erl
Erlang/OTP 21...
Eshell V10.0.5  (abort with ^ G)
1> l(dict_cache).
{module,dict_cache}
```

Note the 1/1 function, that is lower case L, a slash, and the number 1. This shell-specific function will load a module.[12]

Now, start the server:

Listing 7.33 (⇒ >) Don your safety helmets

```
2> dict_cache:start().
true
```

And watch the world burn!

Listing 7.34 (⇒ >) And...Craaash

```
3> dict_cache:get_value(foo).
=ERROR REPORT==== 25-Aug-2015::15:33:40 ===
Error in process <0.38.0> with exit value:
```

---

[12]See the -pa and -pz options in the Erlang man page: http://www.erlang.org/doc/man/erl.html

```
{badarg,[{dict,fetch,
               [foo,
                {dict,0,16,16,8,80,48,

{[],[],[],[],[],[],[],[],[],[],[],[],[],[],[],[]},
{{[],[],[],[],[],[],[],[],[],[],[],[],[],[],[],[]}}}],
               [{file,"dict.erl"},{line,131}]},

{dict_cache,server_loop,1,[{file,"dict_cache.erl"},

{line,12}]}]}]}
```

Yikes! Joker strikes again. Call Batman!

Batman to the rescue.

That—that—error message, Batman. What in the world?

Squint your eyes, young Robin. Simply saying, they passed a badarg, that is, a bad argument, when they called `dict:fetch` with the argument `foo`.

Sorry. Carried away. But did you not notice something HUUGE? The Erlang shell is hung, but VM itself hasn't crashed.

Why is that?

Turns out the shell is waiting for a reply from a server that crashed. Since we never coded a timeout, it'll hang forever—well, at least until we kill the VM and start over.

Press CTRL+C then the A key followed by Enter to do a hard kill of the VM:

Listing 7.35 (⇒ >) **Kill the Erlang shell**

```
BREAK: (a)bort (c)ontinue (p)roc info (i)nfo (l)oaded
       (v)ersion (k)ill (D)b-tables (d)istribution
a (Enter)
```

Watch the world burn slightly less hot but still hot enough

Now for Round Two. Load up `dict_cache2`, that is, the `gen_server` version:

```
$ erl
1> l(dict_cache2).
{module,dict_cache2}
2> dict_cache2:start().
{ok,<0.37.0>}
```

So far, so good. But...

```
3> dict_cache2:get_value(foo).
=ERROR REPORT==== 25-Aug-2015::15:53:57 ===
** Generic server dict_cache2 terminating
** Last message in was {get_value,foo}
** When Server state == {dict,0,16,16,8,80,48,

{[],[],[],[],[],[],[],[],[],[],[],[],[],[],[],[]},

{{[],[],[],[],[],[],[],[],[],[],[],[],[],[],[],[]}}}
** Reason for termination ==
...
```

Where's Batman when we need him?

And you thought the error message for `dict_cache` crash was huge—

In addition to letting us know that an OTP server has crashed, the system complains that we didn't implement a `terminate/2` function.

But note: This time the shell has returned. We can continue working.

If we try now to return a value from our server, however, we see something new:

```
4> dict_cache2:get_value(bar).
** exception exit: {noproc,{gen_server,call,[dict_cache2,
```

```
{get_value,bar}]}} in function  gen_server:call/2

(gen_server.erl, line 204)
5>
```

Well, think. The server crashed, so it's no longer running. We know this because the OTP system has helpfully returned noproc. What happens when we attempt to start the server back up?

Listing 7.39 (⇒ >) gen_server A-OK

```
5> dict_cache2:start().
{ok,<0.44.0>}
6> dict_cache2:set_value(foo, bar).
ok
7> dict_cache2:get_value(foo).
bar
```

Voila! Back from the dead.

Restarting the server brought it back to a known working state (in this case, the known working state is a fresh server with no data yet stored). You can think of it like the classic technical support adage: "Have you tried turning it off and on again?"

Rebooting a computer, router, or what have you brings the system to a known working state.

We did the same thing here.

7.1.8. Let's supervise this sucker!

Repeat: We brought the system to a known working state by starting the server again when it crashed.

OTP *supervisors* do that for us automatically, allowing us an amazing way to ensure availability without having to write a whole mess of code.

Now let's modify the dict_cache2.erl file. Kill the VM if you still have it running:

Listing 7.40 (⇒ >) **Kill the Erlang shell; prepare to edit** `dict_cache2`

```
8> q().
ok
$ vim dict_cache2.erl
```

First, we'll rename start/0 to start_link/0. Then we'll create a terminate/2 function so we can eliminate at least one of those pesky error messages when the server crashes:

Listing 7.41 (⇒ vim) **Modify** `dict_cache2.erl`

```
-module(dict_cache2).
-behaviour(gen_server).
-export([start_link/0, get_value/1, set_value/2]).
-export([init/1, handle_call/3, terminate/2]).

start_link() ->
  gen_server:start_link({local, ?MODULE}, ?MODULE, [], []).

terminate(_Reason, _State) ->
  ok.
```

start vs start_link

The start and start_link functions have separate but related meanings in Erlang:

- **start/1**: Just spawns the server then forgets about it. If the server crashes, it crashes. The process dies and the user mourns.

- **start_link/1**: Starts the server and establishes a link between the calling process and the new process. Given the Swedish origins of Erlang, think of linking as the "viking blood pact" of Erlang. That is, when two processes are linked together, if one one of them dies, the other dies as well.[a]

  However, sometimes you want linked processes to handle a dying process rather than just up and dying itself. In this case, you can do what's called "trapping exits." Then instead of a linked process dying, it will instead receive a message that the other process died.

  This combination of linked processes, trapped exits, and monitors (which are another way of getting notified of a dead process) is ultimately the foundation of the Erlang supervision system.

A great tutorial for the confused:
http://learnyousomeerlang.com/errors-and-processes

---

[a]Rumor has it, Erlang's link/1 was originally called viking_blood_pact/1, but they scrapped it at the last second and renamed it link to save characters.

Given these changes, we don't have to "clean up" after the server if it dies. If the server dies, we just return ok and let it die.

But we mustn't forget to add a supervisor.

Add a supervisor

A supervisor watches other processes and restarts them as necessary. It is universally recommended to keep your supervisors as simple as possible to prevent them from crashing. This is why supervision modules are very short. Let's write one.

By convention, Erlang supervisors are typically named SOMETHING_sup.erl, so we'll call ours dict_cache2_sup.erl:

Listing 7.42 (⇒ $) Create `dict_cache2_sup.erl`

```
$ vim dict_cache2_sup.erl

-module(dict_cache2_sup).
-behaviour(supervisor).
-export([start_link/1, init/1]).
```

Note that the supervisor behaviour, like the gen_server behaviour, warns us if we're missing functions. If we're using Erlang's dialyzer static analysis tool it'll also tell us if we're passing variables of the wrong type.[13]

Now we need to add start/1 and init/1:

Listing 7.43 (⇒ vim) Define `start_link/1` and `init/1` (`dict_cache2_sup.erl`)

```
-export([start_link/1, init/1]).

start_link(_Args) ->
  supervisor:start_link({local, ?MODULE}, ?MODULE, _Args).

init(_) ->
   ChildId = dict_cache2,
   StartFun = {dict_cache2, start_link, []},
   Restart = permanent,
   Shutdown = 2000,
   SupervisorType = worker,
   Modules = [dict_cache2],
```

---

[13]http://erlang.org/doc/apps/dialyzer/dialyzer_chapter.html

```
ChildSpecs = [{ChildId, StartFun, Restart,
        Shutdown, SupervisorType, Modules}],
RestartStrategy = {one_for_one, 15, 60},
{ok, {RestartStrategy, ChildSpecs}}.
```

Erlang supervision is well documented. It's well worth an hour or two of study.[14]

But to translate our code into plain English:

Start a single worker server with `dict_cache2:start_link()` and keep watch for crashes. If the server crashes, restart it. If it crashes more than 15 times in 60 seconds, abort.

7.1.9. Cut to the chase

As my Bostonian friend would say, "This stuff is wicked sweet." So let's compile and test:

Listing 7.44 (⇒ $) **Compile dict_cache2**

```
dict_cache$ erl

1> c(dict_cache2).
dict_cache2.erl:2: Warning: undefined callback function

 code_change/3 (behaviour 'gen_server')
dict_cache2.erl:2: Warning: undefined callback function

 handle_cast/2 (behaviour 'gen_server')
dict_cache2.erl:2: Warning: undefined callback function

 handle_info/2 (behaviour 'gen_server')
{ok,dict_cache2}
2> c(dict_cache2_sup).
{ok,dict_cache2_sup}
```

---

[14]http://erlang.org/doc/design_principles/sup_princ.html,
   https://pdincau.wordpress.com/2010/01/28/supervisors-in-erlang-otp/, 2011,
   Logan, Martin, et. al., *Erlang and OTP in Action*. Manning, Greenwich, pages 125–129.

Now we start the supervisor with a twist:

Listing 7.45 ($\Rightarrow$ >) **Start the supervisor**

```
3> {ok, SupPid} = dict_cache2_sup:start_link([]).
{ok,<0.46.0>}
```

This call links superviser:start_link/1 to the shell process. Why? Since the shell is just another Erlang process, if a process crashes within it, Erlang kills the shell. Since our server is linked to a supervisor, the crashing shell process will trigger the link and bring down the supervisor.

In short, we need to unlink the shell from the supervisor:

Listing 7.46 ($\Rightarrow$ >) **Unlink supervisor**

```
4> erlang:unlink(SupPid).
true
```

Now let's stress on our server:

Listing 7.47 ($\Rightarrow$ >) **Stress the server**

```
5> dict_cache2:set_value(foo, bar).
ok
6> dict_cache2:get_value(foo).
bar
```

So far so good. But:

Listing 7.48 ($\Rightarrow$ >) **Oops!**

```
7> dict_cache2:get_value(bogus).
=ERROR REPORT==== 25-Aug-2015::21:20:41 ===
** Generic server dict_cache2 terminating
** Last message in was {get_value,bogus}
** When Server state == {dict,1,16,16,8,80,48,
```

. . .

Okay, we've seen this before. Hang on:

Listing 7.49 (⇒ >) **Whew! Shell recovered.**

```
8> dict_cache2:set_value(a,b).
ok
9> dict_cache2:get_value(a).
b
```

Way to go! Our server is still operational.

But what about our data? Remember, we'd stored foo:

Listing 7.50 (⇒ >) **But...**

```
10> dict_cache2:get_value(foo).

=ERROR REPORT==== 25-Aug-2015::21:28:00 ===
** Generic server dict_cache2 terminating
** Last message in was {get_value,foo}
** When Server state == {dict,1,16,16,8,80,48,
```

All data stored before the first crash is gone. Trying to access our data causes a crash. Makes sense. When the supervisor restarted the server, it restarted with a blank slate.

7.1.10. Take away

Our gen_server is available immediately after a crash. That's the supervisor at work.

7.1.11. Exercises

1. Fix both dict_cache and dict_cache2 so they don't crash when trying to retrieve a value for a key that doesn't exist. (hint: dict:find/2)

2. Add a delete_key(Key) function to dict_cache2.

7.2. Dets with OTP... For Real this Time

RUSTY: So, with OTP we have the tools we need to make our Dets database both safer and atomic. Let's hear it. Ready?

OLEG: READY!!!

RUSTY: Let's keep it simple by reworking our existing ni_dets module. First, we establish our gen_server behavior and related exports:

Listing 7.51 (⇒ $) Modify `ni_dets.erl`

```
~/dict_cache$ cd ../nindex/site/src
... nindex/site/src$ vim ni_dets.erl

-module(ni_dets).

-behaviour(gen_server).

-export([start/0,
        start_link/0,
        init/1,
        handle_call/3,
        handle_cast/2,
        handle_info/2,
        terminate/2,
        code_change/3
       ]).
-export([init_db/0,
        get_all/0
...
```

MARSHA: Since we won't be changing our API, I'm guessing that we can leave the other exports.

RUSTY: That's right! Nothing will change in the rest of our application.

7.2.1. Initializing the server and some boilerplate

RUSTY: We should know by now that dynamic processes need to be started. So we'll create both start/0 and start_link/0. We won't use start_link/0 until we implement a supervisor:

Listing 7.52 (⇒ vim) **Define start/0 and start_link/0 (ni_dets.erl)**

```
-record(weblink, id, topic, descriptor, url).

start() ->
    gen_server:start({local, ?MODULE}, ?MODULE, [], []).

start_link() ->
    gen_server:start_link({local, ?MODULE}, ?MODULE, [], []).
```

OLEG: We need an init/1 function, right?

RUSTY: 'Deed we do. We need the init/1 function to open the database file. Whereas we opened and closed the database with each request to our non-OTP version of ni_dets, with this version we'll open it when we start the server and close it when we shut it down:

Listing 7.53 (⇒ vim) **Define init/1 (ni_dets.erl)**

```
    gen_server:start_link({local, ?MODULE}, ?MODULE, [], []).

init(_) ->
    open_db(),
    {ok, []}.
```

RUSTY: We know that gen_server expects terminate/2 and code_change/3 functions. The function terminate/2 will close our database file; and, for now, code_change/3 will do nothing.

```
    {ok, []}.

terminate(_Reason, _State) ->
    close_db(),
    ok.

code_change(_OldVsn, State, _Extra) ->
    {ok, State}.
```

STEVIE: But doesn't gen_server expect other functions as well?

RUSTY: You betcha. But for present purposes, the functions handle_cast/2 and handle_info/2 get a free ride:

```
    {ok, State}.

handle_cast(_Msg, State) ->
    {noreply, State}.

handle_info(_Info, State) ->
    {noreply, State}.
```

OLEG: If we're not actually using these functions, why do we even define them?

MARSHA: Yeah, that seems like extra work.

RUSTY: Well, we could forget about these functions and ignore the compile warnings. Our gen_server would still work.

STEVIE: So the only reason to include them is to suppress warnings?

RUSTY: Actually, no. The warnings let us know that we could face real consequences if we fail to define these functions.

OLEG: Like what?

RUSTY. Like if we call gen_server:cast(ni_dets, any_message) and have not defined the handle_cast/2 function, our gen_server will crash.

It will look like this:

Example 7.1 `gen_server:cast` **without** `handle_cast`

```
nindex@127.0.0.1)4> gen_server:cast(ni_dets, something).
ok
nindex@127.0.0.1)5>
=ERROR~REPORT====~28-May-2016::17:35:32~===
** Generic~server ni_dets terminating
** Last message in was {'$gen_cast',something}
** When Server state == []
** Reason for termination ==
** {'function not exported',
    [{ni_dets,handle_cast,[something,[],[]},
    {gen_server,try_dispatch,4,{[{file,"gen_server.erl"},
    {line,615}]
   },
{gen_server,handle_msg,5,[{file,"gen_server.erl"},
{line,681}]},
{proc_lib,init_p_do_apply,3,[{file,"proc_lib.erl"},
{line,240}]}]}]}
```

OLEG: UG...ly!

RUSTY: Anyway, let's not forget to rework init_db/0 function:

Listing 7.56 (⇒ **vim**) **Modify init_db/0 (ni_dets.erl)**

```
handle_info(_Info, State) ->
    noreply, State.

init_db() ->
    open_db(),
    close_db(),
    start().
```

7.2.2. `handle_call` **with our Dets adapter**

RUSTY: Now on to core functionality. Ready for it?

OLEG: Can't wait!

RUSTY: We'll start with the simplest function— get_all/0:

Listing 7.57 (⇒ **vim**) **Modify get_all/0 (ni_dets.erl)**

```
close_db() ->
    dets:close(dets_nindex).

get_all() ->
    open_db(),
    Links = dets:match_object(dets_nindex, '_'),
    close_db(),
    Links.
    gen_server:call(?MODULE, get_all).
```

RUSTY: With power comes great responsibility. Since we're talking gen_server, we need an associated handle_call/3 clause. Note that we'll separate API functions from handlers in our source code:[15]

---

[15]Note: handle_call/3 expects a response and will block until it gets it; handle_cast/2, on the other hand, is asynchronous. See: http://erlang.org/doc/man/gen_server.html

Listing 7.58 ($\Rightarrow$ vim) **Define** `handle_call(get_all...)` **(ni_dets.erl)**

```
    gen_server:call(?MODULE, get_all).

%%*****************************************************
%% gen_server handlers
%%*****************************************************

handle_call(get_all, _From, State) ->
    Links = dets:match_object(dets_nindex, '_'),
    {reply, Links, State};
```

RUSTY: Look familiar?

MARSHA: Sort of. Can I try my hand with get_link/1?

OLEG: Teacher's pet!

MARSHA: Wish me luck!

Listing 7.59 ($\Rightarrow$ vim) **Modify** `get_link/0` **(ni_dets.erl)**

```
get_link(ID) ->
    open_db(),
    Link = case dets:lookup(dets_nindex, ID) of
        [L] -> L;
         [] -> undefined
    end,
    close_db(),
    Link.
    gen_server:call(?MODULE, {get_link, ID}).
```

RUSTY: Lookin' good!

MARSHA: Think I've got the hang:

211

Listing 7.60 (⇒ vim) **Define `handle_call/3` (`ni_dets.erl`)**

```
handle_call(get_all, _From, State) ->
...
handle_call({get_link, ID}, _From, State) ->
    Link = case dets:lookup(dets_nindex, ID) of
        [L] -> L;
        [] -> new
    end,
    {reply, Link, State};
```

RUSTY: You're a natural! Give save_link/1 a shot:

Listing 7.61 (⇒ vim) **Modify `save_link/1` (`ni_dets.erl`)**

```
save_link(Link = #weblink{id=undefined}) ->
    save_link(Link#weblink{id=()});
save_link(Link) ->
    open_db(),
    ok = dets:insert(dets_nindex, Link),
    close_db().
    gen_server:call(?MODULE, {save_link, Link}).
```

RUSTY: Stevie, what next?

STEVIE: A handle_call clause?

RUSTY: Why?

STEVIE: gen_server needs to know what to do with save_link/1.

RUSTY: Right on. Try your hand:

Listing 7.62 (⇒ vim) **Define** `handle_call(save_link...)` (`ni_dets.erl`)

```
handle_call({get_link, ID}, _From, State) ->
...
handle_call({save_link, Link}, _From, State) ->
   ok = dets:insert(dets_nindex, Link),
   {reply, ok, State};
```

RUSTY: Way to go! Want to finish up the API calls?

Listing 7.63 (⇒ vim) **Modify** `delete_link/1` (`ni_dets.erl`)

```
delete_link(ID) ->
   open_db(),
   dets:delete(dets_nindex, ID),
   close_db().
   gen_server:call(?MODULE, {delete_link, ID}).
```

OLEG: How come they get to have all the fun?

RUSTY: Okay, Oleg. Wrap it up for us:

Listing 7.64 (⇒ vim) **Define** `handle_call(delete_link...)` (`ni_dets.erl`)

```
handle_call(delete_link, ID, _From, State) ->

handle_call({delete_link, ID}, _From, State) ->
   dets:delete(dets_nindex, ID),
   {reply, ok, State}.
```

RUSTY: Not bad! Save changes, recompile, fire up our application, and open it in the browser:

Listing 7.65 (⇛ $) **Recompile** `nnindex`

```
nindex/site/src$ cd ../../
nindex$ make && bin/nitrogen console
```

MARSHA: Hey, works. Page loads anyway.

OLEG: Shirts 10 Skins 0.

7.2.3. Starting the Server during Startup

RUSTY: So, Oleg, click the Show All button.

OLEG: Whoa! Crashes. Another big hairy error message in the console. You've got to be Einstein to grok this stuff.

Listing 7.66 (⇛ >) **Oops!**

```
=INFO REPORT==== 28-May-2016::21:34:27 ===
{error,postback_request,
    {url,"127.0.0.1:8000/"},
    {exit,
    {noproc,{gen_server,call,[ni_dets,get_all]}},
    [{gen_server,call,2,
        [{file,"gen_server.erl"},
        {line,204}]},
        ...
```

RUSTY: Buck up. Erlang error messages do take getting used to. Tip: Skim through until you find the relevant line—in this case:

{noproc,{gen_server,call, [ni_dets,get_all]}}.

What do you suppose that means?

STEVIE: noproc—No process?

RUSTY: Indeed! The error message tells us that we're trying to send a request to the gen_server ni_dets, but it can't find a running process. Short answer: We forgot to start our server before we started sending requests.

MARSHA: Ah, do we need a supervisor?

RUSTY: That would be prudent. For now, since we're testing, we can piggyback on init_db/0.

MARSHA: So, then, we should call ni_links:init_db() in the Erlang shell?

RUSTY: We could, and that's fine during development. But we should really start our server during application start-up.

MARSHA: You've lost me?

RUSTY: Fact is, we have quite a few options.[16] My favorite is to put it in the nitrogen_sup.erl file. This way, we can verify that the database has properly started before we start accepting requests.

STEVIE: Can you show us?

RUSTY: Well, first we open up site/src/nitrogen_sup.erl in the editor, then we'll add ni_links:init_db() to nitrogen_sup:init/1:

Listing 7.67 (⇒ $) Add `ni_link_db/0` to `nitrogen_sup:init/1`

```
nindex$ cd site/src
site/src$ vim nitrogen_sup.erl
init([]) ->
    ni_links:init_db(),
    application:load(nitrogen_core),
```

---

[16]The alternative to putting it in nitrogen_sup is to add an associated -eval "ni_links:init_db()" call in etc/vm.args. Or we could put it in the nitrogen_app.erl file as well.

```
application:start(simple_cache),
application:start(crypto),
application:start(nprocreg),
application:start(simple_bridge),
{ok, { {one_for_one, 5, 10}, []} }.
```

RUSTY: Now let's kill Nitrogen, recompile, start it up again, and give it another shot:

Listing 7.68 (⇒ >) Kill and restart

```
2> q().
ok
site/src$ cd ..
nindex$ make && bin/nitrogen console
..
1>
```

MARSHA: Works!

RUSTY: Excellent! Also, note that we use ni_links:init_db() rather than ni_dets:init_db(). Anyone guess why?

OLEG: We don't want to be dependent upon the implementation of the database.

7.2.4. Supervising our Dets adapter

RUSTY: Now let's supervise our server. We don't have time to turn it into a full-blown application, but we could. In fact, that would be an excellent homework assignment.[17] Instead, we'll simply create a supervisor and start it with ni_dets:init_db():

---

[17]http://erlang.org/doc/design_principles/applications.html

---

Listing 7.69 (⇒ $) Define `ni_dets_sup.erl`

```
nindex$ cd site/src
nindex/site/src$ vim ni_dets_sup.erl

-module(ni_dets_sup).
-behaviour(supervisor).

-export([start_link/0,
         init/1
       ]).

start_link() ->
    supervisor:start_link({local, ?MODULE}, ?MODULE, []).
```

OLEG: Man, this `start_link` dooby. So little code, but so confusing.

MARSHA: We've covered that. Weren't you listening?

RUSTY: Take pity. There is indeed a lot hidden under the hood. It definitely took me awhile to get the hang of it. But here's a hint—first, we're starting a *link* between the supervisor and a worker—

STEVIE: Wait! Wait! This supervisor could be linked to another supervisor, couldn't it?

RUSTY: Got me there. It could, but let's focus on the big picture. Next, focus on the parameters. There are only three.

OLEG: That's what confuses me.

MARSHA: We've gone over them, doofus.

STEVIE: Actually, Cesarini and Thompson have a nice explanation. Check it out.[18]

RUSTY: Nice one! If you study how supervisors respond when linked processes die it'll start to become clear.

---

[18]Cesarini, Francesco and Simon Thompson, 2009, *Erlang Programming*, O'Reilly, Sebastapol, CA. page 276.

OLEG: Promise?

RUSTY: I promise. Actually, the Erlang devs threw us a tasty bone with the Erlang 18 release—maps, a hot new way to initialize supervisors. But before we get into that, let's implement one more tweak:

Listing 7.70 (⇒ `vim`) Define `start/0`

```
-export([start/0,
         start_link/0,
         init/1]).

start() ->
    {ok, Pid} = start_link(),
    unlink(Pid),
    {ok, Pid}.
```

MARSHA: Whaa—`unlink`?

RUSTY: In a "real" application, we'd most likely split these modules into their own application and specify them as a rebar dependency. Since supervisors are designed and *expected* to be used within a supervisor tree, or to be started by an application, the supervisor module only has a `start_link` function. Unlike `gen_server`, which does provide a plain, unlinked, start function, supervisors implemented outside a supervision tree don't. So, cut to the chase, we must start a supervisor with `start_link/0`.

STEVIE: I still don't get it.

RUSTY: Recall that linked processes have a "Viking Blood Pact." They kill themselves if one of their brothers die. So we call on the power of Odin to undo the blood pact, that is to `unlink` the calling process from the supervisor. Without unlinking, if the calling process dies, it takes the supervisor with it which, in turn, will take down our `gen_server`.

OLEG: Oh, man, so that `unlink/0` business is just a hack?

RUSTY: Guilty as charged. So don't take away too much and start unlinking supervisors all over your code.

OLEG: Think I get it. But it's a lot to think about for one line of code.

STEVIE: So what's the deal with these maps doohickeys you mentioned?

RUSTY: Maps are a newish syntactical hash-table. They look kind of like records, but are more flexible. For now, I'll just show maps in use, but suggest that you read up:[19]

Listing 7.71 ($\Rightarrow$ `vim`) **Define supervisor**

```
    unlink(Pid),
    {ok, Pid}.

init([]) ->
    SupFlags = #{
        strategy => one_for_one,
        intensity => 1000,
        period => 3600
    },
    Child = #{
        id => ni_dets,
        start => {ni_dets, start_link, []},
        restart => permanent,
        shutdown => 2000,
        type => worker,
        modules => [ni_dets]
    },
    {ok, {SupFlags, [Child]}}.
```

RUSTY: Compare this against the supervisor in an earlier version of nindex. I think you'll agree that it's much cleaner than using all tuples.

STEVIE: It IS much clearer!

---

[19]http://erlang.org/doc/man/maps.html

RUSTY: But there's more. Or should I say, *less?*

OLEG: What?

RUSTY: With the introduction of maps in supervisor declarations, the OTP team was able to introduce sane defaults. This means that we can leave off declarations of things that we otherwise don't care about. So we have a number of completely unnecessary lines:

Listing 7.72 (⇒ `vim`) **Modify `init/1`**

```
init([]) ->
    SupFlags = #{
        strategy => one_for_one,
        intensity => 1000,
        period => 3600
    },
    Child = #{
        id => ni_dets,
        start => {ni_dets, start_link, []},
        restart => permanent,
        shutdown => 2000,
        type => worker,
        modules => [ni_dets]
    },
    {ok, {SupFlags, [Child]}}.
```

STEVIE: Wait! So what are the defaults for `SupFlags`?

RUSTY: The `one_for_one` strategy is a default. For the others, the configuration was overkill. It translated into "if the server crashes more than 1000 times in an hour, kill the supervisor." The default is `intensity=1` and `period=5`, which translates to "If the server crashes more than one time in five seconds, kill the supervisor." This should be completely satisfactory for our server.

STEVIE: I take it `restart=permanent` and `type=worker` are defaults?

RUSTY: *(in an enthusiastic German accent)* Oooooooooooo! That's a bingo!

OLEG: *(picking up on Rusty's reference)* You just say "bingo!"

RUSTY: Bingo! How fun!

MARSHA: Uhhhh, what?

RUSTY: Sorry. Just a bit from Tarantino's *Inglorious Basterds*.

Anyway, our final supervisor is much simpler, wouldn't you say?

STEVIE: Bingo!

RUSTY: Now let's revise the `ni_dets` module so the supervisor starts when we call `ni_links:init_db()`. Save and open up `site/src/ni_dets.erl` and make the following change:

Listing 7.73 (⇒ $) **Modify** `ni_dets:init_db/0` (`ni_dets.erl`)

```
...  site/src$ vim ni_dets.erl
init_db() ->
    start().
    ni_dets_sup:start().
```

RUSTY: Recompile. Fire it up. And everything should be operational.

STEVIE: Looks like that worked. But you mentioned this setup is admittedly a hack. Should we start this properly?

RUSTY: Honestly, that's a good idea.

7.2.5. Properly supervising our supervisor

RUSTY: We made our `ni_dets_sup` supervisor and started it with a hack, but without the link that we so conveniently unlinked we don't actually have a proper supervision tree.

STEVIE: So we're going to supervise the supervisor?

RUSTY: Exactly! In large systems, you might have many servers, state machines, and supervisors linked together. Think about how the supervisor we built will restart our server if it crashes. A natural extension of that is to have multiple servers supervised by a top-level supervisor. What do you think happens if some of the servers are unstable?

STEVIE: My guess—the supervisor will just keep restarting them.

RUSTY: Correct! But if all the servers start crashing regularly as a result of some crazy unpredictable system-wide problem with our state, the supervisor does have a pressure-valve, so to speak. If it's restarting too many things too frequently, the supervisor itself crashes.

OLEG: And that's where we'd want a supervisor for our supervisor, right?

RUSTY: Exactly! If the supervisor of those unstable servers crashes, we can restart the supervisor itself, which will then restart its dependent worker servers, hopefully bringing the system back to a known operational state.

MARSHA: How deep does this rabbit hole go?

RUSTY: Not much deeper. That's kind of it. So let's supervise our supervisor, and then we'll have a true supervision tree, instead of that janky unlinked supervisor we started.

We'll start by saving ni_dets.erl and opening site/src/nitrogen_sup.erl:

Listing 7.74 (⇒ $) **Editing `nitrogen_sup.erl`**

```
site/src$ vim nitrogen_sup.erl

init([]) ->
    ni_links:init_db(),
    application:load(nitrogen_core),
    application:start(simple_cache),
    application:start(crypto),
```

```
application:start(nprocreg),
application:start(simple_bridge),

DetsSup = #{
    id => ni_dets_sup,
    start => {ni_dets_sup, start_link, []},
    shutdown => 2000,
    type => supervisor,
    modules => [ni_dets_sup]
},
{ok, { {one_for_one, 5, 10}, [DetsSup]} }.
```

RUSTY: As you see, we removed the `ni_links:init_db()` call, then defined DetsSup similar to `Child`, defined on page 219.

7.2.6. Summary

RUSTY: So, there you have it. A solid backend-agnostic database adapter. But hang on tight. Next session we'll demonstrate how to use the same API to connect to a world-class relational database.

8. nindex on PostgreSQL

RUSTY: Afternoon, kiddos! Recharged? Ready to experience new planes of existence?

MARSHA: If it's meditation you're selling— not my thing.

OLEG: My idea of meditation is fragging noobs in *Overwatch*.

RUSTY: Today, we're going to install nindex on a rock-solid relational database. And we'll do it with minimal code changes.

OLEG: Which database?

RUSTY: Truth is, we could install any database we want—MySQL, Riak, Mongo, Couch. Or we could install a built-in Erlang database like Mnesia. But I suggest we go for the big daddy in the open source field—PostgreSQL.

OLEG: Dig it!

RUSTY: Turns out, I have the perfect tool to ease the pain—a library called SQL Bridge.[1]

OLEG: What's so cool about SQL Bridge?

RUSTY. The Erlang ecosystem includes adapters to a bunch of popular databases. The SQL Bridge library abstracts away the specifics of each database adapter so you can enter minimal configuration and get to writing your application. It simplifies integration of PostgreSQL and MySQL with Nitrogen applications.

MARSHA: Is PostgreSQL hard to learn?

---

[1] https://github.com/choptastic/sql_bridge

RUSTY: Depends on how deeply you dive in. PostgreSQL can support data requirements of large enterprises. Administration across replicated servers and data centers can be challenging. Indeed, entire careers and countless books are dedicated to database administration (DBA), so we won't dive deep. On the other hand, PostgreSQL is easy to install and run.

OLEG: Says you—

RUSTY: Well, take out your stopwatch big guy. Bet you a dollar to a donut we can install PostgreSQL, get it running, and create a schema in, say, seven minutes. In fact, the schema will be a piece of cake since it will consist of a single table.

OLEG: You're on! Clock is ticking. Counting down.

8.1. Install PostgreSQL

RUSTY: You guys are running Ubuntu Linux, so we'll install PostgreSQL with apt. But you can use your package manager of choice:[2]

Listing 8.1 (⇒ $) **Install PostgreSQL**

```
 ...   /site/src$ sudo apt-get install postgresql
```

RUSTY: We'll need a smattering of SQL commands.[3] If you want to work with relational databases, SQL fluency is essential. Not that hard to learn— volumes out there to help, so we won't get into SQL.

OLEG: Clock is tiiicking—

RUSTY: Right. Now to connect to our database server and create a database:

---

[2]PostgreSQL installation guides: http://bit.ly/install-pg
[3]Structured Query Language

Listing 8.2 (⇒ $) **Create database**

```
...  /site/src$ sudo -u postgres psql
postgres=# create database nindex;
CREATE DATABASE
```

RUSTY: We need to set up credentials to connect to the database. A nice thing about using a tried-and-true database product is that you can configure user credentials to access specific databases in the system. This is handy because if you're running multiple applications on the same database system and one application gets pwned...

OLEG: Pwned?

RUSTY: Sorry, gamer-speak for owned, hacked, compromised... Anyway, if your application gets hacked and you've properly set up credentials, then other databases on the same server are at less risk.

OLEG: Acknowledged. But I remind you, the clock...

RUSTY: Right. To add our first user we need to connect to the new database:

Listing 8.3 (⇒ psql) **Connect to database**

```
postgres=# \c nindex
You are now connected to database "nindex"
as user "postgres".
```

RUSTY: We'll call our user "nindex_user" and give her the super-secure password "nindex_pw"...

Listing 8.4 (⇒ psql) **Add user**

```
postgres=# create user nindex_user with login
                password 'nindex_pw';
```

RUSTY: Now we need to grant user access to the nindex database:

Listing 8.5 (⇒ psql) **Grant user access**

```
nindex=# grant all on database nindex to nindex_user;
GRANT
```

RUSTY: We need to specify which operations are available to our users—in our case the basic CRUD activities: create (insert), read, update, and delete. With larger applications, more intricate permissions can be assigned on a per-user, per-database basis. But for now, we'll go with the following:

Listing 8.6 (⇒ psql) **Grant permissions**

```
nindex=# alter default privileges
nindex-# in schema public
nindex-# grant select, insert, update, delete
nindex-# on tables
nindex-# to nindex_user;
ALTER DEFAULT PRIVILEGES
```

RUSTY: We're also going to grant nindex_user access to use sequences, which are PostgreSQL's method of automatic key creation:

Listing 8.7 (⇒ psql) **Grant permission to use sequences**

```
nindex=# alter default privileges
nindex-# in schema public
nindex-# grant select, usage
nindex-# on sequences
nindex-# to nindex_user;
ALTER DEFAULT PRIVILEGES
```

STEVIE: What's a schema?

RUSTY: A schema describes how data is structured in the database.

Data in a relational database is represented as tables and columns. A schema is a namespace within the database that defines the tables, columns, and various other details of our design. We can add multiple schemas as necessary.

Make sense?

MARSHA: So far so good—

RUSTY: Let's test our connection to the database with a new user. We need to quit the psql shell, then reconnect with new credentials.

When the system asks for a password, enter nindex_pw:

Listing 8.8 (⇒ psql) **Quit and reconnect with new credentials**

```
nindex=# \q
$ psql -U nindex_user -h 127.0.0.1 -W nindex
Password for user nindex_user: nindex_pw
psql (9.3.11)
SSL connection (cipher: DHE-RSA-AES256-GCM-SHA384,
         bits: 256)
Type "help" for help.
nindex=>
```

RUSTY: Success! How we doing for time?

OLEG: Six minutes forty-nine seconds.

RUSTY: You owe me a donut, dude.

OLEG: Rather owe you than cheat you out of it.

STEVIE: Hold it! I'm still trying to get my head around that psql command.

RUSTY: Right. So let's break it down:

- **psql**: name of the executable

- **-U nindex_user**: username nindex_user

- **-h 127.0.0.1**: connect to localhost

- **-W** : prompt for password

- **nindex**: connect to the nindex database.

8.2. Create a Table

RUSTY: Now that we have a user, we need to define a table:

Listing 8.9 (⇒ psql) **Define a table**

```
nindex=> create table link (linkid serial not null primary key,
nindex(> descriptor text,
nindex(> topic text,
nindex(> url text);
CREATE TABLE
```

MARSHA: The text types are obvious, but what is serial?

RUSTY: The serial type is an auto-incrementing integer that's unique to the table. Internally, it's defined by creating a Postgres sequence—

STEVIE: Which explains why we added permissions to sequence in the schema. I was wondering where that was going.

RUSTY: Indeed. You can create your own variety of sequence as well and use that rather than the automatic serial type. That would let you increment your integers by 5, 10, 200, or however you'd like. But that's getting beyond our scope. If you want to look up more, check out the Postgres documentation.[4]

STEVIE: Is our database done—just the one table?

RUSTY: It is. But we need to connect our application.

8.3. Add the `sql_bridge` Dependency

RUSTY: Under the hood, `sql_bridge` uses the popular epgsql[5] driver for Postgres, and `mysql-otp`[6] and, if you use MySQL. It also uses the pooling application poolboy.[7]

STEVIE: So how does all that help us?

RUSTY: Here are the three features I use regularly:

1. Dynamic database connectivity. You specify a {Module, Function} combo, and it'll connect with the proper database.

2. Query result conversion into any format you want: lists, tuples, proplists, maps, dicts.

3. Basic query-construction. It's not quite at the level of an ORM,[8] but it can save maps or proplists with a simple db:save(table_name, RowContents) call.

---

[4]https://www.postgresql.org/docs/
[5]https://github.com/epgsql/epgsql
[6]https://github.com/mysql-otp/mysql-otp
[7]https://github.com/devinus/poolboy
[8]Object-Relational Mapping

MARSHA: Sounds handy.

RUSTY: `sql_bridge` unifies the interface to both MySQL and PostgreSQL. If we want to run MySQL, we only need to change a few configuration settings—no need to write new code unless we write PostgreSQL-specific queries.

OLEG: So is `sql_bridge` built into Nitrogen?

RUSTY: No. We have to add it as a dependency and rebuild the system.

OLEG: You're giving me a headachhhhe.

RUSTY: Hang on—it's simple. Open `rebar.config`[9] in your editor, add the following line to the deps section, then recompile and restart the VM:

Listing 8.10 (⇒ $) **Add `sql_bridge` as dependency (`rebar.config`)**

```
nindex$ vim rebar.config

...
{deps, [
   {cowboy,
      {git,
       "git://github.com/ninenines/cowboy",
       {tag, "2.4.0"}}},
   {sql_bridge,
      {git, "git://github.com/choptastic/sql_bridge",
         {branch, master}}},
...
nindex$ make
...
nindex$ bin/nitrogen console
...  1> sync:go().
```

---

[9]The veteran Erlanger will recognize that we're using rebar 2 style dependencies. As of this writing, Nitrogen still uses rebar 2, but it will be migrating to rebar 3 in the near future.

8.4. Configure `sql_bridge`

RUSTY: Once rebar has downloaded and installed `sql_bridge` you'll see a `sample.config` file which explains all options. But to save time, let's open up a new file in the etc directory called `sql_bridge.config` and enter our configuration:

Listing 8.11 (⇒ vim) **Look at** `sql_bridge.config`

```
[{sql_bridge,
    [{module_alias, db},
     {adapter, sql_bridge_epgsql},
     {host, "127.0.0.1"},
     {port, 5432},
     {user, "nindex_user"},
     {pass, "nindex_pw"},
     {lookup, nindex},
     {connections_per_pool, 10},
     {overflow_connections_per_pool, 10},
     {stringify_binaries, true},
     {replacement_token_style, '$'}
]}].
```

MARSHA: Explain, please.

RUSTY: Should be fairly obvious, but here goes—

- **module_alias**: This gives us a built-in shortcut module alias that we can call in our code instead of typing `sql_bridge:some_function`.

- **adapter**: This is the adapter we will be connecting with. If we were using MySQL, we would specify `sql_bridge_mysql_otp` as the adapter.

- **host, port, user, pass**: No mysteries here—hostname, port, username, and password. The specified port (5432) is the default Postgres port.

- **lookup**: This is the name of our database. We could have specified a {Module, Function} tuple and it would call that before attempting to connect to execute a query.

- **connections_per_pool**: This specifies how many connections we want to spin up simultaneously when sql_bridge first connects to the database. Having a sane number prevents having to set up and tear down connections with each request.

- **overflow_connections_per_pool**: Poolboy manages overflow connections. If you need more than connections_per_pool, Poolboy will both automatically set up overflow connections and tear them down when no longer needed.

- **stringify_binaries**: By default, sql_bridge will return strings as binaries. But since we're doing most of our stuff with plain Erlang strings, we'll autoconvert these binaries to strings. So we set this to *true*.

- **replacement_token_style**: There are two conventions for replacement tokens when writing queries. MySQL tends to use a question mark (?) as the replacement token, and PostgreSQL uses numbered tokens (like $1, $2, $3, etc). We can control which token we prefer to use regardless of the underlying driver. So we say "$" to tell the system we're going to use Postgres style interpolation.

8.5. More on Maps

RUSTY: Let's digress a moment to talk about maps since I want to put them to work in ni_pgsql. A map is a record-style syntax with the pattern matching features of a record, but with an internal structure closer to that of a dict. This means you can add fields dynamically and easily convert to and from a proplist, the former being impossible with records and the latter being inconvenient.

Many languages implement maps. But the Erlang OTP team first implemented them for Erlang with Version 17. It was Erlang's first fundamental syntax change in years.

STEVIE: So how do they work?

RUSTY: A map looks like this:

Example 8.1   Map example

```
MyCharacter = #{
    race  => "Dwarf",
    level => 15,
    name => "Ivan Drago"
}.
```

MARSHA: Definitely more readable than records.

RUSTY: But like records, we can use pattern matching to extract values and bind them to outside variables.

OLEG: How's that?

RUSTY: Say we want to extract the values of race and level from MyCharacter—we can do this:

Example 8.2

```
#{race := Race, level := Level} = MyCharacter.
```

STEVIE: Whoa! Is that ":=" a typo?

RUSTY: No, it's an entirely different operator— => is for setting or updating data in maps, while := is for pulling data out of maps.

STEVIE: Got it. Will this technique work in a function clause definition as well?

RUSTY: You betcha. You could do something like this:

Example 8.3

```
draw_char_level(#{level := Level}) -->
    io:format("My Level: ~p", [Level]).
```

RUSTY: But beware—if you try to use := on a field that doesn't exist, or try to assign a value to the map with it, it'll crash. Similarly, if you try to do => on the left-hand-side of an equals, or in a function clause definition, you'll get an illegal pattern error.

MARSHA: What if I want to change an already assigned value?

RUSTY: Remember that Erlang does not have mutable variables. So we need to update our map and assign it to a new variable. For instance, this won't work:

Example 8.4

```
MyChar = #{race => "Dwarf", level=>15},
MyChar = MyChar#{level=>16}.
```

RUSTY: ...since MyChar is already bound. Instead, we need to assign our updated map to a new variable. So this will work:

Example 8.5

```
MyChar  = #{race => "Dwarf", level => 15},
MyChar2 = MyChar#{level => 16}.
```

STEVIE: Ah, if MyChar was a record, we'd have to reassign it in the same way.

RUSTY: Indeed, as we would with dicts, proplists or any other Erlang variable.

STEVIE: Consistent.

OLEG: Foolish consistency is the hobgoblin of little minds.

STEVIE: (Glaring at Oleg) Speaking of little minds—

MARSHA: Now, now children.

RUSTY: In this case consistency is not foolish in the least. Immutable variables are the heart of functional programming.[10]

RUSTY: Also, you can use variables as keys (as long as the variables are already bound):

Example 8.6

```
> Field = race,
> MyChar = #{Field => "Dwarf"},
> #{Field := Race} = MyChar,
> io:format("Race: ~s~n", [Race]).
```

---

[10]http://miles.no/blogg/why-care-about-functional-programming-part-1-immutability

STEVIE: Way cool!

RUSTY: Does come in handy.

MARSHA: Do keys have to be atoms?

RUSTY: Nope. A key in a map can be any valid Erlang term.

OLEG: This I've got to see.

RUSTY: Well, for example:

Example 8.7

```
#{{a,b,c} => value}.
```

STEVIE: What else can we do with maps?

RUSTY: There is also an Erlang standard library with useful functions for work-ing with maps.[11] For instance, you can convert a map to and from a proplist with maps:to_list/1 and maps:from_list/1.

OLEG: I'm convinced. But what does all this have to do with nindex?

RUSTY: Stay tuned.

8.6. Build `ni_pgsql` with `sql_bridge`

RUSTY: It's taken a bit of setup, but you're going to love the simplicity of ni_psql. We'll start by creating a new file and opening it in our editor at site/src/ni_pgsql.erl:

---

[11]http://erlang.org/doc/man/maps.html

Listing 8.12 (⇒ $) Create ni_pgsql.erl

```
...    /nindex/site/src$ vim ni_pgsql.erl

-module(ni_pgsql).
-export([init_db/0,
         get_all/0,
         get_link/1,
         save_link/1,
         delete_link/1,
         new/3,
         id/1, id/2,
         topic/1, topic/2,
         descriptor/1, descriptor/2,
         url/1, url/2
        ]).
```

RUSTY: Note that these are the same exports we've been using so far. Let's add init_db():

Listing 8.13 (⇒ vim) **Add** init_db/0 (ni_pgsql.erl)

```
         url/1, url/2
        ]).

init_db() ->
    sql_bridge:start().
```

OLEG: Yo! That was simple.

RUSTY: Indeed. That simple command starts up the sql_bridge and epgsql apps, and also sets up the module_alias defined in the configuration (as a reminder, this allows us to use a shorter module name, like db instead of the full sql_bridge). Now we'll add the get_all function. It's equally simple:

Listing 8.14 (⇒ vim) **Add get_all/0 (ni_pgsql.erl)**

```
init_db() ->
    sql_bridge:start().

get_all() ->
    db:maps("select * from link").
```

RUSTY: get_all/0 will run a query that retrieves every row from the link table, puts each field value into a map, and returns the list of maps. Now let's add the most complicated function in our ni_pgsql module:

Listing 8.15 (⇒ vim) **ni_pgsql:get_link/1 (ni_pgsql.erl)**

```
get_all() ->
    db:maps("select * from link").

get_link(ID) ->
    case db:map("select * from link where linkid=$1",[ID]) of
        not_found -> new;
        Map       -> Map
    end.
```

RUSTY: Note that we called db:map instead of db:maps. db:maps returns a list of maps, whereas db:map returns a single map. If none are found, it returns the atom not_found. And just as in the previous versions (Dets and JoeDB), if we don't find a record, we return the atom new.

MARSHA: You're also using string interpolation.

RUSTY: I am! It safely replaces the string $1 with the value of ID, properly escaped in case ID is a string with "dangerous" characters. Very handy when you're working with strings.

MARSHA: What does save_link/1 look like?

RUSTY: We can use db:save/2, which takes a table name and the contents of a record, map, proplist, or dict:

Listing 8.16 (⇒ vim) **Add `save_link/1` (ni_pgsql.erl)**

```
        Map         -> Map
    end.

save_link(Link) ->
    db:save(link, Link).
```

STEVIE: Whoa! That's crazy simple. How does it know whether we're adding a new record or updating an existing one?

RUSTY: Great question! `sql_bridge` looks at the table name (`link`) and makes the assumption that the ID of the table is `TableName ++ "id"`. So the ID for `link` is `linkid`. If the content of the `linkid` field id 0 or `undefined`, `sql_bridge` interprets that as a new record, so it will execute an INSERT query. If, however, linkid has a value other than 0 or `undefined`, it will execute an UPDATE query. Moreover, it will execute those queries with whatever fields, defined in whatever map provided.

MARSHA: How about `delete_link`?

RUSTY: Works much the same way:

Listing 8.17 (⇒ vim) **Add `delete_link/1` (ni_pgsql.erl)**

```
save_link(Link) ->
    db:save(link, Link).

delete_link(ID) ->
    db:delete(link, ID).
```

RUSTY: ...which runs the query: db:q("delete from link where linkid = $1", [ID]).

241

MARSHA: Wicked!

RUSTY: Here, we just need to define our new/3 function.

Listing 8.18 (⇒ vim) **Add** `delete_link/1`

```
delete_link(ID) ->
    db:delete(link, ID).

new(Topic, Descriptor, Url) ->
    #{
        linkid=>0,
        topic=>Topic,
        descriptor=>Descriptor,
        url=>Url
    }.
```

MARSHA: Why did you set `linkid` to 0?

RUSTY: That's a convention in `sql_bridge` - the primary key of 0 is treated as a "new" record - telling the `sql_bridge` to use `INSERT` rather than `UPDATE`.

RUSTY: With that, we turn to the API. I'll blast through quickly since it's so similar to `ni_dets`:

Listing 8.19 (⇒ vim) **Add getters and setters** (`ni_pgsql.erl`)

```
        url=>Url
    }.
id(#{linkid:=ID}) -> ID.
id(W, ID) -> W#{linkid=>ID}.
descriptor(#{descriptor:=Desc}) -> Desc.
descriptor(W, Desc) -> W#{descriptor=>Desc}.
topic(#{topic:=Topic}) -> Topic.
topic(W, Topic) -> W#{topic=>Topic}.
```

```
url(#{url:=Url}) -> Url.
url(W, Url) -> W#{url=>Url}.
```

RUSTY: So that's ni_pgsql. So let's save it, open up site/src/ni_links.erl, and make the following change:

Listing 8.20 (⇒ vim) **Change** DB (ni_links.erl)

```
. . .
site/src$ vim ni_links.erl
-define(DB, ni_dets ni_pgsql).
```

RUSTY: The last thing we need to do is undo the supervisor for our Dets adapter, and reinstate the exeecution of ni_links:init_db(). Open up site/src/nitrogen_sup.erl

Listing 8.21 (⇒ vim) site/src/nitrogen_sup.erl

```
site/src$ vim nitrogen_sup.erl

init([]) ->
    ni_links:init_db(),
    application:load(nitrogen_core),
    application:start(simple_cache),
    application:start(crypto),
    application:start(nprocreg),
    application:start(simple_bridge),

    DetsSup = #{
        id => ni_dets_sup,
        start => {ni_dets_sup, start_link, []},
        shutdown => 2000,
        type => supervisor,
        modules => [ni_dets_sup]
    },
```

```
{ok, { {one_for_one, 5, 10}, [DetsSup ]} }.
```

RUSTY: Alright, that's it.

OLEG: Oh, goodie. I get to recompile and test:

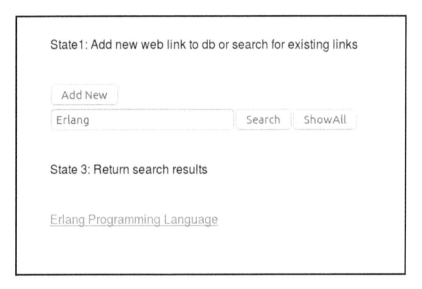

MARSHA: Works! That was easy.

RUSTY: Well, when you're using a professional database, a lot of issues get handled automatically. Makes you appreciate the work of professional database programmers.

8.7. Exercises

1. When we open `localhost:8000/add_edit/new`, we get an error message in the Erlang shell, but our application works without a hitch. This error is from tying to convert `"new"` to an integer. Write a short fix to

`ni_pgsql:get_link/1` (See page 240) to eliminate this warning. Hint: the argument this function is being passed is the atom new.

9. nitroNotes

BOSSMAN: So, Nail, hear you're doing great work with the kids at the high school.

RUSTY: Thanks, sir. They're incredible. Really bright.

BOSSMAN: Listen, my daughter is a freshman up at State College. Sort of floundering.

RUSTY: Didn't do so hot freshman year myself.

BOSSMAN: Well, thing is, the dearheart is not well organized. Think your kids could develop a program to help her organize class notes?

RUSTY: Well, wouldn't be much of a challenge. I mean, probably. But it's so similar to the web link program we just finished—

BOSSMAN: Wait, there's more. My wife teaches over at the university— professor of child psychology. Tells me she needs a program to organize footnotes for her journal articles.

RUSTY: Ah, you're thinking, like, a program that can organize all kinds of notes?

BOSSMAN: You got it!

9.1. And So nnote Came to Be

MARSHA: So will your boss give you a raise if we develop this program—what did you call it, nnote?

RUSTY: Didn't say. But I did get him to promise every member of the team a free Raspberry Pi if we came up with the goods.

MARSHA: Way cool!

STEVIE: I'm in!

OLEG: Awesome!

RUSTY: Okay, Stevie—what's our first step?

STEVIE: Well, nnote is similar in many ways to nindex. I mean, it's just another CRUD program, right?

RUSTY: I agree.

STEVIE: Few changes to the database—few changes to the add/edit form—

RUSTY: Don't be too optimistic. Never know what's going to jump up and bite you. But that said, I've had a few ideas about how we can streamline development.

MARSHA: Still, nnote sounds really cool. I'm always writing short story ideas on scraps of paper.

STEVIE: I could use a notes program to keep track of stuff I find on the web.

RUSTY: That's what I like about this app—has many uses. I keep notes on technical procedures, for instance, and I'm always losing notes I take at conferences.

OLEG: Lots of luck, guys. We're talking totally different kinds of notes. If an app's not super simple, no one will use it. The note part is easy. It's the metadata that makes a note useful. And different kinds of notes require different metadata.

MARSHA: Oleg's right. People keep notes for many reasons. Maybe we need different programs.

RUSTY: Interesting design problem, isn't it?

OLEG: Hold up—I want to hear more about this "streamline development" business.

RUSTY: I've been thinking about how to abstract elements of CRUD programs into generic sequences of code.

OLEG: You mean like some kind of CRUD library?

RUSTY: We may not be able to go that far. Some library functions, yes. But I'm thinking more like scaffolding code. I believe we can significantly reduce the number of keystrokes needed to create a new CRUD program. And, who knows—maybe some of these ideas will even help us deal with Oleg's metadata issue.

9.2. Design—A Brief Aside

STEVIE: Design, ugh! Hate it. I just like to dive in.

RUSTY: That's fine if you're playing around. But maybe you're working under a false assumption.

STEVIE: Like what?

RUSTY: That you're programming a computer.

MARSHA: Well, he is, isn't he?

RUSTY: The computer is a means to an end. In the real world we write programs to solve human problems. As web programmers, we're really programming users.

STEVIE: Users?

RUSTY: The whole point of a web app is to influence the understanding, attitudes, beliefs, or behavior of users—provide or elicit information; motivate click behavior, navigation or purchases; or, simply, entertain.

OLEG: But all that stuff—that's the job of content creators!

RUSTY: Good point. But the web app developer has considerable input into the work flow necessary to use the app. And a successful work flow, in turn, depends on careful programming of the user's eye path.

MARSHA: What's an eye path and how can we program it?

RUSTY: Imagine two boxes on the screen—one, a large red box; the other, a small green box. Where does your eye go first and where from there?

MARSHA: Red to green?

RUSTY: That's an eye path. You control the user's eye path through careful consideration of size, color, placement, and animation of elements on the screen. Think of it this way—you can tell a story about how to interact with the screen by guiding the user's eye path from element to element.

STEVIE: Isn't that what graphic designers do?

RUSTY: Indeed—and good ones get big bucks for creating a compelling user experience. I contend that web developers need to know at least enough about graphic design to create an effective eye path and work flow.

OLEG: Work flow—what's that about?

RUSTY: Choice, placement, and labeling of controls. As web designer Chris Bank puts it, "Like an invisible hand, a web interface should guide users through the experience at the speed of thought."[1]

MARSHA: I'm sold. What's our design goal for this new and improved notes program?

RUSTY: What do you think, Stevie?

STEVIE: Hmmm, I'd say easy to learn and use.

---

[1] Banks, Chris. 2014. *Web UI Design Best Practices*. Chapter 1. http://www.slideshare.net/TheHWD/ux-ui-principles-and-best-practices-20142015

OLEG: Needs to support different kinds of notes.

RUSTY: And I'd add one more thing to the list.

MARSHA: That is...

RUSTY: Programming is fun, but more—programming is an economic activity. Time and cost of development matters in the real world.

OLEG: What does that have to do with us?

RUSTY: As web developers, we should give deep thought to how we can develop our applications as efficiently as possible.

STEVIE: I'm down with that. I've got a thousand programs I'd like to write.

RUSTY: Sounds good. A static grid is a good place to start.

9.3. Static Grid

OLEG: Static grid—Woo-woo! Sounds like "The Matrix."

RUSTY: Here, I've brought up nytimes.com. Squint your eyes until the words are a blur. Pay attention to the shapes on the screen. What do you see?

MARSHA: Boxes.

RUSTY: The screen is composed of boxes within boxes—boxes for news, photos, ads, topical sections. If you follow the site you'll see that the boxes are more or less constant from day to day, but the content changes. The boxes provide a comfortable, consistent, recognizable organization of content—a place for everything and everything in its place. The boxes help brand the site—give it a distinct identity. That's a static grid.

STEVIE: So how do we create a static grid?

OLEG: Templates, man! Don't you remember?

MARSHA: Way ahead of you. While you've been jabbering, I've been sketching out a static grid for nnote:

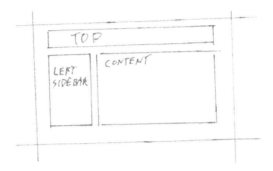

STEVIE: What's with the sidebar?

MARSHA: As a user, it occurs to me that the first thing I'd like to do is to select the type of note I want to enter or retrieve. The sidebar, I think, would be a good place to put a menu to select note type.

RUSTY: Super. Let's see if we can turn it into a template. But first, we need to create a new project. Dataman?

9.4. Create a New Project

OLEG: On it, sir[2]:

Listing 9.1 (⇒ $) Create nnote Project

```
...$ cd ~/nitrogen
.../nitrogen$ make slim_cowboy PROJECT=nnote
.../nitrogen$ cd ../nnote
.../nitrogen/nnote$ git init
```

---

[2]All of the nnotes project's code and changes that cover the next several chapters can be found at https://github.com/BuildItWithNitrogen/nnote/commits

RUSTY: Before we continue, Oleg, how do you bring up nindex in your browser?

OLEG: `localhost:8000`—

RUSTY: Right. Port 8000. Suppose you want to bring up nindex and nnote on your notebook in different tabs at the same time?

OLEG: Oh—I get you. Traffic jam! Both programs will try to serve the browser through the same port. So what can we do about that?

9.5. Any Port in a Storm

RUSTY: Drop into the etc directory, open `simple_bridge.config`, and look for {port, 8000}:

Listing 9.2 (⇒ $) **Locate Port 8000** (`simple_bridge.config`)

```
nnote$ cd etc
etc$ ls
    ...    simple_bridge.config ...
etc$ vim simple_bridge.config
...
{port, 8000},
%% Port to bind
```

RUSTY: Very good. Now change the port to 8001, save the file, start Nitrogen, and open your brower to localhost:8001:

Listing 9.3 (⇒ vim) **Change Port** (`simple_bridge.config`)

```
{port, 8000 8001},
(save)

...nnote/etc$ cd ..
...nnote$ bin/nitrogen console
```

(open browser to `localhost:8001`)

OLEG: Ah, there we are—nindex and nnote side-by-side. Sweet!

9.6. Rusty's Awesome Idea

RUSTY: That gives me an idea. nindex, nnote—feels like we're developing a suite of productivity apps here.

OLEG: So?

RUSTY: Suppose we put our suite under one main menu sharing, basically, the same look and feel?

STEVIE: Should we make it multiuser? I know friends who could use it.

RUSTY: Why not.

OLEG: I don't want anyone reading my notes!

RUSTY: No problemo. We build an access-control system.

MARSHA: Awesome!

RUSTY: So, you're on, girl. Bop over to `site/templates` and copy `bare.html` over to `n_apps.html` so you can implement your static grid.

MARSHA: You really know how to put a girl on the spot!

RUSTY: You can do it!

Listing 9.4   (⇒ $) Create Page Grid Template

```
...nnote$ cd site/templates
...templates$ cp bare.html n_apps.html
```

MARSHA: Okay. We need three `divs`—top, sidebar, and content.

RUSTY: What goes in top?

MARSHA: A navigation menu to switch between programs?

OLEG: No! No! I say top should be reserved for the name of our suite—or maybe even a logo. The navigation menu can go under that. So we need four divs.

MARSHA: On it!

Listing 9.5 (⇒ $) **Define Page Grid Divs** (`n_apps.html`)

```
templates$ vim n_apps.html

[[[page:body()]]]
<div id="contain">
   <div id="top">
      [[[page:top()]]]
   </div>
   <div id="main_menu">
      [[[page:main_menu()]]]
   </div>
   <div id="sidebar">
      [[[page:sidebar()]]]
   </div>
   <div id="content">
      [[[page:content()]]]
   </div>
</div>
...
```

RUSTY: What do you think, Stevie?

STEVIE: Might work.

RUSTY: You've been unusually quiet there, good buddy. What you workin' on?

STEVIE: Oh, making changes to index.erl to see if Marsha's template works.

RUSTY: Way to go! Show us.

STEVIE: I opened index.erl and replaced everything below main/0 with the grid functions Marsha specified in bare.html:

Listing 9.6 ($\Rightarrow$ $) **Edit** index.erl

```
.../templates$ cd ../src
nnote$ vim index.erl
...
main() -> #template { file="./site/templates/n_apps.htmlbare.html" }.

title() ->
    "Welcome to nnote".

top() ->
    #h1 {text="Build it with Nitrogen"}.

main_menu() ->
    #h2 {text="Main Menu"}.

sidebar() ->
    #panel {text="Sidebar"}.

content() ->
    #panel {text="Content"}.
```

RUSTY: Looks promising.

OLEG: Looks bogus on my iPad.

MARSHA: 'Cause he hasn't styled it yet, bozo.

9.7. A Matter of Style

RUSTY: So, Marsha—can you style it?

MARSHA: Think so. But I need to open up `style.css`:

Listing 9.7 (⇒ $) **Open** `style.css`

```
site/src$ cd ../static/css
static/css$ vim style.css
```

MARSHA: I'll put grid styles below body and center the #contain panel:

Listing 9.8 (⇒ `vim`) **Edit** `style.css`

```
body ...

#contain {
    margin-top: 1em;
    margin-left: 10%;
    margin-right: 10%;
    width: 80%;
}
```

MARSHA: Now top:

Listing 9.9 (⇒ `vim`) **Style Top Panel** (`style.css`)

```
#contain ...

#top {
    width: 100%;
    padding-bottom: .5em;
    margin-bottom: 1em;
}
```

MARSHA: Can't forget main_menu:

Listing 9.10 (⇒ `vim`) **Style Main Menu** (`style.css`)

```
#top ...

#main_menu {
    width: 100%;
    padding-bottom: .5em;
    margin-bottom: 1em;
}
```

MARSHA: And, finally, sidebar and content:

Listing 9.11 (⇒ `vim`) **Style Side Bar and Content** (`style.css`)

```
#main_menu ...

#sidebar {
    width: 24%;
    margin-right: 1%;
    float: left;
}

#content {
    width: 75%;
    float: right;
}
```

MARSHA: I think we should tweak the default Nitrogen headline. Find h1 and h2 in that file and we're going to blow away the default styles as well:

Listing 9.12 (⇒ `vim`) **Style Headlines** (`style.css`)

```
.container_12 ...

h1 {
    font-family:  Arial, sans-serif;
    font-weight:  bold;
```

```
      padding-bottom:   7px;
      border-bottom:   dashed 1px #DDD;
      text-transform:  uppaseercase;
      font-size:   1.875em;
      line-height:   1.066667em;
      margin-top:   1.6em;
      margin-bottom:   1.6em;
      margin-top: .3em;
      margin-bottom: .5em;
      padding-top: 0;
      font-style: italic;
      font-weight: 100;
}
h2 {
      font-family:  Arial, sans-serif;
      font-size:   1.5em;
      line-height:   1.333333em;
      margin-top:   1.6em;
      margin-bottom:   1.6em;
      margin-top: 0em;
      margin-bottom: .7em;
      padding: 0;
      font-size: 140%;
      font-weight: lighter;
      text-decoration: underline;
}
```

STEVIE: Looks like the paragraph style could use a tweak.

MARSHA: On it:

Listing 9.13 (⇒ vim) **Style Paragraphs (`style.css`)**

```
h3 ...

p {
    font-size: 1em;
    line-height:2em 1.5em;
    margin-top: 2em;
```

```
    margin-bottom: 2em1em;
 }
```

RUSTY: So how does it look now, Dataman?

(Oleg "the Dataman" directs the browser to ... localhost:8001)

OLEG: It'll pass.

9.8. A Matter of Productivity

RUSTY: Before we continue, let's talk about how we can up our productivity game.

STEVIE: Reuse code?

OLEG: Yeah, but copy-and-paste won't cut it. Change one thing then you have to hunt all over to change it everywhere else.

MARSHA: Ah, so we should abstract functions that we're likely to use more than once—put them in a library module.

RUSTY: Sounds reasonable.

MARSHA: If I'm creating a page that looks like something I've created before, I like to copy the old page and change the name of the module and the various boilerplate functions. But I have to scan through the module to find all the items that need to change.

STEVIE: Use macros. I do that all the time.

RUSTY: Can you show us?

Listing 9.14 (⇒ $) **Define Macros in** `index.erl`

```
.../site/static/css$ cd ../../src
.../src$ vim index.erl

-module(index).
-compile(export_all).
-include_lib("nitrogen_core/include/wf.hrl").
%% **************************************************
%% Macros
%% **************************************************
-define(TEMPLATE,"./site/templates/n_apps.html").
```

OLEG: Way cool! We can create macros for title and top as well:

Listing 9.15 (⇒ vim) **More Macros (**`index.html`**)**

```
-define(TITLE, "Welcome!").
-define(TOP, "Build it with Nitrogen").
```

RUSTY: Aren't you forgetting something?

OLEG: Oh yeah—

Listing 9.16 (⇒ `vim`) **Replace code with macros**

```
-define(TITLE, "Welcome!").
main() -> #template { file=?TEMPLATE "./site/templates/n_apps.html" }.
title() ->
    "Welcome to nnote".
    ?TITLE.
...
top() ->
    #h1 {text=?TOP "Build it with Nitrogen"}.
```

MARSHA: Another thing that bugs me is trying to find the function I'm looking for in a module with lots of functions.

STEVIE: Comments help a lot. I like to group related functions under big bold comments.

RUSTY: Show us.

Listing 9.17 (⇒ `vim`) **Code Organization and Comments(`index.erl`)**

```
-define(TOP, "Build it with Nitrogen").
%% ***************************************************
%% Template and Title
%% ***************************************************
main() -> #template { file=?TEMPLATE}.
title() ->
    ?TITLE.
%% ***************************************************
%% Panel definitions
%% ***************************************************
```

OLEG: Like me mum says, "A place for everything and everything in its place."

RUSTY: I've got to say, you are one impressive bunch.

OLEG: Don't we know it.

9.9. Main Menu

RUSTY: Marsha's point about code abstraction is well taken. The main menu is an excellent case in point. And just so happens, I have code here from another project that I'm happy to share.

OLEG: This should be exciting.

RUSTY: First, I'm going to create a new directory under site/src:

Listing 9.18 (⇒ $) **Create Library Module**

```
site/src$ mkdir n_libs
site/src$ cd n_libs
site/src/n_libs$
```

RUSTY: Next up, create a library module for our menu abstractions:

Listing 9.19 (⇒ $) **Boilerplate** (n_menus.erl)

```
site/src/n_libs$ vim n_menus.erl
...
-module (n_menus).
-compile(export_all).
-include_lib("nitrogen_core/include/wf.hrl").
```

RUSTY: You can build menus in many ways. But they will all have two things in common—a choice offered to the user through a text or image element and a response to that choice. Turns out that Erlang proplists provide a compact way to represent this:[3]

---

[3]http://erlang.org/doc/man/proplists.html

Listing 9.20 ($\Rightarrow$ vim) **Define `main_menu/0` (`n_menus.erl`)**

```erlang
-include_lib("nitrogen_core/include/wf.hrl").

%% ***************************************************
%% Main Menu
%% ***************************************************
main_menu() ->
   [{"home",        "/"},
    {"nindex",      "/nindex"},
    {"nnote" ,      "/nnote"},
    {"Tips & Info", tips}
   ].
```

OLEG: The right side of the tuples—they look like URLs, but `tips` is an atom. Are you doing postbacks?

RUSTY: Can't sneak a thing past you.

OLEG: Not a chance.

RUSTY: I often find it useful to provide context-sensitive help. But be patient and all will be revealed.

MARSHA: Can't wait.

OLEG: The code! The code! The code!

Listing 9.21 ($\Rightarrow$ vim) **Main Menu Executive (`n_menus.erl`)**

```erlang
   {"Tips & Info", tips}
  ].
%% ***************************************************
%% Main Menu Executive
%% ***************************************************
show_main_menu(Selected) ->
   MenuList = main_menu(),
   [show_main_menu_item(MenuItem, Selected) || MenuItem <- MenuList].
```

MARSHA: Ah, I see where this is going. But what's the point of the `Selected` parameter?

RUSTY: Say we need a default selection—

STEVIE: Ah, we can specify it with `Selected`.

RUSTY: Right. The link display function `show_main_menu_item/2` should be straightforward but, as is often the case, we'll need to hack through several complications:

Listing 9.22 (⇒ `vim`) **Main Menu Helper (`n_menus.erl`)**

```
        [show_main_menu_item(MenuItem, Selected) || MenuItem <- MenuList].

%% ***************************************************
%% Main Menu Helpers
%% ***************************************************
show_main_menu_item(MenuItem, Selected) ->
    {Text, Postback} = MenuItem,
    Class = if_selected(Text, Selected),
    #link {class=Class, text=Text, postback=Postback}.
```

RUSTY: Looks good, except for one thing I didn't say. We actually want the postbacks from our main menu to be handled by the `n_menus.erl` module.

OLEG: Won't it already do that? Since we're writing this menu on `n_menus.erl`?

RUSTY: Actually, and perhaps not obviously, no. It won't. This is because the elements here are just being returned back to the index page and, ultimately, rendered there. We need to explicitly tell Nitrogen we want these postbacks to be handled by the n_menus module.

OLEG: Okay... so how do we do that?

RUSTY: The trick is to use the `delegate` attribute. You can actually tell any postback to be handled by any module with this attribute. We can be explicit about it by putting delegate=n_menus, but if we're just having our "self" module handle it (that is, the module in which the function is being defined), I prefer to use the build-in ?MODULE macro.

Listing 9.23 (⇒ vim) **Specify delegate (n_menus.erl)**

```
show_main_menu_item(MenuItem, Selected) ->
   {Text, Postback} = MenuItem,
   Class = if_selected(Text, Selected),
   #link {class=Class, text=Text, postback=Postback, delegate=?MODULE}.
```

STEVIE: Like that?

RUSTY: Perfect!

STEVIE: And here's how I came up with the `if_selected/2` solution.

MARSHA: I'm on pins and needles:

Listing 9.24 (⇒ vim) **More Main Menu Helpers (n_menus.erl)**

```
      #link class=Class, text=Text, postback=Postback, delegate=?MODULE.

if_selected(Text, Selected) ->
   case Text == Selected of
      true -> "mmselected";
      false -> "mm"
   end.
```

MARSHA: I take it that mmselected and mm are class names.

RUSTY: Indeed. We'll add CSS rules in a few moments. While we're at it, let's define event functions to respond to our main menu postbacks:

Listing 9.25 (⇒ vim) **Define event/1 Functions (n_menus.erl)**

```
        false -> "mm"
    end.

%% ********************************************
%% Main menu events
%% ********************************************
event(tips) ->
    ok;
event(logout) ->
    wf:logout(),
    wf:redirect("/");
event(URL) ->
    wf:redirect(URL).
```

MARSHA: Not doing anything with tips yet?

RUSTY: We'll get to that a bit later. That will introduce some new—

OLEG: Wait! We don't HAVE a logout link in our main menu. We don't even have a way to log in.

RUSTY: We agreed that we're building for multiple users, right? Sometimes it pays to think ahead.

STEVIE: So why would we want a dynamic main menu? I mean, wouldn't we want the same menu across all pages of our application?

MARSHA: Maybe we should have hard-wired the main menu into the template. Would have saved code. Right?

RUSTY: Good questions. But imagine that we're offering different features and options to different user categories.

STEVIE: Got it.

OLEG: NOW can we compile and run?

RUSTY: Patience. A confession. I'm harboring ulterior motives.

MARSHA: Like what?

RUSTY: If we're clever, all the code we're building here will serve as building-block code for `nnote.erl` and similar CRUD programs.

STEVIE: You mean like—what did you call it? Scaffolding code?

RUSTY: If it works, it'll save us beaucoup time.

MARSHA: THIS I've got to see!

RUSTY: Patience. First we need to bop into our CSS stylesheet at `site/static/css/style.css` to deck out our menu in all its glory:

Listing 9.26 (⇒ \$) Style Menu Links (`style.css`)

```
.../src/n_libs$ cd ../../static/css
.../static/css$ vim style.css

a:hover, a:active ...

a.mm:link {
   font-size: 140%;
   text-decoration: none;
   color: #666666;
}
a.mm:visited {
   color: #666666;
}
a.mm:hover {
   text-decoration: none;
   color: black;
}
```

STEVIE: Don't forget `mmselected`:

Listing 9.27 (⇒ vim) **Style Selected Link** (`style.css`)

```
      color: black;
}

a.mmselected {
    font-size: 140%;
    text-decoration: underline;
    color: black;
}
```

RUSTY: Finally, this last bit will provide padding around each link and a spacer between them.

Listing 9.28 (⇒ vim) **Add spacing and a separator**(`style.css`)

```
      color: black;
}

a.mmselected, a.mm {
    display:  inline-block;
    padding-left:  15px;
    padding-right:  15px;
    border-right:  1px solid black;
}

a.mmselected:last-child, a.mm:last-child {
    border-right:  none;
}
```

RUSTY: And that's pretty much it. Save it.

9.10. Dare We Say Dynamic?

RUSTY: Let's step back for a second. We have a static grid, but we want to display dynamic content.

OLEG: So what's the big deal?

RUSTY: Two things: How do we know what content goes into which panel when? And how can we change content in a given panel?

STEVIE: Well, there has to be some initial state, like the default content we assign when we program the page.

MARSHA: Ah, but we might want to display different content based on URL variables.

OLEG: Or, maybe a click event triggers a change in content.

STEVIE: Streaming—

RUSTY: Indeed. But we won't go there today. Let's focus on URL variables. If you think about CRUD programs, we're dealing with a set of data objects stored in the database. When we link to a page it wouldn't be unusual to pass along an ID with the URL to uniquely identify a specific object. Or we might pass along a field name to return a group of records. We also frequently pass along tasks—add, edit, delete.

STEVIE: Can you give an example?

RUSTY: Sure. No doubt our notes program will process notes of different types. We may want to select a specific note by id. Or we may want to select a set of notes by type, e.g., retrieve all research notes. Or we may want to edit or delete a specific note record.

This pattern pops up over and over again in CRUD programs. We saw it in nindex. So it's worth considering a generic solution. A good start might be to modify our panel definitions in `index.erl`. We'll start by injecting our newly created main menu:

Listing 9.29 (⇒ $) **Panel Definitions** (`index.erl`)

```
.../site/static/css$ cd ../../src
.../src$ vim index.erl

main_menu() ->
    #h2 {text="Main Menu"}.
    #panel{id=main_menu, body=
        n_menus:show_main_menu(?MMSELECTED)
    }.
```

STEVIE: Oh, okay, our main menu is calling out to the n_menus module we made.

RUSTY: Yep, and the rest will just be stubs for now.

OLEG: We need to add the ?MMSELECTED macro. What is that supposed to be?

RUSTY: It will represent the currently selected menu item for the page that we're on. So let's define it for `index.erl` to be "home".

Listing 9.30 (⇒ `vim`) **Add macros** (`index.erl`)

```
-define(TEMPLATE,"./site/templates/n_apps.html").
-define(MMSELECTED, "home").
-define(TITLE, "Welcome!").
```

RUSTY: And now we can stub in the remaining functions:

9. nitroNotes

Listing 9.31 (⇒ vim) **More Panel Definitions** (`index.erl`)

```
-define(TITLE, "Welcome!").

sidebar() ->
   #panel{text="Sidebar"}.
   #panel{id=sidebar}.

content() ->
   #panel{text="Content"}.
   #panel{id=content}.
```

RUSTY: Here we'll get a little taste of the secret sauce:

Listing 9.32 (⇒ vim) **Define URL Variable Macro** (`index.erl`)

```
-define(TOP, "Build it with Nitrogen").
-define(UVARS, [id, note_type, task]).

%% **************************************************
%% Page state functions
%% **************************************************
get_page_vars() ->
   wf:q_map(?UVARS).
...
```

MARSHA: Oh oh. The plot thickens.

RUSTY: Now we need to tweak our sidebar/0 and content/0 functions:

Listing 9.33 (⇒ vim) **Tweak sidebar and content** (`index.erl`)

```
sidebar() ->
   Vars = get_page_vars(),
   #panel {id=sidebar, body=sidebar(Vars)}.
```

```
content() ->
  Vars = get_page_vars(),
  #panel {id=content, body=content(Vars)}.
```

OLEG: Oh, wow! We're going to update the content panel based on those URL variables as well!

RUSTY: Clever boy. Now let's not forget to define content/1:

Listing 9.34 (⇒ vim) **Define** content/1 (index.erl)

```
       #panel id=content, body=content(Vars).

content(#{}) ->
    greeting().
```

OLEG: An empty map?

RUSTY: An empty map in the function clause basically matches "any map."

STEVIE: I think I see. He's setting up content/1 for pattern matching on the URL variables from the map. I'll bet that greeting/0 is just a chunk of replaceable content.

RUSTY: Sharp cookie!

MARSHA: So you're saying we can display different content when the note type is specified as a field in the Variable map, if we add a clause to content/1— like say, content(#{note_type:=some_note_type})?

RUSTY: We're getting ahead of ourselves, but you're dead on. Here's greeting/0:

Listing 9.35 (⇒ `vim`) Define `greeting/0` (`index.erl`)

```
    greeting().

greeting() ->
   [#h2{text=["Welcome to ", n_utils:get_nickname(), "'s ",
             "Nitrogen Application!"]},
    #p{body="Our motto: <em>\"Build it Fast with Nitrogen\"</em>"}
   ].
```

OLEG: That'll break for sure. Need to make `n_utils:get_nickname()`.

RUSTY: Sure. We'd most likely only show a nickname on an access control page. And we'd probably retrieve it through a database query. For now we can stub in a function that returns a nickname in a new utilities module called, say, `n_utils.erl`. It's just a few lines. We can leave `index.erl` open while we fire up another Unix shell in `n_libs` to define it:

Listing 9.36 (⇒ `$`) Create `n_utils.erl`

```
.../src$ cd n_libs
.../src/n_libs$ vim n_utils.erl

-module(n_utils).
-compile(export_all).

get_nickname() -> "Marsha".
```

STEVIE: The lady goes down in history.

MARSHA: I'm flattered. But I'm interested to see how we define `sidebar(Vars)`.

RUSTY: Okay. Save `n_utils.erl` and bring up `index.erl`. Now, say we want a sidebar menu to display links to our favorite websites. This should do the trick:

Listing 9.37 (⇒ $) **Add sidebar menu** (`index.erl`)

```
.../src/n_libs$ cd ..
.../src$ vim index.erl
greeting() ->
    ...

%% ************************************************
%% Sidebar menus
%% ************************************************
side_menu("WEB SITE") ->
    [{"nitrogen", {goto,
            "http://nitrogenproject.com/"}},
     {"erlang", {goto,
            "http://erlang.org/doc/apps/stdlib/"}},
     {"hacker news", {goto,
            "https://news.ycombinator.com/"}}
    ].
```

MARSHA: This structure looks similar to how we defined the main menu. So these will just be more redirects?

RUSTY: Correct!

STEVIE: So we'll need another event function clause to handle these new {goto, URL} postbacks.

RUSTY: On it:

Listing 9.38 (⇒ vim) **Define event function** (`index.erl`)

```
        "hacker news", goto, "https://news.ycombinator.com/"
    ].

%% ************************************************
%% Sidebar events
%% ************************************************
event({goto, Link}) ->
    wf:redirect(Link).
```

---

9. nitroNotes

RUSTY: We also need to write the `sidebar/1` function:

Listing 9.39 (⟹ vim) Define `sidebar/1` (`index.erl`)

```
event(goto, Link) ->
    wf:redirect(Link).

%% *************************************************
%% Sidebar executives
%% *************************************************
sidebar(#{}) ->
  [ #h3 {text="SELECT"},
    show_side_menu("WEB SITE", unselected)
  ].
```

OLEG: We haven't defined show_menu/2.

RUSTY: Right you are:

Listing 9.40 (⟹ vim) Define `show_menu/2` (`index.erl`)

```
      show_menu("WEB SITE", unselected)
  ].

%% *************************************************
%% Sidebar functions
%% *************************************************
show_side_menu(Menu, Selected) ->
  [ #h4 {class=select, text=Menu},
      [n_menus:show_menu_item(MenuItem, Selected) ||
          MenuItem <- side_menu(Menu)]
  ].
```

MARSHA: Can't we reuse the main menu code?

RUSTY: I think not. There are differences. Let's bop over to `n_menus.erl`:

Listing 9.41   (⇒ $) Open n_menus.erl

```
.../site/src$ cd n_libs
.../src/n_libs$ vim n_menus.erl
...
```

RUSTY: ...and try a road less traveled:

Listing 9.42   (⇒ vim) Revise show_menu_item/2 (n_menus.erl)

```
event(URL) ->
    wf:redirect(URL).
...
%% *************************************************
%% Sidebar menus
%% *************************************************
show_menu_item(MenuItem, Selected) ->
   {Text, Postback} = MenuItem,
   [#radio{name=side_menu_item,
        text=Text,
        checked = (Text==Selected),
        value=Text,
        postback=Postback
      },
    #br{}].
```

OLEG: Radio buttons!!!!

RUSTY: Sure. Why not? I think they look cool.

OLEG: If you say so. But now I definitely want to compile and test.

RUSTY: I need to mention one thing about the radio buttons. You want to make sure they all have the same name attribute.

OLEG: Why?

RUSTY: If they don't have the same name (or they're not wrapped in a #ra-dio_group), then selecting one will NOT deselect the other selected item.

OLEG: Cool. Okay, good to know. Can we compile and test now?

RUSTY: Almost there, so save it. Now a function to display context-sensitive help. We'll plop it in under `greetings/0` in `index.erl`:

Listing 9.43 (⇒ $) Define `index:tips/0` (`index.erl`)

```
.../src_libs$ cd ..
.../src$ vim index.erl

    #p{body = "Our motto:  <em>Build it Fast with Nitrogen</em>"}
].

%% **************************************************
%% Tips
%% **************************************************
tips() ->
    [ #h2{text="Tips & Info"},
      #p{body="The applications in this framework
            were developed by Jesse Gumm and
            Lloyd R. Prentice for their book
            <em>Build it with Nitrogen</em>. These
            applications are available for use and
            modification under the MIT License."}
    ].
```

OLEG: I'm going to jump up and scream if we don't compile and test!

RUSTY: Be my guest.

STEVIE: Hey, *that* looks cool!

MARSHA: And the Tips & Info link doesn't do anything.

STEVIE: That's because we never told it to do anything. Its event clause in n_menus.erl just returns ok.

RUSTY: Good memory. Time to open the floodgates with a super-neat, "you won't believe it, doctor's hate it" trick. We need to make a slight tweak to content/0:

Listing 9.44 (⇒ vim) #flash (index.erl)

```
content() ->
  Vars = get_page_vars(),
  [
   #flash{},
   #panel {id=content, body=content(Vars)}-
  ].
```

RUSTY: Let's bounce back into n_menus.erl, and we'll make this change. This should be interesting:

Listing 9.45 ($\Rightarrow$ $) **Tips (`n_menus.erl`)**

```
.../src$ cd n_libs
.../n_libs$ vim n_menus.erl

event(tips) ->
   ok;
   Mod = wf:page_module(),
   Tips = Mod:tips(),
   wf:flash(Tips);
event(logout) ->
```

RUSTY: Let's save, reload the page, and click "Tips & Info" and see what it does:

RUSTY: Any conjectures on what's going on?

MARSHA: We must be calling the `index:tips()` function.

That `wf:page_module()` function, how does that work?

RUSTY: This gets us into Nitrogen's core. The short answer is that each request to the server maps to a particular module by replacing slashes with underscores. For instance, both /add_edit and /add/edit map to the add_edit module.[4] Nitrogen records a bunch of information while handling the request, including the page module related to the request in what's called the *context*.

The page module is one such thing that's stored in the context. So are the client IP address, request URI, HTTP headers, and so on.

STEVIE: I didn't realize you could use a variable as the module name in a function call.

RUSTY: It's not obvious at first. You can also use a variable for the function name. For example Mod:SomeFun() is perfectly acceptable as long as the variables Mod and SomeFun are bound to atoms.

OLEG: Did we have to use wf:flash()? We could have just done wf:update(content, Tips), couldn't we have?

RUSTY: We could have. And sometimes that's what you want to do. But what if the user is entering data into a form and they click on Tips?

OLEG: Oh, the form would get overridden.

RUSTY: And you'd have an angry customer. But the flash popping up outside of the content panel will merely push the content down, keeping the form intact.

MARSHA: Got it. I would be miffed if I lost information I just entered.

STEVIE: I can see how this wf:page_module() function opens up possibilities.

RUSTY: You ain't seen nothin' yet.

9.11. A Little Refactoring

RUSTY: For our next trick, in the name of optimizing workflow, I'm going to take what we learned in "Tips & Tricks" up a notch.

---

[4]Our request to / is a special case that maps to index.erl

OLEG: That's promising.

RUSTY: Suppose you want to use our `index` module as a template for future tools. How would you do it?

MARSHA: Copy the file and change the things we need to change?

RUSTY: But what about things that would be completely identical, like the `get_page_vars/0` function or the `sidebar/0` and `content/0` functions, both of which just call the related `sidebar/1` and `content/1` functions with the "page vars"? What should we do with those?

OLEG: Keep them as is? Seems simple enough.

RUSTY: If it's copied only once, sure. But as soon as we copy it a second time, we're violating the sacred "Rule of Three"[5] which states: "Three strikes and you refactor."

STEVIE: Ah. If we copy this module multiple times, changing just a few things but creating multiple copies of identical functions, we're headed towards a maintainability nightmare.

RUSTY: Precisely!

Those same 15 lines in two or even three modules—not really a big deal. But imagine 20, 50, or 100 or more page modules, each with identical copy-and-paste functions. Now say you want to update one of those functions.

OLEG: I'd shoot myself!

RUSTY: Yeah. So let's make a new module called `n_common.erl`:

---

[5]`https://en.wikipedia.org/wiki/Rule_of_three_(computer_programming)`

Listing 9.46 ($\Rightarrow$ $) Add common module (n_common.erl)

```
.../n_libs$ vim n_common.erl

-module(n_common).
-include_lib("nitrogen_core/include/wf.hrl").
-compile(export_all).
```

RUSTY: Now let's cut get_page_vars/0 from index.erl:

Listing 9.47 ($\Rightarrow$ $) cut get_page_vars/0 (index.erl)

```
.../n_libs$ cd ..
.../src$ vim index.erl

%% *****************************************************
%% Page state functions
%% *****************************************************
get_page_vars() ->
    wf:q_map(?UVARS).
```

RUSTY: ...and paste it into our new n_common module:

Listing 9.48 ($\Rightarrow$ $) paste get_page_vars/0 (n_common.erl)

```
.../src$ vim n_libs/n_common.erl

get_page_vars() ->
    wf:q_map(?UVARS).
```

OLEG: Well, that's not going to compile. `UVARS` is not defined in this module.

RUSTY: Right you are, Oleg. We will rework `UVARS` in our `index` module to be a function instead of a macro so that we'll have access to it from other modules.

Listing 9.49 (⟹ $) `url_vars/0` (`index.erl`)

```
.../src$ vim index.erl

-define(UVARS, [id, note_type, task]).
url_vars() -> [id, note_type, task].
```

RUSTY: ...then convert the macro invocation in n_common to get our module's url_vars():

Listing 9.50 (⟹ $) `n_common.erl`

```
.../src$ vim n_libs/n_common.erl

get_page_vars() ->
        Mod = wf:page_module(),
        Vars = Mod:url_vars(),
        wf:q_map(?UVARS Vars).
```

MARSHA: Hey, there's that thing we were just talking about. Getting the page module.

RUSTY: Let's do the same with `sidebar/0`:

Listing 9.51 (⇒ $) **cut** sidebar/0 (`index.erl`)

```
.../src$ vim index.erl

sidebar() ->
    Vars = get_page_vars(),
    #panel {id=sidebar, body=sidebar(Vars)}.
```

Listing 9.52 (⇒ $) **paste** sidebar/0 (`n_common.erl`)

```
.../src$ vim n_libs/n_common.erl

sidebar() ->
    Vars = get_page_vars(),
    #panel {id=sidebar, body=sidebar(Vars)}.
```

RUSTY: ...and content/0:

Listing 9.53 (⇒ $) **Cut** content/0 index.erl

```
.../src$ vim index.erl

content() ->
    Vars = get_page_vars(),
    {
     #flash{},
     #panel{id=content, body=content(Vars)}
    }.
```

Listing 9.54 (⇒ $) **Paste** content/0 n_common.erl

```
.../src$ vim n_libs/n_common.erl

...

      #panel{id=sidebar, body=?PAGE:sidebar(Vars)}.

content() ->
   Vars = get_page_vars(),
   [
    #flash{},
    #panel {id=content, body=content(Vars)}
   ].
```

STEVIE: Wait, sidebar/1 and content/1 (the ones that take the Vars argument) aren't defined in this module. So we have to call out to our page module to get them, right?

RUSTY: Exactly! Behold, the glory!

Listing 9.55 (⇒ vim) **Define and use ?PAGE macro** n_common.erl

```
-compile(export_all).
-define(PAGE, (wf:page_module())).

get_page_vars() ->
   Mod = wf:page_module(),
   Vars = Mod:url_vars(),
   Vars = ?PAGE:url_vars(),
   wf:q_map(Vars).

sidebar() ->
   Vars = get_page_vars(),
   #panel{id=sidebar, body=?PAGE:sidebar(Vars)}.

content() ->
   Vars = get_page_vars(),
   [
    #flash{},
```

```
    #panel{id=content, body=?PAGE:content(Vars)}
    ].
```

STEVIE: Whoa! You used that PAGE macro as the module side of a function call. Doesn't that evaluate to (wf:page_module):get_page_vars()? That's valid?

RUSTY: 'tis. It will do the same thing as binding Mod = wf:page_module() then calling Mod:get_page_vars(). It's a more succinct syntax but still readable.

One last thing. We moved sidebar() and content() to n_common. What do you think about moving main_menu() as well?

MARSHA: Might as well. All it's doing is calling n_menus:main_menu/1.

RUSTY: But there's nuance here. We may want to replace these components or even delete them.

So let's take it in two steps: First cut the wrapper panel from index:

Listing 9.56 (⇒ $) **Cut wrapper #panel (index.erl)**

```
.../src$ vim index.erl

main_menu() ->
    #panel{id=main_menu, body=
      n_menus:show_main_menu(?MMSELECTED)
    }.
```

RUSTY: Don't forget the dot at the end of that function! Then make a new function in n_common:main_menu/0:

```
.../src$ vim n_libs/n_common.erl
...
main_menu() ->
   #panel{id=main_menu, body=?PAGE:main_menu()}.
```

MARSHA: I see. This still gives our index page control over the menu, if we need it. Maybe we don't want a main menu on one page, or maybe we want a completely different main menu. We can just call a different function in index:main_menu().

RUSTY: Nailed it!

RUSTY: We have one more critical change to make here. We moved the sidebar/0 and content/0 functions out of our index module and reworked main_menu/0 in index, but our template is still calling page:sidebar(), page:content(), and page:main_menu(), .

MARSHA: Oh yeah, I completely forgot.

OLEG: I'm on this one. Just got to open n_apps.html:

```
.../src$ cd ../templates
.../site/templates$ vim n_apps.html

  <div id="main_menu">
    [[[page:main_menu()]]]
    [[[n_common:main_menu()]]]
  </div>
  <div id="sidebar">
```

```
  [[[page:sidebar()]]]
  [[[n_common:sidebar()]]]
</div>
<div id="content">
  [[[page:sidebar()]]]
  [[[n_common:content()]]]
</div>
```

RUSTY: Great job! Speaking of templates, there's one more nit I'd like to pick. In index.erl we defined a path to a page template as a macro called ?TEMPLATE. We then instantiated index:main/0 with our macro. It's likely that our application will have only a few templates at most. Suppose we take our abstraction one step further?

STEVIE: Like defining a tmplate function in n_common?

MARSHA: Oooh, I like that. Then we don't have to define our #template on every page. Plus, if we ever decide to rename or reorganize our template file, we can do so in st_common rather than editing the TEMPLATE macro on every page.

RUSTY: Now you're getting it! Let's see what you can whip up.

MARSHA: Okay, I'll remove ?TEMPLATE macro from index and replace the #template element with a call to a new function in n_common:

Listing 9.59 (⇒ $) Use common module for template (index.erl)

```
.../site/templates$ cd ../src
.../src$ vim index.erl

-define(TEMPLATE,"./site/templates/n_apps.html").
-define(MMSELECTED, "home").
...
main() ->
    #template{file=?TEMPLATE}.
```

```
n_common:template().
```

OLEG: That's really not that much shorter.

RUSTY: True, but it's fewer concepts—fewer "tokens." The old one is a record, with an attribute assigned to a macro while the new one is a simple function call—easily scannable and easily grokable. And we've removed the template macro which is just another line that would otherwise be copied and pasted on each page.

MARSHA: And now I'll put that removed code into n_common.

Listing 9.60 (⟹ $) **Drop ?TEMPLATE into common module (n_common.erl)**

```
.../site/src$ vim n_libs/n_common.erl

-define(PAGE, (wf:page_module())).
-define(TEMPLATE, "./site/templates/n_apps.html").

template() ->
   #template{file=?TEMPLATE}.
```

RUSTY: Now we're cookin'! Give it all a save and refresh the page. It should look and work exactly the same.

OLEG: Looks completely unchanged. That was a lot of work for a whole lotta nothin'.

RUSTY: You're a funny guy, Oleg. What comes next is where our work will pay off.

9.12. Challenge!

RUSTY: Now we're getting down to the nitty gritty. Let me throw out a challenge.

OLEG: Love a challenge.

RUSTY: Bet a donut that I can set up the landing page for nnote.erl in less than 60 seconds.

OLEG: You're on, baby!

RUSTY: First I'll make a subdirectory in our project tree and copy index.erl:

Listing 9.61 (⇒ $) **Create subdirectory and copy** `index.erl`

```
site/src$ mkdir nnote
site/src$ cp index.erl nnote/nnote.erl
site/src$ cd nnote
site/src/nnote$ vim nnote.erl
...
-module(index nnote).
```

RUSTY: Next I'll update the macros:

Listing 9.62 (⇒ vim) **Update macros (**nnote.erl**)**

```
-module(nnote).
...
-define(MMSELECTED, "home" "nnote").
-define(TITLE, "Welcome!" "Welcome to nnote!").
-define(TOP, "Build it with Nitrogen" "nnote").
url_vars() -> [id, note_type, task].
```

RUSTY: Stub in content. Let's change greeting/0 to content_headline/0, and replace the entire body of the old greeting/0:

Listing   9.63   (⇒ vim)   greeting/0   to   content_headline/0   (nnote.erl)

```
content(#{}) ->
    greeting().
    content_headline().
...
greeting() ->
...
    }.
content_headline() ->
    [#h2 {class=content, text="My Notes"}].
```

RUSTY: ...click the nnote link on the main menu and—voila! What's the time, Stevie?

STEVIE: Forty-four seconds.

OLEG: Cheater! You didn't update the sidebar.

RUSTY: Be easy enough to change the sidebar menu if we knew what we wanted.

STEVIE: Awesome! But we go down in flames if we click on nindex.

OLEG: Have to change the main menu event functions so the nindex link vectors off to our nindex code.

RUSTY: Not if you morph nindex into our new framework. But I'll leave that as a homework assignment.

STEVIE: So, can I get a jump on my homework—stub in a landing page for our morphed nindex code?

RUSTY: Give it a go.

Listing 9.64 (⇒ $) **Create** `nindex.erl`

```
site/src/nnote$ cd ..
site/src$ mkdir nindex
site/src$ cp index.erl nindex/nindex.erl
site/src$ cd nindex
site/src/nindex$ vim nindex.erl
...
-module(index nindex).
...
-define(MMSELECTED, "nindex" "nindex").
-define(TITLE, "Welcome!" "Welcome to nindex!").
-define(TOP, "Build it with Nitrogen" "nindex").
url_vars() -> [id, note_type, task].
```

OLEG: Fifty-four seconds.

MARSHA: Shouldn't think it would take him that much longer to copy over the sidebar menu and content blocks.

STEVIE: Let you know tomorrow.

OLEG: *That*'s what I'm talking about. Productivity!

9.13. Oh Behave!

RUSTY: I'm gonna fill you in on a little secret here—the work we've done here, making our pages require a handful of specific functions so that our n_common module can call them—we've basically started using OTP behaviors without even knowing it.

MARSHA: That's like those -behavior lines when we used gen_server and supervisors?

RUSTY: Exactly like that. If you remember, we got compilation warnings when we tried compiling our gen_servers without defining a terminate/2 function. This is the same thing. Here, if our module is going to use the n_common module, which functions do we expect it to export?

STEVIE: Let's see. main/0, url_vars/0, main_menu/0, sidebar/1, content/1.... I think that's it.

RUSTY: We could probably also argue that we need a tips/0 function.

STEVIE: Maybe, but our page's main_menu/0 calls n_menus:main_menu(). If we use a different main menu on our page, one that doesn't try calling tips(), it would be misleading and unnecessary, I think.

RUSTY: You make a great argument, and I agree. If we were to call our n_menus:main_menu() function in every use of this type of module, I would say we should include tips/0, but given that we haven't, I agree with you completely.

OLEG: Okay then. How do we make a behavior?

RUSTY: It's actually quite easy. What should we call our behavior?

OLEG: We called our template n_apps.html, so how about we call our behavior n_apps?

RUSTY: Perfect! Let's create a new module and call it n_apps.erl and include our normal Nitrogen module definitions:

Listing 9.65 (⇒ $) **Create behavior module (n_apps.erl)**

```
...site/src$ vim n_apps.erl

-module(n_apps).
-include_lib("nitrogen_core/include/wf.hrl").
-compile(export_all).
```

RUSTY: Now that that's out of the way, time to define the meat of our new behavior by defining which callbacks we want to expect our n_apps modules to export:

Listing 9.66 (⇒ vim) **Add main() to (n_apps.erl)**

```
-callback main() -> body().
```

OLEG: What is that body() function? We're definitely not expecting our main() function to immediately call body(). It should return a #template element.

RUSTY: The body() above isn't actually a function here—it's a *type* in Erlang. While body() isn't a standard type in Erlang, it is in Nitrogen. We haven't really talked about typespecs at all so far, and I'll leave it up to you to look into how typespecs work[6], but we have to tell our callbacks what kind of arguments our functions expect and the expected type return.

MARSHA: So what does body() actually mean then?

RUSTY: The body() type is defined mostly like this:

---

[6]http://erlang.org/doc/reference_manual/typespec.html

Example 9.1 Sample body() type definition

```
-type body_element() -> tuple() | string() | binary() | iolist().
-type body() -> body_element() | [body_element()].
```

STEVIE: That looks pretty complicated.

RUSTY: I can respect that. Put more straightforwardly, the body() type means a string, binary, or tuple—or a list of any combination of those three items.

MARSHA: Why a tuple?

STEVIE: Don't you remember? Nitrogen records are really tuples.

MARSHA: Oh right. Forgot.

RUSTY: To be precise...*Erlang* records are tuples and Nitrogen records are Erlang records. In essence you're right. They are just tuples.

We want our main() function to return one of the types in the type specification. Since it will return a #template element, that works.

Let's add our url_vars callback. What do you think this should look like? What does our url_vars function return?

OLEG: A list.

RUSTY: A list of what?

STEVIE: Atoms.

RUSTY: Precisely. So here's the callback definiton of url_vars():

Listing 9.67 (⇒ `vim`) **Add `url_vars()` (`n_apps.erl`)**

```
-callback url_vars() -> [atom()].
```

RUSTY: That term, `[atom()]`, means a "list of atoms." Let's add the remaining functions:

Listing 9.68 (⇒ `vim`) **Add more callback (`n_apps.erl`)**

```
-callback main_menu() -> body().

-callback sidebar(map()) -> body().

-callback content(map()) -> body().
```

RUSTY: That's it for our behavior. Let's save this, then add the behavior to our page modules. Open up `index.erl` again:

Listing 9.69 (⇒ `$`) **Use the new behavior in `index.erl`**

```
site/src$ vim index.erl

-module(index).
-include_lib("nitrogen_core/include/wf.hrl").
-behavior(n_apps).
-compile(export_all).
```

RUSTY: That's it. If we save our module, it should recompile. And if we were to remove the `sidebar/1` function from our module, the compiler would yell at us. Let's do the same to the `nindex.erl` and `nnote.erl` files we just made:

Listing 9.70 (⇒ $) Use the new behavior in `nindex.erl`

```
site/src$ vim nindex/nindex.erl

-module(nindex).
-include_lib("nitrogen_core/include/wf.hrl").
-behavior(n_apps).
-compile(export_all).
```

Listing 9.71 (⇒ $) Use the new behavior in `nnote.erl`

```
site/src$ vim nnote/nnote.erl

-module(nnote).
-include_lib("nitrogen_core/include/wf.hrl").
-behavior(n_apps).
-compile(export_all).
```

RUSTY: All done. Going forward, this behavior construct will help us with more modules that follow this pattern. We'll keep using it going forward.

What do types do?

Well, nothing. But, the long answer is that they support a powerful tool called Dialyzer.[a] Dialyzer analyzes your code and reports when you're violating type contracts. It points out potential bugs that could add up to customer frustration and considerable debugging time in future.

By default, Nitrogen apps include a handy `dialyzer` Makefile rule. To see if your app, Nitrogen elements, and function calls follow the type rules that you and others have specified, run this from the command line in the root of your project:

```
make dialyzer
```

Make sure you have plenty of RAM—8 GB minimum recommended. You'll see a bunch of stuff scroll by; it will take a while. Dialyzer messages are notoriously cryptic, but well worth digging in and learning how to interpret.

---

[a]http://erlang.org/doc/man/dialyzer.html

9.14. Notes Notes and More Notes

MARSHA: From what I see, it should be a snap to update the sidebar in nnote. Just have to decide what we want.

RUSTY: Point well taken! Quick, let's list all the different kinds of notes we can think of.

STEVIE: Research notes—

MARSHA: Conference notes—random ideas.

OLEG: Interview notes—lectures.

RUSTY: Terrific!

STEVIE: Web.

MARSHA: Lab notes?

RUSTY: That's enough to get us started. So, our list looks like this:

```
NOTE TYPE
conference note
idea
interview note
lab note
lecture note
research note
web note
```

9.14.1. Update the sidebar

MARSHA: Oh, goodie! Can I update the sidebar menu in nnote.erl?

RUSTY: You have the conn:

Listing 9.72 (⇒ $) **Update sidebar menu (nnote.erl)**

```
site/src$ vim nnote/nnote.erl

side_menu("WEB SITE" "NOTE TYPE") ->
    [{"nitrogen" "conference", {goto,
        ...   },
```

MARSHA: Ah, me thinks we do need another event clause. The event ({goto, wherever}) links us to a site on the web. We want to pass the note type back to nnote.erl.

RUSTY: Most astute. Let's try something like this:

300

Listing 9.73 (⇒ vim) **Revise** `side_menu/1` **(**`nnote.erl`**)**

```
side_menu("NOTE TYPE") ->
   [{"conference",{select,"conference"}},
    {"idea",      {select,"idea"}},
    {"interview", {select,"interview"}},
    {"lab",       {select,"lab"}},
    {"lecture",   {select,"lecture"}},
    {"research",  {select,"research"}},
    {"web",       {select,"web"}}
   ].
```

RUSTY: Let's see if this will do for an event function:

Listing 9.74 (⇒ vim) **Define sidebar event (**`nnote.erl`**)**

```
%% **************************************************
%% Sidebar events
%% **************************************************
event({goto, Link}) ->
   wf:redirect(Link).
event({select, NoteType}) ->
   Redirect = [wf:path(), "?",
       wf:to_qs([ {note_type, NoteType} ]) ],
   wf:redirect(Redirect).
```

STEVIE: Waaay to go!

RUSTY: Now, sleight of hand, we wave our magic wand over `sidebar/1`:

Listing 9.75 (⇒ vim) **Revise** `sidebar/1` **(**`nnote.erl`**)**

```
sidebar(#{note_type:=NoteType}) ->
   [ #h4 {text="SELECT"},
     show_side_menu("WEB SITE" "NOTE TYPE",unselected NoteType)
   ].
```

9.14.2. Don't forget content

RUSTY: …and pop content out of a hat:

Listing 9.76 (⇒ vim) **Revise** `content/1` (`nnote.erl`)

```erlang
content(#{}) ->
    [content_headline(),
     #p{text="Select note type."}
    ];
```

STEVIE: Ah, a user prompt…

RUSTY: I think it's appropriate since this is the first time the user has landed on the page.

STEVIE: Sold.

RUSTY: Now, what else would we like to display on this page?

MARSHA: Well, we need to do three things: add, edit, and search for notes.

OLEG: I'm thinking that add and edit forms along with save functions are a hefty chunk of code. Maybe we should factor them off onto another page.

RUSTY: I agree. What are we searching for?

STEVIE: Notes that contain certain key words, definitely.

MARSHA: How about searching for notes by date?

RUSTY: So, in addition to `welcome/0`, we want to display three user controls in the content box on this page—a link to an add-a-note form, a form for entering key words, and a form for selecting search dates…

```
welcome/0
search_by_tag/n
search_by_date/n
search_results/n
```

MARSHA: We need a panel to display search results, right?

STEVIE: But we don't want search results to display until we've entered our search terms.

RUSTY: Right you are. So we really have four different page states here.

OLEG: How so?

RUSTY: Let's jot them down. It'll help us define the functions we need:

```
State 1: Note type unselected - no results
State 2: Note type selected - no results
State 3: Search-by-tag selected - show results
State 4: Search-by-date selected - show results
```

OLEG: Okayyyy—This is getting *comp...* licated.

RUSTY: Not really. Page state can be selected by URL variables or postbacks. So, behold:

Listing 9.77 (⇒ vim) **Display selected note type (nnote.erl)**

```
menu("NOTE TYPE") ->
...
%% ***************************************************
%% Content executives
%% ***************************************************
content(#{note_type:=undefined, task:=undefined}) ->
  [content_headline(),
   #p{text="Select note type."}]
  ];
content(#{note_type:=NoteType, task:=Task}) ->
  io:format("~p selected with task:  ~p", [NoteType, Task]).
```

MARSHA: Ah, so... we can use pattern matching to determine what we want to show.

303

RUSTY: You've got it. So let's suppose we have a content display function that looks like this:

Listing 9.78 (⇒ vim) **Content display function (nnote.erl)**

```
%% **************************************************
%% Content
%% **************************************************
display_forms(NoteType, Records) ->
   [content_headline(),
    add_note_button(NoteType),
    search_by_tag(),
    search_by_date(),
    search_results(Records)
   ].
```

RUSTY: The trick is to modify the content/1 to correctly call display_forms/2.

STEVIE: I still don't get it.

RUSTY: It all comes down to what we pass to search_results/1:

- We're in state 1 or 2; show nothing

- The search turns up empty; inform the user

- Search returns results; display them

STEVIE: Ah, the light dawns.

RUSTY: So this should do the trick:

Listing 9.79 (⇒ vim) **Revise content/1 (nnote.erl)**

```
content(#{note_type:=NoteType, task:=Task}) ->
   io:format("~p selected with task:  ~p", [NoteType, Task])}.
   Records = case Task of
```

```
    undefined -> undefined;
    search_by_tag -> tag_search(NoteType);
    search_by_date -> date_search(NoteType)
  end,
  display_forms(NoteType, Records).
```

MARSHA: Brilliant! We saw something like this in `nindex`. We need to pattern match the `Record` parameter in `display_forms/2`.

RUSTY: Yes, but before we do that, let's just quickly stub in our `tag_search` and `date_search` functions. We'll just return empty lists for now, and when we actually implement our database, we'll pull actual results:

Listing 9.80 (⇒ `vim`) **Stub in search functions (`nnote.erl`)**

```
  display_forms(NoteType, Records).

tag_search(NoteType) ->
  [].
date_search(NoteType) ->
  [].
```

RUSTY: Now, back to pattern matching the `Record` parameter. Care to show us?

Listing 9.81 (⇒ `vim`) **Pattern match record parameters (`nnote.erl`)**

```
date_search(NoteType) ->
  [].

search_results(undefined) ->
```

```
   io:format("Show nothing");
search_results([]) ->
   io:format("No notes found");
search_results(Records) ->
   io:format("Display results").
```

RUSTY: Can you polish it off?

STEVIE: I can! I was reviewing the nindex stuff last night.

RUSTY: Go for it.

STEVIE: I'm assuming we have a draw_link/1 function in n_utils:

Listing 9.82 (⇒ vim) **Revise search_results/1(nnote.erl)**

```
search_results(undefined) ->
   io:format("Show noting");
   [];
search_results([]) ->
   io:format("No notes found");
   [#hr{},
    #h2{text="Search Results"},
    #p{text="No notes found"}
   ];
search_results(Records) ->
   io:format("Display results").
   [#hr{},
    #h2{text="Search Results"},
    [n_utils:draw_link(Record) || Record <- Records]
   ].
```

OLEG: Hate to break it to you, comrades. But we still need to define the work-horse functions in display_forms/2.

RUSTY: Simple enough:

Listing 9.83 (⇒ vim) **Define** `display_forms/2` **helpers** (`nnote.erl`)

```
content_headline() ->
...
add_note_button(NoteType) ->
   ButtonText = ["Enter new ",NoteType," note"],
   #button{text=ButtonText, postback={add_note, NoteType}}.

search_by_tag() ->
   [#label{text="enter search words"},
    #textbox{id=search_words},
    #button{text="Search", postback=search_by_tag},
    #button{text="Info", postback={info, search_by_tag}}
   ].

search_by_date() ->
   io:format("Search by date~n"),
   [].
```

RUSTY: And so, test that puppy, Oleg, and tell us what you see.

OLEG: Totally cool. But what's that `Info` button?

RUSTY: Let me add a tad more code then you tell me:

Listing 9.84 (⇒ vim) Define `search_by_tag` **event** (`nnote.erl`)

```
event(search_by_tag) ->
   NoteType = wf:q(note_type),
   Content = content(#{note_type=>NoteType, task=>search_by_tag}),
   wf:update(content, Content);
%% **************************************************
%%  Info events
%% **************************************************
event({info, Function}) ->
   wf:flash(info(Function));
%% **************************************************
%% Sidebar Events
%% **************************************************
```

Listing 9.85 (⇒ vim) Define info/1 (`nnote.erl`)

```
tips() ->
...
%% **************************************************
%% Info
%% **************************************************

info(search_by_tag) ->
   [ #h2{body=["<i>Search Words</i>"]},
     #p{text=["Search word documentation goes here"]}
   ].
```

STEVIE: I like it! I like it!

MARSHA: Aren't we forgetting search-by-date?

OLEG: How would that work? User has to enter an exact date?

MARSHA: Maybe, like, return all notes between two dates?

OLEG: That would require two date entries. Bogus.

STEVIE: Suppose the user enters a date and the system returns all notes dated a week before and a week after?

MARSHA: Might work.

STEVIE: Can we use the `datepicker` element from nitroBoard?

9.15. Datepicker

RUSTY: We can. But let's create a function so we don't muck up our form—call it `datepicker/2`. Best to put it in a library module:

Listing 9.86 ($\Rightarrow$ `vim`) **Create date library module (`n_dates.erl`)**

```
site/src/n_libs$ vim n_libs/n_dates.erl
...
-module(n_dates).
-include_lib("nitrogen_core/include/wf.hrl").
-compile(export_all).

datepicker(Id, Text) ->
   #datepicker_textbox{
      id=Id,
      text=Text,
      options=[
         {dateFormat, "yy-mm-dd"},
         {showButtonPanel, true}
      ]
   }.
```

MARSHA: Okay—so how do we install it?

RUSTY: We've already stubbed it in. We just need to save `n_dates.erl` and update `search_by_date/0` in `index/0`:

Listing 9.87 (⇒ vim) **Edit** `search_by_date` **(nnote.erl)**

```
site/src$ cd ../nnote
site/src$ vim nnote/nnote.erl
...
search_by_tag() ->
...
search_by_date() ->
   io:format("Search by date~ n").
   [ #label{text="enter date"},
     n_dates:datepicker(search_date, ""),
     #button{text="Search", postback=search_by_date},
     #button{text="Info", postback={info, search_by_date}}
   ].
```

RUSTY: And we've already called it in `display_forms/2`, so no worry there:

Listing 9.88 (⇒ vim) **Review** `search_by_date/0` **(nnote.erl)**

```
display_forms(NoteType, Record) ->
    ...
      search_form(ButtonText, TextValue),
      search_by_date(),
      search_results(Records)
    ]
  }].
```

STEVIE: But we need an event function for search_by_date/0.

RUSTY: Easy enough:

Listing 9.89 (⇒ vim) **Add** `search_by_date` **handler (nnote.erl)**

```
event(search_by_tag) ->
...
event(search_by_date) ->
```

```
NoteType = wf:q(note_type),
Content = content(#{note_type=>NoteType, task=>search_by_date}),
wf:update(content, Content);
```

STEVIE: And we should probably handle the `info` button for date searching as well.

Listing 9.90 (⇒ `vim`) **Add date search info event (`nnote.erl`)**

```
info(search_by_tag) ->
  ...
  ];-    %% just replacing the dot with a semicolon
info(search_by_date) ->
  [ #h2{body="<i>Search Date</i>"},
    #p{text="Search date documentation goes here"}
  ].
```

RUSTY: Alright! Load up the page and click on the search date field.

9. nitroNotes

OLEG: Sweet!

MARSHA: Does clicking the "Info" button work?

OLEG: Mega-sweet!

RUSTY: With that, we've covered a ton of ground and we're out of time. So let's polish off nnotes next session.

OLEG: Wait! How can we search anything? We haven't even decided on a database.

MARSHA: My vote: mnesia! We've explored everything else.

9.15.1. mnesia it is

RUSTY: So, mnesia it is. I suggest you read up.[7]

OLEG: Oh, man—I've got a bodacious history test coming up.

RUSTY: To keep you out of mischief, try your hand at the search_by_date/0 info event in your spare time.

OLEG: Slave driver!

STEVIE: Wait a minute. We defined a URL variable, id, but never used it.

RUSTY: Well, strip it out. But it'll come in handy when we build the add/edit form.

---

[7]http://erlang.org/doc/apps/mnesia/mnesia_chap1.html
http://learnyousomeerlang.com/mnesia
Cesarini, Francesco & Simon Thompson. 2009. *Erlang Programming*. O'Reilly. Sebastapol, CA. pp 295–305
Logan, Martin et. al. 2011. *Erlang and OTP in Action*, Manning. Stamford, CT. pp 213–241
http://www.developer.com/db/article.php/3864331/Mnesia-A-Distributed-DBMS-Rooted-in-Concurrency.htm

10. nitroNotes II

RUSTY: Great progress last session! But thinking back, it occurs to me that we're getting ahead of ourselves.

OLEG: Yeah, like we talk about notes, but don't know what we're talking about. Is a note just a blob of text or does it have structure? We talk about metadata, but what's that? How can we begin to define a record structure, design user input forms, or database functions if we don't know what we're dealing with?

RUSTY: How about it, gang?

STEVIE: Well we know we need to uniquely identify every note. So we need an ID.

OLEG: And a date field.

RUSTY: Got it.

MARSHA: We need a note field, obviously.

STEVIE: And a subject field.

OLEG: "Topic" is better. That's what we used in nindex.

STEVIE: Bust my chops. Topic it is.

MARSHA: A conference note needs an event field.

STEVIE: But an idea doesn't.

RUSTY: We could just leave the event field undefined for idea-type notes.

MARSHA: Research notes need a source field—like, maybe, footnotes.

OLEG: My history teacher is super finicky about footnotes. It's a can of worms. Like, when you quote an author, you're supposed to cite the source in a footnote. And there are a gazillion different footnote styles, each one formatted just so.[1]

RUSTY: Good point. Maybe we need a generic field for source data and a set of display routines to generate different footnote styles. Now that you mention it, I think that's an excellent homework assignment.

MARSHA: I'm thinking that research notes should also have a question field. The answer would go in the note field.

STEVIE: Maybe the question should go into the topic field.

OLEG: No, no— If I'm studying for a history final, here's how I want my notes organized— Topic: history. Question: "Who won the War of 1812?" Note: Americans think they won, but Canadians remained part of the British Empire. Native people were pushed off their lands.

STEVIE: So you're saying Americans didn't win the War of 1812?

OLEG: Straight from Google.

STEVIE: Smart aleck.

RUSTY: I vote for a question field. Why not? Easy enough to do.

STEVIE: Web notes need a URL.

MARSHA: URLs could go into the source field, couldn't they?

STEVIE: So I'm wondering, can we store our different note types in one record structure?

RUSTY: Looks that way— if we're creative. What next?

STEVIE: Seems comprehensive. So where should we define the record?

---

[1] http://www.plagiarism.org/citing-sources/citation-styles/

10.1. Record Definitions

RUSTY: We could define it in a `*.hrl` file in the `include` directory and import the file into our modules when needed. Or it could go at the top of the module where we define the database table and access queries.

OLEG: Oh brother—OTOH alert!

RUSTY: OTOH?

STEVIE: On The One Hand, but on the other—

RUSTY: Gotcha. Well, here's the issue. Suppose we have record access functions scattered throughout our source code—

MARSHA: Oh, so the `*.hrl` file is better. We can import it wherever needed.

RUSTY: But what happens when we need to change the record structure—like move a field to a new location in the record?

STEVIE: No problemo. Just change the `*.hrl` file.

RUSTY: What happens then to our access functions?

MARSHA: I get it. We need to find all the record access functions in our source and change them to reflect the new record structure.

RUSTY: Bingo! Erlang guru Jesper Louis Andersen argues that it's always better to use "loose coupling" between persisted data structures and application code. That's why we implemented a facade in nindex.

OLEG: I don't know. We could use grep to find all the access functions. Shouldn't be hard.

RUSTY: Well, as I recall, Jesper put it this way: "...control the scope of records harshly, for they breed like rabbits in a grassy field."[2]

---

[2]`http://erlang.org/pipermail/erlang-questions/2015-July/085139.html`

MARSHA: My head hurts. Can you just tell us where to put the darn record definitions?

RUSTY: Right. I suggest that we put them in the same module as the table access functions and put that module in a separate directory along with all of our other persistence modules:

Listing 10.1 (⇒ vim) **Define** `nnote_db_mnesia`

```
...  /site/src$ mkdir n_dbs
...  /site/src$ cd n_dbs
...  /n_dbs$ vim nnote_db_mnesia.erl
...
-module(nnote_db_mnesia).
-record(nnote, {
    id = n_utils:create_id(),
    user_id,
    type,
    date,
    event,
    source,
    topic,
    question,
    tags,
    note
}).
```

STEVIE: We need to copy `create_id/0` over from nindex, right?

10.2. `create_id/0`—Another Take

RUSTY: Just for fun, here's another take on `create_id/0`:

Listing 10.2 (⇒ $) create_id/0—**Another Take (n_utils.erl)**

```
site/src/n_dbs$ cd ../n_libs
site/src/n_libs$ vim n_utils.erl
...
get_nickname() -> "Marsha".

create_id() ->
    Rand = rand:uniform(1000000000),
    Seconds = qdate:unixtime(),
    GigaSeconds = Seconds * 1000000000,
    ID = GigaSeconds + Rand,
    integer_to_list(ID, 16).
```

OLEG: How does *that* work?

RUSTY: On the slim chance that two users generate ids at the exact same time to the second, they still have to beat a billion[3]-to-one odds that they'll generate the same Rand value.

OLEG: Wouldn't it be easier to simply use rand:uniform with a big number like we did in nindex?

RUSTY: Point taken. But consider this:

Listing 10.3 (⇒ vim) **Define id_created/1 (n_utils.erl)**

```
create_id() ->
...
id_created(ID) ->
    IntID = list_to_integer(ID, 16),
    Seconds = IntID div 1000000000,
    qdate:to_date(Seconds).
```

STEVIE: So cool! We can pinpoint to the second when a record was created.

---

[3]The American billion: 1,000,000,000

RUSTY: But, let me warn you—the more records you're creating per second, the more likely you are to run into a collision. The billion multiplier is the absolute *minimum* you'd ever want to use, and even that low of a number makes me a little uncomfortable. But if we want to figure out to the second when our ID was generated, this is the system we'd have to use.

STEVIE: So what do you think is a safe multiplier for most applications, if a billion makes you uncomfortable?

RUSTY: Honestly, if you're going to roll your own ID creation mechanism, do exactly what Oleg suggested: `rand:uniform(X)` where X is a big integer (like 10^{40}) or maybe use something a little more standardized like a UUID[4]. Otherwise, you have to constantly tune your ID generation algorithm to scale for growth, whereas UUID is practically guaranteed to generate a unique number every time (at least if you use UUID Version 4). If appropriate, you could also consider natural `ids`.[5]

OLEG: Natural `ids`—*was ist das?*

RUSTY? Any data item that uniquely defines our record naturally rather than something that's randomly generated —like say, `username` or a social security number.

MARSHA: Back to the record definition—what's with `user_id`?

RUSTY: We're designing for multiple users are we not?

10.3. Speaking of *mnesia*

STEVIE: We ready to define database queries yet?

MARSHA: Maybe we should define the add/edit form first.

---

[4]UUID version 4 is basically a random number from 0 to 10^{39}. `https://en.wikipedia.org/wiki/Universally_unique_identifier`

[5]`https://en.wikipedia.org/wiki/Natural_key`

OLEG: Chicken and egg. I vote for database queries. I spent half the night reading up.

STEVIE: I second that. I want to see how mnesia works.

RUSTY: So, Oleg, what can you tell us?

OLEG: Logan says we need to do several things before we can create tables.[6]

- Initialize mnesia

- Start a node

- Create a schema

- Start mnesia

- Create database tables

- Populate tables

- Perform test queries on the data

RUSTY: You're the man—

OLEG: Since we're developing a productivity suite, we need to control multiple mnesia tables. We need to initialize the database, start, and stop it. The mnesia docs you inflicted on us spell out different ways to do this, so I sort of mixed and matched and came up with my own.

MARSHA: Prepare to be amazed.

OLEG: I put it in a module called n_mnesia.erl which contains the functions we need to create and manage the database:

---

[6]Logan, op cit, p 221.

Listing 10.4 (⇒ $) **Create** `n_mnesia.erl`

```
site/src/n_libs$ cd ../n_dbs
site/src/n_dbs$ vim n_mnesia.erl
...
-module(n_mnesia).
-export([init_tables/0,
         one_time/0,
         start/0,
         info/0,
         stop/0
    ]).
```

STEVIE: Here's `init_tables/0`. We haven't defined nnote access functions yet, so I had to fudge it:

Listing 10.5 (⇒ vim) **Define** `init_tables/0` (`n_mnesia.erl`)

```
init_tables() ->
   nnote_db_mnesia:init_table().
```

MARSHA: Hey, should have asked—I have a definition for `init_table/0`. While you were reading last night, I was programming.

RUSTY: Let's let Oleg finish.

STEVIE: No, hold it. You're leaving us in the dust, Oleg good buddy. What's that `one_time/0` about?

OLEG: Actually, I stole it from Joe Armstrong:[7]

---

[7] Armstrong, Joe. *Programming Erlang: Software for a Concurrent World*, Pragmatic Bookshelf, 2007, p 325.

Listing 10.6 (⇒ vim) **Define** one_time/0 **(n_mnesia.erl)**

```
init_tables(Define one_time/0) ->
...
one_time() ->
  schema(),
  init_tables().
```

STEVIE: So why do we need it?

OLEG: According to the mnesia docs, before we do anything, we need to define a schema and initialize our tables.

STEVIE: Ah, yes, read about that. So what does schema/0 look like?

OLEG: It's fairly simple actually. I cobbled it up from the mnesia docs:

Listing 10.7 (⇒ vim) **Define** schema/0 **(n_mnesia.erl)**

```
one_time_per_node() ->
...
schema() ->
  mnesia:create_schema([node()]),
  mnesia:start().
```

RUSTY: Very good. But do be careful here. The system will throw an error if someone calls mnesia:create_schema/1 when it already exists.

OLEG: So what can I do about that?

RUSTY: Here's a trick:

Listing 10.8 (⇒ vim) **Revise** schema/0 **(n_mnesia.erl)**

```
schema() ->
  case mnesia:create_schema([node()]) of
    ok                            -> ok;
    {error, {_, {already_exists, _}}} -> ok;
    Other                         -> exit(Other)
  end,
  mnesia:start().
```

OLEG: Ah, so.

STEVIE: OK, got it. Trap the return value of create_schema/1 and exit if something goes south.

MARSHA: What about init_tables/0? What happens if someone calls that more than once? I mean, you trapped that case in schema/0.

RUSTY: Turns out there's no harm in calling mnesia:create_table/2 if a table already exists. Instead of crashing, it just returns a handy error message: {aborted, {already_exists,TableName}}.

STEVIE: What happens if we change a record structure?

RUSTY: Ah—you'll need to back up all records in the table associated with my_stuff, call mnesia:delete_table(my_stuff), then you need to recreate the table with a call to n_mnesia:init_tables/0.

MARSHA: You'll also have to convert the old records into the new format won't you?

RUSTY: Indeed. That's the hard part.

OLEG: Can I get on with it?

RUSTY: Go for it.

OLEG: The remaining functions in n_mnesia.erl are dead simple:

Listing 10.9 (⇒ vim) start/0, info/0, and stop/0 (n_mnesia.erl)

```
start() ->
   mnesia:start().

info() ->
   mnesia:info().

stop() ->
   mnesia:stop().
```

RUSTY: Way to go, Oleg. Proud of you.

STEVIE: Show off!

10.4. mnesia Queries

RUSTY: So, Marsha—what were you saying about init_table/0?

MARSHA: That I've already defined it:

Listing 10.10 (⇒ $) Export init_table/0 (nnote_db_mnesia.erl)

```
src/n_dbs$ vim nnote_db_mnesia.erl

-module(nnote_db_mnesia).
-record(nnote, {
...
-export([ init_table/0
          % More to come
      ]).

-include_lib("stdlib/include/qlc.hrl").

-define(TABLE, nnote).
```

RUSTY: Whoa, hold up! You guys *have* been doing your homework. What's that `include_lib/1` all about?

MARSHA: I did an all-nighter to understand this stuff. So, qlc is a query interface to table-like data structures. It's cool—uses list comprehensions.[8]

RUSTY: Okay. So let's see your definition for `init_table/0`:

Listing 10.11 (⇒ vim) `init_table/0` (`nnote_db_mnesia.erl`)

```
-define(TABLE, nnote).
init_table() ->
  mnesia:create_table(?TABLE,
    [ {disc_copies, [node()] },
      {attributes,
            record_info(fields, ?TABLE)}
    ]).
```

RUSTY: Can you explain what you've done?

MARSHA: It's pretty simple once you get the hang. The first parameter in `create_table/2`, ?TABLE is a macro that names the table we're creating. Then, we have a configuration list. The first item says that we want to persist a copy of the table on the node defined by our schema.

RUSTY: Do we have other choices?

MARSHA: So happens that `disc_copies` also keeps a copy of the table in RAM. But we could specify `ram_copies` if we want a copy only in RAM or `disc_only_copies` if we want a copy only on disc. Anyway, all these options are explained in the mnesia docs.[9]

RUSTY: So why would we choose `disc_copies` over `ram_copies`?

---

[8]http://erlang.org/doc/man/qlc.html

[9]http://erlang.org/doc/man/mnesia.html

MARSHA: Queries respond faster out of RAM, but if power goes down or the system crashes, we lose the table.

OLEG: So what kind of table are we talking about here—set, bag, ordered set?

MARSA: Come on, Oleg. Read the documentation. You know that set is the default table type.

STEVIE: Yeah, put a bag over your head, Oleg. Anyway, what's a bag?

OLEG: Read the docs.

RUSTY: Children. Children. Before we continue, it might be interesting to see if we can start up mnesia and create the notes table in the nnote shell:

Listing 10.12 (⇒ >) **Create notes table**

```
(nnote@127.0.0.1)6> n_mnesia:one_time().
{atomic,ok}
(nnote@127.0.0.1)7> n_mnesia:info().
---> Processes holding locks <---
---> Processes waiting for locks <---
---> Participant transactions <---
---> Coordinator transactions <---
---> Uncertain transactions <---
---> Active tables <---
nnote   : with 0  records occupying 299  words of mem
schema  : with 2  records occupying 539  words of mem
...
ok
```

MARSHA: I get it! The function one_time/0 tells us that mnesia started properly. And info/0 gives us detailed information about our database.

RUSTY: You've got it! We ready to build access functions?

10.5. nnote Access Functions

MARSHA: We need an export attribute.

STEVIE: Done.

RUSTY: Can you show us?

Listing 10.13 (⇒ vim) **Export functions (nnote_db_mnesia.erl)**

```
-export([ init_table/0,
         % More to come
         put_record/1,
         get_all_values/1,
         get_all/0,
         get_record/1,
         delete/1,
         populate_record/1,
         get_records_by_type/2,
         get_records_by_date/3,
         search/3,
         id/1,
         user_id/1,
         date/1,
         type/1,
         event/1,
         source/1,
         topic/1,
         question/1,
         tags/1,
         note/1,
         id/2,
         user_id/2,
         date/2,
         type/2,
         event/2,
         source/2,
         topic/2,
         question/2,
         tags/2,
```

```
          note/2
]).
```

RUSTY: That's impressive! Why did you list them in that order?

STEVIE: Well, I've been playing with the productivity ideas we discussed last session. Wondering how they apply to database access modules.

RUSTY: Terrific! What have you come up with?

STEVIE: Not much. Probably bogus.

RUSTY: Can you show us?

STEVIE: Well the basic idea is to minimize keystrokes, right?

RUSTY: Okay—

STEVIE: We discussed several ways to do that—code abstraction, macros, and thoughtful code layout.

OLEG: So how do those techniques apply to the database access functions?

STEVIE: I was playing around with mnesia the other night. I realized that several essential functions are completely generic—they'd be the same regardless of the table we're accessing.

MARSHA: Like?

STEVIE: Take put_record/1, for instance:

Listing 10.14 (⇒ vim) **Revise** init_table/0 **(**nnote_db_mnesia.erl**)**

```
init_table() ->
    ...
%% Copy and paste the following functions
put_record(Record) ->
```

```
Insert =
   fun() ->
      mnesia:write(Record)
   end,
{atomic, Results} = mnesia:transaction(Insert),
Results.
```

STEVIE: Same for get_all_values/1 and get_all/0:

```
get_all_values(Record) ->
   [_|Tail] = tuple_to_list(Record),
   Tail.
get_all() ->
   Query =
      fun() ->
         qlc:eval( qlc:q(
            [ Record || Record <- mnesia:table(?TABLE) ]
         ))
      end,
   {atomic, Results} = mnesia:transaction(Query),
   Results.
```

STEVIE: So we can cut and paste these functions whenever we create a new mnesia function.

OLEG: Makes sense. What about init_table/0?

STEVIE: Sometimes we can also cut and paste, but we have to be careful since the list of options may vary across different tables.

MARSHA: Why didn't you use mnesia:dirty_write/1 for put_record/1? It would be faster.

OLEG: Oooo—Sounds salacious. What's a dirty write?

MARSHA: Ah, so you DIDN'T read the mnesia docs. Dirty functions write and read data directly to and from the database.

STEVIE: I read about that. But I wanted to get the hang of mnesia transactions.

RUSTY: Besides, the dirty functions are not so smart if you have concurrent users. You can end up with inconsistencies in the database. In such cases, transactions are better. So what else, Stevie?

STEVIE: With slight loss of clarity, get_record/1 and delete/1 can be copied directly over as well:

Listing 10.16 (⇒ vim) **get and delete (nnote_db_mnesia.erl)**

```
get_record(Key) ->
   Query =
      fun() ->
         mnesia:read({?TABLE, Key})
      end,
   {atomic, Results} = mnesia:transaction(Query),
   case length(Results) < 1 of
      true  -> [];
      false -> hd(Results)
   end.

delete(Key) ->
   Insert =
      fun() ->
         mnesia:delete({?TABLE, Key})
      end,
   {atomic, Results} = mnesia:transaction(Insert),
   Results.
```

RUSTY: Key is more abstract than ID or Username. So clarity does indeed suffer. But I see your point.

OLEG: So why not use ID or Password, as the case may be? Easy enough to change—or not—when you copy over the function.

STEVIE: Your choice. No big deal. But this is where I got stuck.

RUSTY: How so?

STEVIE: Well, say we're creating a new record—we might do something like this to suck values out of a form:

Example 10.1   Form values (do not reproduce in your modules)

```
Params = wf:mq([user_id, n_type, date, event, source,
                topic, question, tags, note]),
```

STEVIE: Given this, we could define a save function that looks something like:

Example 10.2   Define save (do not reproduce in your modules)

```
save_note(Params) ->
   Record = populate_record(Params),
   put_record(Record).
```

RUSTY: So what's the problem?

STEVIE: Well, now we need populate_record(Params):

Example 10.3   Define populate_record/1 (do not reproduce in your modules)

```
%% Big changes required here for different tables
populate_record([ID, UserID, Type, Date, Event, Source, Topic,
        Question, Tags, Note]) ->
```

```
#nnote{user_id  = UserID,
    type      = Type,
    date      = Date,
    event     = Event,
    source    = Source,
    topic     = Topic,
    question  = Question,
    tags      = Tags,
    note      = Note
    }.
```

RUSTY: Looks fine to me.

STEVIE: But what a productivity buster! All those repetitive keystrokes—

RUSTY: What else can you do?

10.6. Stevie Takes a Flyer

STEVIE: I thought I could do something with `record_info(fields, Record)`. I tried to include it in a function, but I got an error message—"Error: illegal record info." When I executed it in the Erlang shell, however, it gave me a list of field names:

Listing 10.17 (⇒ >) **Stevie strikes out**

```
5> rr(nnote_db_mnesia).
[nnote]
6> Fields = record_info(fields, nnote).
[id,user_id,date,type,event,source,topic,question,tags,note]
```

STEVIE: So I wrote two utility functions—one to convert the atoms in Fields to Erlang strings, and another to capitalize the strings:

Listing 10.18 (⇒ $) **Utility functions to the rescue (n_utils.erl)**

```
src/n_dbs$ cd ../n_libs
src/n_libs$ vim n_utils.erl

id_created() ->
...
field_names(FieldList) ->
   [atom_to_list(FieldName) || FieldName <- FieldList].

cap_field_names(FieldNames) ->
   [string:titlecase(String) || String <- FieldNames].
```

STEVIE: From there, it was easy to synthesize the function head:

Listing 10.19 (⇒ vim) **Synthesize function head (n_utils.erl)**

```
fieldnames_to_params(FieldNames) ->
   Caps = cap_field_names(FieldNames),
   string:join(Caps, ", ").

to_function_head(FieldList) ->
   FieldNames = field_names(FieldList),
   Params = fieldnames_to_params(FieldNames),
   lists:flatten(["populate_record([", Params, "]) ->"]).
```

STEVIE: And here's what I get when I execute to_function_head/1 in the Erlang shell:

Listing 10.20 (⇒ >) **Calling to_function_head/1 in the Erlang shell**

```
7> n_utils:to_function_head(Fields).
"populate_record([Id, User_id, Type, Date, Event, Source,
Topic, Question, Tags, Note]) ->"
```

OLEG: So you just copy and paste that into the n_utils module?

STEVIE: Exactly.

MARSHA: That's way cool, Stevie!

RUSTY: So what's the bottom line here, Stevie?

STEVIE: Took me awhile to figure how to synthesize to_function_body/2, but when I did, I was able to define this:

Listing 10.21 (⇒ $) synthesize_populate_record (n_utils.erl)

```
src/n_libs$ vim n_utils.erl
...
to_function_head(fieldList) ->
...
synthesize_populate_record(Record, FieldList) ->
    Head = to_function_head(FieldList),
    Body = to_function_body(Record, FieldList),
    io:format("~s~n~s~n", [Head, Body]).
```

STEVIE: And here's to_function_body/2:

Listing 10.22 (⇒ vim) **Define** to_function_body/2 (n_utils.erl)

```
to_function_head(FieldList) ->
...
to_function_body(Record, FieldList) ->
    FieldNames = field_names(FieldList),
    Caps = cap_field_names(FieldNames),
    Zip = lists:zip(FieldNames, Caps),
    Assignments = lists:map(fun({Name, Cap}) ->
        Name ++ " = " ++ Cap
    end, Zip),
    Delimited = string:join(Assignments, ", "),
    lists:flatten(["   #", Record, "{", Delimited, "}."]).
```

335

```
synthesize_populate_record(Record, FieldList) ->
```

OLEG: Gnarly—

MARSHA: Awesome!

RUSTY: It's clever, Stevie. I like the way you used `lists:map` and `lists:zip`. Can you tell us how long it took you to program `synthesize_populate_record/2`?

STEVIE: Uh, don't know—two, three hours?

RUSTY: Do you really think it was worth it?

STEVIE: Well, yeah, but I mean—I have a bunch of CRUD programs I want to write so it will save me time in the long run.

OLEG: Who cares! I want to see what it does!

STEVIE: Well, here's what I get when I run it in the Erlang shell:

Listing 10.23 (⇒ >) Call **synthesize_populate_record**

```
8> n_utils:synthesize_populate_record("nnote", Fields).
populate_record([Id, User_id, Type, Date, Event, Source, Topic,
Question, Tags, Note]) ->
    #nnote{id = Id, user_id = User_id, type = Type, date = Date,
event = Event, source = Source, topic = Topic, question = Question,
tags = Tags, note = Note}.
ok
```

STEVIE: So now I can copy and paste that into nnote_db_mnesia.erl and do a touch of reformatting to get this:

Listing 10.24 (⇒ \$) populate_record (nnote_db_mnesia.erl)

```
src/n_libs$ cd ../n_dbs
src/n_dbs$ vim nnote_db_mnesia.erl
...
delete(ID) ->
...
populate_record([Id, User_id, Type, Date, Event, Source,
    Topic, Question, Tags, Note]) ->
  #nnote{id = Id,
         user_id = User_id,
         type = Type,
         date = Date,
         event = Event,
         source = Source,
         topic = Topic,
         question = Question,
         tags = Tags,
         note = Note
        }.
```

STEVIE: That's as far as I got. Ran out of time.

RUSTY: That's great work. But before we continue, allow me to shed a little light. You are correct. You cannot call record_info(fields, Variable) when Variable is *actually* a variable. The second argument of record_info has to be an atom literal. Even a variable bound to an atom will fail to compile, because record_info/2 is a compile-time-only construct (just like records).

Knowing that, you can actually create an elaborate set of setters, getters, and format conversions for records, and there are some pretty good libraries that exist that can this for you. The most common is dynarec.[10] Using a library like that will eliminate the need for you to generate code on the command line that you have to copy-and-paste into your modules.

---

[10]https://github.com/dieswaytoofast/dynarec

That said, the work you've done is a noble effort to address a common pain point for those new to Erlang. Indeed, it's quite common for new Erlang developers to write something like synthesize_populate_record/2 on their own when they start working with records.

10.7. Search and Select Functions

RUSTY: I see that our time is running short. So let me try my hand at the search and select functions we'll need. There's definitely a pattern:

Listing 10.25 (⇒ vim) **Search-and-select (nnote_db_mnesia.erl)**

```
populate_record([ID, UserID, Type, Date, Event, Source,
                 Topic, Question, Tags, Note]) ->
...
get_records_by_type(UserID, Type) ->
   Query =
      fun() ->
         qlc:eval( qlc:q(
            [Record || Record <- mnesia:table(?TABLE),
                Record#nnote.id == UserID,
                Record#nnote.type == Type]
         ))
      end,
      {atomic, Results} = mnesia:transaction(Query),
      Results.

get_records_by_date(UserID, Type, Date) ->
   DateTime = qdate:to_date(Date),
   {FirstDate, LastDate} = n_dates:date_span(DateTime, 7),
   Query =
      fun() ->
         qlc:eval( qlc:q(
            [Record || Record <- mnesia:table(?TABLE),
                qdate:between(FirstDate, Record#nnote.date, LastDate),
                Record#nnote.user_id == UserID,
                Record#nnote.type >= Type
         ]))
      end,
```

```
        {atomic, Results} = mnesia:transaction(Query),
        Results.
    search(UserID, NoteType, SearchList) ->
        Query =
            fun() ->
                qlc:eval( qlc:q(
                    [Record || Record <- mnesia:table(?TABLE),
                               Record#nnote.user_id == UserID,
                               Record#nnote.type == NoteType,
                               n_search:filter(SearchList, Record)]
                ))
            end,
            {atomic, Results} = mnesia:transaction(Query),
            Results.
```

OLEG: I see the pattern, but I don't quite see the point of all the boilerplate leading up to mnesia:transaction/1.

RUSTY: Note that each of these functions has at heart a list comprehension which, as we've learned, is a powerful way to process every value in a list. The qlc functions apply list comprehensions to our mnesia table. Wrapping the qlc functions in a fun-to-create a headless function provides a generic way to pass any access operation as a parameter to mnesia:transaction/1.

MARSHA: I think I get it.

RUSTY: Keep in mind that mnesia queries may access several tables, records, and fields within those records before finishing their work. Indeed, when you perform an operation on one copy of the schema, it is automatically propagated to all other replicas and fragments. If a query fails, we definitely don't want to leave unfinished business in the records and tables involved—that is, in case of error we want to return every database touched to the state it was in before we initiated the query.

This is called Atomicity.

OLEG: Sounds hard core.

RUSTY: It's a fundamental requirement for data integrity.

In the same vein, we want every transaction to bring the database from one valid state to another, that is, to maintain `Consistency`.

STEVIE: That leaves Oleg out.

OLEG: I didn't hear that.

RUSTY: When transactions are coming in fast and furiously, we certainly don't want one transaction to interfere with another. They should be executed one after another. We want Isolation.

And finally, once a transaction is successfully completed, we want the result to be Durable, that is, to be retained even in the case of power loss, system crash, or error.

The `mnesia:transaction/1` function enforces these ACID properties, that is, guarantees atomicity, isolation, consistency, and durability.

Make sense?

OLEG: Sort of—er, maybe, with a flurry of hand-waving.

RUSTY: Yeah. Know what you mean.

10.8. A bit about date handling

OLEG: I wonder, this is the second time you've used these qdate functions...

RUSTY: Ah, yes, the qdate functions. Working with dates, times, date strings, and time zones can be pesky. But tell you what, we have to face up to date conversions sooner or later. Out-of-the-box Nitrogen comes with qdate[11], a nifty library written by Jesse Gumm, the Nitrogen Project Lead. Here are a few examples:

---

[11]https://github.com/choptastic/qdate

Listing 10.26 ($\Rightarrow$ >) **Test date functions in Erlang shell**

```
1> DateTime = calendar:universal_time().
{{2020,9,12},{19,18,22}}
2> EarlyDate = qdate:add_days(-7,DateTime).
1599333538
3> Earliest = qdate:to_date(EarlyDate).
{{2020,9,5},{19,18,58}}
4> LateDate = qdate:add_days(7,DateTime).
1600543138
5> Latest = qdate:to_date(LateDate).
{{2020,9,19},{19,18,58}}
6> qdate:to_string("Y-m-d g:ia", Latest).
"2020-09-19 7:18pm"
```

OLEG: Oh, man— wish I knew about this before. I've gnashed teeth writing date conversion functions.

STEVIE: What are those long integers returned by add_unit/2?

RUSTY: Unix timestamps. The number of seconds since 12:00AM GMT, January 1st, 1970. qdate can work with the date/time tuples we've seen, Unix timestamps, the output of os:timestamp() (generally referred to as the now format), and can convert to and from most date and time strings. Its formatting functions use the PHP's date[12] format strings.

MARSHA: Ah, I get it! May I try my hand at date_span/2?

RUSTY: Go for it!

Listing 10.27 ($\Rightarrow$ $) **Define** date_span/2 **(n_dates.erl)**

```
src/n_dbs$ cd ../n_libs
n_libs$ vim n_dates.erl
...
datepicker(Id, Text) ->
```

---

[12]https://www.php.net/manual/en/datetime.format.php

```
...
date_span(DateTime, N) ->
   StartRange = qdate:add_days(-N, DateTime),
   EndRange = qdate:add_days(N, DateTime),
   {StartRange, EndRange}.
```

RUSTY: Way to go! Keep up the good work and there's a job waiting for you at Erlingo!.

OLEG: The girl rocks!

MARSHA: I'm thinking pre-med.

RUSTY: Definite loss to the Nitrogen community.

10.9. Filter Functions Revisited

MARSHA: Hey, n_search:filter/2 in search/3—should we copy over the filter functions from n_index?

RUSTY: Fancy you mention that. I was polishing up those functions just the other day. Here. I'll SCP over the new-and-improved versions:[13]

> **Listing 10.28** (⇒ $) **Filter functions (n_search.erl)**

```
/site/src/n_dbs$ cd ../n_libs
/site/src/n_libs$ vim n_search.erl
...
-module(n_search).
-compile(export_all).
%% ------------------------------------------------
%% @doc Search by keyword
%% ------------------------------------------------
unique_words_from_string(String) ->
```

---

[13]https://haydenjames.io/linux-securely-copy-files-using-scp/

```
    Normalized = normalize(String),
    Tokens = string:lexemes(Normalized, " "),
    sets:from_list(Tokens).

unique_words_from_record(Record) ->
    Values = nnote_api:get_all_values(Record),
    Sets = [unique_words_from_string(Value)
            || Value <- Values, is_list(Value)],
    sets:union(Sets).

normalize(String) ->
    Clean = re:replace(String, "[,.?!()-]", "", [global,{return, list}]),
    string:to_upper(Clean).

filter(SearchString, Record) ->
    NoteSet = unique_words_from_record(Record),
    SearchSet = unique_words_from_string(SearchString),
    SharedWords = sets:intersection(NoteSet, SearchSet),
    sets:size(SharedWords) > 0.
```

10.10. Field Access Functions

RUSTY: So, Stevie, I see you tapping away.

STEVIE: Oh, just trying to finish off the field access functions.

RUSTY: Outstanding! What can you show us?

Listing 10.29   (⇒ $) Field access functions (nnote_db_mnesia.erl)

```
src/n_libs$ cd ../n_dbs
src/n_dbs$ vim nnote_db_mnesia.erl

search(UserID, NoteType, SearchList) ->
...
%% GETTERS
id(Record) -> Record#nnote.id.
```

```
user_id(Record) -> Record#nnote.user_id.
date(Record) -> Record#nnote.date.
type(Record) -> Record#nnote.type.
event(Record) -> Record#nnote.event.
source(Record) -> Record#nnote.source.
topic(Record) -> Record#nnote.topic.
question(Record) -> Record#nnote.question.
tags(Record) -> Record#nnote.tags.
note(Record) -> Record#nnote.note.
```

OLEG: Hmmm—beaucoup repetitive keystrokes. Couldn't we use Stevie's function synthesis idea here?

RUSTY: Possibly. The better solution would be to use the previously mentioned dynarec library to generate the setters and getters without you having to define them at all. But I'll leave either of those to you as a homework assignment.

STEVIE: They do get a tedious:

Listing 10.30 (⇒ `vim`) **More functions (`nnote_db_mnesia.erl`)**

```
%% SETTERS
id(Record, ID) ->
    Record#nnote{id=ID}.
user_id(Record, UserID) ->
    Record#nnote{user_id=UserID}.
date(Record, Date) ->
    Record#nnote{date=Date}.
type(Record, Type) ->
    Record#nnote{type=Type}.
event(Record, Event) ->
    Record#nnote{event=Event}.
source(Record, Source) ->
    Record#nnote{source=Source}.
topic(Record, Topic) ->
    Record#nnote{topic=Topic}.
question(Record, Question) ->
```

```
    Record#nnote{question=Question}.
tags(Record, Tags) ->
    Record#nnote{tags=Tags}.
note(Record, Note) ->
    Record#nnote{note=Note}.
```

RUSTY: Looking good! So, we ready to test what we have so far?

Listing 10.31 (⇒ >) **And more tests**

```
8> rr(nnote_db_mnesia).
[nnote]
9> Record = #nnote{id="1", note="Our test note."}.
#nnote{id = "1",user_id = undefined,type = undefined,
    date = undefined,event = undefined,source = undefined,
    topic = undefined,question = undefined,tags = undefined,
    note = "Our test note."}
10> nnote_db_mnesia:put_record(Record).
ok
11> Record1 = nnote_db_mnesia:get_record("1").
#nnote{id = "1",user_id = undefined,type = undefined,
    date = undefined,event = undefined,source = undefined,
    topic = undefined,question = undefined,tags = undefined,
    note = "Our test note."}
12> nnote_db_mnesia:get_all_values(Record1).
["1",undefined,undefined,undefined,undefined,undefined,
undefined,undefined,undefined,"Our test note."]
13> nnote_db_mnesia:get_all().
[#nnote{id = "1",user_id = undefined,type = undefined,
    date = undefined,event = undefined,source = undefined,
    topic = undefined,question = undefined,tags = undefined,
    note = "Our test note."}]
```

OLEG: *That*'s what I'm talking about!

RUSTY: One last thing—we should probably make sure we start mnesia and load our database when our application starts up.

MARSHA: Good call. I don't want to have to start it manually every time. We can put that in the supervisor, right?

RUSTY: Sure, that's fine:

Listing 10.32 (⇒ $) **Initialize database (`nitrogen_sup.erl`)**

```
src/n_dbs$ cd ..
src$ vim nitrogen_sup.erl
...
init([]) ->
    n_mnesia:one_time(),
    application:load(nitrogen_core),
    application:start(simple_cache),
    ...
```

OLEG: `one_time()`?

MARSHA: Sure. Rusty said it's safe to re-initialize if the table is already there, and this will then initialize a new database if one doesn't already exist.

OLEG: Solid.

10.11. A Facade for nnote

RUSTY: So who's up for cranking out the facade?

MARSHA: I'm on it:

Listing 10.33 (⇒ $) **Facade functions**

```
site/src$ vim n_dbs/nnote_api.erl
...
-module(nnote_api).
```

```
-define(DB, nnote_db_mnesia).

-export([ init_table/0,
    put_record/1,
    get_all_values/1,
    get_all/0,
    get_record/1,
    delete/1,
    populate_record/1,
    get_records_by_type/2,
    get_records_by_date/3,
    search/3,
    id/1,
    user_id/1,
    date/1,
    type/1,
    event/1,
    source/1,
    topic/1,
    question/1,
    tags/1,
    note/1,
    id/2,
    user_id/2,
    date/2,
    type/2,
    event/2,
    source/2,
    topic/2,
    question/2,
    tags/2,
    note/2
    ]).

init_table() ->
    ?DB:init_table().
put_record(Record) ->
    ?DB:put_record(Record).

get_all_values(Record) ->
```

```
      ?DB:get_all_values(Record).
   get_all() ->
      ?DB:get_all().

   get_record(ID) ->
     ?DB:get_record(ID).
   delete(ID) ->
      ?DB:delete(ID).
   populate_record(Values) ->
     ?DB:populate_record(Values).
   get_records_by_type(UserID, Type) ->
      ?DB:get_records_by_type(UserID, Type).

   get_records_by_date(UserID, Type, Date) ->
      ?DB:get_records_by_date(UserID, Type, Date).

   search(UserID, Type, SearchList) ->
      ?DB:search(UserID, Type, SearchList).

   id(Record) ->
      ?DB:id(Record).

   user_id(Record) ->
      ?DB:user_id(Record).

   date(Record) ->
      ?DB:date(Record).

   type(Record) ->
      ?DB:type(Record).

   event(Record) ->
      ?DB:event(Record).

   source(Record) ->
      ?DB:source(Record).

   topic(Record) ->
      ?DB:topic(Record).

   question(Record) ->
```

```
    ?DB:question(Record).

tags(Record) ->
    ?DB:tags(Record).

note(Record) ->
    ?DB:note(Record).

id(Record, ID) ->
    ?DB:id(Record, ID).

user_id(Record, UserID) ->
    ?DB:user_id(Record, UserID).

date(Record, Date) ->
    ?DB:date(Record, Date).

type(Record, Type) ->
    ?DB:type(Record, Type).

event(Record, Event) ->
    ?DB:event(Record, Event).

source(Record, Source) ->
    ?DB:source(Record, Source).

topic(Record, Topic) ->
    ?DB:topic(Record, Topic).

question(Record, Question) ->
    ?DB:question(Record, Question).

tags(Record, Tags) ->
    ?DB:tags(Record, Tags).

note(Record, Note) ->
    ?DB:note(Record, Note).
```

RUSTY: What do you think, Oleg?

OLEG: Smokin'!

349

10.12. Add/Edit Form

RUSTY: What's next?

MARSHA: The add/edit form?

RUSTY: So Dataman, want to stub it in?

OLEG: Your wish, sir, is my command. Any objection if I morph nnote.erl?

RUSTY: Go for it:

Listing 10.34 (⇒ $) **Morph nnote.erl**

```
src$ cd nnote
src/nnote$ cp nnote.erl nnote_add_edit.erl
src/nnote$ vim nnote_add_edit.erl
...
%% @doc nnote add/edit
...
-module(nnote_add_edit).
```

OLEG: Can't forget the title macro:

Listing 10.35 (⇒ vim) **Macros (nnote_add_edit.erl)**

```
-define(TITLE, ~~"Welcome to nnote!"~~ "Add/edit note").
```

OLEG: Sidebar menu should stay the same, I think. But we need to tweak the select event that goes with it. Let's just say if we click one of the sidebar items that it immediately brings us to the create new note form for that note type:

Listing 10.36 (⇒ vim) **Tweak select event** (`nnote_add_edit.erl`)

```
event({select, NoteType}) ->
   Redirect = [wf:path(), "?",
                  wf:to_qs([{id, "new"}, {note_type, NoteType} ]) ],
   wf:redirect(Redirect);
```

OLEG: And we definitely need to completely redo content/1:

Listing 10.37 (⇒ vim) **Redo** content/1 (`nnote_add_edit.erl`)

```
context(#{note_type:=undefined, task:=undefined}) ->
   ...
   display_forms(NoteType, Records).
content(#{id:=undefined, note_type:=undefined}) ->
   #h2{class=content, text="My Notes"};
content(#{id:=ID, note_type:=NoteType}) ->
   add_edit_form(ID, NoteType).
```

OLEG: Since we haven't designed an add/edit form yet, I'll just fake it:

Listing 10.38 (⇒ vim) **Fake add/edit form** (`nnote_add_edit.erl`)

```
add_edit_form(ID, NoteType) ->
   #p{text="In this space soon: One Bodacious
                     Add/Edit Form for nnotes"}.
```

STEVIE: Clever. But you still need to link to your add/edit page from `nnote.erl`.

OLEG: You've read my mind:

Listing 10.39 (⇒ $) **Link add/edit page to nnote.erl**

```
site/src/nnode$ vim nnote.erl
...
event(search_by_date) ->
...
event({add_note, NoteType}) ->
   Redirect=["/nnote/add_edit?",
             wf:to_qs([{id,"new"}, {note_type,NoteType}])],
   wf:redirect(Redirect);
%% **************************************************
%% Info events
%% **************************************************
```

RUSTY: I see that you're following along, Marsha. Does it work?

MARSHA: So far so good.

OLEG: The time has come to actually create the add/edit form. So back to add_edit.erl.

RUSTY: I like your enthusiasm, but before we do that, let's just clean out the unneeded functions in nnote_add_edit.erl. We can safely blow away: tag_search/1, date_search/1, search_results/1, display_forms/2, content_headline/0, add_note_button/1, search_by_tag/0, search_by_date/0, info/1:

Listing 10.40 (⇒ $) **Unnecessary functions (nnote_add_edit.erl)**

```
src/nnote$ vim nnote_add_edit.erl
...
tag_search(NoteType) ->
...
date_search(NoteType) ->
...
search_results(undefined) ->
...
```

```
display_forms(NoteType, Records) ->
    ...
content_headline() ->
    ...
add_note_button(NoteType) ->
    ...
search_by_tag() ->
    ...
search_by_date() ->
    ...
info(search_by_tag) ->
    ...
```

RUSTY: ... and a couple clauses from event/1:

Listing 10.41 (⇒ vim) **More deletions** (nnote_add_edit.erl)

```
event(search_by_tag) ->
    ...
event(search_by_date) ->
    ...
event(info) ->
    ...
```

OLEG: Now can we make the add/edit form?

RUSTY: Let's do it!

10.13. A Tricky Form

RUSTY: Here's where things get tricky. We have a list of note types and a set of note attributes. But not all attributes are appropriate across all note types. The event attribute, for instance, applies only to conference and lecture notes.

OLEG: Just as I feared— we need several different input forms and save functions.

STEVIE: I've made a table to help us out. Note that for conference and lecture notes we override the event and source fields with labels more appropriate to the note type.

	id	date	type	event	source	topic	ques	note
conference	-	x	-	conf.	speaker	x	x	x
idea	-	x	-	/	/	x	/	x
interview	-	x	-	/	x	x	x	x
lab	-	x	-	/	/	x	x	x
lecture	-	x	-	lect.	speaker	x	x	x
research	-	x	-	/	x	x	x	x
web	-	x	-	/	URL	x	/	x

MARSHA: I don't grok the symbols.

STEVIE: So, each row is a type of note. Each column is a field in the note record. A hyphen means we never display this field in the add/edit form. An 'x' indicates cases where the record-field name and add/edit form-field label are the same. Otherwise, I show an alternative label for the field.

MARSHA: Ah, I take it backslashes tell us to suppress the field for that note type since it's not needed.

STEVIE: Bingo!

OLEG: This is getting way more complicated than `nindex`. Just as I predicted, we're headed down a rabbit hole.

RUSTY: Maybe not. Let's take our lead from `nindex`. Take a few minutes to review what we did there. Then let's see how it applies to this puppy.

Okay Stevie—looks like you're chomping at the bit.

STEVIE: We need a function to handle the (ID, NoteType) case:

```
Listing 10.42  (⇒ $) Define add/edit form (nnote_add_edit.erl)

src/nnote$ vim nnote_add_edit.erl
...
add_edit_form(ID, NoteType) ->
    #p{text="In this space soon: One Bodacious
                       Add/Edit Form for nnotes"}.
    form(ID, "", NoteType, "", "", "", "", "", "").

form(ID, UserID, NoteType, Date, Event, Source, Topic,
              Question, Tags, Note) ->
    [ #label{text="Date"},
      #textbox{id=date, text=Date},
      #label{text="Event"},
      #textbox{id=event, text=Event},
      #label{text="Source"},
      #textbox{id=source, text=Source},
      #label{text="Topic"},
      #textbox{id=topic, text=Topic},
      #label{text="Question"},
      #textbox{id=question, text=Question},
      #label{text="Search Words"},
      #textbox{id=tags, text=Tags},
      #label{text="Note"},
      #textarea{id=note, text=Note},
      #br{},
      #button{id=save_note, text="Submit", postback={save_note}},
      #button{text="Cancel", postback=cancel}
    ].
```

MARSHA: So where will UserID come from?

RUSTY: We'll need a function to pull it out of the session, but that'll have to wait until we create an access control system.

OLEG: Hold it! Since ID, UserID, and NoteType are all given when we enter the form, shouldn't they be hidden fields?

STEVIE: My bad...

RUSTY: Hold up! Do not do that!

OLEG: Wait, what? Why?

RUSTY: There are uses for hidden fields, but if you recall, those #hidden fields are actually converted to <input type=hidden> HTML tags and are sent to the client. And even though they aren't rendered on the page, the values still exist in the DOM. Anyone have a theory why that's bad?

MARSHA: Because internal values can be leaked? Maybe you want to keep the values concealed from the user?

RUSTY: Well, yes, but that's not the worst part.

MARSHA: Can those values be tampered with somehow?

RUSTY: That's the one. If you're using wf:q to capture the value from a form field, that raw value can easily be changed by anyone with even a moderate amount of technical savvy. If you press CTRL+SHIFT+I on your keyboard in most modern browsers, that brings up the developer tools or DOM inspector. Using that, even with a hidden field, you can change the value of anything on the page, including changing the value of an ID. And if a user changes the ID of a note to the value of another ID that already exists in the system, you will have just allowed that user to overwrite another user's note.

OLEG: Whoa...

RUSTY: The better solution is to encode the ID and other hidden fields like it into the postback itself, like this:

Listing 10.43 (⇒ vim) **Encode values (nnote_add_edit.erl)**

```
...
     #br{},
```

```
#button{id=save_note, text="Submit",
        postback={save_note, ID, UserID, NoteType}},
#button{text="Cancel", postback=cancel}
```

STEVIE: But doesn't that also expose the data on the page to tampering?

RUSTY: Good question. No, it doesn't! Whereas form fields, like textboxes, dropdowns, and hidden elements, are all typically presented in unencrypted plain text, all postback values are signed and encrypted. So unless an attacker somehow gets the encryption key, you're safe. So it's very important to keep that encryption key safe.

STEVIE: Got it! That's great to know!

RUSTY: And it helps with cutting down on code as well. You don't have to make #hidden elements, so you don't have to collect those values with wf:q(). And because you can trust the postback, you might not even have to add extra checks like "does the current user have access to the note with this ID?" and so on. Instead, you just pattern match the values from the event clause and carry on.

MARSHA: We should probably use the datepicker widget we wrote in n_dates. Also, we need validators.

STEVIE: On it:

Listing 10.44 (⇒ vim) **Define validators (nnote_add_edit.erl)**

```
form(ID, UserID, NoteType, Date, Event, Source, Topic,
            Question, Tags, Note) ->
  wf:defer(save_note, topic, #validate{validators=[
        #is_required{text="Topic required"}]}),
  wf:defer(save_note, note, #validate{validators=[
        #is_required{text="Note required"}]}),
  wf:defer(save_note, event, #validate{validators=[
        #is_required{text="Event required"}]}),
```

```
wf:defer(save_note, source, #validate{validators=[
        #is_required{text="Source required"}]}),
  [ #label{text="Date"},
    #textbox{id=date, text=Date},
    n_dates:datepicker(date, Date),
  ...
```

MARSHA: I think we need a headline over the form.

STEVIE: You're right:

Listing 10.45 (⇒ vim) **Headline (nnote_add_edit.erl)**

```
content(#{id:=ID, note_type:=NoteType}) ->
  [
    content_headline(ID, NoteType),
    add_edit_form(ID, NoteType)
  ].
```

OLEG: Don't forget to define content_headline/2.

STEVIE: Yes, yes, I'm on it:

Listing 10.46 (⇒ vim) content_headline/2 (nnote_add_edit.erl)

```
content_headline(ID, NoteType) ->
  Action = case ID of
    "new" -> "Enter";
    _ -> "Edit"
  end,
  #h2{class=content, text=[Action, " ",NoteType," Note"]}.
```

OLEG: Style check! NoteType comes off the URL in lowercase. But as displayed in h2, shouldn't the first character be in uppercase?

RUSTY: Well, for sake of consistency, looking back at the headline in nnote.erl, it should. Simple solution: string:titlecase/1 will do that for us:

Listing 10.47 (⇒ vim) **Title case** (nnote_add_edit.erl)

```
content_headline(ID, NoteType) ->
    Action = case ID of
        "new" -> "Enter";
        _ -> "Edit"
    end,
    #h2{class=content, text=[Action," ",string:titlecase(NoteType)," Note"]}.
```

OLEG: Maybe the "Submit" button should say something more specific—you know, like "Enter" and "Save."

STEVIE: If you insist:

Listing 10.48 (⇒ vim) **Revise button labels** (nnote_add_edit.erl)

```
        #br{},
        #button{id=save_note, text="Submit" button_text(ID),
                postback={save_note, ID, UserID, NoteType}},
        #button{text="cancel", postback=cancel}
].
%% ****************************************************
%% Content helpers
%% ****************************************************
button_text("new") -> "Enter new note";
button_text(_ID) -> "Submit changes".
```

MARSHA: Do we have an event to handle the cancel postback?

OLEG: We haven't handled the save_note postback yet, but the cancel postback is easy. I can do that:

Listing 10.49 (⇒ vim) **Cancel postback (nnote_add_edit.erl)**

```
event(select, NoteType)
    ...
    wf:redirect(Redirect)-;
event(cancel) ->
    wf:redirect("/nnote").
```

STEVIE: The date field bugs me. Shouldn't we provide the current date as default in the date field?

RUSTY: Good call. But we may run into date conversion issues.

OLEG: Tough it out.

RUSTY: No—qdate to the rescue:

Listing 10.50 (⇒ $) **Revise add_edit_form/2 (nnote_add_edit.erl)**

```
src/nnote$ vim nnote_add_edit.erl
    ...
add_edit_form(ID, NoteType) ->
    Date = qdate:to_string("Y-m-d"),
    form(ID, "", NoteType, "" Date, "", "", "", "", "").
```

MARSHA: That doesn't look right. If we're editing a note, it will still put in today's date, no?

RUSTY: Good catch. Time to break add_edit_form/2 function into 2 clauses:

Listing 10.51 (⇒ vim) **Revise functions (nnote_add_edit.erl)**

```
add_edit_form(ID "new", NoteType) ->
    Date = qdate:to_string("Y-m-d"),
    form(ID "new", "", NoteType, Date, "", "", "", "", "")-;
```

```
add_edit_form(ID, NoteType) ->
    %% We'll do more here when we set up editing
    [].
```

STEVIE: I still don't like that date format. Y-m-d? Yuck!

RUSTY: That's the ISO standard format! It's wonderfully unambiguous.

OLEG: I like it...

STEVIE: You would!

RUSTY: Tell ya what, I'll leave it as a homework assignment for you to rework the date format. Keep in mind, you'll also need to tell the #datepicker_textbox in n_dates.erl to use the alternate format. It's not as obvious as you'd think. #datepicker_textbox's date format is based on the Jquery UI's format strings,[14] while qdate uses PHP's formatting.[15]

MARSHA: Okay. Shouldn't we also instantiate the user_id field?

RUSTY: Right. We won't know that until we've developed the user-access system. But we can stub in a function to tide us over:

Listing 10.52   (⇒ $) Stub in user id (n_utils.erl)

```
...   site/src/nnote$ cd ../n_libs
...   src/n_libs$ vim n_utils.erl
...
get_nickname() -> "Marsha".
...
get_user_id() -> "123".
```

RUSTY: Now to install it:

---

[14]https://jqueryui.com/datepicker/
[15]https://www.php.net/manual/en/function.date.php

Listing 10.53 (⇒ $) **Install add/edit form (`nnote_add_edit.erl`)**

```
...   src/n_libs$ cd ../nnote
...   src/nnote$ vim nnote_add_edit.erl
...
add_edit_form("new", NoteType) ->
    UserID = n_utils:get_user_id(),
    Date = qdate:to_string("m/d/Y"),
    form("new", ⊥ UserID, Date, NoteType, "", "", "", "", "", "");
```

10.14. Swing Back to Metadata

OLEG: I like it. I like it. But I hate to inform you, Fearless Leader— we still haven't dealt with the metadata issue.

RUSTY: Thought you'd never ask. So I took the liberty of translating Stevie's table into a set of functions. First the labels:

Listing 10.54 (⇒ `vim`) **Metadata functions (`nnote_add_edit.erl`)**

```
button_text(_ID) -> "Submit changes".

event_label("conference") -> "Conference";
event_label("lecture") -> "Event";
event_label(_) -> "".

source_label("conference") -> "Speaker";
source_label("idea") -> "";
source_label("lab") -> "";
source_label("lecture") -> "Speaker";
source_label("web") -> "URL";
source_label(_) -> "Source".

question_label("conference") -> "";
question_label("idea") -> "";
question_label("web") -> "";
question_label(_) -> "Question".
```

RUSTY: Now a set of functions to suppress unnecessary fields:

Listing 10.55 ($\Rightarrow$ vim) **Suppress fields (nnote_add_edit.erl)**

```erlang
show_event("conference") -> true;
show_event("lecture") -> true;
show_event(_) -> false.

show_source("idea") -> false;
show_source("lab") -> false;
show_source(_) -> true.

show_question("interview") -> true;
show_question("lab") -> true;
show_question("lecture") -> true;
show_question("research") -> true;
show_question(_) -> false.
```

MARSHA: The suspense is killing me.

RUSTY: Last step— install these functions in our form:

Listing 10.56 ($\Rightarrow$ vim) **Metadata functions (nnote_add_edit.erl)**

```erlang
form(ID, UserID, NoteType, Date, Event, Source, Topic, Question, Tags,
Note) ->
    ShowEvent = show_event(NoteType),
    ShowSource = show_source(NoteType),
    ShowQuestion = show_question(NoteType),
    wf:defer(save_note, topic, #validate{validators=[
        #is_required{text="Topic required"}]}),
    ...
    wf:defer(save_note, source, #validate{validators=[
        #is_required{text="Source required"}]}),
  [ #label{text="Date"},
    #datepicker_textbox{id=date, text=Date},
    #label{text="Event" event_label(NoteType), show_if=ShowEvent},
    #textbox{id=event, text=Event, show_if=ShowEvent},
```

```
#label{text="Source" source_label(NoteType), show_if=ShowSource},
#textbox{id=source, text=Source, show_if=ShowSource},
#label{text="Topic"},
#textbox{id=topic, text=Topic},
#label{text="Question" question_label(NoteType), show_if=ShowQuestion},
#textbox{id=question, text=Question, show_if=ShowQuestion},
#label{text="Search Words"},
...
```

RUSTY: So Oleg—how we looking in the browser?

OLEG: A-OK! Love the way the form changes depending upon note type.

RUSTY: So what's next, troopers?

MARSHA: "Edit" form to go with our "Add" form?

STEVIE: I know how to do that! Here we go:

Listing 10.57 (⇒ vim) **Revise add/edit form (`nnote_add_edit`)**

```erlang
add_edit_form("new", NoteType) ->
    ...
    form("new", UserID, NoteType, Date,  "", "", "", "", "", "");
add_edit_form(ID, NoteType) ->
    %% We'll do more here when we set up editing
    [].
    Record = nnote_api:get_record(ID),
    [ID, UserID, NoteType, Date, Event, Source, Topic,
        Question, Tags, Note] = nnote_api:get_all_values(Record),
    form(ID, UserID, NoteType, Date, Event, Source, Topic,
        Question, Tags, Note).
```

RUSTY: Who wants to tackle the save function?

OLEG: I'm in:

Listing 10.58 (⇒ vim) **Define save function (`nnote_add_edit`)**

```erlang
side_menu("NOTE TYPE") ->
    ...
%% ************************************************
%% Saving Things
%% ************************************************
save(ID, UserID, NoteType) ->
    Params = wf:mq([date, event, source, topic, question, tags, note]),
    Params2 = [ID, UserID, NoteType | Params],
    Record = nnote_api:populate_record(Params2),
```

```
nnote_api:put_record(Record),
Redirect = ["/nnote", "?",
    wf:to_qs([{note_type, NoteType} ]) ],
wf:redirect(Redirect).
```

MARSHA: Beep Beep. Point of order. Found a bug!

RUSTY: Just one?

MARSHA: We never made the handler for the save_note event.

OLEG: Need that, for sure:

Listing 10.59 (⇒ vim) **save_note clause (nnote_add_edit.erl)**

```
event({select, NoteType}) ->
 ...
%% ***************************************************
%% Save Events
%% ***************************************************
event({save_note, ID, UserID, NoteType}) ->
  wf:wire(#confirm{text="Save?",
                   postback={confirm_save, ID, UserID, NoteType}});
event({confirm_save, ID, UserID, NoteType}) ->
  save(ID, UserID, NoteType);
event(cancel) ->
  wf:redirect("/nnote").
```

MARSHA: Okay! It worked! I managed to save a conference[16] note with no problem, but...

---

[16]Be sure to test *only* a *conference* note for now. All will be revealed...

10.15. Loose Ends

10.15.1. Exposing the Note Search

MARSHA: ... but there's a problem: I can't find the saved record when I search from the main nnote page.

OLEG: We never filled in the tag_search and date_search functions in nnote.erl. We just stubbed them in and left them alone.

RUSTY: That is a problem. Let's finish that up so we can see our handy work in action:

Listing 10.60 (⇒ $) **Tag and date search (nnote.erl)**

```
src/nnote$ vim nnote.erl
-module(nnote).
...
tag_search(NoteType) ->
    [].
    UserID = n_utils:get_user_id(),
    SearchList = wf:q(search_words),
    nnote_api:search(UserID, NoteType, SearchList).
date_search(NoteType) ->
    [].
    UserID = n_utils:get_user_id(),
    Date = wf:q(search_date),
    nnote_api:get_records_by_date(UserID, NoteType, Date).
```

RUSTY: Try searching now.

OLEG: Crashes.

10.15.2. Debug Search Crash

RUSTY: What's the error?

OLEG: It's giving us {error,undef, [{n_utils,draw_link,...]. We never built the draw_link function in n_utils?

STEVIE: Looks like we're trying to call n_utils:draw_link(Record), which we built before the Record or the database stuff. So we didn't know how to build it.

OLEG: But we know now how we can do it, soooo...

MARSHA: I got this:

Listing 10.61 (⇒ $) **Add n_utils:draw_link/1**

```
...$ vim ../n_libs/n_utils.erl
-module(n_utils).
-include_lib("nitrogen_core/include/wf.hrl").
...
synthesize_populate_record(Record, FieldList) ->
...

draw_link(Record) ->
   ID = nnote_api:id(Record),
   NoteType = nnote_api:type(Record),
   Date = nnote_api:date(Record),
   Topic = nnote_api:topic(Record),
   EditUrl = ["/nnote/add_edit?",
             wf:to_qs([{id, ID}, {note_type, NoteType}])],
   Menuid = wf:temp_id(),
   [
      #link {
         body = [Date, " ", "&#8212;", " ", Topic],
         click=#toggle{target=Menuid}
      },
      #panel{id=Menuid, style="display:none", body=[
         #link {text="edit", url=EditUrl},
         " | ",
         #link {text="delete", postback={delete, ID}}
      ]},
      #br{}
   ].
```

MARSHA: Okay, saving, and clicking "Search" again . . . and it works!

OLEG: What happens if you click the search result?

MARSHA: Seems to work.

RUSTY: Does clicking "edit" work?

STEVIE: Oh weird. . .

10.15.3. Debug Save Issue

STEVIE: . . . it doesn't seem to show any info in any of the fields when I click "edit."

MARSHA: But it saved, right?

OLEG: Seemed like it did? Maybe it didn't. Can we check what's in the database?

STEVIE: We totally can! We have the `nnote_api:get_all()` function:

Listing 10.62 (⇒ >) **Inspect the database**

```
15> nnote_api:get_all().
[#nnote{id = "1",user_id = undefined,type = undefined,
    date = undefined,event = undefined,source = undefined,
    topic = undefined,question = undefined,tags = undefined,
    note = "Our test note."},
 #nnote{id = "new",user_id = "123",type = "conference",
    date = "2020-09-12",event = "CEUG",source = "Joe Arms",
    topic = "Programming Tips",question = undefined,tags = "erlang",
    note = "don't use gotos, it's not 1970 anymore."}]
```

MARSHA: We never deleted that test record with `id="1"`.

STEVIE: That's not the cause of the error though. The conference note is there and it looks fine to me.

OLEG: Whoa, our conference note says `id="new"`. That can't be right.

RUSTY: Good eye. Also, look at the URL bar on the page.

OLEG: It says `id=new` in the URL as well. What the heck?

MARSHA: I'm scanning over our code—not seeing why our record is saving with `id` being set to new.

RUSTY: Have a closer look at `nnote_db_mnesia:populate_record/1`.

STEVIE: I'm still not seeing it.

RUSTY: I'll give you a hint: what are we doing with `id`?

STEVIE: Oh, we're just passing the `id` from the function head into the record. We're not letting it assign the id automatically, so it stored `id` as new, which we've treated as a value. How should we fix this?

RUSTY: First, let's stop passing id to the populate_record functions altogether. We'll start in nnote_db_mnesia, and work from there:

Listing 10.63 (⇒ $) **Remove id**

```
src/nnote$ cd ../n_dbs
src/n_dbs$ vim nnote_db_mnesia.erl
...
populate_record([id, User_id, Date, Type, Event, Source,
    Topic, Question, Tags, Note]) ->
  #nnote{id = Id,
         user_id = User_id,
         date = Date,
         type = Type,
...
```

RUSTY: We don't have to make any changes to nnote_api:populate_record/1
since that's just a blind pass-thru to nnote_db_mnesia:populate_record/1.
So, we'll modify nnote_add_edit.erl and remove the ID item from pop-
ulate_record:

Listing 10.64 (⇒ $) **Tweak nnote_add_edit:save/3**

```
src/n_dbs$ cd ../nnote
src/nnote$ vim nnote_add_edit.erl
...
save(ID, UserID, NoteType) ->
  Params = wf:mq([date, event, source, topic, question, tags, note]),
  Params2 = [ID, UserID, NoteType | Params],
  Record = nnote_api:populate_record(Params2),
    ...
```

RUSTY: ...then use nnote_api:id/2 to manually specify the record ID for
pre-existing records:

371

Listing 10.65 ($\Rightarrow$ vim) **More Tweaks**

```
. . .
Params2 = [UserID, NoteType | Params],
Record = nnote_api:populate_record(Params2),
Record2 = case ID of
    "new" -> Record;
    _ -> nnote_api:id(Record, ID)
end,
nnote_api:put_record(Record Record2),
Redirect = ["/nnote", "?",
    wf:to_qs([{note_type, NoteType} ]) ],
wf:redirect(Redirect).
```

RUSTY: Since we've polluted our database a bit, let's delete that test item, and the old value we added way back when we first tested our database. We can do it directly from the Erlang shell:[17]

Listing 10.66 ($\Rightarrow$ >) **Delete bad item (Erlang Shell)**

```
16> nnote_api:delete("new").
ok
17> nnote_api:delete("1").
ok
18> nnote_api:get_all().
[]
```

RUSTY: Let's try it again now with those changes in place. Add a new conference note, then search for it. Does it work?

MARSHA: It does!

---

[17]If results show in the return of get_all(), they're just test data left over from previous tests. The important thing is that no results have the ID "new".

RUSTY: And clicking "edit" takes you to the proper note with all the information?

MARSHA: It does!

RUSTY: Great!

10.15.4. Debugging Validators

MARSHA: Now when I tried to save an idea it wouldn't save.

RUSTY: Did you try an io:format statement in the postback event to prove the postback actually made it to the server?

MARSHA: What do you mean?

RUSTY: Like this:

```
%% **************************************************
%% Content events
%% **************************************************
event({save_note, ID, UserID, NoteType}) ->
    io:format("Save~n"),
    wf:wire(#confirm{text="Save?",
                     postback={confirm_save, ID, UserID, NoteType}});
```

Listing 10.67 (⇒ vim) **Debug with** io:format/1 (nnote_add_edit)

RUSTY: Save again and tell me if the io:format statement shows up in the Erlang console.

MARSHA: Nothing.

RUSTY: Oh, wait... I think I see the problem.

We have show_if statements in the add/edit form to conditionally show certain form fields, right?

MARSHA: We do—event, source, and question fields.

RUSTY: OK—we have validators on the "event" and "source" fields.

OLEG: Uh oh—I smell a rat.

RUSTY: Or a bug, at least. First, the system draws the add/edit field. Then the wf:defer functions look for event, source, and question fields so they can wire the validators to them.

MARSHA: But the forms don't display event or source fields. So—

RUSTY: One or the other throws an error.

OLEG: So why doesn't the system crash?

RUSTY: This is actually a client-side error, so there is a crash, but it's not on the Erlang console. Press CTRL+SHIFT+I in the browser. This should bring up developer tools. Then click the "Console" tab:

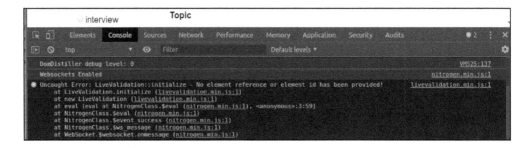

MARSHA: Oh, there's an error there about LiveValidation.

RUSTY: Alas, there is! Javascript crashed while trying to validate values for fields that aren't there.

MARSHA: So what can we do about it?

RUSTY: The trick here is to make sure we're validating only on fields that exist. We could just wrap them in case expressions, but there's a slightly more concise method. If you've coded in C, PHP, or Ruby,[18] you might be familiar with the concept of the "Ternary If," "Inline If," or just the ?: syntax in some languages.

MARSHA: Yeah. Does Erlang have that too?

RUSTY: Nope! But Nitrogen provides a simple macro for it: ?WF_IF. It works like:

```
?WF_IF(TrueOrFalse, DoIfTrue, DoIfFalse).
```

RUSTY: It's equivalent to:

```
case TrueOrFalse of
    true -> DoIfTrue;
    false -> DoIfFalse
end.
```

RUSTY: You can also leave off the DoIfFalse clause like this:

```
?WF_IF(TrueOrFalse, DoIfTrue).
```

RUSTY: ...which works like this:

```
case TrueOrFalse of
    true -> DoIfTrue;
    false -> ""
end.
```

RUSTY: So, if my theory is right, we can do it like this:

---

[18]Or one of a couple dozen more programming languages: https://en.wikipedia.org/wiki/%3F:

Listing 10.68 (⇒ vim) **Use ?WF_IF/3**

```
form(ID, UserID, NoteType, Date, Event, Source,
     Topic, Question, Tags, Note) ->
  ...
  ?WF_IF(ShowEvent, wf:defer(save_note, event, #validate{validators=[
    #is_required{text="Event required"}]}) ),
  ?WF_IF(ShowSource, wf:defer(save_note, source, #validate{validators=[
    #is_required{text="Source required"}]}) ),
```

RUSTY: Give the page a reload and try saving again. Can you save your "idea" note?[19]

MARSHA: I can. It works!

RUSTY: Let's save this! Then for next week's club meeting we'll have a special guest.

10.16. Code Review with a Special Guest

RUSTY: Welcome back, everyone! As promised, this week we have a special guest, Paula Soiker. Paula is the organizer of our local Erlang User Group and was my mentor when I first got into programming. Last year, her Nitrogen-based web startup was acquired by MegaCorp, Inc. She's been working with them since, integrating her system into their larger product line.

I've asked Paula to review our nnotes code as if we were submitting it for review in a business environment.

Oleg: *Whispers to Stevie:* Oh oh...

---

[19] If the idea of a macro for this feels icky, you could alternatively take advantage of the fact that the andalso and orelse keyword operators both short-circuit. This would allow you to do this: ShowEvent andalso wf:defer(save_note, event, #validate{...}). That is, if ShowEvent evaluates to false, the whole expression short-circuits and just returns false without evaluating the expression on the right-hand side of andalso.

PAULA: Thanks for the kind introduction, Rusty! Before we get started—
questions anyone?

MARSHA: How long did you work on your project before it was acquired?

PAULA: Oh, let me think...Seven years I'd say. Time flies.

OLEG: How long have you been a programmer?

PAULA: Professionally? Twenty years now.

STEVIE: Wow! You must have seen amazing progress.

PAULA: I've seen programming trends rise and fall: hot languages, development
methodologies, and fancy libraries and frameworks.

What brings me back to Erlang is the consistency of the language and environment. Erlang is a rock-solid platform, and the language itself changes
slowly, so you're not constantly having to keep up with the Jones's. Also,
the friendly and intelligent community is amazing. There are world-class
computer scientists and programmers on the Erlang mailing lists.

OLEG: What's your absolute favorite thing about Erlang?

PAULA: Good question. I'd say Erlang processes—how quickly they can be
spawned, how no process can interfere with another's memory. Crashed
process don't take down the whole VM. I love that errors can be captured
and handled by the supervision system. The whole language and VM are
built around these concepts. It's beautiful in its cohesiveness. Every piece
just fits.

RUSTY: Thanks for that, Paula. You can see how passionate Paula is about
Erlang. So let's get to...

STEVIE: Wait, wait, one more question, please!

PAULA: Ask away!

STEVIE: What's your least favorite part about Erlang?

PAULA: Easily my least favorite thing is that Erlang is not more mainstream. I know that might sound like a bit of a cop-out, but one of the great benefits of working in a language like Javascript, Ruby, PHP, Python, C, C#, C++, or any of the other top 10 most used languages is that there are helper libraries for just about every task you want to do. Companies provide official libraries to interact with their services.

MARSHA: But not Erlang?

PAULA: Libraries are often left to the Erlang ecosystem to solve on its own. That said, it's getting better. The rebar3 build system is now able to compile Elixir packages alongside Erlang.[20]

RUSTY: So Paula, how can we improve our code?

10.16.1. Paula's critique

PAULA: Well first, let me say that you guys have put together an interesting project here. I like your use of behaviors. Your CRUD forms look good. You validate the values, retrieve them from postback, and store them in mnesia. Mnesia is not the most straightforward of database systems, so kudos to you for working through it!

MARSHA: It was fun!

Oleg: But...

PAULA: That said, if this were submitted by one of the my programmers, I'd be asking for revision. But keep in mind, every professional programmer I know revises first-draft code at least once or even several times. So...

MARSHA: We're all ears!

---

[20]https://www.rebar3.org/docs/using-available-plugins#section-elixir-dependencies

10.16.2. User Interface

PAULA: The most obvious problem, but easiest to fix, is that you never actually set up the "delete" postback event handler.

OLEG: Oh, I can handle that.

PAULA: Be a good idea. You set it up in `nnote_db_mnesia.erl`.

10.16.3. Dynamic Content

MARSHA: What's next.

PAULA: When you click either of the search buttons in `nnote.erl`, the entire `contents` element redraws. This is a two-fold problem.

MARSHA: How so?

PAULA: First, you lose the content of the search field. If you had a typo in your search string, say, then clicked "search," you wouldn't be able to make a quick correction. The field would be completely redrawn and reset. You'd have to type the whole search string all over again.

OLEG: How can we fix that?

PAULA: With Nitrogen you can selectively replace certain parts of the page when you update dynamic content. This means that search results, say, replace only a selected area of the page.

STEVIE: Makes sense.

PAULA: I'll show you. First, let's pull the case expression out of the `content/1` function:

Listing 10.69 (⇒ $) **Revise case expression** (`nnote.erl`)

```
nnote$ cd site/src/nnote
src/nnote$ vim nnote.erl
...
content(#{note_type:=NoteType, task:=Task}) ->
   Records = case Task of
      undefined -> undefined;
      search_by_tag -> tag_search(NoteType);
      search_by_date -> date_search(NoteType)
   end,
   Records = records_from_task(NoteType, Task),
   display_forms(NoteType, Records).

records_from_task(_, undefined) -> undefined;
records_from_task(NoteType, search_by_tag) -> tag_search(NoteType);
records_from_task(NoteType, search_by_date) -> date_search(NoteType).
```

PAULA: Then we'll wrap our `search_results` function with a `#panel` so we can update the contents on the fly:

Listing 10.70 (⇒ `vim`) **Update** `display_forms/2` (`nnote.erl`)

```
display_forms(NoteType, Records) ->
   [content_headline(),
    add_note_button(NoteType),
    search_by_tag(),
    search_by_date(),
    #panel{id=search_results, body=search_results(Records)}
   ].
```

PAULA: Change the search_by_tag and search_by_date events to update only the relevant part:

Listing 10.71 (⇒ vim) **Update the search events (nnote.erl)**

```
event(search_by_tag) ->
  NoteType = wf:q(note_type),
  Content = content(#{note_type=>NoteType, task=>search_by_tag}),
  Records = records_from_task(NoteType, search_by_tag),
  wf:update(content, Content);
  wf:update(search_results, search_results(Records));
event(search_by_date) ->
  NoteType = wf:q(note_type),
  Content = content(#{note_type=>NoteType, task=>search_by_date}),
  Records = records_from_task(NoteType, search_by_date),
  wf:update(content, Content);
  wf:update(search_results, search_results(Records));
```

STEVIE: Those two clauses look almost exactly the same except for one argument to the records_from_task function. Can that be condensed?

PAULA: Quick pupil you have here, Rusty!

RUSTY: Told ya!

PAULA: Stevie, is it? Yes, Stevie, that's the next step:

Listing 10.72 (⇒ vim) **Condense the search events (nnote.erl)**

```
event(search_by_tag) ->
event(SearchTask) when SearchTask==search_by_tag;
                       SearchTask==search_by_date ->
  NoteType = wf:q(note_type),
  Records = records_from_task(NoteType, search_by_tag SearchTask),
  wf:update(search_results, search_results(Records));
event(search_by_date) ->
  NoteType = wf:q(note_type),
  Records = records_from_task(NoteType, search_by_date),
  wf:update(search_results, search_results(Records));
```

PAULA: Nice! At this point, I'm pretty comfortable. Now when you click the search button search fields aren't blown away. You've also eliminated a fair bit of duplicated code.

10.16.4. A structural issue

PAULA: A structural issue is bothering me. We've already pulled the note_type from the URL, so rather than pulling that *again* when we search, we can include it in the postback:

```
display_forms(NoteType, Records) ->
  [content_headline(),
   add_note_button(NoteType),
   search_by_tag(NoteType),
   search_by_date(NoteType),
   #panel{id=search_results, body=search_results(Records)}
  ].
...
search_by_tag(NoteType) ->
  [#label{text="enter search words"},
   #textbox{id = search_words},
   #button{text="Search", postback={search_by_tag, NoteType}},
   #button{text="Info", postback={info, search_by_tag}}
  ].

search_by_date(NoteType) ->
  [#label{text="enter date"},
   n_dates:datepicker(search_date, ""),
   #button{text="Search", postback={search_by_date, NoteType}},
   #button{text="Info", postback={info, search_by_date}}
  ].
```

```
event({SearchTask, NoteType}) when SearchTask==search_by_tag;
                                   SearchTask==search_by_date ->
  NoteType = wf:q(note_type),
  Records = records_from_task(NoteType,SearchTask),
  wf:update(search_results, search_results(Records));
```

OLEG: I'm not sure I understand how that's better. You blew away one line of code, but inserted it in a whole bunch more places. Overall, it increased the number of keystrokes in our code.

PAULA: True. We did increase the number of keystrokes. But true to functional programming principles, we removed reliance on external "state."

Pulling the `note_type` from the URL is essential to the functionality of nnote. But we're *not* validating it. This means that a user could just enter `note_type=some_garbage` in our URL.

OLEG: And cause a crash.

PAULA: Right. In a real customer-facing application, you should never trust the user. You should validate, sanitize, or convert URL variables. But we want to minimize the number of validations. So we pass `NoteType` with the postback just as if we were calling a function.

OLEG: But what about keystrokes?

PAULA: Efficient programming is about more than saving keystrokes. Otherwise, all our variables and function names would be one or two characters long, and our programs would look like APL.[21] Programs must be maintained into the future—grokkable by other programmers. This means well-named functions, variables, and modules. But, it also means adopting common conventions when possible. Maintenance is inevitable. A big part of being an effective programmer is minimizing friction for maintenance, both for you *and* others.

MARSHA: I can see how the change improved readability.

PAULA: It did. Significantly. The `search_by_X` events now have their full context in the function definition. When a maintainer sees `event({SearchTask, NoteType})`, they don't have to figure out where `NoteType` is coming from. Compare that with `NoteType = wf:q(note_type)`. The programmer now has to ask: "Where is `note_type` coming from? Is it from the URL, or is it from a form field, and if so, where in the code is this form? Should this value be validated before working with it?"

These questions go away by including `NoteType` directly in the postback.

---

[21]`https://youtu.be/a9xAKttWgP4`

Circling back to keystrokes, duplicating work unnecessarily makes maintenance that much more difficult. If you have to make the same change in several places because you've copied and pasted code, you're wasting valuable time and cultivating bugs like a Petri dish.

Make sense?

OLEG: Whew! A lot of chew on.

PAULA: Sorry about the lecture, guys. But it comes from years of experience. Anyway, let's move on.

10.16.5. IDs

PAULA: I think your use of the Unix timestamp in your custom ID generation system is interesting. But I would rather add a timestamp to the record definition and use a large random number for the ID. Given your existing mechanism, there are two small tweaks I'd suggest. First, I'd add a much larger random number than $1,000,000,000$, after creating an ID then verify that the ID is unused. That is only feasible, however, in low-traffic environments. Secondly, if you do choose to use a large random number, you might want to adopt base36 or even base62.

STEVIE: Base36? What is base36 or base62?

PAULA: Base36 is like hexadecimal except that all A-Z characters are used instead of just A-F. Base62 continues that trend by making upper and lower-case characters have different value as well. For base62, you'll either need to get a library or roll your own converter. Base36, however, is built into Erlang, and you just need to change this in n_utils.erl:

Listing 10.75 (⇒ $) Base 16 to base 36 (n_utils.erl)

```
src/nnote$ cd ../n_libs
src/n_libs$ vim n_utils.erl
create_id() ->
```

```
    Rand = rand:uniform(1000000000),
    Seconds = qdate:unixtime(),
    GigaSeconds = Seconds * 1000000000,
    ID = GigaSeconds + Rand,
    integer_to_list(ID, 16 36).

id_created(ID) ->
    IntID = list_to_integer(ID, 16 36),
    Seconds = IntID div 1000000000,
    qdate:to_date(Seconds).
```

PAULA: That small change would shorten your IDs. I'd use the savings to increase the random number modifier from $1,000,000,000$ to something like 10^{30} or more. Your final IDs would have more characters but so much entropy that you'd never encounter a duplicate even if you made a million IDs per second. Finally, if you must have IDs that are strings, I'd be inclined to store them in the database as binaries rather than lists.

10.16.6. Data Type Issues

PAULA: One thing I've noticed is a heavy reliance on `strings` for things that should either be `atoms` or `integers`. You're treating NoteType as a string for instance. It's pulled from the URL query string in `n_common.erl` then jammed into a map. From there, it's either passed around in the map or retrieved with `wf:q()` and pattern matched without ever converting it to an atom. Erlang thrives on pattern matching, but string list matching is slow by comparison to atom matching. Internally, an atom is ultimately mapped to an integer lookup table, so a match on an atom is basically instant, while a string match must traverse the whole string.

Atoms and strings are different types. Static analysis tools like Dialyzer can warn you of a bug even before you run your code. With NoteType represented as a string throughout your application, however, Dialyzer will be kneecapped. Bugs related to invalid assignments of NoteType will be invisible.

MARSHA: We talked about Dialyzer, but didn't go into details.

PAULA: Dialyzer takes getting used to, but it will find bugs in your code. Even if you don't define the type specs, it can infer types just from code usage. But explicitly defining your type specs will really help to pinpoint bugs.

10.16.7. Date Formats

PAULA: Related— you're storing dates as a date string. I'd suggest storing dates and times as Unix timestamps. Timestamps are time zone neutral so you can easily convert from one time zone to another.

MARSHA: But we're not using times.

PAULA: You could store the date as a date tuple: {Year, Month, Day}. This would be a conventional format. The problem is that qdate needs more than just the date tuple.[22]

You can pull out the Date part when necessary like this:
{Date, _} = qdate:to_date(DateString):
If you absolutely must store the date as a string, be sure to use the ISO format: YYYY-MM-DD. This is an international standard format and easily parsed by basically everything.

10.16.8. The Map that's parsed and passed to each page

PAULA: This discussion has been leading up to a key issue. NoteType is a string but should really be an atom. IDs (Note IDs and User IDs) are currently strings, but we could be anything—strings, binaries, or integers. The key is that everything right now is a string. Except Task. The task argument is parsed as a string in n_common, but it's used in nnote.erl as an atom. This works. But by accident. Let's try. Load this page in the browser:

---

[22] A date tuple is {Year, Month, Day} while a now() tuple is {MegaSeconds, Seconds, MicroSeconds}. Both are 3-tuples and there's no safe way to distinquish one from the other. So qdate treats a 3-tuple as a now() tuple. To feed a Date tuple into qdate, just add midnight: {Date, {0,0,0}}.

```
localhost:8001/nnote?note_type=conference&task=search_by_tag
```

What do you think will happen?

OLEG: It would load the search page with no results because we haven't specified search values.

PAULA: That's certainly what it should do.

MARSHA: It doesn't though. It crashes.

⚠ **There was an error processing this page** ⚠

```
error:function_clause
------------------------
[{nnote,records_from_task,
        ["conference","search_by_tag"],
        [{file,"/home/gumm/www/nitrogen-git/nnote/site/src/nnote/nnote.erl"},
         {line,120}]},
 {nnote,content,1,
        [{file,"/home/gumm/www/nitrogen-git/nnote/site/src/nnote/nnote.erl"},
         {line,117}]},
 {n_common,content,0,
           [{file,"/home/gumm/www/nitrogen-git/nnote/site/src/n_libs/n_common.erl"},
            {line,25}]},
 {element_function,call_next_function,1,
                   [{file,"src/elements/other/element_function.erl"},
                    {line,35}]},
 {wf_render_elements,call_element_render,3,
                     [{file,"src/lib/wf_render_elements.erl"},{line,151}]},
 {wf_render_elements,prepare_and_render,3,
                     [{file,"src/lib/wf_render_elements.erl"},{line,120}]},
 {wf_render_elements,'-inner_render_elements/1-lc$^0/1-0-',1,
                     [{file,"src/lib/wf_render_elements.erl"},{line,40}]},
 {wf_render_elements,'-inner_render_elements/1-lc$^0/1-0-',1,
                     [{file,"src/lib/wf_render_elements.erl"},{line,40}]}]
```

STEVIE: In the code, it looks like it should work. That's the chunk you pulled out of content/1 and turned into the function records_from_task/2:

Listing 10.76 ($\Rightarrow$ `vim`) **Revisit** `nnote.erl`

```
records_from_task(_, undefined) -> undefined;
records_from_task(NoteType, search_by_tag) -> tag_search(NoteType);
records_from_task(NoteType, search_by_date) -> date_search(NoteType).
```

STEVIE: `search_by_tag` here and `search_by_tag` there. What am I missing?

MARSHA: The error message[23] says it's trying to match against the arguments (`"conference"`,`"search_by_tag"`). The second argument there is the string `"search_by_tag"`. But the actual second argument should be the *atom* `search_by_tag`, not a string.

STEVIE: Ohh, totally missed that.

PAULA: Exactly!

OLEG: So let's make a special case in `n_common:get_page_vars()` that looks for the task URL variable and converts it to an atom.

PAULA: Hang on. That would work. But not long-term. What if we allow *each page* to specify the type it wants each of its `url_vars()` to be? Like this:

Listing 10.77 ($\Rightarrow$ `$`) **Add type to** `url_vars` (`nnote.erl`)

```
src/n_libs$ cd ../nnote
src/nnote$ vim nnote.erl
...
url_vars() -> [id, note_type, {task, atom}].
```

---

[23]`{nnote, records_from_task, ["conference","search_by_tag"]...`

389

PAULA: Now we can just rework n_common:get_page_vars() to handle our new type tag. Any item in the list that's just an atom will be treated like a string, but if the item is a tuple, the second element specifies the type. This'll require a few more lines of code than just wf:q_map(), but it's gonna be pretty slick!

Listing 10.78 (⇒ $) **Handle new type (n_common:get_page_vars)**

```
src/nnote$ cd ../n_libs
src/n_libs$ vim n_common.erl
...
get_page_vars() ->
   Vars = ?PAGE:url_vars(),
   wf:q_map(Vars).
   lists:foldl(fun(Var, Map) ->
      {VarName, Value} = get_url_var(Var),
      maps:put(VarName, Value, Map)
   end, #{}, Vars).

get_url_var({Var, atom}) ->
   {Var, wf:to_existing_atom(wf:q(Var))};
get_url_var({Var, int}) ->
   {Var, wf:to_integer(wf:q(Var))};
get_url_var(Var) ->
   {Var, wf:q(Var)}.
```

OLEG: What is foldl?

RUSTY: Sorry Paula, we haven't covered folding.

PAULA: It's okay. Folding is a way to iterate over a list. But unlike lists:map, which returns a list with one item for each item passed in, folding has an accumulator that could be modified each iteration. If you were to do the above in an imperative-type language, the above lists:foldl might be done like this:

Example 10.4 Fold alternative - pseudocode

```
Map = [];
foreach(Var in Vars) {
  {VarName, Val} = get_url_var(Var);
  Map[VarName] = Val;
}
```

OLEG: Ohh, I get it. Not sure I could write one yet, but I get it.

PAULA: It takes getting used to. We start with an empty map (#{}), then iterate over every item in Vars. In each iteration, we update one key of Map (maps:put/3), then return that newly updated Map, passing it to the next iteration of the fold. When the iteration is complete, we return the fully filled-in Map.

MARSHA: So are we ready to run it? Any other changes?

PAULA: I think we're ready. Give the page a reload.

MARSHA: New error!

```
⚠ There was an error processing this page ⚠

error:{badmatch,
          {aborted,
              {badarg,
                  [{re,replace,
                      [undefined,"[..?!()-]",[],[global,{return,list}]],
                      [{file,"re.erl"},{line,362}]},
                  {n_search,normalize,1,
                      [{file,
                           "/home/gumm/www/nitrogen-git/nnote/site/src/n_libs/n_search.erl"},
                       {line,17}]},
                  {n_search,unique_words_from_string,1,
                      [{file,
                           "/home/gumm/www/nitrogen-git/nnote/site/src/n_libs/n_search.erl"},
                       {line,12}]},
                  {n_search,filter,2,
                      [{file,
                           "/home/gumm/www/nitrogen-git/nnote/site/src/n_libs/n_search.erl"},
                       {line,22}]},
                  {nnote_db_mnesia,'-search/3-fun-13-',9,
                      [{file,
                           "/home/gumm/www/nitrogen-git/nnote/site/src/n_dbs/nnote_db_mnesia.erl"},
                       {line,145}]},
                  {qlc,collect,1,[{file,"qlc.erl"},{line,1367}]},
                  {qlc,eval,2,[{file,"qlc.erl"},{line,299}]},
                  {mnesia_tm,apply_fun,3,
                      [{file,"mnesia_tm.erl"},{line,836}]}]}}}
--------------------------
[{nnote_db_mnesia,search,3,
      [{file,"/home/gumm/www/nitrogen-git/nnote/site/src/n_dbs/nnote_db_mnesia.erl"},
       {line,148}]},
  {nnote,content,1,
      [{file,"/home/gumm/www/nitrogen-git/nnote/site/src/nnote/nnote.erl"},
       {line,117}]},
  {n_common,content,0,
      [{file,"/home/gumm/www/nitrogen-git/nnote/site/src/n_libs/n_common.erl"},
       {line,35}]}
```

OLEG: It's passing undefined into the n_search:normalize/1 function. How? That never happened before.

PAULA: If you dig into the error, you'll see it highlights nnote_db_mnesia:search as one of the functions. Remember when we run the search_by_tag task, we're doing wf:q(search_words), except we haven't submitted anything, since this is the initial page load, so wf:q(search_words) returns undefined.

MARSHA: So we want to tell nnote_db_mnesia:search to return immediately with an empty list if SearchList is undefined?

PAULA: Check!

Listing 10.79 (⇒ $) Fix the crash in nnote_db_mnesia.erl

```
src/n_libs$ cd ../n_dbs
src/n_dbs$ vim nnote_db_mnesia.erl
...
search(_, _, undefined) -> [];
search(UserID, NoteType, SearchList) ->
   Query = fun() ->
            qlc:eval( qlc:q(
...
```

PAULA: Try it now!

MARSHA: Works!

PAULA: Perfect!

STEVIE: With all you've said about NoteType not being an atom we could also replace note_type with {note_type, atom} in url_vars(), couldn't we? That would make NoteType an atom by default.

PAULA: Absolutely. It's the right move, but it would require a fair bit to rework all the functions that rely on NoteType being a string. nnote_add_edit.erl, in particular, has all those functions that change labels or toggle certain fields—those are all assuming NoteType is a string. I'll leave that up to you to fix it—it's a lot of little changes, but they are easy.

MARSHA: Ah, Ms. Soiker, I noticed that you added an int converter to the url_page_vars(). Is that just in case we wanted to convert URL variables to integers automatically?

PAULA: Precisely!

10.16.9. Hard-coded NoteTypes

OLEG: Wow. So many issues. We must have really screwed up.

PAULA: No. You did well. nnote is not a simple program. No programmer I know nails it on first draft. But we do still have a few issues.

OLEG: Sock it to us.

PAULA: NoteType is the common denominator between the two main nnote pages. The definition of side_menu shows up in both nnote.erl and nnote_add_edit.erl. Looks like it's copy-and-pasted. What happens if you decide to add another note type?

MARSHA: Add it to both pages?

PAULA: Okay. But suppose we add more pages with sidebars to nnote?

MARSHA: Got it. Maybe we need to define side_menu in a new module.

PAULA: Moving the definition to n_menus would certainly simplify future maintenance or modifications. But there's another problem.

OLEG: (*Mutters*) Of course there is. Always is.

STEVIE: Don't mind Oleg. Cranky is his middle name.

PAULA: (*Smiles*) Take a look at `side_menu("NOTE TYPE")`. If you want to change the text on the screen from `"NOTE TYPE"` to anything else, you'll have to edit the function definition to match. That's fragile code: easy to break and Dialyzer won't catch it. Fact is, you're not really using the parameter so it should just be its own function. Something like `n_menus:note_type_side_menu()`, dropping the parameter altogether.

Want to try?

STEVIE: Can I?

PAULA: Of course!

STEVIE: First, make a new function in n_menus called `note_type_side_menu()` and paste into the same body as the `side_menu/1` function from `nnote.erl`:

Listing 10.80 (⇒ $) **Add `note_type_side_menu()` to `n_menus.erl`**

```
src/n_dbs$ cd ../n_libs
src/n_libs$ vim n_menus.erl
...
%% ******************************************************
%% Sidebar menus
%% ******************************************************
note_type_side_menu() ->
    [{"conference",{select,"conference"}},
     {"idea", {select,"idea"}},
     {"interview", {select,"interview"}},
     {"lab", {select,"lab"}},
     {"lecture", {select,"lecture"}},
     {"research", {select,"research"}},
     {"web", {select,"web"}}
    ].

show_menu_item(MenuItem, Selected) ->
    ...
```

STEVIE: Then I'll blow away the `side_menu()` functions from both `nnote.erl`
and `nnote_add_edit.erl`:

Listing 10.81 (⇒ $) Delete `side_menu()`

```
src/n_libs$ cd ../nnote
src/nnote$ vim nnote.erl
...
%% ***************************************************
%% Sidebar menus
%% ***************************************************
side_menu("NOTE TYPE") ->
    [{"conference",{select,"conference"}},
     {"idea", {select,"idea"}},
     {"interview", {select,"interview"}},
     {"lab", {select,"lab"}},
     {"lecture", {select,"lecture"}},
     {"research", {select,"research"}},
     {"web", {select,"web"}}
    ].
...
show_side_menu(Menu, Selected) ->
    [#h4{class=select, text=Menu},
     [n_menus:show_menu_item(MenuItem, Selected) ||
      MenuItem <- side_menu(Menu) n_menus:note_type_side_menu()]
    ].
```

Listing 10.82 (⇒ $) More deletions (`nnote_add_edit.erl`)

```
src/nnote$ vim nnote_add_edit.erl
...
%% ***************************************************
%% Sidebar menus
%% ***************************************************
side_menu("NOTE TYPE") ->
    [{"conference",{select,"conference"}},
     {"idea", {select,"idea"}},
```

```
  {"interview", {select,"interview"}},
  {"lab", {select,"lab"}},
  {"lecture", {select,"lecture"}},
  {"research", {select,"research"}},
  {"web", {select,"web"}}
].
  ...
show_side_menu(Menu, Selected) ->
  [#h4{class=select, text=Menu},
   [n_menus:show_menu_item(MenuItem, Selected) ||
    MenuItem <- side_menu(Menu) n_menus:note_type_side_menu()]
  ].
```

STEVIE: That should be it, I think.

OLEG: Checked and working.

PAULA: So, Stevie. want a job?

10.16.10. Passing Lists of Values for Records

PAULA: This last issue I see could be a maintenance nightmare. The code in its current form *works*. But it is a maintenance disaster waiting to happen. Problem is, you've tightly coupled nnote_db_mnesia:get_all_values() functions and nnote_db_mnesia:populate_record() functions to the specific definition of the #nnote record.

OLEG: I'm confuzzled.

PAULA: Say we decide to change the order of fields in our #nnote record definition. What will happen to nnote_db_mnesia:get_all_values()?

OLEG: It will return items in a different order.

PAULA: And what relies on that?

OLEG: Oh, of course, the values to put in the form in nnote_add_edit.erl.

PAULA: Exactly.

OLEG: That's not that bad, though.

PAULA: Well what happens to the `nnote_db_mnesia:populate_record()` function?

OLEG: We'd have to update the order of the items in the function head, I guess.

PAULA: Seeing it yet?

OLEG: Not really. These are all easy fixes.

PAULA: Fair enough. So say you change the order of items in `populate_record()`. Which other functions call `populate_record()`?

OLEG: `nnote_add_edit.erl`. When we save.

PAULA: Precisely.

OLEG: Still, that's also not a hard thing to do.

PAULA: Well, so far I haven't been specific. Let's look at two snippets of code to nail this down. First, let's look at the definition of the #nnote record:

Listing 10.83 (⇒ vim) **#nnote definition in nnote_db_mnesia.erl**

```
-record(nnote, {
    id = n_utils:create_id(),
    user_id,
    type,
    date,
    event,
    source,
    topic,
    question,
    tags,
    note
}).
```

PAULA: ...then save/3 from nnote_add_edit.erl:

Listing 10.84 (⇒ vim) nnote_add_edit:save/3

```
save(ID, UserID, NoteType) ->
   Params = wf:mq([date, event, source, topic, question, tags, note]),
   Params2 = [UserID, NoteType | Params],
   Record = nnote_api:populate_record(Params2),
   Record2 = case ID of
      "new" -> Record;
      _ -> nnote_api:id(Record, ID)
   end,
   nnote_api:put_record(Record2),
   Redirect = ["/nnote", "?",
               wf:to_qs([{note_type, NoteType} ]) ],
   wf:redirect(Redirect).
```

PAULA: Now, with those bits of code on the screen, let's consider a concrete example. What if we decided to swap the order of the type and date fields in the #nnote definition? What would we need to do in nnote_add_edit:save/3?

OLEG: Okay, so, uh...Oh. That'd be a mess. Umm, I'm actually not sure what to do here.

STEVIE: We'd have to peel off the Date field from the beginning of the return value of wf:mq(), then re-insert it into Params2 before NoteType, kinda like this: [Date|Params] = wf:mq([...]).

PAULA: That works.

OLEG: That was trickier, but Stevie figured it out in like five seconds, so it can't be that bad. Honestly though, how frequently are we going to be re-ordering the fields of our record?

PAULA: Once it's in production, probably not frequently—maybe never. But during development, it'll happen fairly often. And having to make simple changes in multiple modules every time you redefine the record definition? That will slow you to a crawl. However, the same problems arise if we decide to add a field to the record, don't they?

OLEG: Guess so.

STEVIE: For sure! If we're adding new features later, we're no doubt going to add new fields.

PAULA: And that's the looming threat of this inefficiency. Making changes that requires changing lots of code and the code it relies on and fixing the bugs you're likely to introduce will ruin your day. So what about n_utils:draw_link(Record)? It uses an #nnote record as well:

Listing 10.85 (⇨ vim) n_utils:draw_link **refresher**

```
draw_link(Record) ->
    ID = nnote_api:id(Record),
    NoteType = nnote_api:type(Record),
    Date = nnote_api:date(Record),
    Topic = nnote_api:topic(Record),
    EditUrl = ["/nnote/add_edit?",
                wf:to_qs([{id, ID}, {note_type, NoteType}])],
    Menuid = wf:temp_id(),
    [
        #link {
            body = [Date, " ", "&#8212;", " ", Topic],
            click=#toggle{target=Menuid}
        },
        #panel{id=Menuid, style="display:none", body=[
            #link {text="edit", url=EditUrl},
            " | ",
            #link {text="delete", postback={delete, ID}}
        ]},
        #br{}
    ].
```

OLEG: It doesn't look like we need to change anything there. I don't get it. Is there something to change?

MARSHA: Oleg! Don't you see? That's the point she's making! There is a way to build it *without* having to know the order of the fields in the #nnote record. `draw_link()` works regardless of the record definition.

PAULA: Slam dunk, Marsha!

STEVIE: So should we use setters and getters for all the values in the Record? Like we do in `draw_link()`?

PAULA: Not necessarily. Consider the `dict` module.

STEVIE: `dict`?

PAULA: Short for dictionary.[24] Another key-value data structure, similar to a map. You can make a new dict with `dict:new()`, add key-value pairing with `dict:store(Key, Value, Dict)`, and retrieve a value with `dict:find(Key, Dict)`. Internally, a `dict` is actually just a record, but you never interact directly with the record itself, nor do you care about the order of the fields, or even which fields it has at all. I don't even have to know the fields of a `dict` record. All that matters to me is that it works when I call the `dict` functions. I don't care at all about the internal implementation of `dict`.

MARSHA: That's super interesting.

PAULA: I'm glad you think so! But again, calling `dict:store()` a bunch of times is not the only way to populate one. You can also create a new, fully-populated dict with `dict:from_list(List)`. Here List is a proplist of key-values.

MARSHA: And I bet it has the opposite, a `dict:to_list()` function as well?

---

[24]`https://erlang.org/doc/man/dict.html`

PAULA: Right, Marsha! So my primary beef is not that your code depends on the field names from your database (which is largely unavoidable in a CRUD-type application), but that your code is *heavily* dependent on the *internal* implementation of #nnote, particularly the field order.

OLEG: Ooooookay, I think I get it.

PAULA: Excellent! My proposal is to eliminate populate_record() while adding conversion functions: convert an #nnote record to a map, and back, and call these new functions record_to_map(Record) and map_to_record(Map). Using this, make sure to update nnote_add_edit to use both of these.

MARSHA: That will require quite a bit of rewriting.

PAULA: But it'll save you countless hours in the future. And your application will be far more easily expanded and maintained! I'll leave the implementation of this up to you. But I'll send you my revisions tomorrow so you can see how I'd do it.

10.16.11. Thoughts on the Facade

PAULA: I have one final thought for your project, and it's about your nnote_api module.

RUSTY: We've been calling it a *facade*, as an entry point to the database.

PAULA: Okay, sure. For now, I'd probably just ditch the facade. As written, it doesn't do anything except redirect calls to nnote_db_mnesia.

MARSHA: But we've been doing that in case we change the database backend.

PAULA: Interesting. I see how that might be useful as a learning tool. But, in production you almost never change your backend database. That's a huge undertaking—so much code rewrite that your facade module won't be of help. If you don't like how long the module name is for nnote_db_mnesia, it'd probably just be worth renaming nnote_db_mnesia to a shorter name, even just nnote_db.

You could add the `erlias`[25] dependency to make an alias module from `nnote_db_mnesia` to `nnote_api` if you want to stick with the facade by calling `erlias:build(nnote_api, nnote_db_mnesia)`. This library can automatically create the `nnote_api` module exactly as written, but you don't have to write or maintain any code.

10.16.12. That's All for Now

RUSTY: Well, it's 4:30, time to wrap up.

PAULA: Thanks a lot for having me. Rusty, you've got some bright young minds here. I'm so glad to see you steering them toward Erlang!

MARSHA: Thanks, this was illuminating.

OLEG: Yeah—most excellent!

STEVIE: Yes, thanks Ms. Soiker, this was wonderful.

PAULA: Ms. Soiker is my mother. Call me Paula.

STEVIE: Thanks Paula!

RUSTY: Yes, Thanks Paula! As always, you're a beacon of light!

PAULA: Aww, thanks Rusty! And you guys are welcome to join and attend our Erlang User Group any time you like.

10.17. Homework

If you want a shortcut to the state of the nnotes before the homework section, you can get it with:

---

[25]https://github.com/choptastic/erlias

Example 10.5 (⇒ $) Download a mostly finished nnotes

`$ git clone -b end_chapter_10 git://github.com/BuildItWithNitrogen/nnote`

1. Implement the "delete note" feature we forgot to add.

   Solution: https://github.com/BuildItWithNitrogen/nnote/commit/5bf9c7

2. Convert all date string formats in nnote.erl, nnote_add_edit.erl, and n_dates.erl from ISO Format (YYYY-MM-DD) to either an American format (MM/DD/YYYY) or a more worldly format: (DD-MM-YYYY). It's your choice. Hint: American format should use slashes (/) and the European should use dashes (-) as delimiters. The qdate parser engine[26] uses those delimiters to figure out which format is which.

   Solution: https://github.com/BuildItWithNitrogen/nnote/commit/311a79

3. Rework the storage system for our note dates to store dates in the database either with the ISO format string ("YYYY-MM-DD") or a date tuple ({Y,M,D}). Your call.

   Solution: https://github.com/BuildItWithNitrogen/nnote/commit/d0cfa1

4. Update the url_vars() functions so that NoteType is universally converted to an atom. Make sure all pages and related source properly handle the newly atomized NoteType values.

   Note: After this problem is solved, your previously stored notes will likely not show up when you search. This is because the new NoteTypes are atoms, while the old NoteTypes are strings.

   Solution: https://github.com/BuildItWithNitrogen/nnote/commit/f908f9

5. Eliminate the nnote_api.erl file by adding erlias as a dependency, then, during Nitrogen's startup, establishing an alias from nnote_api to nnote_db_mnesia.

---

[26]qdate's parsing engine is ec_date from Erlware Commons: https://github.com/erlware/erlware_commons

Get Erlias from `https://github.com/choptastic/erlias`.

Solution: `https://github.com/BuildItWithNitrogen/nnote/commit/b8de31`

6. Rework save and retrieve functions from the current method to passing maps instead. To do this, make two new functions in `nnote_db_mnesia.erl`: `record_to_map(Record)` which converts an #nnote record to a map, and `map_to_record()` which does the reverse. Next remove `populate_record()` from `nnote_db_mnesia`. Finally, update any code in `nnote_add_edit.erl` that previously relied on `get_all_values()` and `populate_record()` to use the new functions. The use of `get_all_values()` in `n_search.erl` can stay.

Solution: `https://github.com/BuildItWithNitrogen/nnote/commit/691031`

Follow-up: `https://github.com/BuildItWithNitrogen/nnote/commit/f2ddbd` – This modifiction to the first solution does not require the `record_to_maps()` functionality at all.

11. Simple Login

Note: This chapter uses code from the last homework assignment in Chapter 10. If you haven't done that problem (saving using `map_to_record()`*), you can get the code here:*

Listing 11.1 (⇒ $) **Download an up-to-date nnotes**

```
~$ git clone -b end_chapter_10_hw git://github.com/BuildItWithNitrogen/nnote
...
~$ cd nnote
~/nnote$ make
...
```

MARSHA: Obi-Wan—we've been talking. If we put our productivity suite online, we don't want just anyone mucking about in our private notes.

OLEG: Especially my little sister.

STEVIE: We need login.

OLEG: Access control.

RUSTY: So, let's build it.

MARSHA: Now, you mean?

11.1. Bird's Eye View

RUSTY: Why not? It's simply a matter of determining who gets to see what.

OLEG: Oh, is that all.

RUSTY: Well, we could get fancy and design in user roles and access groups.[1] And we could implement two-factor authentication[2] or OAuth.[3] Or we could require biometric authentication.[4]

OLEG: Oh, brother.

RUSTY: But we'll keep it simple.

OLEG: I'm relieved.

RUSTY: There's not much here that you haven't been through a jillion times. First, you register a username and password. Next, to access the site, you enter your user name and password into a form.

MARSHA: So we need a registration form and a table in our database to store usernames and passwords. That shouldn't be hard.

STEVIE: Hey, piece of cake. We can morph `index.erl`.

MARSHA: The login stuff should be simple—a form to enter username and password; a table look-up function to see if they match. Am I right?

RUSTY: More or less.

OLEG: It's the less part that worries me.

RUSTY: Well, how do we determine which pages are public and which private?

STEVIE: Hmmm—

RUSTY: What happens if someone gains access to our database and downloads all the passwords?

---

[1] https://en.wikipedia.org/wiki/Role-based_access_control
[2] https://en.wikipedia.org/wiki/Multi-factor_authentication
[3] https://en.wikipedia.org/wiki/OAuth
[4] https://en.wikipedia.org/wiki/Biometrics

OLEG: Kill 'em.

RUSTY: Gotta catch 'em.

STEVIE: I've read that cyber crime is a trillion-dollar-a-year business.

OLEG: If you believe the security firms.

RUSTY: Seriously, cyber crime *is* serious business.

MARSHA: So, jabber jabber guys, but I have a dance lesson at six.

RUSTY: Righto. To set the stage, let me show you an easy way to distinguish public pages from private.

11.2. More Things to Behave

RUSTY: Let's assume that `index.erl` is a public page, that is, no login required. We can make a function to declare that:

Listing 11.2 (⇒ `vim`) **Define public page (`index.erl`)**

```
~/nnote$ cd site/src
.../site/src$ vim index.erl

url_vars() -> [id, record_type, task].

access() -> public.
```

RUSTY: On the other hand, we no doubt want users to log in before they can access our productivity tools so in `nnote.erl` we instantiate access/0 as private:

Listing 11.3 (⇒ vim) **Define access-controlled page (nnote.erl)**

```
.../site/src$ cd nnote
.../src/nnote$ vim nnote.erl

url_vars() -> [id, note_type, task, atom].

access() -> private.
```

RUSTY: ...and save.

STEVIE: So we need to define access on every page.

RUSTY: Bear with me. We'll get there. The next issue is to determine whether or not a user is logged in. We don't need anything all that special for that, we'll just use the built-in `wf:user()` function.

OLEG: How does `wf:user()` know if the user is logged in?

RUSTY: When a user logs in, we set a Nitrogen authentication variable by declaring `wf:user(User)`. We call `wf:user()` to authenticate the user. For a logged in user `wf:user()` will return the value we previously passed into it. Otherwise it returns `undefined`. This information is temporarily stored in the session and expires automatically if the user is idle for about 20 minutes. That time limit is configurable.

STEVIE: Ah, I get it. We'll call `access()` and `wf:user()` to either open the page or redirects to a login page.

RUSTY: Let me show you. First, we need to tell our n_apps behavior to expect an `access()` function on each page.

Listing 11.4 (⇒ vim) **Add `access()` to `n_apps.erl`**

```
.../src/nnote$ cd ..
.../src$ vim n_apps.erl
```

```
-compile(export_all).
-optional_callbacks([access/0]).

-callback main() -> body().

-callback access() -> private | public.
...
```

OLEG: Whoa, that's new. Optional callbacks, interesting.

MARSHA: And how do we actually handle the access() call?

RUSTY: Right in our n_common module. If you recall, the main() function in all our pages starts by calling n_common:template(), so let's handle it there. If the user should have access, we'll return the template, and if not, we'll redirect to a login page. So first save n_apps.erl, then:

Listing 11.5 (⇒ vim) **Add access control to n_common.erl**

```
.../src$ cd n_libs
.../src/n_libs$ vim n_common.erl

-define(TEMPLATE,"./site/templates/n_apps.html").

template() ->
    #template{file=?TEMPLATE}.
    Access = get_access(),
    case can_access(Access) of
       true -> #template{file=?TEMPLATE};
       false -> wf:redirect_to_login("/register")
    end.
```

OLEG: Straightforward so far. get_access() should call ?PAGE:access().

RUSTY: Yes, but with a slick little twist:

Listing 11.6 ($\Rightarrow$ `vim`) **Add access control to `n_common.erl`**

```
         false -> wf:redirect_to_login("/register")
      end.

get_access() ->
   case erlang:function_exported(?PAGE, access, 0) of
      true -> ?PAGE:access();
      false -> public
   end.
```

OLEG: Oh, dang! So that checks if the page actually defines the function before calling it?

RUSTY: Practically, yes. Technically, no. It checks if our page *exports* the function. If we had defined the function but not exported it, it would return `false`. But our page has `-compile(export_all)` so all functions are exported.

STEVIE: And if the page doesn't export `access/0`, we assume it's public.

RUSTY: Bingo! This, of course, is customizable. It's totally up to you how you want to handle it. No function exported could default to `private`. Up to you.

MARSHA: What's that zero that's the third argument of `function_exported/3`?

STEVIE: I'll bet that's the number of arguments in the `access` function.

MARSHA: Oh yeah, that would make sense.

RUSTY: Great deduction, Stevie. As a reminder, the word for the number of arguments is *arity*. Anyway, now we need a function to lock in our user access control system. We'll call it `can_access/0`. It will return `true` if we should have access and `false` if not:

Listing 11.7 ($\Rightarrow$ `vim`) **More access control to** `n_common.erl`

```
      false -> public
   end.

can_access(public) ->
   true;
can_access(private) ->
   wf:user()=/=undefined.
```

OLEG: Slick! public is always available, but private is only accessible if wf:user/0 isn't undefined.

STEVIE: So, just to confirm—we don't have to add an access/0 function to every page of our system?

RUSTY: Well, only the private pages. But no harm if it's added to public pages. In fact, I'd recommend adding it to every page, just to be explicit about who can access what. So let's save our work and click on "nnote" on the menu to see our new access control system at work.

11.3. Registration Page

MARSHA: On the topic of pages, I've created a new directory, copied over index.erl, and renamed it register.erl:

11. Simple Login

```
.../src/n_libs$ cd ..
.../site/src$ mkdir n_access
.../site/src$ cp index.erl n_access/register.erl
```

MARSHA: Now, presto chango, a little scaffolding for our registration page:

```
.../src$ cd n_access
.../site/n_access$ vim register.erl

-module(index register).

...
-define(MMSELECTED, "home").
-define(TITLE, "Welcome!" "Registration Page").
-define(TOP, "Build it with Nitrogen").

url_vars() -> [id, record_type, task].
```

MARSHA: We don't need the side menu. So I'll nix that, and the functions it
relies on:

```
side_menu("WEB SITE") ->
   [{"nitrogen", {goto, "http://nitrogenproject.com/"}},
    {"erlang", {goto, "http://erlang.org/doc/apps/stdlib/"}},
    {"hacker news", {goto, "https://news.ycombinator.com/"}}
   ].
...
```

```
sidebar(#{}) ->
    [
    #h3 {text="SELECT"},
    show_side_menu("WEB SITE", unselected)
    ].
...
show_side_menu(Menu, Selected) ->
    [ #h4 {class=select, text=Menu},
    [n_menus:show_menu_item(MenuItem, Selected) ||
    MenuItem <- side_menu(Menu)]
    ].
```

MARSHA: And, voilà, we're well on our way toward a registration page.

STEVIE: I presume we should delete greeting/0?

MARSHA: We'll replace the body of greeting/0 with a registration form.

STEVIE: We could just put the registration form directly in content/1. Less clutter in the source.

MARSHA: Granted. But suppose we have a reason to redraw the form. Would be real nice to just go wf:update(content, greeting()).

OLEG: Girl has a point.

STEVIE: Okay! I'm sold. Actually, greeting() is a pretty terrible name for a registration form. Let's rename it something more relevant, like say, new_account_form.

Now, after that wicked form we built in nnotes_add_edit.erl, the registration form should be a walk in the park:

Listing 11.11 (⇒ `vim`) **Define registration form**

```
content(#{}) ->
    greeting().
    new_account_form().

greeting() ->
    [#h2{class=content, text=["Welcome to ", n_utils:get_nickname(),
                             "'s ", "Nitrogen Applications!"]},
     #p{body = "Our motto: <em>Build it Fast with Nitrogen</em>"}
    ].

new_account_form() ->
    wf:defer(save, username, #validate{validators=[
        #is_required{text="Username Required"}]}),
    wf:defer(save, password, #validate{validators=[
        #is_required{text="Password Required"}]}),
    wf:defer(save, password2, #validate{validators=[
        #confirm_same{text="Passwords do not match",
                      confirm_id=password}]}),
    [#h1{text="Create Account"},
     #label{text="Username"},
     #textbox{id=username},
     #label{text="Password"},
     #password{id=password},
     #label{text="Confirm Password"},
     #password{id=password2},
     #br{},
     #button{id=save, text="Save Account", postback=save}
    ].
```

RUSTY: Bring up `localhost:8001/register`, Oleg. Let's see what we've got.

```
Build it with Nitrogen

home | nindex | nnote | Tips & Info

            Create Account

        Username

        _____

        Password

        _____

        Confirm Password

        _____

        [ Save Account ]
```

STEVIE: Awesome!

OLEG: But thinking ahead, shouldn't we snag the user's email address so we can implement password recovery?

OLEG: And maybe a link back to the homepage?

MARSHA: The main menu has a link back to the homepage already.

OLEG: Oh, yeah.

RUSTY: Now you're cookin', guys. Who wants to make the changes?

Listing 11.12 (⇒ vim) **Revise** `new_account_form/0` (`register.erl`)

```
new_account_form() ->
    wf:defer(save, username, #validate{validators=[
        #is_required{text="Username Required"}]}),
    wf:defer(save, email, #validate{validators=[
        #is_required{text="Email Required"}]}),
    ...
    #label{text="Username"},
    #textbox{id=username},
    #label{text="Email"},
```

415

```
    #textbox{id=email},
    ...
    #button{id=login, text="Save Account", postback=save},
].
```

RUSTY: Let's drop in some placeholders, too:

Listing 11.13 (⇒ vim) **Revise `new_account_form/0` (`register.erl`)**

```
new_account_form() ->
    ...
    #label{text="Username"},
    #textbox{id=username, placeholder="Your Username"},
    #label{text="Email"},
    #textbox{id=email, placeholder="your@email.com"},
    ...
].
```

STEVIE: Done. Now how does it look?

OLEG: *That*'s the way I like it!

RUSTY: I agree. What's next?

MARSHA: We need a save function.

RUSTY: We do. But we can't save passwords in clear text.

MARSHA: What does that mean?

RUSTY: We need to hash the passwords so they'll be protected if someone breaks into the database.

OLEG: Hash? Is that like encrypting them?

RUSTY: In a way. The big difference is that you can convert an encrypted string back into the original string. A hashed string, not so much.

STEVIE: How do we do that?

11.4. Rebar Dependency: `erlpass`

RUSTY: First, we need a decent hashing mechanism.[5]

MARSHA: Is that like—a Nitrogen element?

RUSTY: No. No. Think of it this way. Imagine throwing our password through a magic door.

OLEG: Here we go.

RUSTY: As it passes through the door, it's transformed in a way that makes it nearly impossible to recover it's original form.

MARSHA: Will it turn me into a beautiful princess?

OLEG: Sounds like some kind of quantum wave/particle experiment.

---

[5]More about proper password hashing and security on page 459

STEVIE: So we have a hashing function that magically transforms our password into something else. What good does that do us?

RUSTY: We can store the hashed value in the database without revealing the password itself.

STEVIE: I'm still confused.

RUSTY: Say the registered user decides to log in. She enters her password. We run that password through the hashing function and compare the result with the hash stored in the database.

OLEG: Oh clever clever. Where do we get this magic function?

RUSTY: There are a bunch of them, but my favorite is called bcrypt. And it's handled by an excellent third-party library called erlpass. We have to add it as a dependency to rebar.config, so let's kill the Nitrogen system (CTRL-C. then A):

Listing 11.14 (⇒ >) **Kill the Nitrogen system**

```
(nnote@127.0.0.1)15> q().
ok
~/nnote$
```

RUSTY: Now we open rebar.config and add the erlpass dependency:

Listing 11.15 (⇒ $) **Edit rebar.config**

```
nnote$ vim rebar.config
...
{deps, [
    {cowboy, {git, "git://github.com/ninenines/cowboy", {tag, "2.4.0"}}},
    {erlpass,  {git, "git://github.com/ferd/erlpass", {branch,  master}}},

...
```

RUSTY: Turns out that `erlpass` has a dependency of it's own—an Erlang application called `bcrypt`. It gets loaded along with `erlpass` but, since it's an application, it needs to be started before we can call it.

STEVIE: Started—how?

RUSTY: We could start it from the command line when we restart Nitrogen. But it's more convenient to let Nitrogen do the deed.

Open up `site/src/nitrogen_sup.erl` and you'll see a list of applications started by default. We're just going make sure erlpass and its dependencies start when we start the virtual machine.

Listing 11.16 (⇨ $) Open `nitrogen_sup.erl`

```
~/nnote$ vim site/src/nitrogen_sup.erl
...
init([]) ->
  n_mnesia:one_time(),
  erlias:build(nnote_db_mnesia, nnote_api),
  application:load(nitrogen_core),
  application:start(simple_cache),
  application:start(crypto),
  application:start(nprocreg),
  application:start(simple_bridge),
  application:ensure_all_started(erlpass),
  {ok, { {one_for_one, 5, 10}, []} }.
```

MARSHA: What exactly does `application:ensure_all_started/1` that do?

RUSTY: It traverses the dependency tree under `erlpass` and starts any of its dependencies, and any of its dependencies' dependencies, and so on. Once all of those are started, it starts `erlpass`.

A supervisor that doesn't supervise anything?

The Erlang veteran will notice that the supervisor above isn't actually supervising anything. Starting these apps would probably be better served in the `nitrogen_app.erl` file.

Nitrogen provides a blank supervisor for when you wish to create supervised servers. For example, perhaps you have an aggregation server as core part of your system. In this case, starting the apps as shown in Listing 11.16 works. Starting them in the `nitrogen_app.erl` file also works.

RUSTY: Finally, we need to recompile the system to bring in `erlpass` and its dependencies:

Listing 11.17 (⇒ $) Recompile

```
~/nnote$ make
~/nnote$ bin/nitrogen console
...
1> sync:go().
Starting Sync (Automatic Code Compiler / Reloader)
Scanning source files...
Growl notifications disabled
ok
```

RUSTY: And now—a quick test:

Listing 11.18 (⇒ >) Test password

```
2> MyHash = erlpass:hash("This is my password").
<<"$2a$12$wgnIVpAM2Pm.01EmaBP3Tu3F0ChVkZAanfVK.CNj5/8mphunXjYPS">>
```

OLEG: Whoa! That's a bucket of worms.

RUSTY: Odds are slim to nothing that a different text string will produce the same hash value. Now observe:

```
2> MyHash = erlpass:hash("This is my password").
<<"$2a$12$wgnIVpAM2Pm.01EmaBP3Tu3FOChVkZAanfVK.CNj5/8mphunXjYPS">>
3> erlpass:match("This is my password", MyHash).
true
4> erlpass:match("This isn't my password", MyHash).
false
```

STEVIE: Must be some gnarly math behind that puppy.

RUSTY: You could earn a PhD. But tell you what, Marsha's worried about her dance class. So, guys, up for a challenge?

OLEG: That being?

RUSTY: Before we can write a save event for our registration form we need a user account database. So I challenge you to see how fast you can morph nnote_db_mnesia.erl into account_db_mnesia.erl.

STEVIE: You're on!

11.5. User Accounts

OLEG: We can morph nnote_db_mnesia.erl:

```
...nnote$ cd site/src/n_dbs
...src/n_dbs$ cp nnote_db_mnesia.erl account_db_mnesia.erl
```

```
...src/n_dbs$ vim account_db_mnesia.erl
...
-module(nnote_db_mnesia account_db_mnesia).
```

MARSHA: Wait. We need to define a record structure.

RUSTY: Think you can do it?

MARSHA: Think so. I'll blow away the nnote record definition and make a new n_account record:

Listing 11.21 (⇒ vim) **Define record (**`account_db_mnesia.erl`**)**

```
-module(account_db_mnesia).
...
-record(n_account, {}
...
}).

-record(n_account, {
    id = n_utils:create_id(),
    username,
    email,
    date = qdate:unixtime(),
    pwhash
}).
```

STEVIE: There're no changes to the export list up through map_to_record/1 and record_to_map.

RUSTY: Nice.

We'll need two functions that you haven't seen before—new_account/2 and attempt_login/2.

OLEG: The man has a crystal ball.

RUSTY: Been down this path before:

Listing 11.22 (⇒ vim) **Exports** (`account_db_mnesia.erl`)

```
export([init_table/0,
    put_record/1,
    get_all_values/1,
    get_all/0,
    get_record/1,
    delete/1,
    map_to_record/1,
    record_to_map/1,
    get_records_by_type/2,
    get_records_by_date/3,
    search/3,
    id/1,
    user_id/1,
    date/1,
    type/1,
    event/1,
    source/1,
    topic/1,
    question/1,
    tags/1,
    note/1,
    id/2,
    user_id/2,
    date/2,
    type/2,
    event/2,
    source/2,
    topic/2,
    question/2,
    tags/2,
    note/2
    new_account/3,
    attempt_login/2,
```

STEVIE: We need to replace all field access functions, so we can bulk delete all the exports after `attempt_login/2` and replace with:

Listing 11.23 (⇒ vim) **Replace functions** (`account_db_mnesia.erl`)

```
    . . .
    attempt_login/2,
    id/1,
    username/1,
    email/1,
    date/1,
    pwhash/1,
    id/2,
    username/2,
    email/2,
    date/2,
    pwhash/2
]).
```

STEVIE: Let's make sure we've told mnesia which table we're using:

Listing 11.24 (⇒ vim) **Replace functions** (`account_db_mnesia.erl`)

```
-define(TABLE, n̶n̶o̶t̶e̶ n_account).
```

STEVIE: In the code, no need to change init_table(), put_record() or
   get_all_values(), get_all(), get_record() or delete().

MARSHA: That's a ton of code that was left in place from copy-and-paste.
   Shouldn't we move that to a general purpose library?

RUSTY: I'm so glad you noticed. You're completely right. Every one of those
   functions should be made more general. For now, let's just get an understanding of our authentication system. You can refactor to eliminate the
   copy-and-paste for homework.

MARSHA: Sounds good. map_to_record/1 and record_to_map/1 should both
   specify the new record:

Listing 11.25 (⇒ vim) **Revise functions** (`account_db_mnesia.erl`)

```
map_to_record(Map) ->
  n_utils:map_to_record(#nnote{} #n_account{},
                        record_info(fields, nnote n_account), Map).

record_to_map(Record) ->
  n_utils:record_to_map(Record,
                        record_info(fields, nnote n_account)).
```

MARSHA: And we can blow away get_records_by_type(), get_records_by_date(), and search().

RUSTY: Ya know what, keep get_records_by_type() around. We're going to cannibalize it. But axe the others you mentioned:

Listing 11.26 (⇒ vim) **Blow away copied functions** (`account_db_mnesia.erl`)

```
get_records_by_type(UserID, Type) ->
  ...
  Results.
  {atomic, Results} = mnesia:transaction(Query),

get_records_by_date(UserID, Type, Date) ->
  ...
  {atomic, Results} = mnesia:transaction(Query),
  Results.

search(_, _, undefined) -> [];
search(UserID, NoteType, SearchList) ->
  ...
  {atomic, Results} = mnesia:transaction(Query),
  Results.
```

MARSHA: Done.

RUSTY: And now, to speed things along, let me define new_account/3 and
attempt_login/2:

Listing 11.27 (⇒ vim) **Define** new_account/3 **and** attempt_login/2
(account_db_mnesia.erl)

```
get_records_by_type(UserID, Type) ->
...
new_account(Username, Email, Password) ->
   PWHash = erlpass:hash(Password),
   Record = #n_account{username=Username,
                       email=Email,
                       pwhash=PWHash},
   put_record(Record),
   Record.

attempt_login(UserName, Password) ->
   Records = get_records_by_username(UserName),
   case Records of
      [] -> undefined;
      [Record] ->
         PWHash = Record#n_account.pwhash,
         case erlpass:match(Password, PWHash) of
            false -> undefined;
            true -> Record
          end
   end.
```

RUSTY: Now I'm going to rework the get_records_by_type() function.

MARSHA: I bet you're converting it to get_records_by_username().

RUSTY: Your intuition serves you well:

Listing 11.28 (⇒ vim) **Make get_records_by_username()** (`account_db_mnesia.erl`)

```
get_records_by_type(UserID, Type) ->
get_records_by_username(Username) ->
  Query = fun() ->
    qlc:eval( qlc:q(
        [Record || Record <- mnesia:table(?TABLE),
                        Record#nnote.id == UserID,
                        Record#nnote.type == Type]
                        Record#n_account.username == Username]
    ))
  end,
  atomic, Results = mnesia:transaction(Query),
  Results.
```

RUSTY: Note that `attempt_login/2` is the workhorse of our login system. It matches the hash value entered by the user at login with the stored hash value. It returns the match `#n_account` record if it succeeds and `undefined` if there is no matching username and password.

OLEG: Hey! I could've done that.

STEVIE: In a million years.

RUSTY: So, Oleg, maybe then you can replace all the setters and getters.

Listing 11.29 (⇒ vim) **Blow away getters and setters** (`account_db_mnesia.erl`)

```
%% GETTERS
id(Record) -> Record#nnote.id.
user_id(Record) -> Record#nnote.user_id.
date(Record) -> Record#nnote.date.
type(Record) -> Record#nnote.type.
event(Record) -> Record#nnote.event.
```

```
source(Record) -> Record#nnote.source.
topic(Record) -> Record#nnote.topic.
question(Record) -> Record#nnote.question.
tags(Record) -> Record#nnote.tags.
note(Record) -> Record#nnote.note.

%% SETTERS
id(Record, ID) ->
  Record#nnote{id=ID}.
user_id(Record, UserID) ->
  Record#nnote{user_id=UserID}.
date(Record, Date) ->
  Record#nnote{date=Date}.
type(Record, Type) ->
  Record#nnote{type=Type}.
event(Record, Event) ->
  Record#nnote{event=Event}.
source(Record, Source) ->
  Record#nnote{source=Source}.
topic(Record, Topic) ->
  Record#nnote{topic=Topic}.
question(Record, Question) ->
  Record#nnote{question=Question}.
tags(Record, Tags) ->
  Record#nnote{tags=Tags}.
note(Record, Note) ->
  Record#nnote{note=Note}.
```

MARSHA: Done it already.

OLEG: Whoa! Speed demon.

MARSHA: Took me two minutes:

Listing 11.30 (⇒ vim) **Replace functions** (`account_db_mnesia.erl`)

```erlang
%% GETTERS
id(Record) ->
    Record#n_account.id.
username(Record) ->
    Record#n_account.username.
email(Record) ->
    Record#n_account.email.
date(Record) ->
    Record#n_account.date.
pwhash(Record) ->
    Record#n_account.pwhash.

%% SETTERS
id(Record, ID) ->
    Record#n_account{id=ID}.
username(Record, Username) ->
    Record#n_account{username=Username}.
email(Record, Email) ->
    Record#n_account{email=Email}.
date(Record, Date) ->
    Record#n_account{date=Date}.
pwhash(Record, PWHash) ->
    Record#n_account{pwhash=PWHash}.
```

RUSTY: So what's our total time?

OLEG: Twelve minutes 14 seconds.

STEVIE: Smokin'!

OLEG: Yeah, but maybe we should test before we claim bragging rights.

RUSTY: Give it a go:

Listing 11.31 (⇒ >) **Test accounts in database**

```
26> account_db_mnesia:init_table().
{atomic,ok}
27> account_db_mnesia:get_all().
[]
28> account_db_mnesia:new_account("rusty","rusty@example.com","mypassword").
{n_account,"C24NXXAVX2DP","rusty","rusty@example.com",
1587246546,
<<"$2a$12$qn9b3FGn4LtzKawSXetKwuhax7uW8T0km.w.AW2jmZ2aCZylaMMey">>}
29> account_db_mnesia:get_all().
[{n_account,"C24NXXAVX2DP","rusty","rusty@example.com",
1587246546,
<<"$2a$12$qn9b3FGn4LtzKawSXetKwuhax7uW8T0km.w.AW2jmZ2aCZylaMMey">>}]
```

OLEG: Awesome!

11.5.1. Another Dependency: Erlias

RUSTY: Based on Paula's recommendation last time, we're going to use Erlias[6] to automatically make our facade this time, just like we did for `nnote_api` in the homework at the end of the Chapter 10.

MARSHA: Oooooooo! Sounds cool!

RUSTY: Let's kill our VM and add the Erlias dependency:

(Note: If you did the homework in Chapter 10, adding Erlias, some of these instructions will seem redundant).

Listing 11.32 (⇒ $) **Add erlias dependency (if you didn't do it in the Chapter 10 homework)**

```
~/nnote$ vim rebar.config
...
{deps, [
```

---

[6]https://github.com/choptastic/erlias

```
...
{erlpass, {git, "git://github.com/ferd/erlpass", {branch, master}}},
{erlias, {git, "git://github.com/choptastic/erlias", {branch, master}}},
...
```

RUSTY: Then we're going to make Erlias create its aliases during startup in
nitrogen_sup.erl:

Listing 11.33 (⇒ $) Set up aliases (n_mnesia.erl)

```
~/nnote$ cd site/src
site/src$ vim nitrogen_sup.erl
...
init([]) ->
    n_mnesia:one_time(),
    erlias:build(nnote_db_mnesia, nnote_api), %% skip if you did it already
    erlias:build(account_db_mnesia, account_api),
    application:load(nitrogen_core),
...
```

Listing 11.34 (⇒ $) Initialize account table (n_mnesia.erl)

```
site/src$ cd n_dbs
src/n_dbs$ vim n_mnesia.erl
...
init_tables() ->
    nnote_db_mnesia:init_table(),
    account_db_mnesia:init_table().
```

RUSTY: Finally, let's delete nnote_api.erl, since we don't need it anymore.
Then we'll make and startup again:

Listing 11.35 (⇒ $) **Clean up unnecessary modules**

```
...src/n_dbs$ rm nnote_api.erl
...src/n_dbs$ ../../..
...nnotes$ make && bin/nitrogen console
...
Erlias:  Building alias nnote_api ==> nnote_db_mnesia.
Erlias:  Building alias account_api ==> account_db_mnesia.
...
1>
```

RUSTY: Somewhere in the startup message will be a notification that Erlias is building the aliases above. If you see warnings about export_all, you can ignore them.

11.6. Save the Day

MARSHA: Oh, goodie! Now we get to write a save event for our registration form. Shall I do the honors?

OLEG: Glory hog.

MARSHA: That goto event is not needed. It's toast!

Listing 11.36 (⇒ $) **Define event functions (`register.erl`)**

```
~/nnote$ cd site/src/n_access
src/n_access$ vim register.erl
...
-module(register).
...
event({goto, Link}) ->
   wf:redirect(Link).
...
event(save) ->
```

432

```
[Username, Email, Password] = wf:mq([username, email, password]),
Record = account_api:new_account(Username, Email, Password),
wf:user(Username),
wf:redirect("/").
```

RUSTY: A recommendation...

OLEG: Yeah?

RUSTY: Instead of storing the Username in the `wf:user()` field, let's store the UserID and we can store the username in a different session variable.

OLEG: Oh?

RUSTY: Honestly, we could just store the UserID and if we need to display the username, we pull it from the database, but this will save us from writing a new query for this. But you can store anything you want in any session variables.

Also, we should use `wf:redirect_from_login/1` instead of `wf:redirect/1`.

MARSHA: What does that do?

RUSTY: If you've redirected to this page with `wf:redirect_to_login/1`, it remembers which page you were on and redirects you back there. But if there is no information (like if you directly opened the `/register` page in the browser), then it defaults to redirecting to the provided argument.

MARSHA: Neat! Let's the user stay in the groove.

Listing 11.37 (⇒ vim) **Store UserID and Username (`register.erl`)**

```
...
Record = account_api:new_account(Username, Email, Password),
UserID = account_api:id(Record),
wf:user(Username UserID),
```

433

```
wf:session(username, Username),
wf:redirect_from_login("/").
```

RUSTY: So, what say? Should we test registration?

OLEG: Been there. Done that.

RUSTY: And?

OLEG: It works!

MARSHA: I have a question.

RUSTY: Shoot.

MARSHA: Why did we use `new_account/3` instead of the `map_to_record(Map)` approach we took in nnote?

RUSTY: For most CRUD-like uses, `map_to_record()` or any other system you might cook up (passing around proplists, dicts, or records) will work. Account creation is a little trickier because you want to make sure you don't overwrite the password hash unless you're changing the password. Under no circumstances should pwhash ever be revealed to the customer, or anywhere. It should only be accessed when creating, changing, or validating the password. So it's safer to to use functions like `create_account()`, `save_account()`, `change_password()`, and `attempt_login()`, and a `verify_password()` option when you create an account.

That said, if we add fields to login, I'd recommend adopting `map_to_record()` because I wouuldn't want to be deal with passing around so many arguments. I'd do something like pass in a map, check for the presence of a `password` field, hash it if it's present, and store it in pwhash.

11.7. Login!

RUSTY: What are we forgetting?

STEVIE: We need a sign-in page.

MARSHA: Should just take a minute or two. We can copy over register.erl and modify the registration form.

RUSTY: Suggestion—suppose we rename register.erl to login.erl and add tasks to the url_vars() to distinguish when we're registering, signing in, or signing out. We can add menu options on the sidebar to switch tasks.

MARSHA: Like it! We can add task=login or task=create. And if no task is provided, it'll ask if we want to "create an account" or "sign in."

RUSTY: Show us the way:

Listing 11.38   (⇒ $) Rename `register.erl` to `login.erl`

```
src/n_access$ mv register.erl login.erl
src/n_access$ vim login.erl
...
-module(register login).
...
url_vars() = [{task, atom}].
```

MARSHA: Start with filling in the sidebar:

Listing 11.39   (⇒ vim) Build the Sidebar (`login.erl`)

```
sidebar(#{}) ->
    [].
    SignedOut = (wf:user()==undefined),
    [
     #h2{text="Account Menu"},
```

435

```
    #button{show_if=SignedOut, text="Create Account",
            postback={open, create}},
    #br{},
    #button{show_if=SignedOut, text="Sign In", postback={open, signin}},
    #br{},
    #button{show_if=not(SignedOut), text="Log Out", postback=logout}
].
```

MARSHA: We need to add the events to handle our new button postbacks.

OLEG: You didn't use the radio buttons we've been using

MARSHA: I felt like using actual buttons, so sue me:

Listing 11.40 Add event handlers for our open events (`login.erl`)

```
event({open, Task}) ->
    UrlVars = #{task=>Task},
    wf:update(content, content(UrlVars));
event(logout) ->
    UrlVars = #{task=>undefined},
    wf:logout(),
    wf:update(content, content(UrlVars)),
    wf:update(sidebar, sidebar(UrlVars));
event(save) ->
    ...
```

STEVIE: The girl's on a tear!

RUSTY: You even properly handled the `logout` event. I'm impressed.

MARSHA: Told you—I have a dance class tonight.

STEVIE: Don't let us hold you up.

MARSHA: Okay, let's build some of those task handlers in content/1:

Listing 11.41 (⇒ vim) **Update** content/1 (login.erl)

```
content(#{task:=undefined}) ->
    #h3{text="Choose an option from the left"};
content(#{task:=create}) ->
    new_account_form();
content(#{task:=signin}) ->
    signin_form().
```

Listing 11.42 (⇒ vim) **Build the sign-in form** (login.erl)

```
new_account_form() ->
    ...
signin_form() ->
    wf:defer(signin, username, #validate{validators=[
        #is_required{text="Username Required"}]}),
    wf:defer(signin, password, #validate{validators=[
        #is_required{text="Password required"}]}),
    [
        #h1{body="Sign In"},
        #label{text="Username"},
        #textbox{id=username},
        #label{text="Password"},
        #password{id=password},
         #br{},
        #button{id=signin, text="Sign In", postback=signin}
    ].
```

OLEG: Whoa! Virtuoso performance!

MARSHA: You should see me dance.

RUSTY: But the sixty-four dollar question—does it work?

OLEG: I vote to do the sign-in event before test.

RUSTY: Go for it:

Listing 11.43 (⇒ vim) **Define sign-in event (login.erl)**

```
event(save) ->
    ...
event(signin) ->
    [Username, Password] = wf:mq([username, password]),
    case account_api:attempt_login(Username, Password) of
        undefined ->
            wf:flash("No Matching Username or Password.  Please Try Again");
        Record ->
            UserID = account_api:id(Record),
            wf:user(UserID),
            wf:session(username, Username),
            wf:redirect_from_login("/")
    end.
```

RUSTY: So, Stevie, open up `localhost:8001/login`. What's the verdict?

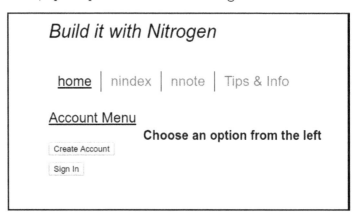

RUSTY: What if you click "Sign In" on the side menu?

STEVIE: Works like a charm!

RUSTY: See if you can break it while I go answer this phone call.

11.8. Ten Minutes Later

RUSTY: So guys, what did you find?

STEVIE: Well, if not logged in, clicking nnote on the menu directs to the login page, but it's missing the side menu. Not sure why.

RUSTY: Show me.

MARSHA: The address it's directing to is http://localhost:8001/register? But there isn't even a register module anymore. We renamed register.erl to login.erl. What gives?

RUSTY: So true, but the old compiled byte-code for register remains. Remember that site/ebin directory with all the .beam files? register.beam is still in there, and loaded into the VM.

MARSHA: Can we remove it?

RUSTY: Yup. We need to delete register.beam, then unload it from the VM.

Listing 11.44 (⇒ vim) **Delete register.beam**

```
src/n_access$ cd ../../ebinᵃ
nnote/ebin$ rm register.beam
```

---

[a]With the release of Nitrogen 3.0, which will use rebar3, this file will actually located in nnote/_build/default/rel/APPNAME/lib/APPNAME-X.Y.Z/ebin, where APPNAME will be nitrogen by default

OLEG: Deleting the .beam file isn't enough?

RUSTY: We only changed the contents of the disk. The code is loaded into the memory of the VM, so now we need to *unload* it from the Erlang shell:

Listing 11.45 (⇒ >) Unload code from Erlang shell

```
2> code:purge(register).
false
3> code:delete(register).
true
```

RUSTY: Now try it.

MARSHA: Getting a 404 error now.

RUSTY: That's good. It means the `register` module is now fully gone.

MARSHA: But we shouldn't be loading the register page. It should be `login`, not `register`.

RUSTY: Have a look in n_common.erl.

OLEG: Oh dude, forgot to change automatic redirect if they're not logged in.

Listing 11.46 (⇒ $) Change the login redirect (n_common.erl)

```
...ebin$ cd ../src/n_libs
...n_libs$ vim n_common.erl

-module(n_common).
...
template() ->
    Access = get_access(),
    case can_access(Access) of
```

```
    true -> #template{file=?TEMPLATE};
    false -> wf:redirect_to_login("/register" "/login")
end.
```

MARSHA: Well, works now. We're not logged in so it redirects to the right login page. So the problem was trying to make multiple accounts with the same username. The login page crashed when we tried to sign in.

OLEG: That reminds me. When we're viewing the login page, we should see the username we're logged in as, like in the sidebar.

RUSTY: Solid idea. Go for it.

OLEG: Okay. We used wf:session(username, Username) to store the username in the session. Can we retrieve it with wf:session(username)?

RUSTY: We can indeed!

Listing 11.47 (⇒ $) Add Username to Sidebar

```
...n_libs$ cd ../n_access
...n_access$ vim login.erl
...
%% **************************************************
%% Sidebar executives
%% **************************************************
logged_in_msg(undefined) -> "Not Logged In";
logged_in_msg(Username) -> ["Logged In as ",Username].

sidebar(#{}) ->
   SignedOut = (wf:user()==undefined),
   Username = wf:session(username),
   [
    #h2{text="Account Menu" logged_in_msg(Username)},
    #button{show_if=SignedOut, text="Create Account",
            postback={open,create}},
```

RUSTY: Load it up in the browser at /login. What do you think?

MARSHA: Looks good. I like it.

RUSTY: Stevie, you've been clicking furiously over there. Whatcha up to? Find something interesting?

STEVIE: I did. I made two different accounts, and I see the same notes regardless of which account I'm logged in as. In fact, I only see notes we made before we even made the login system.

RUSTY: Well, we *did* write the nnotes stuff before we had an account system in place.

STEVIE: Oh right, we stubbed in user stuff in n_utils.erl, but it was all hard-coded. I'll change it.

Listing 11.48 (⇒ $) **Edit n_utils.erl for user management**

```
...n_access$ cd ../n_libs
...n_libs$ vim n_utils.erl
-module(n_utils).
...
get_nickname() -> "Marsha" wf:session(username).
get_user_id() -> "123" wf:user().
```

RUSTY: And since we're making this change, we should probably reflect it when we call wf:user() and wf:session(username) directly. First in n_common.erl:

Listing 11.49 (⇒ $) Add Username to `login.erl` Sidebar

```
...n_libs$ vim n_common.erl
-module(n_common).
...
can_access(public) ->
    true;
can_access(private) ->
    wf:user() n_utils:get_user_id()=/=undefined.
```

RUSTY: ...and in `login.erl`:

Listing 11.50 (⇒ $) Add Username to `login.erl` Sidebar

```
...n_libs$ cd ../n_access
...n_access$ vim login.erl
-module(login).
...

sidebar(#{}) ->
    SignedOut = (wf:user() n_utils:get_user_id()==undefined),
    Username = wf:session(username), n_utils:get_nickname(),
    [
     #h2{text=logged_in_msg(Username)},
     ...
```

MARSHA: The last thing that bugged me, and it's not really a bug, but we should have an "Account" item on the main menu that takes us to the login page. Maybe down the road, that login page could be modified further to let us change our profile information (like change username, email, password, or add more fields like real name, phone number, etc.)

RUSTY: Good thinking. For now, you can just add an option to redirect to the login page.

MARSHA: Sounds easy enough:

Listing 11.51 (⇒ $) Add Account to menu (n_menus.erl)

```
...n_access$ cd ../n_libs
...n_libs$ vim n_menus.erl
-module(n_menus).
...
main_menu() ->
    [{"home", "/"},
     {"nindex", "/nindex"},
     {"nnote" , "/nnote"},
     {"Tips & Info", tips},
     {"Account", account}
    ].
...
event(tips) ->
   Mod = wf:page_module(),
   wf:flash(Mod:tips());
event(logout) ->
   wf:logout(),
   wf:redirect("/");
event(account) ->
   wf:redirect_to_login("/login");
event(URL) ->
```

MARSHA: Give it a shot.

OLEG: Me likey!

RUSTY: You guys knock me out! What a talented bunch.

MARSHA: Thanks to a talented mentor!

11.9. Closing thoughts

RUSTY: Well, you know you can't get away without a homework assignment.

OLEG: Oh man! I've got to study for my college entrance exams.

RUSTY: There are still important things missing from our login system. How do users update passwords? And what happens if they forget their password? How can they recover it?

Hint: Password update is relatively easy, especially with `erlpass:change/3` and `erlpass:change/4` functions. Password recovery is more difficult because you have to deal with email, which we haven't had time to cover. But give some thought to how you might go about it.

You can also tie your system to third-party login systems like Google, Facebook, Twitter, and the like. But for most business applications, you're likely to want to keep your password and user management system internal.

STEVIE: Thanks again, man. You're the best.

11.10. Homework

1. Refactor `nnote_db_mnesia.erl` and `account_db_mnesia.erl` to eliminate the code duplication, particularly for the functions `put_record/1`, `get_all_values/1`, `get_all/1`, `get_record/1`, and `delete/1`. This will likely require making a helper module called something like `mnesia_utils.erl`, with the bodies of these functions. They'll need the table name passed along. For example, `nnote_db_mnesia:get_all()` should end up calling `mnesia_utils:get_all(?TABLE)`.

2. Implement change password. The function should ask for the user's current password, validate it then, if it's correct, change the password.

3. Experiment with sending a confirmation email when the user creates an account. The simplest way to get started is to create to a free test account at Sparkpost[7] and to use the Sparkler[8] Erlang library.

---

[7]https://sparkpost.com
[8]https://github.com/choptastic/sparkler

4. Once you have the system sending email, try to build a password recovery system. User will enter their email address, and the system will email them their username and a link to change their password, specific to their account. Add "Forgot your Password" button to the sidebar on `login.erl`.

5. Allow users to change username. Add an "Edit Username" option to the sidebar on `login.erl`.

6. If you happen to create two users with the same username, you're going to run into some crashes. Add a custom validator[9,10] on account creation (and the "change username" interface from the last problem). This validator will check if the desired username already exists.

---

[9]Validator demo (includes a sample custom validator):
   http://nitrogenproject.com/demos/validation.
[10]Documentation for custom validators:
   http://nitrogenproject.com/doc/validators/custom.html

12. But is it Secure?

Rusty Nail searched high and low but finally found Jesse James sunning behind the erlingo! building.

JESSE: 'Sup?

RUSTY: The kids are pushing to deploy the Nitrogen apps we've been developing. I'm concerned about security. Any tips?

JESSE: Regardless of framework, security should be based on standard best practices.

But hey, this might help. I recorded this Nitrogen web security presentation last year.

(*Opens Dell XPS*)

12.1. Trust No One!

(Queue *X-Files* theme)

Trust No One!

Never trust data sent from a client. Form input such as POST variables, URL paths, characters found after a question mark in the URL query string, and even headers are all easy to spoof.

Nitrogen cryptographically signs and validates postback requests, preventing Cross-Site Request Forgery (CSRF) attacks. Given a postback request, Nitrogen will not execute an event/1 function if it fails to decode the page_state token.

But while signed postbacks close that particular attack vector, there's still plenty left to do.

12.1.1. Prevent HTML Injection

Spammers and others often inject HTML into data input fields in an attempt to break into a system. If input is not sanitized they may well succeed.

A user, in all innocence, may enter formatting tags such as <b> or <i> or a friendly link rather than a long and ugly URL. But a malicious actor could just as well inject an image known to exploit a security hole in the browser. If successful, this would enable the attacker to run malicious code. Or, they could inject a <script> tag.

Consider a forum. If an attacker can successfully inject:

Example 12.1

```
<script>location.href="http://evil-forum-clone.com/fakethread"</scipt>
```

...then every user who opens the post would be redirected to the attacker's fake site, which could well be a visual clone of the forum. Now, say, a user replies to the fake post, not noticing that the domain name has changed. After all, her screen perfectly replicates the forum! She clicks Sign In. This takes her to a perfectly legitimate-looking login screen. Now she attempts to log in by entering her email address and password.

BOOM! USER COMPROMISED

The user has just sent her email address and password to the malicious site. To be extra sneaky, the fake page could, upon login form submission, immediately redirect back to the legitimate site's login form since the login itself will fail. The user is completely unaware that she's been scammed and her account information harvested. This is similar to credit card skimmers—everything works as expected. Except now the malicious actor has harvested sensitive information.

This is just one of the dangers users face when you fail to sanitize data from HTML or JavaScript injection.

There are several ways to protect them.

Easiest option: Element text attribute

Most Nitrogen elements have both a body and a text attribute. The body attribute will display data as presented. But the text attribute will apply HTML encoding before rendering. Here's a simple example:

Example 12.2

```
MaliciousText = "<script>alert('HAHA! Gotcha')</script>",
#panel{body=MaliciousText}.
```

Since MaliciousText is not properly encoded, the injected JavaScript is sent to the client and executed in the browser. The simplest way to defeat MaliciousText is to use the text attribute:

Example 12.3

```
MaliciousText = "<script>alert('HAHA! Gotcha')</script>",
#panel{text=MaliciousText}.
```

Another easy option: HTML encoding

A second easy option is to employ Nitrogen's built-in HTML encoding function wf:html_encode/1. Calling wf:html_encode("<i>my awesome words</i>") will return "<i>my awesome words</i>". This will completely eliminate the possibility of injecting HTML.

Other options

- **HTML sanitizing**: Strip out potentially damaging tags or attributes. This will allow users to enter HTML into form fields without threat of malicious input. The Erlang CMS Zotonic offers an HTML sanitizer you can use—the z_html:sanitize function from:

https://github.com/zotonic/z_stdlib.

- **Markdown**: Markdown is simple and ubiquitous—used from Github to book production to presentation slidedecks like Reveal.js. You can find a solid Erlang Markdown encoder currently maintained by Erlware:

  https://github.com/erlware/erlmarkdown

- **BBCode**: BBCode is a formatting markup language popularized by the phpBB forum. It looks like HTML and, when run through a BBCode parser, gets converted to HTML while all actual HTML gets encoded. BBCode encoding is not standardized. But it is simple. You can find a BBCode parser and converter that converts between BBCode, Textile, RTF, and HTML here:

  https://github.com/evanmiller/jerome

But even with the Markdown or BBCode solutions, it's still a good idea to sanitize HTML after converting Markdown/BBCode to HTML. Otherwise, a malicious user could enter BBCode that looks like:

Example 12.4 Unsanitized BBCode

```
[url=javascript:alert('Your Gibson is hacked')]See my homepage[/url]
```

This would unfortunately render as:

Example 12.5 HTML-Rendered Unsanitized BBCode

```
<a href="javascript:alert('Your Gibson is hacked')">See my homepage</a>
```

This would allow an attacker to execute arbitrary JavaScript on the client.

Under most circumstances, simply encoding HTML is the appropriate solution. The other methods should be used only when you absolutely need to allow users to arbitrarily format text, such as forum posts or pages of a Content Management System (CMS).

12.1.2. Prevent JavaScript injection

The previous section illustrates the hazards of allowing users to enter `<script>` tags containing JavaScript. Beware, however. There are other ways that a malicious user can execute JavaScript on your site. If your page contains a script with JavaScript strings, it's essential to escape quotes. This prevents the script from ending prematurely. Consider this code circa 1996, complete with `<blink>` tags, animated dripping blood dividers, and background MIDI music:

Example 12.6

```
<a href="javascript:alert('Welcome to my site, Jesse')Click to welcome</a>
```

The script looks innocuous enough. But obviously you can't hardcode a user's name. Joe doesn't want to be called Jesse. So you might be tempted to build something like this on the server and send it to the client:

Example 12.7

```
Name = wf:user(),
wf:f("<a href=\"javascript:alert('Welcome to my site, ~s')\">
     Click to welcome</a>", [Name]).
```

This would work in most cases. But suppose the user's name is D'Angelo? Here's what the server would send to the client:

Example 12.8

```
<a href="javascript:alert('Welcome to my site, D'Angelo')">
  Click to welcome
</a>
```

Nasty! The apostrophe in D'Angelo will precipitate a crash—not a nice way to treat users but, *worse,* a gaping security hole.

Imagine if a malicious user set their username to the crazy string: `"');do_something_naughty("`. It would render as:

Example 12.9

```
<a href="javascript:alert('Welcome to my site,
    ');do_something_naughty();">
  Click to welcome
</a>
```

Now, following the "Welcome to my site" alert, the user can execute whatever they want on the client.

Here are several solutions:

- You could incur the wrath of geeks and user-experience folks everywhere by preventing users from adding non-alphanumeric characters to their names. But that's dumb. Don't do that.

- You could escape JavaScript using `wf:js_escape(Name)`. Your solution would look like this:

Example 12.10

```
wf:f("<a href="javascript:alert('Welcome to my site, ~s')\">Click to
    welcome</a>", [wf:js_escape(Name)]).
```

- The best option is to use Nitrogen elements with text attributes:

Example 12.11

```
#link{text="Click to welcome", click=[
  #alert{text=wf:f("Welcome to my site, ~s", [Name])}
]}.
```

This approach is superior because you don't have to call escape functions—escaping is automatic with the text attributes. Nor do you have to escape anything in HTML, \\" for instance. Further, your code will be syntactically consistent since you're likely using Nitrogen elements everywhere already. Why muddle your codebase with hand-rolled HTML?

12.1.3. Prevent SQL Injection

SQL injection is similar to JavaScript injection, but with even greater potential for damage. The famous XKCD Cartoon "Little Bobby Tables" tells the tale. Check it out:

http://xkcd.com/327

Simply put, it's one thing to execute arbitrary JavaScript on a client's browser. It's another altogether to let random strangers execute full SQL queries on your production database. A random stranger could alter or delete data or harvest information from your database. Either way—bad.

SQL injection is the most common technique for breaking into computers. It mostly goes unnoticed since it rarely breaks the system. It just ends up as another line-item in the log files.

So employ best practices from the get-go. This way you won't need to retrofit your site with proper SQL escaping.

Consider old-style PHP from books that recommended doing silly things like:

12. But is it Secure?

Example 12.12

```
mysql_query("Select * from login where loginid=$loginid").
```

While direct string interpolation is no longer recommended for dealing with SQL in PHP, it's still quite common in the wild.[1]

Bottom line: make sure that whatever database library you use properly escapes inputs. Most of them do. It's easy. Here we'll use `sql_bridge`,[2] an SQL library,to demonstrate the right and wrong way to do it:

Example 12.13

```
%% WRONG!
db:q("Select firstname, lastname
      from login where loginid="
      ++ Loginid).

%% RIGHT
db:q("Select firstname, lastname
      from login where loginid=?",
      [Loginid]).
```

Most SQL drivers escape variables correctly as shown in the RIGHT example. Indeed, had the user specified the `loginid` (which would be expected to be an integer) as the string `"loginid"` as shown in the WRONG example, the final SQL string would be:

---

[1] Recently a client asked me to overhaul their PHP website. I found unescaped string interpolation in SQL statements everywhere. This site was a candy shop for malicious users.

[2] https://github.com/choptastic/sql_bridge

Example 12.14

```
db:q("Select firstname, lastname
    from login where loginid=loginid").
```

Sweet! We just returned all users in the whole system. How convenient[3]. But let's take it a step further. What if the login variable was bound to `"0 union select credit_card_number, expiration from client_credit_cards"`.

Uh oh—serious problem! The query will be called as:

Example 12.15

```
db:q("Select firstname, lastname
    from login where loginid=0
    union
    select credit_card_number, expiration
    from client_credit_cards").
```

... and return the full list of credit card numbers and expiration dates. Not nice![4]

Bottom line: always escape variables to avoid serious data leaks. Use methods provided by your SQL driver. Here's an example:

Example 12.16

```
db:q("Select firstname, lastname
    from login where loginid=?", [Loginid]).
```

---

[3]I hope the sarcasm is clear

[4]Of course, you should *never* store credit card information in plaintext. And with most modern systems, you should not even store any credit card numbers at all, certainly not in a server that's directly accessible from your webserver with open database access.

In this example `sql_bridge` properly escapes `Loginid`. If the variables are malicious, `sql_bridge` will just return zero records.

12.1.4. Be careful with file paths

You should also sanitize inputs when presenting files directly from the file system. Do not allow users to specify arbitrary paths. You're headed for trouble if you allow a user to request a file with input like `?file=/etc/passwd`.

Attackers frequently use trial and error to break into systems. But once an attacker figures out that they can navigate the file system by entering arbitrary file paths, it's only a matter of time before they break in.

So strip out slashes and periods from user-specified file paths. It's not enough to remove only leading slashes or leading double-dots (..) because an attacker can always add a string like `?file=random/../../../etc/passwd` to the URL.[5]

12.1.5. Be mindful of the atom table

Erlang atoms are quite useful, but there is a limit to the number of atoms that can exist in the system. Once an atom is created, it's never destroyed. This is referred to as the atom table limit. The atom table is never garbage collected. The benefit is that atoms enable super fast pattern matching and comparison. But the upper limit is a potential vulnerability.

By default, Erlang will allow 1,048,576 or 2^{20} atoms.[6] This limit can be changed (increased or decreased) when first starting the Erlang VM by specifying the `+t` command-line switch.

You can easily crash the VM by executing the following list comprehension in the Erlang shell:

---

[5] Challenge: Write an Erlang function that escapes all characters in a file path—except dashes, numbers and alphanumeric characters—to underscores. Here's how it might be done in Rails— `https://makandracards.com/makandra/1309-sanitize-filename-with-user-input`

[6] See: `http://erlang.org/doc/efficiency_guide/advanced.html`.

Example 12.17 How to crash the Erlang Virtual Machine

```
[list_to_atom(integer_to_list(X)) || X <- lists:seq(1, 2000000))].
```

Try it and you'll find that the atom table limit is exhausted in a matter of minutes. The Erlang VM will crash even though the memory usage is completely normal.

The lesson here is this: never, ever allow user data to pass unfiltered through erlang:list_to_atom/1.[7]

The Erlang function erlang:list_to_existing_atom/1 is the way to plug the atom table limit vulnerability.[8] If the atom 'Erlang' is in the atom table, it will convert the list "Erlang" to the atom 'Erlang'. Otherwise, it will raise an exception.

Nitrogen also provides slightly more forgiving versions of the above functions: wf:to_atom/1 and wf:to_existing_atom/1. Both will convert any term to an atom if it can.

12.2. Hash Passwords

Never, *ever* store passwords in plaintext—that is, in the same form received over the wire. If your database is compromised and attackers see plaintext passwords you will likely cause unknown but not insignificant harm to your users. Think you're immune to break ins? Check the news. Even internet giants like eBay and LinkedIn have been compromised.

Use a hash function to store passwords.[9]

A hash function takes an input and returns a unique term called a hash. It requires formidable computing power to reverse a hash, that is, get the original input from the hash. But that said, clever cryptographers have found some hash functions weaker than others. Given advances in computing power, it's only a

---

[7]Seriously, this is the single easiest way to take down the VM.

[8]http://erlang.org/documentation/doc-5.7.4/erts-5.7.4/doc/html/erlang.html# list_to_atom-1

[9]https://en.wikipedia.org/wiki/Hash_function

matter of time before the weaker hash functions will be broken, that is, if they haven't been already.

Hashing is one of the few areas in computer technology where there's benefit in slowing down.

Enter bcrypt.

Bcrypt is a slow-by-design hash function. And it's designed to stay slow for the conceivable future, even with advances in computing power. Every bcrypt hash contains a work factor, which tells bcrypt how hard it has to work to produce a hash. It also contains a `salt`, which is an additional random term added to the input to produce a unique hash even if the input value is the same.

The Erlang library erlang-bcrypt[10] can do the heavy lifting for us. But even more useful is the erlpass library,[11] which we introduced in the previous chapter. For more examples of working with `erlang-bcrypt` and erlpass, check out this blog post:

http://sigma-star.com/blog/post/proper-password-hashing-in-erlang-with

12.3. Verify Logged-in Status in User-Specific Postbacks

While Nitrogen verifies that requests are valid postbacks from the server, it does not automatically validate if a user's session has expired or whether a user has logged out or logged in as a different user. We need to consider this when postbacks contain user-specific data or require user-specific permissions.

For instance:

Example 12.18   Can you find the bug?

```
main()->
    case wf:role(admin) of
        true  -> #template{file="./templates/admin.html"};
        false -> wf:redirect_to_login("/login")
```

---

[10]https://github.com/smarkets/erlang-bcrypt
[11]https://github.com/ferd/erlpass

```
    end.

body()->
    Userid=wf:to_integer(wf:q(userid)),
    #button{
        text="Delete User",
        postback={delete, Userid}
    }.

event({delete, UseridToDelete})->
    MyUserid = wf:user(),
    my_database:delete_something(MyUserid, UseridToDelete),
    wf:wire(#alert{text="User Deleted"}).
```

This example harbors a bug.

Assume that an administrator wants to delete a user. The `main()` function indeed checks that the administrator is logged in and correctly redirects to login if not.

Further assume that `Userid` has been correctly instantiated.

But say the administrator leaves her computer idle for an hour and the system automatically logs her out. She returns and clicks the "Delete User" button. The system correctly deletes the user but `MyUserid` is now `undefined`. If the system logs who deletes things, this will report as a user deleted by an `undefined` user. Who knows what problems this may create down the line?

Bottom line: check role status in user-sensitive or role-sensitive postbacks. Consider the following change:

Example 12.19   Confirm admin role is true

```
event(E) ->
    case wf:role(admin) of
        true -> admin_event(E);
        false -> wf:redirect_to_login("/login")
    end.

admin_event({delete, UseridToDelete}) ->}
```

```
MyUserid = wf:user(),
my_database:delete_something(MyUserid, UseridToDelete),
wf:wire(#alert{text="User Deleted"}).
```

Note the changes: This simple fix confirms that the admin role is true prior to processing postbacks. If the user had gone idle, or logged out in another tab, this will ensure that the user is still logged in as an administrator before deleting the user.

But even this may not be sufficient. Conceivably, we may want to guarantee that we haven't logged out as one admin and logged in as another. We could guarantee this by putting the initial role into the page state with wf:state/2, and comparing it against the return value of wf:user/0.

Consider the final version:

Example 12.20   Final version

```
main() ->
    wf:state(original_user, wf:user()),
    case wf:role(admin) of
        true  -> #template{file="./templates/admin.html"};
        false -> wf:redirect_to_login("/login")
    end.

body() ->
    UserToDeleteid = wf:to_integer(wf:q(userid)),
    #button{
        text="Delete User",
        postback={delete, UserToDeleteid}
    }.

event(E) ->
    IsSameUser = wf:state(original_user)==wf:user(),
    IsAdmin = wf:role(admin),
    case wf:role(admin) of
    case IsSameUser andalso IsAdmin of
        true -> admin_event(E);
        false -> wf:redirect_to_login("/login")
```

```
    end.

admin_event({delete, UseridToDelete}) ->
    MyUserid = wf:user(),
    my_database:delete_something(MyUserid, UseridToDelete),
    wf:wire(#alert{text="User-Deleted"}).
```

Now, if the user logs out of the system or has not been assigned an admin role, the system will redirect to the login module.

12.4. Hidden doesn't mean gone

One thing to be particularly aware of is that hiding Nitrogen elements either with #hide{} or CSS (e.g. "display:none") is not the same thing as removing or not rendering.

Consider this module:

Example 12.21 Example Of Insecure Info

```
-module(sensitive_user_info).
-include_lib("nitrogen_core/include/wf.hrl").
-compile(export_all).

main() ->
    #template{file=?TEMPLATE}.

body() ->
    ?WF_IF(wf:role(admin), wf:wire(content, #show{})),
    Userid = wf:q(userid),
    {Name, SSN, Address} = db_user:get_pii_from_database(Userid),
    #panel{id=content, actions=#hide{}, body=[
        #label{text="Name"},
        #panel{text=Name},
        #label{text="Social Security Number"},
        #panel{text=SSN},
        #label{text="Address"},
```

463

```
        #panel{text=Address}
    ]}.
```

Maybe you have this page for admins to view sensitive PII (Personally Identifiable Information) that you have on the user, for compliance with the CCPA[12] or the GDPR.[13] You might think this is secure. After all, it's hiding the PII by default and checking if the user has an admin role before showing the information.

This is a massive security hole—the worst kind of security hole.

Even if a user isn't an admin, it will still send the information. It just won't render on the browser screen. But right click the page, click "View Page Source," and all the information is there, plain as the nose on your face.

12.4.1. Simply redirecting isn't enough either

So what to do? You could direct the user away from the page by doing something like this:

Example 12.22 Example Of Insecure Info

```
main() ->
    ?WF_IF(not(wf:role(admin)), wf:redirect("/login")),
    #template{file=?TEMPLATE}.


    ...
```

Surely, that's sufficient, right?

WRONG!

"But the page doesn't even load, it just instantly redirects," you say.

Sort of. But before it redirects, it sends the *entire* the content of the body() function to the client because you still returned the #template{} from main(). So this is still a serious security hole.

---

[12]https://www.oag.ca.gov/privacy/ccpa
[13]https://gdpr-info.eu/

Here's the proper solution:

Example 12.23   Example Of Insecure Info

```
main() ->
    case wf:role(admin) of
        true -> #template{file=?TEMPLATE};
        false -> wf:redirect_to_login("/")
    end.
```

Key takeaway: if the user does not have permission, we should not send the template. This way, there is no danger of exposing sensitive information to unauthorized users.

If you're unsure about where to implement your security checks, put them in the main() function. More advanced users can tap into Nitrogen's security handlers[14] to check who should have access to what.

12.5. Conclusion and Recommendations for System-wide Security

An application developer needs to do many things to ensure security. But if you design your site with security in mind from the start, you should be good. To rehash:

- Never trust data from the client

- Escape, encode, or sanitize everything user-generated

- Use proper password hashing

- Build security into each page or build a security handler to control data access.

---

[14]http://nitrogenproject.com/doc/handlers/security.html

12. But is it Secure?

There are other systemwide things you can do to lock down your systems—general recommendations regardless of your programming language or tech stack. Here are a few:

1. **Use SSH:** Disable root[15] and password access. Use only public key login.[16].

   Do not use FTP; it is an insecure plain-text protocol.

2. **Configure a reverse proxy and use SSL:** Use a reverse proxy[17] in front of Nitrogen, rather than exposing Nitrogen directly to the customer. That means not binding Nitrogen to port 80 or 443. Configure your application to use SSL (ideally, use SSL exclusively, and set up your reverse proxy to instantly redirect from HTTP to HTTPS). Either use LetsEncrypt[18] or buy a cheap SSL certificate.

3. **Add a Firewall:** Use a firewall to limit port access to only 80 (HTTP) and 443 (HTTPS). On Linux, the built-in firewall is called iptables.[19]. Ideally, limit access to port 22 (SSH) from certain white-listed IP addresses.[20]

4. **Do NOT run Nitrogen as root:** If there happens to be a bug in your application or in Erlang itself, running Nitrogen as root exposes your server to unlimited exploits.

---

[15]https://www.howtogeek.com/howto/linux/security-tip-disable-root-ssh-login-on-linux
   (Short Version: https://bit.ly/ssh-disable-root)

[16]https://linux-audit.com/using-ssh-keys-instead-of-passwords
   (Short Version: https://bit.ly/ssh-public-key-only)

[17]To learn more about reverse proxies, check out: https://www.nginx.com/resources/glossary/reverse-proxy-server. Nginx (https://www.nginx.com) is the recommended reverse proxy with Nitrogen. You can find Nginx configuration steps in http://nitrogenproject.com/doc/config.html. There are reverse proxies that will do the job, however. Choose the one you prefer

[18]https://letsencrypt.org

[19]https://www.howtogeek.com/177621/the-beginners-guide-to-iptables-the-linux-firewall (Short Version: https://bit.ly/intro-to-iptables) If you're running a flavor of BSD, look into PF or ipfilter.

[20]https://unix.stackexchange.com/q/145929

5. **Use different passwords for everything:** Your system login password should be different from the root password, which should be different from your database password, and so on. If your system password and database password are the same, and somehow your codebase leaks, you don't want the code or config files from your application to expose the entire system.

6. **Apply regular security updates from your OS distribution:** This one should be obvious.

Please be aware: the above advice are low-hanging fruit in system security. They are easy to address and fix. But this list is hardly exhaustive. System security is an entire field of computing, so be ready to ask questions and get advice, and if your company starts to grow, a competent system administrator will help tremendously. With luck and pluck you will one day be large enough to hire a full-time security engineer.

Eventually, maybe you'll be large enough that you can justify hiring a full-time security engineer.

Part III.

Going Further

13. Stockticker

STEVIE: So what's our next awesome project, Obi-Wan?

RUSTY: Nitrogen delivers cool features we haven't touched on.

MARSHA: Like what?

RUSTY: Like the other day Bigboss asked if we could display real-time weather data on nitroBoard. Dude's a weather freak. Problem is, weather data changes frequently.

STEVIE: So what did you say?

RUSTY: Nitrogen is a fantastic tool for pushing data to the browser without user intervention. But...

OLEG: Way cool— a weather app! We could hook up a temperature sensor to a Raspberry Pi.

RUSTY: ...pushing weather data to nitroBoard would require extra hardware. Better to walk before we run.

STEVIE: But still, I'd really like to learn how to push data to the browser.

RUSTY: It's useful to know. My work buddy Lloyd London suggested a stock ticker app.

MARSHA: Stock ticker[1]— love it! We're going to get richhhh.

OLEG Wouldn't count on it.

---

[1]The entirety of this project's code can be found here: https://github.com/BuildItWithNitrogen/stockticker/commits

RUSTY: For bonus points, we could integrate Bootstrap into our app.

STEVIE: Bootstrap?

RUSTY: Bootstrap is a popular HTML, CSS, and JavaScript library. It can help make our apps mobile friendly.

MARSHA: Like on my iPhone?

RUSTY: Exactly. Much to be gained. Once you know how to integrate Bootstrap, you'll find that other custom template frameworks are same-ol' same-ol'.

OLEG: There goes Marsha— checking her stocks. Glued to her iPhone.

STEVIE: There goes Marsha's GPA.

MARSHA: But I'll be rich. I vote for a stock ticker app.

STEVIE: I second the motion.

13.1. Getting Started

RUSTY: So let's set up a new project. What should we call it?

OLEG: "How to lose your inheritance?"

MARSHA: How about "stockticker."

STEVIE: Good by me.

RUSTY: So, Stevie, show us the way. Suggest we use the MochiWeb web server.

MARSHA: Why MochiWeb?

RUSTY: No particular reason. Nitrogen supports five different web servers. We've deployed Cowboy. So now, let's install Mochiweb. Honestly, I'd be inclined to install Yaws, except that will require installing a handful of OS Applications and compiling some C code, and we'll avoid that for now.

STEVIE: I'll give it a shot:

Listing 13.1 (⇒ $) **Create stockticker project**

```
.../nitrogen$ make slim_mochiweb PROJECT=stockticker
...
**********************************************
Generated a slim-release Nitrogen project
in ../stockticker, configured to run on yaws.
**********************************************
make[1]: Leaving directory '/home/gumm/www/nitrogen-git/nitrogen'

$ cd ../stockticker
$ bin/nitrogen console
...
=INFO REPORT==== 10-Aug-2016::18:37:36 ===
Yaws: Listening to 0.0.0.0:8000 for <1> virtual servers:
 - http://simple_bridge:8000 under ./site/static

(stockticker@127.0.0.1)1> sync:go().
Starting Sync (Automatic Code Compiler / Reloader)
Scanning source files...
ok
```

RUSTY: As my cat Loki says, "Purrrrrrr-fect!"

13.2. Introducing `httpc`

MARSHA: We need market data, right?

RUSTY: Alpha Vantage provides what we need.[2] Their free tier imposes usage
limits, but that shouldn't matter.

STEVIE: How do we connect?

---

[2]You'll need your own API Key. Download it from https://www.alphavantage.co/support/
#api-key

473

RUSTY: Through the Alpha Vantage HTTP web API.

MARSHA: Could we use `curl`?

RUSTY: We could. But let's use the Erlang HTTP client provided by the `inets` application.

Inets provides a bunch of handy tools for working with HTTP, including a web server, parsers, encoders— we'll use `httpc`, the HTTP/1.1 client.

OLEG: Do show the way, Big Chief.

RUSTY: Since inets is an Erlang application, we need to start it. We can do that in `nitrogen_sup:init/1`. So, first, open up a new UNIX terminal:

Listing 13.2 (⇒ $) **Start inets**

```
.../stockticker$ cd site/src
.../site/src$ vim nitrogen_sup.erl

init([]) ->
    application:start(simple_cache),
    application:start(crypto),
    application:start(nprocreg),
    application:start(inets),
    application:start(simple_bridge),
```

RUSTY: So, done and saved.

Now, since we're changing the startup procedure, typically we'd want to stop our Erlang VM and restart it. But for now, let's turn to our Erlang terminal and force start it:

Listing 13.3 (⇒ >) **Start inets**

```
(stockticker@127.0.0.1)1> application:start(inets).
```

RUSTY: ...then, returning to our UNIX shell, create an API module called `stock.erl`, and export a function called `lookup(Symbol)`:

Listing 13.4 (⇒ $) **Create stock module**

```
.../stockticker$ cd site/src
.../site/src$ vim stock.erl

-module(stock).
-export([lookup/1]).
```

RUSTY: Oh, can't forget to snag our API Key for Alpha Vantage. Head over to `https://www.alphavantage.co/support/#api-key` to generate an API Key.

STEVIE: Done.

RUSTY: Great. Now define a macro called `API_KEY` in `stock.erl` and paste in our new API key[3] as its key:

---

[3] Alpha Vantage has kindly approved this key to be published in this book, but if too many of you use this same key as you're testing, you'll step on each others' toes. We strongly urge you to get your own API Key and use that key instead.

Listing 13.5 (⇒ `vim`) **Alpha Vantage API key (`stock.erl`)**

```
-export([lookup/1]).
%% Note:  replace example key with your own.
-define(VA_API_KEY, "BVJ2JHQY6MLAOWGZ").
```

RUSTY: Alpha Vantage docs give us a sample API endpoint:

> https://www.alphavantage.co/query?function=GLOBAL_
> QUOTE&symbol=MSFT&apikey=demo

Point your browser to that URL to see what it looks like. Or you could use curl to see it in your terminal:

Example 13.1 (⇒ `$`) **Alpha Vantage response (NOTE: URL should be unbroken on one line)**

```
site/src$ curl "https://www.alphavantage.co/query?function=GLOBAL_QUOTE
        &symbol=MSFT&apikey=demo"

{
        "Global Quote": {
                "01. symbol": "MSFT",
                "02. open": "179.5000",
                "03. high": "180.0000",
                "04. low": "175.8700",
                "05. price": "178.6000",
                "06. volume": "52273542",
                "07. latest trading day": "2020-04-17",
                "08. previous close": "177.0400",
                "09. change": "1.5600",
                "10. change percent": "0.8812%"
        }
}
```

MARSHA: Oh, nice. A simple JSON response.[4]

RUSTY: Yep. Now let's see what it looks like in the Erlang shell:

Listing 13.6 (⇒ >) **JSON in Erlang shell**

```
2> URL="https://www.alphavantage.co/query?function=GLOBAL_QUOTE&symbol=MSFT&a
pikey=demo".
3> httpc:request(URL).
{ok,{{"HTTP/1.1",200,"OK"},
     [{"connection","keep-alive"},
      {"date","Mon, 22 Apr 2019 19:14:17 GMT"},
      {"via","1.1 vegur"},
      {"server","gunicorn/19.7.0"},
      {"vary","Cookie"},
      {"allow","GET, HEAD, OPTIONS"},
      {"content-length","385"},
      {"content-type","application/json"},
      {"x-frame-options","SAMEORIGIN"}],
      "{\n    \"Global Quote\": {\n       \"01. symbol\": \"MSFT\",\n
\"02. open\": \"122.6200\" ... \"10. change percent\": \"0.1203%\"\n
\}\n}"}}
```

STEVIE: Whoa! That's ominous.

RUSTY: Does look intimidating. But much can be ignored. The general response is simply:

{ok, {ResponseCode, Headers, ResponseBody}}

ResponseCode is {"HTTP/1.1",200,"OK"}

Headers is that long list that starts [{"connection","keep-alive"},...]

And finally, ResponseBody is the goofy string that starts with a curly brace and "Global Quote"...

---

[4]If you're using Firefox to see the response, you need to click "Raw Data" to see the raw JSON.

We only care about the ResponseBody, so we'll discard the rest by calling it like this:

{ok, {_, _, ResponseBody}} = httpc:request(URL).

Try it in the shell:

Listing 13.7 (⇒ >) **Display Body in the Erlang shell**

```
4> {ok, {_, _, Body}} = httpc:request(URL),
4> Body.
"{\n    \"Global Quote\": {\n          \"01. symbol\": \"MSFT\",\n
\"02. open\": \"122.6200\" ... \"10. change percent\": \"0.1203%\"\n
\}\n}"
```

RUSTY: Now we have Body. Let's use Nitrogen's built-in JSON decoder to see how it decodes:

Listing 13.8 (⇒ >) **Decode JSON in the Erlang shell**

```
5> wf:json_decode(Body).
{<<"Global Quote">>,
      [{<<"01. symbol">>,<<"MSFT">>},
      {<<"02. open">>,<<"122.6200">>},
      {<<"03. high">>,<<"124.0000">>},
      {<<"04. low">>,<<"122.6100">>},
      {<<"05. price">>,<<"123.5900">>},
      ...
```

RUSTY: Voilà! A proplist with binaries for keys and values.

You've seen proplists before. Think you can build the lookup(Symbol) function?

STEVIE: Think so! I still have stock.erl open in my editor. Just need to add the definition:

Listing 13.9 (⇒ $) **Define** lookup/1 **(**stock.erl**)**

```
site/src$ vim stock.erl
...
-define(VA_API_KEY, "BVJ2JHQY6MLAOWGZ").

lookup(Symbol) ->
  BaseURL = "https://www.alphavantage.co/query?",
```

STEVIE: Anything after the ? in the URL, as I recall, is a query string. So we can build the full request URL with the help of wf:to_qs():

Listing 13.10 Full request URL (stock.erl**)**

```
lookup(Symbol) ->
  BaseURL = "https://www.alphavantage.co/query?",
  QS = wf:to_qs([
    {function, "GLOBAL_QUOTE"},
    {apikey, ?VA_API_KEY},
    {symbol, Symbol}
  ]),
  URL = BaseURL ++ QS,
```

RUSTY: Outstanding! Now let's fetch the results from Alpha Vantage:

Listing 13.11 (⇒ vim) **Fetch data from Alpha Vantage** (stock.erl)

```
URL = BaseURL ++ QS,
{ok, {_, _, Body}} = httpc:request(URL),
```

RUSTY: Great! Now we need to decode the JSON and extract the price:

Listing 13.12 (⇒ vim) **Decode JSON and extract price** (stock.erl)

```
{ok, {_,_,Body}} = httpc:request(URL),
Quote = wf:json_decode(Body),
GlobalQuote = proplists:get_value(<<"Global Quote">>, Quote),
proplists:get_value(<<"05.   price">>, GlobalQuote).
```

RUSTY: Looking good. Give it a shot.

Save the file, then call stock:lookup/1 from the Erlang shell:

Listing 13.13 (⇒ >) **Save and call** stock:lookup/1 **from Erlang shell**

```
5> stock:lookup("MSFT").
<<"178.7600">>
```

RUSTY: Works! Way to go.

Note that our stock module is quite simple. Should be easy to rewrite if you want to shift to another public API.

MARSHA: But it returns a binary. Should we convert the return value to a float?

RUSTY: Nah. We're going to display it on the page, so binaries are fine. Actually, floats are less precise.

STEVIE: I've heard that you should never use floats when dealing with money.

RUSTY: Good advice. It's a good idea to convert money to integer representation.

MARSHA: Interesting.

RUSTY: Indeed, in the U.S., it's common to convert dollar amounts to cents.

OLEG: Guys... Can we get back to business?

RUSTY: OK. Let's install and configure Bootstrap.

13.3. Bootstrap

STEVIE: Remind me. What does Bootstrap do for us?

RUSTY: Bootstrap[5] is a popular presentation framework. Mostly CSS with a bit of JavaScript thrown in. The big win for our purposes is that Bootstrap is responsive.

MARSHA: Meaning?

RUSTY: The display adjusts to smaller screens automatically.

MARSHA: Like on my mobile phone.

RUSTY: Exactly.

Plus, Bootstrap simplifies site design. Businesses often use uncustomized, completely-off-the-shelf Bootstrap for internal apps. Custom web development shops can publish attractive websites with minimal cost and effort.

OLEG: Sounds boring. March of the website zombies.

---

[5]http://getbootstrap.com

RUSTY: No. No. You can find scores of well-designed Bootstrap themes on the web. And you can modify them. It's easy to change color schemes. Many graphic designers start with Bootstrap and customize from there.

OLEG: But what if I don't want to get locked into some graphic design silo?

RUSTY: Hey, with Bootstrap under your belt, you'll find the gazillion other design frameworks out there a piece of cake.[6]

MARSHA: So how hard is it to integrate Bootstrap into our apps?

RUSTY: Quite easy, actually.

13.3.1. A matter of choice

RUSTY: Bootstrap themes are mostly powered by HTML classes.

OLEG: Oh, brother. You mean we need to write a bunch of HTML?

RUSTY: Not quite. You can either download the Bootstrap class definition files from https://getbootstrap.com/, unzip them, and serve them from the stockticker/site/static directory or you can link to the the Bootstrap CDN.[7]

OLEG: You've confused me already. How are we supposed to decide which way to go?

RUSTY: I like to use the Bootstrap CDN during development. But production sites will be more stable if you serve the Bootstrap files from the site/static. That way, your site won't be compromised if Bootstrap's CDN goes down.

MARSHA: So, since we're developers, we use Bootstrap's CDN, right?

RUSTY: Maybe. But installing Bootstrap files in site/static demonstrates nicely how to work with static files in Nitrogen.

---

[6] Check out http://wrapbootstrap.com and http://themeforest.com

[7] Content Delivery Network. http://bootstrapcdn.com

STEVIE: We're here to learn, so I vote for installing the files in site/static.

RUSTY: OK. Point your browser to http://getbootstrap.com. Click on the download button. This links to the download page. Scan your eye down to the "Compiled CSS and JS" section and, again, click on "Download."

STEVIE: Way ahead of you. It's done.

13.3.2. Install Bootstrap files

RUSTY: OK. Downloading from command line:

Listing 13.14 (⇒ $) **Install Bootstrap files**

```
.../site/src$ cd ..
.../stockticker$ cd static
.../site/static$ wget https://github.com/twbs/bootstrap/releases/
        download/v4.3.1/bootstrap-4.3.1-dist.zip
.../site/static$ unzip bootstrap-4.3.1-dist.zip

 Archive:  bootstrap-4.3.1-dist.zip
   creating: bootstrap-4.3.1-dist/css/
   inflating: bootstrap-4.3.1-dist/css/bootstrap.css
   inflating: bootstrap-4.3.1-dist/css/bootstrap.css.map
   ...
.../site/static$ ln -s bootstrap-4.3.1-dist bootstrap
.../site/static$ rm bootstrap-4.3.1-dist.zip
```

RUSTY: If we peek into .../site/static, we see, among other things, the Bootstrap directory:

Listing 13.15 (⇒ $) **list ../site/static**

```
site/static$ ls
bootstrap  bootstrap-4.3.1-dist  css  images  js  nitrogen
```

MARSHA: What was that `ln` command? Was that like making a shortcut on the desktop?

RUSTY: Pretty much. It creates a a symbolic link or symlink from the fake directory `bootstrap` to the actual directory `bootstrap-4.3.1-dist`. Very similar to the Windows concept of shortcuts.

MARSHA: Why do that?

RUSTY: Version 4.3.1 of Bootstrap will almost certainly not be the last version of Bootstrap to be released. So when it comes time to upgrade your Bootstrap, you can do the same steps, download the latest version, unzip it, then update the symlink to point to the new version with `ln -sf new-bootstrap-dist bootstrap`. That means you don't have to change any code that points to the files in question.

13.3.3. Configure SimpleBridge

RUSTY: We need to tell SimpleBridge to recognize Bootstrap as one of our static directories. To do this, open up the SimpleBridge `config file`. but first, let's assign a new port number to our new project.

Listing 13.16 (⇒ $) Open `simple_bridge.config`

```
$ cd ../..
$ vim etc/simple_bridge.config
  ...
  {port, 8000 8002},
  ...
```

RUSTY: Now we can update the static directories. Note that most of the items in the SimpleBridge config list are the same as the list of directories in `.../site/static`. Let's add `bootstrap`:

Listing 13.17 (⇒ `vim`) **Add Bootstrap** (`simple_bridge.config`)

```
...
{static_paths, ["js/", "css/", "images/",
  "nitrogen/", "favicon.ico", "bootstrap/"]},
...
```

RUSTY: Since we changed configuration, we need to shut down Nitrogen and restart it before we continue:

Listing 13.18 (⇒ `>`) **Add Bootstrap**

```
9> q().
stockticker$ bin/nitrogen console
...
1> sync:go().
```

MARSHA: Oookay— what, exactly, did we just do in that config file?

RUSTY: SimpleBridge configures and connects Nitrogen to the underlying web server. We just specified that requests to `bootstrap/*` should be automatically handled by the underlying web server rather than passing through Nitrogen code. This allows the system to handle static files more efficiently.

Nitrogen is actually smart about static files. If a request ends with a file extension like *.html, Nitrogen will assume that it's a static file and try to pass it off to the server on its own. But requests to `bootstrap/*` short-circuits it.

MARSHA: So, if after this change, we made a Nitrogen module called `bootstrap_whatever.erl`, the path `/bootstrap/whatever` wouldn't point to that module?

RUSTY: Precisely. Way to connect the dots there, Marsha!

OLEG: Why do I feel there's more to this story?

RUSTY: Because there is. We still need to:

1. Update our page template.

2. Specify Bootstrap classes in our Nitrogen elements.

13.3.4. Call Bootstrap files from template

We're running short on time. We still have a lot to cover. So bear with me. I'm going to modify bare.html with a fair amount of code. Follow along. If you get lost, check the Bootstrap docs when you get home tonight:

Listing 13.19 (⇒ $) **Edit** `site/templates/bare.html`

```
stockticker/site$ cd site/templates
site/templates$ vim bare.html
  ...
  <meta http-equiv="Content-Type" content="text/html; charset=UTF-8" />
  <meta charset="utf8">
  <meta name="viewport" content="width=device-width, initial-scale=1">
  <title>[[[page:title()]]]</title>
  <script src='/nitrogen/jquery.js' type='text/javascript'
          charset='utf-8'></script>
  <script src='/nitrogen/jquery-ui.min.js' type='text/javascript'
          charset='utf-8'></script>
  <script src='/nitrogen/livevalidation.min.js' type='text/javascript'
          charset='utf-8'></script>
  <script src="/nitrogen/nitrogen.min.js"></script>
  <script src="/nitrogen/bert.min.js"></script>
  <script src="/bootstrap/js/bootstrap.bundle.min.js"></script>
  <link rel="stylesheet" href="/nitrogen/jquery-ui/jquery.ui.all.css">
  <link rel="stylesheet" href="/bootstrap/css/bootstrap.min.css">
  <link rel="stylesheet" href="/nitrogen/nitrogen.css">
  <link rel="stylesheet" href="/css/style.css">
</head>
<body style="padding-top:5em">
  [[[page:body()]]]
```

```
<nav class="navbar navbar-expand-md navbar-dark bg-dark fixed-top">
  <a class="navbar-brand" href="/">
    Stock Ticker
  </a>
  <button type="button" class="navbar-toggler"
      data-toggle="collapse"
      data-target="#main-menu">
    <span class="navbar-toggler-icon"></span>
  </button>
  <div class="collapse navbar-collapse" id="main-menu">
    [[[st_common:menu()]]]
  </div>
</nav>
<main role="main" class="container">
  <div class=row>
    <div class="col-md-offset-2 col-md-4">
      [[[page:body_left()]]]
    </div>
    <div class="col-md-4">
      [[[page:body_right()]]]
    </div>
  </div>
</main>
</body>
  ...
```

OLEG: Oh, man! That *is* a lot of code.

RUSTY: Most of it should be obvious.

STEVIE: Says you.

RUSTY: Come on guys. You're better than this. What are you going to do when I'm not around to hold your hands?

MARSHA: I think I get it. Rusty's code:

- Adds style sheet links to the Bootstrap CSS files.

- Removes the page:body() callout and replaces it with two new callouts: page:body_left() and page:body_right().

- Adds a new callout for `st_common:menu()`, which will, I presume, display a menu. It also defines a new module called `st_common`. I'm guessing that st is an acronym for Stock Ticker).

RUSTY: Not bad!

OLEG: Show off.

RUSTY: Note that the `collapse navbar-collapse` class implements a hamburger menu[8] for mobile users.

Also, the `container` and `col` classes set up the Bootstrap grid system.

But I can't stress enough— Bootstrap classes[9] will give you superpowers.

STEVIE: Like what?

RUSTY: Well, the classes I specified in `bare.html` are a good start. But the Bootstrap class `form-control` is a great way to style form-type elements such as textboxes and dropdowns. You can create cool buttons with the base class `btn` and a subclass like `btn-warning`.

You can find everything you need to know about Bootstrap classes in the documentation.

13.4. Stock Quotes

OLEG: So we ready to snag stock quotes?

RUSTY: We are indeed! Let's delete the existing `index.erl` file and start from scratch:

---

[8]https://apptimize.com/blog/2015/07/the-ultimate-guide-to-the-hamburger-menu/
[9]https://getbootstrap.com

Listing 13.20 (⇒ $) **Revise** (`index.erl`)

```
site/templates$ cd ../src
site/src$ rm index.erl
site/src$ vim index.erl
```

RUSTY: First, we enter the basic boilerplate stuff:

Listing 13.21 (⇒ vim) **Add boilerplate code** (`index.erl`)

```
-module(index).
-include_lib("nitrogen_core/include/wf.hrl").
-compile(export_all).

main() ->
  #template{file="site/templates/bare.html"}.

title() ->
  "Home".
```

MARSHA: Will the stockticker user interface go on this page?

RUSTY: Eventually. But first let's code what we know so far— click something, something happens.

Once we've got that working, we'll modify it with live-update code.
This is how I usually build live-update applications. Simplifies debugging:

Listing 13.22 (⇒ vim) **Live-update code** (`index.erl`)

```
title() ->
  "Home".

body_left() ->
```

489

```
[
  #label{text="Stock Symbol"},
  #textbox{id=symbol},
  #br{},
  #button{
    text="Show Quotes",
    postback=get_quotes
  }
].
```

RUSTY: Nothing mysterious here. We've added a textbox and a button that calls a postback. All familiar stuff.

STEVIE: Didn't you tell us to use Bootstrap classes for buttons and textboxes?

RUSTY: I did. But I want to show you what the form looks like without Bootstrap classes. Before we can check it out in the browser, I've got to stub in st_common:menu() or our template will crash:

Listing 13.23 (⇒ $) **Stub in** st_common:menu() (st_common.erl)

```
site/src$ vim st_common.erl
...
-module(st_common).
-include_lib("nitrogen_core/include/wf.hrl").
-compile(export_all).

menu() -> [].
```

RUSTY: Now, let's take a look in the browser. Open up localhost:8002:

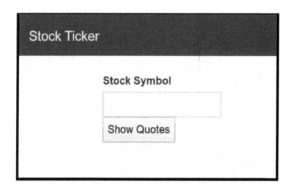

RUSTY: Now, back in index.erl, let's add Bootstrap classes:

Listing 13.24 (⇒ $) **Add Bootstrap classes** (`index.erl`)

```
site/src$ vim index.erl
...
body_left() ->
  [
    #label{text="Stock Symbol"},
    #textbox{id=symbol, class='form-control'},
    #br{},
    #button{
      text="Show Quotes",
      postback=get_quotes,
      class=[btn,'btn-success']
    }
  ].
```

RUSTY: And again, check it out in the browser:

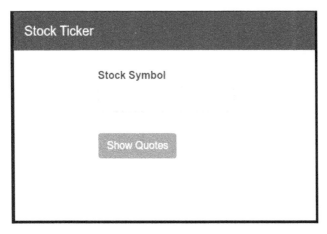

RUSTY: Looks a bit nicer, don't you think?

OLEG: Marginally.

MARSHA: Be nice, Oleg.

OLEG: Kidding. Does look great.

RUSTY: Now let's add body_right():

Listing 13.25 (⇒ vim) **Add body_right (index.erl)**

```
body_left() ->
...

body_right() ->
  #panel{id=quotes}.
```

MARSHA: That's just an empty panel.

STEVIE: Yes, but we'll update it with info from the postback.

MARSHA: OK.

RUSTY: Now we need to get a quote. An event function will do the trick:

Listing 13.26 (⇒ vim) **Define event function (`index.erl`)**

```
body_right() ->
...
event(get_quotes) ->
  Symbol = wf:q(symbol),
  get_quote(Symbol).
```

MARSHA: Why are we implementing a separate get_quote/1 function instead of just doing it all in event/1?

RUSTY: Good question. We could definitely do it all in event/1. But defining a separate function will simplify things when we start periodically polling for results. Also, it's generally good practice to shorten event clauses with a separate function, if only to make the source more readable.[10] Highly complex pages can generate lots of event clauses, and it can really start getting out of hand.

Anyway, what should our stock quotes look like?

STEVIE: We need to show the stock price.

OLEG: Duh.

RUSTY: Well, that's given. What else?

STEVIE: A timestamp would be a good idea.

RUSTY: Great. Anything else?

MARSHA: We should definitely display the stock symbol.

RUSTY: Simple enough. So, we ready to build our get_quote/1 function?

Oleg: I'm on it:

---

[10]https://youtu.be/CQyt9Vlkbis

Listing 13.27 ($\Rightarrow$ **vim**) **Define** `get_quote/1` (`index.erl`)

```erlang
event(get_quotes) ->
...
get_quote(Symbol) ->
  Quote = stock:lookup(Symbol),
  QuoteTime = qdate:to_string("g:i:sa"),
  Body = #panel{text=[
    Symbol,
    " (",
    QuoteTime,
    "): ",
    Quote
  ]},
  wf:insert_top(quotes, Body).
```

STEVIE: Why do I think get_quote is not a good name for this function? After all, the function does two things—retrieves quote data and inserts it into the quotes #panel{}. Wouldn't something like get_and_insert_quote/1 be more descriptive?

RUSTY: Descriptive names definitely make it easier to maintain code:

Listing 13.28 ($\Rightarrow$ **vim**) **Rename** `get_quote/1` (`index.erl`)

```erlang
event(get_quotes) ->
  Symbol = wf:q(symbol),
  get_quote(Symbol).
  get_and_insert_quote(Symbol).

get_quote(Symbol) ->
get_and_insert_quote(Symbol) ->
  Quote = stock:lookup(Symbol),
  ...
```

RUSTY: You good with that, Oleg?

OLEG: Whatever.

RUSTY: Great! Let's test.

Open `http://localhost:8002`, enter a known stock symbol and click "Show Quotes:[11]"

MARSHA: Hey! It works!

OLEG: Yeah, but we want live updates.

RUSTY: Patience, my man.

13.4.1. Live updates with Comet

RUSTY: Nitrogen has supported live updates from the very beginning with a technique called Comet.

---

[11]Be sure to give it a second or two, since it's querying an external source.

495

MARSHA: Comet?

RUSTY: Yeah. Comet... was cutting-edge awesome back in the Web 2.0 days.

STEVIE: Hold up, Grandpa. Please define... Comet?

RUSTY: Comet allows a web server to push data to a browser without the browser explicitly requesting it.

STEVIE: So how does it work?

RUSTY: Comet is actually an umbrella term for several real-time practices used by web frameworks.[12] I'll take a step back to give you brief history of time. Around the year 2000, there was basically no real-time updating of anything in browsers.[13] Every page request, update, or posted form required a full page load or crazy hackery with frames.

Microsoft introduced access to the `IXMLHttpRequest` function in Internet Explorer 5. This function could make a background request to an XML document. Mozilla built this functionality into their eponymously named browser. Folks picked up on this capability and the practice spread like a virus. AJAX was born, the term being short for "Asynchronous Javascript with XML." Basically, a JavaScript call queries the server and the server responds with an XML document. Keep in mind, this is before JSON. The browser traverses the XML doc to make the relevant updates. This was the beginning of Web 2.0.

MARSHA: OK.

RUSTY: It was cool, but it was still a hassle. You had to write special cases for different browsers. Working with XML was, and still is, a drag.

But it was the first time you could update the DOM in real time using data from the server (again, unless you were doing hackery with frames).

MARSHA: I messed around with frames when I first learned HTML.

---

[12] https://www.quora.com/How-does-a-comet-webserver-work
[13] Aside from things like Java applets, Macromedia Flash, and various other plugins.

RUSTY: Comet was an evolution of AJAX.

OLEG: Sounds like a Pokémon card.

MARSHA: Get real, Oleg.

RUSTY: Keep in mind, it was the Stone Age. Native, real-time push to the browser was a pipe dream. Ajax came along and changed everything. Smart folks started using XMLHTTPRequest to retrieve not just XML, but plain text, raw JavaScript and, eventually, JSON.

JavaScript libraries like JQuery abstracted the tedious browser-specific hijinks into a single Ajax call. Really simplified things.

OLEG: So what does that have to do with Comet?

RUSTY: Comet puts Ajax in a loop of long-polling requests. The browser is in a perpetual loop waiting for the server to respond. When the server responds, the client updates something, starts the next request, and waits for more changes.

So, instead of "click something, get a single response," the process became "when data changes on the server, change it on the browser, and wait for more changes."

STEVIE: So is this how Nitrogen handles live updates these days?

RUSTY: Yes and no. Nitrogen can use Comet if necessary. But by default, modern Nitrogen uses websockets. If websockets are unavailable for any reason,[14] Nitrogen falls back to using Comet. Even though Nitrogen uses websockets, the term "Comet" is still used within Nitrogen to represent long-running processes.

MARSHA: How does it work?

---

[14] Websockets would be unavailable if a reverse proxy is misconfigured or outdated, a firewall blocks them, or the user is using a browser so old it doesn't support websockets (like Internet Explorer 9). They can also just be manually disabled.

RUSTY: It uses `wf:comet/1`. Spins up a long-running process then updates data as it becomes available. Sort of like Erlang's `erlang:spawn/1`. This makes it ideal for projects like chat rooms, stock symbol updates, auctions, and the like.

OLEG: The code... The code...

RUSTY: Coming right up:

Listing 13.29 (⇒ `vim`) **Coming right up... Comet** (`index.erl`)

```
event(get_quotes) ->
  Symbol = wf:q(symbol),
  wf:comet(fun() ->
    get_and_insert_quote(Symbol)
  end).
```

STEVIE: That's it?

RUSTY: Almost. Our `get_and_insert_quote/1` function currently runs once then ends. We need to keep it running:

Listing 13.30 (⇒ `vim`) **Revise** `get_and_insert_quote/1` (`index.erl`)

```
get_and_insert_quote(Symbol) ->
  Quote = stock:lookup(Symbol),
  QuoteTime = qdate:to_string("g:i:sa"),
  Body = #panel{text=[
    Symbol,
    " (",QuoteTime,"): ",
    Quote
  ]},
  wf:insert_top(quotes, Body),
  wf:flush(),
  timer:sleep(10000),
  get_and_insert_quote(Symbol).
```

RUSTY: *That*, however, is it. Let me break down what's going on:

- wf:flush()—tells Nitrogen "send all currently queued up actions to the browser." Without the wf:flush() call, no actions will get sent to the browser until the process dies. As it's written, the process will never die naturally; it will just continue looping.

- timer:sleep(10000)—pauses the process for 10 seconds (10,000 milliseconds).

- get_and_insert_quote(Symbol)—loops the process.

STEVIE: Correct me if I'm wrong, but isn't this just an infinite loop? There's no "end process" or base case. In a language like C or PHP, this would eventually fill up the call stack in RAM and crash.

RUSTY: Ah, now you're identifying one of the beating hearts of functional programming— tail-call optimization. The compiler recognizes the result of the last call in a function as the return value. It executes the last call, returns the value, and drops the function from the call stack.

This trick, among other optimizations, makes functional programming possible. Tail-call optimization is well explained in *Learn You Some Erlang.*[15]

MARSHA: But we haven't written anything into our function to make it terminate. What happens if our user closes the browser? Won't the process run forever? Sounds like wasted cycles to me.

RUSTY: Great question! Nitrogen has you covered. When you spawn a function with wf:comet, Nitrogen starts a process that periodically checks if the user is connected. If Nitrogen determines that the user is no longer connected, or their browser has hung, then Nitrogen terminates any and all Comet processes associated with that particular page. There is a short window to accommodate temporary connection loss of say 10 to 20 seconds, but once the allotted time passes, Nitrogen terminates all orphaned long-running processes.

---

[15]http://learnyousomeerlang.com/recursion

MARSHA: Way cool!

STEVIE: Hey! Wait! While you were babbling on, I added one stock, clicked "Show Quotes," then entered another stock and clicked it again. Look what it's doing!

OLEG: Whoa, it seems to be flipping back and forth between showing the two different stocks.

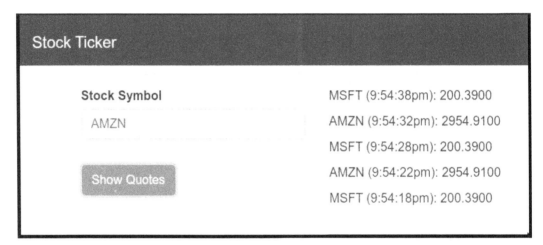

RUSTY: Great catch, Stevie. We didn't tell our system to cancel the original lookup process, so it has several processes running in parallel. Let's make tweaks to kill the process.

13.4.2. Track and kill a Comet process

RUSTY: We need to know which process to kill. So we need a way to track processes. `wf:comet` returns a tuple in the format `{ok, Pid}`, where `Pid` is a `Process ID`. We can store the `Pid` with a call to `wf:state/2`:

Listing 13.31 (⇒ vim) **Track the Comet process** (`index.erl`)

```
event(get_quotes) ->
  Symbol = wf:q(symbol),
  {ok, Pid} = wf:comet(fun() ->
    get_and_insert_quote(Symbol)
  end),
  wf:state(stock_pid, Pid).
```

MARSHA: `wf:state/2`? That's new.

RUSTY: A Nitrogen session stores user information, like username, user ID, etc. These values comprise "page state."

The initial request and postbacks change the page state. No user can view another user's page state. Page state values are cleared when the page is reloaded. Think of page state as a hyper-localized key-value store.

The `wf:state` command enables us to determine if the session is active or dormant.

MARSHA: So the `wf:state` call stores Pid, the Process ID, in a session variable?

RUSTY: Close, but not quite. It stores it in the page state, which goes away when the page is navigated away from or reloaded. It's actually eventually stored on the client's browser.

STEVIE: How do we retrieve it?

RUSTY: Behold:

Listing 13.32 (⇒ vim) **Retrieve Comet process** (`index.erl`)

```
event(get_quotes) ->
  OldPid = wf:state(stock_pid),
  Symbol = wf:q(symbol),
```

```
{ok, Pid} = wf:comet(fun() ->
  get_and_insert_quote(Symbol)
end),
wf:state(stock_pid, Pid).
```

RUSTY: We've captured the `Pid` in the variable `OldPid`. Now we build a function to kill our processes:

Listing 13.33 ($\Rightarrow$ vim) **Kill the old Comet process** (`index.erl`)

```
event(get_quotes) ->
  OldPid = wf:state(stock_pid),
  maybe_kill(OldPid),
  Symbol = wf:q(symbol),
  {ok, Pid} = wf:comet(fun() ->
    get_and_insert_quote(Symbol)
  end),
  wf:state(stock_pid, Pid).

maybe_kill(undefined) -> ok;
maybe_kill(Pid) -> erlang:exit(Pid, kill).
```

MARSHA: Why did you make a separate kill function instead of just calling `erlang:exit` directly?

STEVIE: The first time we enter the page there won't be a `Pid` to kill, right?

RUSTY: Spot on, Stevie. When we enter the page the process id is undefined. `erlang:exit/2` will crash if we call it with anything other than a process id.

STEVIE: So we need to catch when the process ID is undefined and do nothing.

RUSTY: Exactly. The site will update indefinitely until the user leaves the page, at which point Nitrogen will terminate the running process.

That, in a nutshell, is how Comet works in Nitrogen.

13.4.3. User interaction

OLEG: But what about applications like chat or games where users interact with one another?

RUSTY: Great question. But I'm not sure why users of our stock ticker would want to interact with one another.

MARSHA: Well, investors like to know what other investors are thinking.

STEVIE: Hey, yeah, maybe users can share their favorite stock picks with other users.

RUSTY: We *could* implement a simple "favorites" system. Shouldn't be too hard.

MARSHA: How would it work?

RUSTY: Suppose we broadcast a notification to the effect of "A user has added a favorite stock XYZ." How does that sound?

OLEG: Awesome!

MARSHA: Does that mean that every user has a list of favorite stocks?

RUSTY: Easy enough to do:

Listing 13.34 (⇒ `vim`) **Add favorites list** (`index.erl`)

```
event(get_quotes) ->
    ...
  wf:state(stock_pid, Pid);
event({favorite, Symbol}) ->
```

```
    add_favorite(Symbol).

  add_favorite(Symbol) ->
    Favorites = wf:session_default(favorites, []),
    NewFavorites = [Symbol | Favorites],
    wf:session(favorites, NewFavorites).

maybe_kill(undefined) -> ok;
maybe_kill(Pid) -> erlang:exit(Pid, kid).
```

RUSTY: Note the `wf:session` calls.

> `wf:session_default(favorites, [])` attempts to return the list of current favorites from the session store. If the list of favorites is not found, it returns an empty list.

`add_favorite/1` then appends the new favorite stock symbol to the favorites list and stores the updated list back into the session database.

MARSHA: But where's the user interaction?

RUSTY: We're getting there. We just need to add a `#flash` to `index.erl`:

Listing 13.35 (⇒ vim) **Add #flash element (index.erl)**

```
body_right() ->
  [
    #panel{id=quotes},
    #panel{id=favorite_holder},
    #flash{}
  ].
```

MARSHA: Remind me. What does the `#flash{}` element do again?

RUSTY: Honestly, nothing yet. The flash element is merely a container for flash messages we wire to the page. We'll wire the messages by-and-by.

STEVIE: We need a button to mark favorites, don't we?

RUSTY: We do. We can add the button to the get_quotes event:

Listing 13.36 (⇒ vim) **Add button to get_quotes event** (index.erl)

```
event(get_quotes) ->
  OldPid = wf:state(stock_pid),
  maybe_kill(OldPid),
  Symbol = wf:q(symbol),
  {ok, Pid} = wf:comet(fun() ->
    get_and_insert_quote(Symbol)
  end),
  wf:state(stock_pid, Pid),
  wf:update(favorite_holder, favorite_button(Symbol));
event({favorite, Symbol}) ->
  add_favorite(Symbol).

favorite_button(Symbol) ->
  #button{
    class=[btn, 'btn-info'],
    text=["Favorite ", Symbol],
    postback={favorite, Symbol}
  }.
```

RUSTY: Last but not least, we need to start a global Comet process.

MARSHA: Do tell, oh guru.

13.4.4. Start a global Comet process

RUSTY: Basically, we give our Comet process a name so other users can connect to it.

Let's do this in body_left/0:

Listing 13.37 (⇨ vim) **Give Comet process a name** (`index.erl`)

```
body_left() ->
  wf:comet_global(fun notify/0, stock_notify),
  [
    #label{text="Stock Symbol"}
    ...
```

RUSTY: Now, for this to work, we need to define the `notify/0` function:

Listing 13.38 (⇨ vim) **Define** `notify/0` (`index.erl`)

```
title() ->
  "Home".

notify() ->
  receive
    {favorite, Symbol} ->
      wf:flash(wf:f("A user has favorited the symbol ~s", [Symbol]))
  end,
  wf:flush(),
  ?MODULE:notify().

body_left() ->
  ...
```

OLEG: Wheels within wheels.

RUSTY: It's not as bad as it looks. The only thing that's new here is the receive block. This tells the current process to wait until we receive a message that looks like {favorite, Symbol}. If that message fails to come, the process will patiently wait until the session ends. But it won't block any other processes, so it's perfectly safe.

MARSHA: Sort of looks like a case statement.

RUSTY: Technically, the terminology is "case expression." But yes. It's just like a case expression, including the ability to specifiy multiple matching clauses.

You can even add a timeout in the form `after` X, where X is some non-negative integer including zero which says "If nothing is received after X seconds, evaluate this chunk instead." It's pretty neato-burrito.

STEVIE: Ah, if the receive block receives the message `{favorite, Symbol}`, it sticks a message in the `#flash{}` element we defined earlier.

RUSTY: Bingo!

MARSHA: I think I see. But how do we actually send messages?

RUSTY: This will blow your mind! We use the `wf:send_global` function.

MARSHA: Ah, that's it?

RUSTY: Sorry. I exaggerate to make a point. But the `wf:send_global` function is straightforward. Let's update add_favorite/0:

Listing 13.39 (⇒ vim) **Update** `add_favorite/0` (`index.erl`)

```
add_favorite(Symbol) ->
  wf:send_global(stock_notify, {favorite, Symbol}),
  Favorites = wf:session_default(favorites, []),
  NewFavorites = [Symbol | Favorites],
```

RUSTY: That's it. Now add_favorite/1 will broadcast the {favorite, Symbol} message to everyone connected to the global Comet pool called stock_notify.

Let's give it a try. We'll have to open the page in two tabs to see the messaging. Even better, we do it on two different machines.

Marsha, want to open it up on your tablet?

MARSHA: Can do. Looks great!

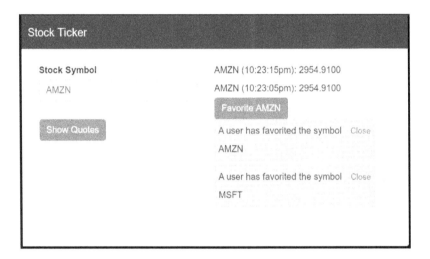

13.5. A menu for stockticker

OLEG: Let's add our menu now. We stubbed it in, but it doesn't do anything.

MARSHA: Know what? I'd love to put stockticker, nindex, and nnotes together into one master application.

RUSTY: Easy to do. You already know most of what you need to know so I'll leave it as a homework assignment.

OLEG: Guys... `st_common:menu()`? Can we get on with it?

STEVIE: Menus are kind of a pain, Mr. Nail. Any tips?

RUSTY: Bootstrap is your friend. Offers more than we can cover today. Plenty of help on the web.[16]

A Brief Tangent to a `favorites` Function

RUSTY: But to get you started, let's create a function to list favorite stocks and call it from st_common:menu/0:

Listing 13.40 (⇒ $) **Add favorites export (`st_common.erl`)**

```
site/src$ vim site/src/st_common.erl

-module(st_common).
-include_lib("nitrogen_core/include/wf.hrl").
-compile(export_all).
-export([favorites/0, menu/0]).

menu() -> [].

favorites() ->
```

RUSTY: As you'll recall, we defined the favorites list as a session variable. No time to get fancy, so we'll just call it up and display it in all it's raw glory:

Listing 13.41 (⇒ vim) **Define `favorites/0` (`st_common.erl`)**

```
...
-export([favorites/0, menu/0]).

menu() -> [].

favorites() ->
  wf:session_default(favorites, []).
```

---

[16]https://www.w3schools.com/bootstrap/bootstrap_navbar.asp

MARSHA: Why did we make this? I thought we were making the menu.

RUSTY: Just adding a helper function to pull our favorites. If we ever decide to add favorites to a database (which we should), then we can call `st_common:favorites()` to pull our list of favorites rather than relying specifically on the session variable.

Back on Task: Our Menu

RUSTY: So, help me out. What links do we need in our menu?

MARSHA: Well, we definitely need a Home link.

RUSTY: Good. What next?

OLEG: Duh. Favorites.

MARSHA: Oh, that's why you defined the `favorites()` function. I get it.

RUSTY: Anything else?

STEVIE: Should be good. Maybe eventually we'll add a login system.

MARSHA: If we merge it into nnotes, we can just use the login system from there.

RUSTY: Here are our menu items then:

Listing 13.42   (⇒ `vim`) **Specify menu items (`st_common.erl`)**

```
menu() -> [].

menu_items() ->
  [
    {"Home", "/"},
    {"Favorite Stocks", "/favorites"}
  ].
```

OLEG: Tuples! How can we turn tuples into Bootstrap menus?

STEVIE: We don't even have a page named "favorites" to display our favorite stocks.

RUSTY: I'm going to leave adding the favorites page up to you for homework. As for tuples, there are at least three common ways that pop to mind. First, menus in Bootstrap are just hyperlinks, so we'll use the #link{} element.

OLEG: Oh, I didn't realize they were just links. That should be easy enough to handle.

RUSTY: Yep. But for the sake of completeness, I'll show you three different ways of iterating to make menus or lists of items in Nitrogen: the #bind{} element, the function lists:map/2, or list comprehensions.

OLEG: Choices. Choices. Don't we just love choices.

RUSTY: Totally up to you which one you choose. Simple matter of style or convenience.

STEVIE: So how can we make an informed choice if we don't know how to do all of them? We've done lists:map and list comprehensions, but we haven't seen #bind before.

RUSTY: Fair enough. I'll start with #bind.

13.5.1. The #bind element

RUSTY: To help us quickly illustrate the different iterations, we're going to make a new function for each. We'll call this one menu_bind/1.

Listing 13.43 (⇒ vim) **Make `menu_bind/1` (`st_common.erl`)**

```
menu() -> [].
  Items = menu_items(),
  menu_bind(Items).

menu_bind(Items) ->
```

RUSTY: Nitrogen's #bind{} element makes it easy to display lists of data on a Nitrogen page. To quote the docs, "...you define a set of 'data', a 'body' containing one or more elements, and a 'map' that tells the bind element how to map a data row into the body."[17]

Clearly, Items qualifies as a "set of data." The links in Items "map" labels to links, e.g., {Label, URL}. At risk of confusing you, we can state this in another way:

Listing 13.44 (⇒ vim) **Map labels to links (`st_common.erl`)**

```
menu_bind(Items) ->
    Map = {menu_link@text, menu_link@url},
```

RUSTY: Follow me?

MARSHA: Nope. Lost me.

STEVIE: Same.

OLEG: Maybe it'll make more sense if you show us the rest of the code.

RUSTY: OK. I'll start with the #list{} element, since we need this whether or not we use #bind{}:

---

[17]http://nitrogenproject.com/doc/elements/bind.html

Listing 13.45 (⇒ vim) **Define list element** (`st_common.erl`)

```
menu_bind(Items) ->
  Map = {menu_link@text, menu_link@url},
  #list{class='navbar-nav', body=[
```

RUSTY: nav and 'navbar-nav' are Bootstrap classes. They configure a list inside a navigation bar.

Next, we call #bind{}, which will loop over our tuples:

Listing 13.46 (⇒ vim) **Use #bind{}** (`st_common.erl`)

```
menu_bind(Items) ->
  Map = {menu_link@text, menu_link@url},
  #list{class='navbar-nav', body=[
    #bind{data=Items, map=Map, body=[
      #listitem{class='nav-item', body=[
        #link{class='nav-link', id=menu_link}
      ]}
    ]}
  ]}.
```

MARSHA: Ooooooh, okay. Getting interesting. You made a single #listitem{} containing a single #link{} element, and gave it an ID, but didn't define anything else.

STEVIE: Oh, I think I get it. The first element of the Map tuple is transformed into the #link{}'s text attribute, and the second element is transformed into the #link{}'s url attribute.

RUSTY: Bingo!

STEVIE: Oh, then #bind.body gets repeated for every item assigned to #bind.data.

OLEG: You've left me behind.

RUSTY: Read the #bind{} docs. Should clear it up for you.

MARSHA: Just loaded the page, and it looks great:

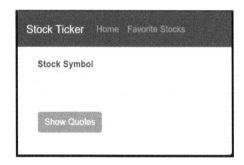

13.5.2. Iterating with `lists:map/2`

RUSTY: The function `list:map/2` provides another way to implement our menu. Let's make a new function called menu_map/1:

Listing 13.47 (⇒ vim) **Add `menu_map/1` (`st_common.erl`)**

```erlang
menu() ->
  Items = menu_items(),
  menu_bind(Items).
  menu_map(Items).

menu_map(Items) ->
  #list{class='navbar-nav',body=[
    lists:map(fun({Label, Url}) ->
      #listitem{class='nav-item', body=[
        #link{class='nav-link', text=Label, url=Url}
      ]}
    end, Items)
  ]}.

menu_bind(Items) ->
  ...
```

MARSHA: This is odd. Seems like it should be simpler.

RUSTY: Maybe. Probably because of the intermixing of elements and `lists:map`. I find it jarring too. But there are situations where I'd rather use a `lists:map/2` or a list comprehension than `#bind{}`.

For instance, if I'm wiring actions to the repeated elements, I prefer to use a map or list comprehension.

If I want more readable source code, I'll gravitate toward `#bind{}`.

MARSHA: How would you use a list comprehension?

13.5.3. Iterating with a list comprehension

RUSTY: I tend to use list comprehensions when combined with other functions. If our data was slightly more complicated, I'd write it like this:

Listing 13.48 ($\Rightarrow$ `vim`) **Make `menu_bind/1` (`st_common.erl`)**

```
menu() ->
  Items = menu_items(),
  menu_map(Items).
  menu_list_comp(Items).

menu_list_comp(Items) ->
  #list{class='navbar-nav',body=[
    [draw_item(Item) || Item <- Items]
  ]}.

draw_item({Label, Url}) ->
  #listitem{class='nav-item', body=[
    #link{class='nav-link', text=Label, url=Url}
  ]}.

menu_map(Items) ->
```

MARSHA: Why didn't we just hard code the list as a series of #listitem{} elements and define the contents that way? It would be shorter code.

RUSTY: It definitely would be, especially with only the two menu items, but if we had more items, then the code would start getting copy-pasty, and we don't want that. Employing #bind, lists:map, or list comprehensions sets us up for future scaling. Maybe we want to use a different list of menu options for different pages. Or maybe we want to load the menu options from our application's database.

13.6. Stub in the Favorites Page

RUSTY: Lastly, let's stub in our "favorites" page:

Listing 13.49 ($\Rightarrow$ $) Create `favorites.erl`

```
site/src$ vim favorites.erl

-module(favorites).
-include_lib("nitrogen_core/include/wf.hrl").
-compile(export_all).

main() ->
  #template{file="site/templates/bare.html"}.

title() -> "Favorites".
```

RUSTY: We need body_left():

Listing 13.50 (⇒ vim) **Define** `body_left/0` (`favorites.erl`)

```erlang
title() -> "Favorites".

body_left() ->
  Favorites = st_common:favorites(),
  wf:join(Favorites, #br{}).
```

RUSTY: Should be good to test in your browser: `localhost:8002`. Clicking "Favorite Stocks" should take us to this page:

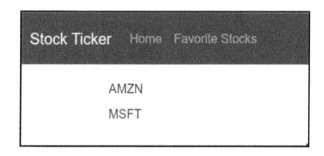

13.7. Homework

Possible improvements:

1. Update the Favorite button to show when a stock is already in the favorites list. (Hint: Use `lists:member/2`). If it is, change the button's behavior to be an "Unfavorite" button. When a user unfavorites a stock, it should also notify all connected clients.

2. Our favorites page is very sparse. It should list our favorite stocks (pulling the list from the session) and display each stock's current price next to it. Try making a table with the `#table{}` element.

517

3. There is a bug in our API. Stockticker crashes when stock lookup fails. (Hint: `wf:json_decode` will return `undefined` if it encounters invalid JSON or if the internet goes down.)

4. There is an exploit we did not fix that notifies users that other users have favorited a stock symbol. To see the exploit in action, enter the following ticker symbol: `<script>alert("gotcha")</script>`, then click Show Quotes then the Favorite button. A JavaScript alert box will pop up on every connected client. Your task here is to close this exploit. Refer to Chapter 12 for how to fix this.

14. Custom Elements

On this fine day we find the intrepid Erlingo! dev team sprawled around a make-shift conference table littered with notebook computers and lunch leavings, Lloyd London pecking at his keyboard.

BOSSMAN: So, London, what do you have for us today?

LLOYD: A tuna fish sandwich?

BOSSMAN: No. No. Bag-Lunch Presentation Day, remember? You drew the short straw.

RUSTY: We await your wisdom with bated breath, Big Man.

LLOYD: Then prepare for enlightenment. Nitrogen elements. Wouldn't you love to roll your own?

RUSTY: We can do that?

LLOYD: We can. And it's not that hard.

Notebooks to the ready, o ye brave tech warriors.

14.1. A Simple Element: #b{}

Part of the power of Nitrogen is its "Erlang-Record-As-Element" abstraction.

If you find a repetitive pattern in your code, the DRY[1] principle suggests it's time to abstract it. Nitrogen elements do just that. But, suppose existing Nitrogen elements don't fit the bill. The answer is to create your own custom Nitrogen element.

---

[1]DRY = Don't Repeat Yourself.

So, for learning purposes, let's create the Nitrogen #b{} element from scratch. As you all know, the HTML tag transforms normal text into bold<b>.[2] The #b{} element will be an abstraction of that tag.

To get this show on the road, we'll make a new app:[3]

Listing 14.1 (⇒ $) **Create a new app and let's edit the port number**

```
~/nitrogen$ make slim_cowboy PROJECT=custom_elements
...
*******************************************************
Generated a slim-release Nitrogen project
in ../custom_elements, configured to run on yaws.
*******************************************************
~/nitrogen$ cd ../custom_elements
custom_elements$ vim etc/simple_bridge.erl
...
{port, 8000 8003}
...
```

Fire up the Nitrogen system:

Listing 14.2 (⇒ $) **Start Nitrogen**

```
custom_elements$ bin/nitrogen console
...
1> sync:go().
```

Then open up .../site/include/records.hrl, add the following line, then save:

---

[2]We understand styling tags are deprecated, but this is a useful tag for demonstration purposes.

[3]All the code and changes for this chapter can be found at
https://github.com/BuildItWithNitrogen/custom_elements/commits

Listing 14.3 (⇒ $) **Create a new sample app**

```
.../custom_elements$ cd site/include
.../site/include$ vim records.hrl

%% Include any application-specific custom elements, actions, or valida-
tors below

-record(b, {?ELEMENT_BASE(element_b), text="", html_encode=true}).
```

Okay, what does this mean?

- **-record(b**—You'll recognize this as a plain vanilla record definition.

- **?ELEMENT_BASE(element_b)**—Invokes an ?ELEMENT_BASE macro, which creates the base element fields. Base element fields include id, class, style, and title attributes among others. The macro takes the name of the module that will actually render our element as its only argument. In our case, we're going to call our module element_b.

- **text="", html_encode=true**—This establishes which custom attributes we'd like to use when creating our element. We want the user to be able to specify a text value with an empty string as the default value for text and true the default value for html_encode.

So that's the first step.

Now we need to create a module. By convention, custom elements go into the directory site/src/elements. Since we specified element_b as our module in our record definition, we must call our module element_b.erl. This module must export two functions:

- **reflect/0**—returns a list of the fields used in the element. These fields are mostly called internally by Nitrogen.

- **render_element/1**—this is the function that transforms the values in our element record into user interface code that can be executed by the browser.

Listing 14.4 (⇒ $) Define `element_b.erl`

```
.../site/include$ cd ../src
.../site/src$ vim element_b.erl

-module(element_b).
-include_lib("nitrogen_core/include/wf.hrl").
-include("records.hrl").
-export([reflect/0, render_element/1]).
```

Note `nitrogen_core/include/wf.hrl` and `records.hrl`. These enable us to invoke other Nitrogen elements in `render_element/1`. You can define Nitrogen elements in terms of other Nitrogen elements. But, eventually, you must return HTML.

Here's the definition of `reflect/0`:

Listing 14.5 (⇒ vim) Define `reflect/0` (`element_b.erl`)

```
...
-export([reflect/0, render_element/1]).
reflect() -> record_info(fields, b).
```

Erlang records are converted to plain tuples at compile time. But suppose we need to know field names at run time? The function `record_info(fields, RecordName)` makes that possible. Here's the secret sauce—`render_element/1`:

Listing 14.6 (⇒ vim) Define `render_element/1` (`element_b.erl`)

```
reflect() -> record_info(fields, b).

render_element(Rec = #b{}) ->
    Text = Rec#b.text,
    Encode = Rec#b.html_encode,
    Body = wf:html_encode(Text, Encode),
    wf_tags:emit_tag(b, Body, [
        {class, Rec#b.class},
        {title, Rec#b.title},
```

```
      {style, Rec#b.style},
      {data_fields, Rec#b.data_fields}
  ]).
```

Save it. Now note that render_element executes text attributes specified by wf:html_encode. The parameter Rec = #b{} ensures that render_element can be called only by a #b{} record. The function wf_tags:emit_tag/3 produces the desired HTML tags.

The arguments for wf_tags:emit_tag are:

```
wf_tags:emit_tag(TagName, Content, Attributes)
```

- **TagName** should be b, since we're making a <b> tag. Substitute blink and it would produce the long-deprecated <blink> tag and simultaneously transport us back to 1995.

- **Content** is the text that goes between the opening and closing tags. In our case, it ends up being the HTML-encoded version of our text field.

- **Attributes** is a proplist, which gets converted into the attribute="value" pairs found inside an HTML tag.

We can experiment with this in the shell:

Listing 14.7 (⇒ $) **Test** wf_tags:emit_tag/3 **in the Erlang shell**

```
.../site/src$ cd ../../
.../custom_elements$ erl

1> wf_tags:emit_tag(blink, "Welcome to 1995",
      [{class, my_blink}]).
["<","blink",
  [[" ","class","=\"","my_blink","\""]],
  ">","Welcome to 1995","</","blink",">"]
```

523

Note that Nitrogen's `emit_tag` function returns an Erlang IOList. Erlang IOLists are an optimization that speedup string building.[4]

For more readable output, wrap the previous call with `iolist_to_binary/1`:

Listing 14.8 (⇒ >) **Experiment with `iolist_to_binary/1`**

```
> iolist_to_binary(v(-1)).
<<"<blink class=\"my_blink\">Welcome to 1995</blink>">>
```

RUSTY: Whoa! Hold up! What's that `v(-1)` business?

LLOYD: Oh that. It's a shell function to retrieve the last return value from the shell. Handy now and again—a convenience function available only in the Erlang shell. It cannot be used inside a module. Whatever negative number you assign to the function `v/1` will take you back that many return values.[5] So `v(-1)` retrieves the last return value, `v(-2)` retrieves the second-to-last return value, and so on.

RUSTY: Learn something every day. Trudge on good friar.

LLOYD: By your leave.

All that's left is to compile our module and use it in our application. So let's create a sample page called "sweettag" to test our sweet new tag:

Listing 14.9 (⇒ $) **Create `sweettag.erl`**

```
.../site/src$ vim sweettag.erl

-module(sweettag).
-include_lib("nitrogen_core/include/wf.hrl").
-include("records.hrl"). %% bring in our custom element
```

---

[4]See String Building and IOLists on page 551 for more about strings and IO Lists.
[5]See `http://www.erlang.org/doc/man/shell.html` for more sneaky Erlang shell-only commands.

```
-compile(export_all).

main() ->
  #template{file="site/templates/bare.html"}.

body() ->
  #panel{body=[
    #h2{text="Are you ready for the awesome?!"},
    #h1{text="I said: ARE YOU READY FOR THE AWESOME?!"},
    #br{},
    #br{},
    #b{text="BOOM BABY, THIS IS THE AWESOME!"}
  ]}.
```

And there it is! Our custom #b{} element and a sample of its usage from start
to finish! I'll let you compile and test on your own time.

RUSTY: Not so fast! Couldn't we use pattern matching to eliminate extra lines
in render_element/2?

LLOYD: We could. But I referenced the fields with Record#b.fieldname for
sake of readability.

But you're right. In the wild it's quite common to use pattern matching to
shorten code.

Switching back to element_b.erl, we could redefine render_element/1 as:

Listing 14.10 (⇒ $) **Redefine** render_element/1 (element_b.erl)

```
.../site/src$ vim element_b.erl
...
render_element(Rec = #b{text=Text, html_encode=Encode}) ->
    Text = Rec#b.text,
    Encode = Rec#b.html_encode,
    Body = wf:html_encode(Text, Encode),
    wf_tags:emit_tag(b, Body, [
        {class, Rec#b.class},
        {title, Rec#b.title},
```

```
        {style, Rec#b.style},
        {data_fields, Rec#b.data_fields}
    ]).
```

LLOYD: The variables Text and Encode get bound in the function definition, cutting down on the lines of code.

Here's how it looks, opening up **localhost:8003/sweettag**:

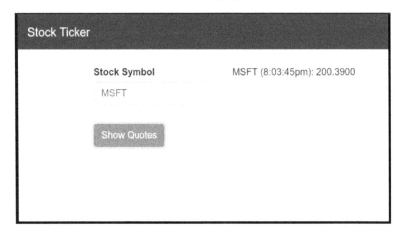

LLOYD: But let me get on with my presentation. Be prepared to be blown away with a more advanced custom element.

14.2. Advanced Custom Element #time_selector{}

LLOYD: Bear with me as I pick up the pace since we all have work to do.

First, we create a record in site/include/records.hrl. You've been here, done that:

Listing 14.11 (⇒ $) Define `time_selector` record (records.hrl)

```
.../site/src$ cd ../include
.../site/include$ vim records.hrl
...
-record(b, {...}).

-record(time_selector, {?ELEMENT_BASE(element_time_selector),
        start=0, finish=1440, increment=60, value}).
```

Now we create site/src/elements/element_time_selector.erl:

Listing 14.12 (⇒ $) Create `elements_time_selector.erl`

```
.../site/include$ cd ../src/elements
.../site/src/elements$ vim element_time_selector.erl

-module(element_time_selector).
-include_lib("nitrogen_core/include/wf.hrl").
-include("records.hrl").
-export([reflect/0, render_element/1]).

reflect() -> record_info(fields, time_selector).
```

So much for boilerplate. Now to the heart of the matter:

Listing 14.13 (⇒ vim) Define `render_element/4`
(`element_time_selector.erl`)

```
reflect() -> record_info(fields, time_selector).

render_element(Rec = #time_selector{start=Start,
        finish=Finish, increment=Inc, value=Value}) ->
    Times = lists:seq(Start, Finish, Inc),
    Options = [format_time_option(T) || T <- Times],
    #dropdown{
        options=Options,
        value=Value,
```

527

```
    class=Rec#time_selector.class,
    style=Rec#time_selector.style,
    title=Rec#time_selector.title,
    data_fields=Rec#time_selector.data_fields
  }.
```

RUSTY: Note that we've passed the values of Start, Finish, Inc, and Value into render_element/1. We've used lists:seq/3 to create a list of times from Start to Finish incremented by Inc. Finally, we've iterated through the Times list with the as-of-yet undefined function format_time/1. This gives us a list of optional times to pass into the #dropdown element.

RUSTY: Hold it, compadre. Looks like your take on render_element returns a Nitrogen element instead of HTML. Isn't that kind of weird?

LLOYD: Not at all. This is the beauty of Nitrogen. Everything can be programmed as Nitrogen elements. The Nitrogen rendering engine will recognize the function has returned *more* Nitrogen elements and render those elements accordingly. Indeed, there are several built-in Nitrogen elements that are actually composed of multiple elements.

That said, this could lead to problems. Let's say you make two custom elements. We'll call them #x{} and #y{}. #x{}'s render_element/1 function returns a #y{} and #y{}'s render_element/1 function returns a #x{}. In this situation, the Nitrogen renderer could get stuck in an infinite loop, either never returning or, in certain conditions, running out of memory and unceremoniously bringing down the system.

Anyway, let's finish up by creating format_time_option/1. The solution is simple enough to code it directly. But if we were coding something more complicated, like accounting for time zones or formats, you'd definitely want to use the previously introduced qdate:

Listing   **14.14** (⇒ vim)   format_time/1
(element_time_selector.erl)

```
        data_fields=Rec#time_selector.data_fields
    }.

format_time_option(Time) ->
    TimeStr = format_time(Time),
    #option{text=TimeStr, value=wf:to_list(Time)}.

format_time(Time) ->
    Hour = Time div 60,
    Minute = Time rem 60,
    wf:f("~2..0w:~2..0w", [Hour, Minute]).
```

Integer division with the Erlang function `div` and integer modulo with the
Erlang function `rem` will fix this in short order.[6] But I'll leave that to your
genius and curiosity.

14.2.1. Testing `#time_selector`

Does it work?

Let's test it in the `sweettag.erl` module. We can leave the header as is, but
we need to redefine the body() function:

Listing **14.15** (⇒ $) Test #time_selector (sweettag.erl)

```
.../src/elements$ cd ../
.../site/src$ vim sweettag.erl

...
body() ->
  #panelbody=[
    #h2{text="Are you ready for the awesome?!"},
    #h1{text="I said: ARE YOU READY FOR THE AWESOME?!"},
    #br{},
    #br{},
```

---

[6]https://www.erlang.org/doc/reference_manual/expressions.html, Section 8.12

```
#b{text="BOOM BABY, THIS IS THE AWESOME!"}
#h1{text="Pick a time during the business day"},
#time_selector{start=480, finish=1020, increment=30}
].
```

We can test it now.

PICK A TIME DURING THE BUSINESS DAY

08:00 ▼

Our dropdown shows times from 8:00 through 17:00 in half-hour increments. But we need a postback to see the return value:

Listing 14.16 (⇒ vim) **Add button and event/1 (sweettag.erl)**

```
body() ->
  [
    #h1{text="Pick a time during the business day"},
    #time_selector{id=time, start=480, finish=1020,
                   increment=30},
    #button{text="I've decided", postback=select_time}
  ].

event(select_time) ->
  Time = wf:to_integer(wf:q(time)),
  FormattedTime = element_time_selector:format_time(Time),
  wf:wire(#alert{text=["You picked: ", FormattedTime]}).
```

A click on the button "I've made my decision" will pop up a JavaScript alert with the text "You picked: 9:30," or whatever time you've selected.

BOSSMAN: Ah, London, my boy, You forgot to export format_time/1 from element_time_selector.

LLOYD: Ah, good catch. Grey Beards 1, Skins 0:

Listing 14.17 (⇨ $) **Export** elements_time_selector:format_time/1

```
site/src$ vim elements/element_time_selector.erl
...
-export([reflect/0, render_element/1, format_time/1]).
```

That should work! Just need to compile and point to http://localhost:8003/sweettag in your browser. Then pick a time and click the "I've decided" button.

14.3. X-Treme `#time_selector{}`! Custom Postbacks

LLOYD: Some Nitrogen elements generate their own postbacks rather than using the usual event/1 function. The function #inplace_textbox{}, for instance, generates the call inplace_textbox_event/2.

Here's the trick: Generate a postback and use the delegate attribute to redirect the postback to your element's render module. Then handle the postback from that module and make a call back to our page module.

RUSTY: Well that's clear as mud.

LLOYD: Mea culpa.

Let's say we want to have the #time_selector{} element automatically generate a postback called time_selector_event(Tag, FormattedTime), where FormattedTime is a string representation of the time: "8:00" rather than the integer 480.

To do this, we need to modify our record definition to include a tag attribute that will identify our element on the page; that is, disambiguate it from other #time_selector{} elements we might have on the page:

Listing 14.18 (⇒ $) **Add `tag` attribute to `time_selector` record (`records.hrl`)**

```
src/elements$ cd ../include
site/include$ vim records.hrl

-record(time_selector, {?ELEMENT_BASE(element_time_selector),
        start=0, finish=1440, increment=60, value, tag}).
```

...And revise the time_selector element code:

Listing 14.19 (⇒ $) Revise `element_time_selector.erl`

```
.../site/include$ cd ../src/elements
.../src/elements$ vim element_time_selector.erl

...
-export([reflect/0, render_element/1, format_time/1, event/1]).

reflect() -> record_info(fields, time_selector).

render_element(Rec = #time_selector{start=Start,
    finish=Finish, increment=Inc, value=Value, tag=Tag}) ->
  Times = lists:seq(Start, Finish, Inc),
  Options = [format_time_option(T) || T <- Times],
  ID = wf:temp_id(),
  #dropdown{
    options=Options,
    value=Value,
    id=ID,
    postback={Tag, ID},
    delegate=?MODULE,
    class=Rec#time_selector.class,
    style=Rec#time_selector.style,
    data_fields=Rec#time_selector.data_fields
  }.

event({Tag, ID}) ->
  Time = wf:to_integer(wf:q(ID)),
  FormattedTime = format_time(Time),
  Page = wf:page_module(),
  Page:time_selector_event(Tag, FormattedTime).
```

RUSTY: Phew!

LLOYD: Yes, there is a bit to unpack here.

1. We bound the Tag attribute into render_element/1.

2. We generated a temporary id, which is necessary for these kinds of "internal postbacks."

3. We assigned the temporary id to #dropdown and {Tag, ID} to the postback and changed the postback delegate to ?MODULE, that is, the element_time_selector module.

4. We created an event/1 handler function.

RUSTY: Oh, that's all? But why?

LLOYD: Bust my chops. The event/1 handler function:

1. Retrieves the Tag and the ID.

2. Uses the ID to get the value of the #dropdown{} and converts it to an integer.

3. Formats the time into a usable string.

4. Gets the current page module, wf:page_module/0.

5. Calls the time_selector_event/1 function on our page.

We do need to change our page to handle the new #time_selector element, however. Our new function is called time_selector_event(Tag, Formatted-Time), so let's add it.

Just need to open up site/src/sweettag.erl in our editor and modify it:

Listing 14.20 (⇒ $) Use #time_selector event (sweettag.erl)

```
site/src/elements$ cd ..
site/src$ vim sweettag.erl

body() ->
  [
    #h1{text="Pick a time during the business day"},
    #time_selector{id tag=time, start=480, finish=1020,
                increment=30},
    #button{text="I've decided", postback=select_time}
  ].
```

534

```
event(select_time) ->
  Time = wf:to_integer(wf:q(time)),
  FormattedTime = element_time_selector:format_time(Time),
  wf:wire(#alert{text=["You picked: ", FormattedTime]}).
time_selector_event(Tag, FormattedTime) ->
  Msg = io_lib:format("You picked: ~s with tag ~p",
                      [FormattedTime, Tag]),
  wf:wire(#alert{text=Msg}).
```

RUSTY: Save the changes and we should be ready to go. When you select a time, it will trigger the time_selector_event/2 event and produce a JavaScript alert.

BOSSMAN: Can you clarify, London? I may have missed something.

LLOYD: tag is a common convention for tracking postbacks for elements that generate their own custom postbacks. Because these elements will likely be using their own internal ids for tracking a value throughout postbacks, we need some way to keep track of the value.

In many cases, there may be only one such field on a page, in which case tag remains mostly unused, though matched against _. However, in plenty of cases, you may have more than one of the same type of event-generating element on a page, in which case `tag` is essential. You can think of `tag` as an alternate field for postback when an element uses its own custom event.

Any other questions?

RUSTY: Outstanding, man. Very helpful. Thank you.

BOSSMAN: Best yet, London.

LLOYD: So, can I have a raise?

15. Nitrogen Plugins

RUSTY: Hey, London— loved your bag lunch gig on custom elements. Can we create our own custom plugins as well?

LLOYD: Piece of cake. Buy me a cold one and we can discuss.

RUSTY: You're on.

15.1. So Now in a Crufty Booth...

...in the back of the dev team's favorite hang out, we find Lloyd London in earnest lecture mode.

LLOYD: In general you want to avoid copy and paste as much as possible. The good news is that you can package up your custom element into a plugin to make it easy to use across multiple applications.

RUSTY: Just to be clear... A plugin is an Erlang application that contains both the record definition and the code of a custom element.

LLOYD: You've got it.

Reformatting custom elements into distributable plugins is actually quite simple.

Let me bring up the #time element. Recall that we modified the following files:

- site/include/records.hrl

- site/src/elements/element_time_selector.erl

To create a plugin, we need to create an application. Let's give it the same name we gave the time element, `element_time_selector`.

Conveniently, Nitrogen provides a `make_plugin` script to initialize a new plugin application from existing code.

From our `custom_elements` application directory, type the following:

Listing 15.1 (⇨ $) **Create `element_time_selector` plugin**

```
custom_elements$ ~/nitrogen/make_plugin site/src/elements/element_time_selector.erl
...
element_time_selector initialized.
Next Step:  copy the element records into element_time_selector/include/records.hrl
```

We need the element record definition from `.../site/include/records.hrl` so we can paste it into our plugin library application.

Let's create the directory and cut the record:

Listing 15.2 (⇨ $) **Create plugin application directory**

```
custom_elements$ vim site/include/records.hrl
-include("plugins.hrl").
-record(time_selector, {?ELEMENT_BASE(element_time_selector),
        start=0, finish=1440, increment=60, value, tag}).
```

Next, paste the definition into `records.hrl` then save:

Listing 15.3 (⇨ $) **Paste record definition into records.hrl**

```
custom_elements$ cd ../element_time_selector
element_time_selector$ vim include/records.hrl

-record(time_selector, {?ELEMENT_BASE(element_time_selector),
        start=0, finish=1440, increment=60, value, tag}).
```

Once this is done, we can review the final structure of our plugin:

Listing 15.4 ($\Rightarrow$ $) **Structure of our plugin**

```
element_time_selector$ tree
    include
        records.hrl
    nitrogen.plugin
    src
        element_time_selector.erl
        element_time_selector.app.src
```

Let's push our new plugin to GitHub so others can use it. If you prefer GitLab or whatever, be my guest:

Listing 15.5 ($\Rightarrow$ $) **Push plugin to GitHub**

```
element_time_selector$ git init
Initialized empty Git repository in /home/user/element_time_selector/.git/
element_time_selector$ git add .
element_time_selector$ git commit -m "Initial Commit"
[master (root-commit) 585a960] Initial Commit
 4 files changed, 159 insertions(+)
 create mode 100644 include/records.hrl
 create mode 100644 nitrogen.plugin
 create mode 100644 src/element_time_selector.erl
 create mode 100644 src/element_time_selector.app.src
element_time_selector$ git remote add origin \
    git@github.com:YourUsername/element_time_selector.git
element_time_selector$ git push origin master
```

RUSTY: Can we try it out?

LLOYD: Why not? We just need to add our new plugin to our app's re-bar.config file and rebuild:

Listing 15.6 (⇒ $) **Add plugin to** `rebar.config`

```
element_time_selector$ cd ../custom_elements
custom_elements$ vim rebar.config
{deps, [
...
   {simple_cache,
      {git, "git://github.com/nitrogen/simple_cache", {branch, master}}},
   {element_time_selector,
      {git, "git://github.com/YourUsername/element_time_selector",
        {branch, master}}},
   ...
]}.
```

LLOYD: You remember how to rebuild, right?

Listing 15.7 (⇒ $) **Compile plugin**

```
custom_elements$ make
```

Now you can test by pointing your browser to http://localhost:8003/ sweettag It should look no different.

With another future project, all you have to do is add your plugin to rebar.config, then simply refer to #element_time_selector{} like any other Nitrogen element.

Related links

- Code for the above element_time_selector plugin:
  https://github.com/choptastic/element_time_selector

- Official plugin documentation:
  http://nitrogenproject.com/doc/plugins.html

- Other plugins:
  `https://github.com/nitrogen/nitrogen/wiki/Nitrogen-Plugins`

- Code for the plugin handling code, which is also an alternative source of plugin documenation
  `http://j.mp/plugincode`

- Jesse's blog post describing the introduction of the plugin system:
  `http://sigma-star.com/blog/post/why-nitrogen-plugins`

- Sample Nitrogen Plugin:
  `https://github.com/nitrogen/sample_nitrogen_plugin`

16. The Wide World is Waiting

Rusty Nail strides into the classroom, frowns, scratches his head, and checks his watch.

The classroom is empty.

Here it is two days before graduation, last chance to say goodbye to his young friends before they scatter off to great things—Marsha to Juilliard, Oleg to MIT, and Stevie to Sweden's Uppsala University where he hopes to meet the greats of the Erlang world.

But his computer club tutees are AWOL. Suddenly...

THREE VOICES: SURPRISE!

Three heads pop up from behind the teacher's desk.

RUSTY: Whoa! Almost gave me a heart attack.

OLEG: Gotcha!

Oleg sets out plastic cups. Stevie starts pouring out Club-Mate.

STEVIE: Won't believe what we went through to get this stuff.

Marsha plops a pizza box on the desk, opens it. Pepperoni with at least six extra toppings.

MARSHA: Get it while it's hot.

RUSTY: Well, I have a surprise for you.

At that, a tall, lanky man dressed in black with black hair pulled back into a pony tail steps into the room followed by two slightly pudgy sidekicks. The bald one is carrying two pizza boxes and the one with shaggy hair is carrying a large cardboard box.

RUSTY: Kids, I'd like you to meet my boss, the guy who got me into this gig in the first place. And these two characters are Erlang programmers extrodinaire—Jesse James and Lloyd London.

LLOYD: Man, we've heard awesome things about you characters.

JESSE: Heard you're amazing.

OLEG: Aw, shucks!

MARSHA: Obi Wan here is the amazing one.

BOSSMAN: I just wanted to thank you guys for the superb notes program you kids programmed to help my wife and daughter. Heard that Rusty promised you each a Raspberry Pi.

Oleg gives Rusty a dirty look.

OLEG: Now that you mention it. . .

BOSSMAN: But we thought these would be much more useful as you head out into the wide world.

And at that, Lloyd London reaches into the cardboard box and pulls out three brand-new gleaming System 76 Galago Pro notebook computers.

RUSTY: Yeah, troopers. It's been real. You've earned 'em.

Part IV.

Appendices

A. Erlang from top down

In our humble opinion, syntax is not Erlang's greatest charm. No, we're not of the "hate Erlang syntax" school. Cast habit and prejudice aside and Erlang syntax offers treasures enough—first-class functions, immutable variables, pattern matching, list comprehensions. Erlang binaries are wicked cool. Truth be told, Erlang syntax is not that difficult to learn.

No, we vote for OTP.

Indeed, OTP is so boffo we won't even let you in on what the acronym OTP stands for—it oh-so-shortchanges the range of applications.[1]

OTP is a collection of libraries and an underlying philosophy that significantly slaps down the pain that accompanies development of highly scalable, reliable, distributed software systems.

Here's a flyover.

Erlang Release

The whole point of the development enterprise is to produce and ship a software product that installs and runs with ease and satisfaction on client hardware.

In Erlang parlance, this is called a release.

Superficially, a release looks like a directory with a bunch of code in it. Compress it, ship it, uncompress it it, start it, and it runs—and runs.

Consider that most Erlang programs coordinate swarms of light-weight processes, all actively processing messages according to grand design.

Bug? (Tell us your software doesn't have bugs.)

Simply do a hot-code update. That is, install a patch without taking the program out of service.

---

[1]OK. We give in: Open Telecom Platform.

Tell us that's not cool! While you're going about surgery, the processes just keep doing their thing without pause.

Stop the whole buzzing crew when you wish with a single command.

Think for a moment and you'll understand why every Erlang release ideally has a version number. Hint: makes hot-code updates possible.

Erlang releases are an artful construction of Erlang applications plus the Erlang VM, e.g., virtual machine. Note that the word *application* is a technical term in Erlang—it means what it means, no more nor less.

```
http://www.erlang.org/doc/design_principles/release_
structure.html
```

Erlang Application

An Erlang application is a set of `*.beam` files plus a `*.app` resource file. You met up with `*.app` files back in Chapter 2, recall? App files contain explicitly structured metadata that tells the outside world what it needs to know to play nice.

You can think of an Erlang application as a more-or-less stand-alone high-level component of an Erlang release. The functionality of an Erlang application is hammered out and lives as a set of Erlang modules.

As you may have surmised in Chapter 2, Erlang applications start life as a collection of `*.erl` source files.

By convention, all elements of an application are organized in the following subdirectories:

- **src**—contains the Erlang source code.

- **ebin**—contains the Erlang object code, the BEAM files. The `.app` file is also placed here.

- **priv**—used for application-specific files. For example, custom scripts, C executables, or specific static resources might be placed here. The function `code:priv_dir/1` should be used to access this directory.

- **include**—used for include (`*.hrl`) files.

Erlang applications can be active or static. Active applications implement, monitor, and control active processes such as servers, state machines, or event handlers. Active applications need to be started and stopped, thus they include a module that defines start and stop procedures. The callback module is usually named, simply, `<application name>.erl`, e.g., `my_awesome_app.erl`.

Active applications also need to be monitored or supervised. You'd hate to have your whole system die sudden death if an active process fails. So here's one of the keys behind Erlang's touted reliability: active Erlang applications include monitor and/or supervisory modules that take appropriate action should a process choke on a bug or bad data. Supervisors usually have a name in the form of `<application name>_sup.erl`, e.g., `my_application_sup.erl`.

Most Erlang systems implement a hierarchical tree of supervisors, where a master supervisor monitors and controls minion supervisors who, in turn, supervise lesser supervisors and workers. Supervisors take appropriate action when processes fail to limit nasty consequences. Phew! Now you know the deep secret of Erlang reliability.

Library applications are composed solely of static functions that do support and grunt work. Since they do not need to be started or stopped, they don't need application callbacks or supervisory support.

```
http:
//www.erlang.org/doc/design_principles/applications.html
http:
//www.erlang.org/doc/design_principles/sup_princ.html
```

Modules

Modules are the building blocks of Erlang. Open any `*.erl` source file and you will see distinctive similarities: comments, a short set of attributes, and a sequence of functions.

By convention, comments take several forms: [2]

```
%%% This is a comment.
```

---

[2]https://docs.2600hz.com/dev/doc/engineering/erlang-documentation/

```
%% As is this.
% And this.
```

Attributes look like this:

```
-Tag(Value).
```

Every Erlang module starts like this:

```
-module(Module).
```

Note that `Tag` is the name of an attribute and `Module` is the name of the module. As you may know by now, the name of an Erlang variable always starts with an uppercase letter or an underscore (_).

The module attribute could follow any number of comments in the file but must come before other attributes and functions.

Dig into Erlang docs to discover other important attributes; in particular, note `-export(...)`, `-compile(...)`, and `-behaviour(...)`. [3]

Functions

Functions execute sequential logic and spawn active processes. They're the worker-bees of Erlang. Functions take zero or more parameters; the number of parameters designates the function's arity.

In code, a function looks like this:

```
<function_name>(<param1>, <param2>) -> <function body>.
```

There's that period at the end again. It's important. In documentation, the function above would be written `<function_name>/2`.

Note that `my_function/0` is totally distinct from `my_function/1` which, in turn, is totally distinct from `my_function/2`.[4]

---

[3] http://www.erlang.org/doc/reference_manual/modules.html
[4] http://www.erlang.org/doc/reference_manual/functions.html

BIFs

Erlang comes complete with a set of built-in functions called BIFs. BIFs save considerable effort. Fact is, you couldn't even write most of these in Erlang if you tried.[5]

Data Types

Erlang supports a rich set of data types including, as you'd expect, integers and floats. Named constants are called atoms. Maps, tuples, and lists make it possible to process related data items in powerful ways including construction of yet more sophisticated data structures.

Useful aside: whenever you see the word *term* in Erlang documentation, the author is most likely talking about an item of data.[6]

String Building and IOLists

IOLists are Erlang's unique way of efficiently building strings. An IOList is a list of any combination of binaries, "word-sized" integers (0-255) and, recursively, other IOLists. Erlang does fantastic things in the name of optimization with large binaries.

In other languages, when you append elements to a string, you have to copy string1 and string2 and combine them producing string3. Or you're resizing string1 to accommodate the additional bytes in string2. In Erlang, you should rarely do normal string concatenation with the ++ operator. The ++ copies the data you wish to append and traverses the list on the left side of the ++ operator, a potential perfomance hit.

Instead, you'll want to use IOLists, which, so far as we know, are unique to Erlang.

Say you have:

```
A = <<"Hello ">>.
```

---

[5]http://www.erlang.org/doc/man/erlang.html
[6]http://www.erlang.org/doc/reference_manual/data_types.html

```
B = "World".
```

And you want to send the message "Hello World" over the wire or save it to a file.

If you try this in an Erlang shell:

```
Msg = A ++ B.
```

... you're courting an exception. We'll let you puzzle out why.

Try this instead:

```
Msg = [A, B]. [<<"Hello ">>,"World "]
```

OK. Returns a list... not exactly what we want. But, let's simulate sending `Msg` over the wire:

```
io:format(Msg).
Hello World ok
```

Bingo!

When IOLists such as `Msg` get sent to a database, a file, over the network, or to the browser, Erlang sequentially and recursively reads through the list and transmits the bytes it finds, essentially dropping whatever recursive structure they were in. The IOList ends up being transmitted as a byte string, in our case, "Hello World".

The Erlang Shell

We could write a whole booklet on the Erlang shell. It enables you to enter and execute Erlang code interactively, and it's a damned useful—if not essential— tool for Erlang and Nitrogen development.[7]

Fire it up. Experiment:

---

[7]http://erlang.org/doc/man/erl.html

```
my_directory$ erl

Erlang/OTP 22 [erts-10.4] [source] [64-bit] [smp:4:4] [ds:4:4:10] [async-
    threads:1] [hipe]

Eshell V10.4  (abort with ^G)
1> 1 + 1.
2
2> 1 + 1
2>
```

The line that starts with "1>" is your cue to start typing.

Note that line 2> did not return a result. Now why would that be? Hint: Look at line 1>.

Important: Spend time learning how to exit the Erlang shell. Hint: There's more than one way and each has its advantages.[8]

And Much, Much More

```
http://www.erlang.org/doc/man/ets.html
http://www.erlang.org/doc/man/dets.html
http://www.erlang.org/doc/man/mnesia.html
http://erlang.org/doc/apps/stdlib/
http://www.erlang.org/faq/libraries.html
```

---

[8]http://www.erlang.org/doc/man/shell.html
   http://erlang.org/doc/man/erl.html

B. Erlang Resources

Most definitely start here: http://www.erlang.org/

Bedside Reading:

- *The bible:* Armstrong, Joe. *Programming Erlang: Software for a Concurrent World, 2nd Ed.,* Pragmatic, 2013

- *Gentle introduction:* St. Laurent, Simon. *Introducing Erlang,* O'Reilly, 2013

- *Fun and instructive:* Hebert, Fred. *Learn You Some Erlang for Great Good!: A Beginner's Guide,* Pragmatic, 2013

- *Rigorous:* Cesarini, Francesco, and Simon Thompson. *Erlang Programming,* O'Reilly Media, 2009

- *OTP Emphasis:* Logan, Martin; Eric Merritt; and Richard Carlsson. *Erlang and OTP in Action,* Manning Publications, 2010

- *Advanced ninja-mode:* Hebert, Fred. *Stuff Goes Bad: Erlang in Anger,* Heroku eBook (erlang-in-anger.com), 2014

Websites

- Erlang tutorial: https://www.tutorialspoint.com/erlang/index.htm

- Download Erlang packages: https://www.erlang-solutions.com/resources/download.html

- Erlang online resources: https://gist.github.com/macintux/6349828

B. Erlang Resources

- Conferences and consulting: `https://www.erlang-solutions.com/`

- As always, Google is your friend: `https://erlangcentral.org/`

- Mailing lists: `http://www.erlang.org/static/doc/mailinglist.html`

C. Just Enough Git

Computer programming is a creative art. Programmers transform imagination and vision into tools, entertainment, and toys that augment and expand human mind and muscle.

But seldom does the programmer get it right in one pass. Typos, syntax errors, faulty logic, blind alleys, and garden paths are inevitable. Requirements evolve and technology advances.

For these reasons and others, version control is an essential programming tool. With version control, a programmer far down a garden path can easily morph back to an earlier known-correct state of development.

Git is a distributed version control system built by Linus Torvalds to handle the thousands of concurrent GNU Linux kernel hackers. Since then, and with the rise of github.com, Git has become the go-to choice of open source developers throughout the world.

Git can be intimidating to one new to version control. Here we distill Git down to the "need to know" basics for Nitrogen developers.

If you're a veteran Git user and have had to resolve merge conflicts, feel free to skip this Appendix.

Gittin' Started

Git is a command-line program. It maintains trees of commits, e.g., changes, in files called Git repositories. Each project has a master repository. Repositories can be cloned and updated separately, and merged back into the master repository. This eanbles development teams to work unhindered on different branches of the master program.

C. Just Enough Git

Here we'll hit the basics, but by all means review the Git Reference Manual.[1] You can also find many fine tutorials on the web.

Initialize a Repository

First thing, let's create a repository:

> **Listing C.1** ($\Rightarrow$ $) **Initialize a repository**

```
$ mkdir my_project
$ cd my_project
$ git init
Initialized empty Git repository in /home/gumm/
     my_project/.git/
```

Every Git project starts this way.

Your First Commit

The next step is to create files and add them to the repository:

> **Listing C.2** **Add files to the repository**

```
$ touch a
$ touch b
$ ls
a  b
$ git add a b
$ git status
On branch master
Initial commit
Changes to be committed:
    (use "git rm --cached <file>...  " to unstage)
        new file:    a
        new file:    b
```

---

[1]https://git-scm.com/doc

So, we've created files a and b, added them to our Git index, and run Git status to show us the state of our repository. Git's index is a temporary location for changes you plan to commit. In our case, we've added files a and b to the index, but we haven't yet committed them. Changes added to the index are said to be staged. Note that Git hints at this by letting us know how we can unstage our files:

(use "git rm --cached <file>..." to unstage)

So let's commit them:

Listing C.3 Commit files

```
$ git commit

*** Please tell me who you are.
Run
  git config --global user.email "you@example.com"
  git config --global user.name "Your Name"

to set your account's default identity.
Omit --global to set the identity only in this
      repository.
fatal: unable to auto-detect email address
      (got 'gumm@my-laptop.(none)')
```

What the heck? Ah, Git doesn't know who we are. Every commit must be attributed to someone. Let's fix that:

NOTE: Replace user.mail and user.name with your own credentials.

Listing C.4 Define account identity

```
$ git config --global user.email "gumm@sigma-star.com"
$ git config --global user.name "Jesse Gumm"
```

OK. Git now knows who we are. Let's try that commit again:

Listing C.5 Commit—second attempt

```
$ git commit -m "Initial Commit"
[master (root-commit) 9731d0e] Initial Commit
 2 files changed, 0 insertions(+), 0 deletions(-)
 create mode 100644 a
 create mode 100644 b
```

Sweet! Our first commit.

---

git commit vs git commit -m

Git provides a choice as to how you attach messages to your commits.
For brevity, we'll stick with git commit -m "Some message."
If you type git commit without the -m, git commit will bring up your
text editor and let you type an extended message to attach to the commit.
It might look something like this:

```
This is the commit message

This is the extended message, it contains extra information and allows
you to describe the purpose of this commit in greater detail.

# Please enter the commit message for your changes. Lines starting
# with '#' will be ignored, and an empty message aborts the commit.
# On branch master
# Your branch is up-to-date with 'origin/master'.
#
# Changes to be committed:
#       new file:    blah
#
```

The first line is the commit. The second is blank, and the third and
fourth lines are the extended message.
Lines starting with # are comments.

Change History and Git Commit Identifiers

Let's check our commit history:

```
$ git log
commit 9731d0edf87d6c6fca5e3aa924ab3bba84dd0805
Author: Jesse Gumm <gumm@sigma-star.com>
Date:   Sat Jun 7 18:19:56 2014 -0500
    Initial Commit
```

As we'd hoped, our commit shows up.

But, wait! What is that   9731d0edf87d6c6fca5e3aa924ab3bba84dd0805 string telling us?

That eye-crossing string uniquely identifies a Git commit. Indeed, it's an SHA hash of the contents of the commit, kind of a fingerprint. Note that the first seven characters are the same as in the string that popped up when we submitted the git commit command.

We can refer to commits by that string. For instance, to see the details of our last commit, we could enter:

```
$ git show 9731d0edf87d6c6fca5e3aa924ab3bba84dd0805
commit 9731d0edf87d6c6fca5e3aa924ab3bba84dd0805
Author: Jesse Gumm <gumm@sigma-star.com> Date:
        Sat Jun 7 18:19:56 2014 -0500
    Initial Commit
diff --git a/a b/a
new file mode 100644
index 0000000..e69de29
diff --git a/b b/b
new file mode 100644
index 0000000..e69de29
```

Hmmm... We see "new file" twice. More later.

It's worth noting that you do not need to refer to the commit by its whole hash string. You can refer to it by the first few unambiguous characters. Usually the first five to seven characters are plenty. For instance, the following will return the same result as the previous, longer, command:

Listing C.8   See commit details via partial SHA hash

```
$ git show 9731d0
```

There is a special commit called HEAD. HEAD is a "moving commit." Whenever you add a new commit, HEAD advances to point to this latest commit.

Try it:

Listing C.9   Show HEAD

```
$ git show HEAD
```

Here's a useful trick. If our repository has more than one commit, we can refer to them in relation to HEAD or any other specified commit:

Listing C.10   Show commits relative to HEAD

```
$ git show HEAD~1  # show commit before HEAD
$ git show 9731d0~1 # show commit before 9731d0
$ git show 973d0^1 # show commit after 9731d0
```

Commit More Changes

Let's add actual data to our files. Fire up vim and edit the file called a. Add and save the following text:

Listing C.11 Edit file a

```
$ vim a
This is my file.
It contains some lines.
Of text.
That last line was not a complete sentence.
```

Git has a concept called working directory. Let's look into it:

Listing C.12 Examine working directory

```
$ git status
On branch master
Changes to be committed:
  (use "git reset HEAD <file>...  " to unstage)
modified:   a
Untracked files:
  (use "git add <file>...  " to include in what
      will be committed)
a~
```

Git sees that the file a has changed, but it also sees a file called a~. When you save a vim file, vim saves a backup with ~ appended to the filename. We'll get back to this, but let's commit the changes we care about:

Listing C.13 Commit changes to file a

```
$ git add a
$ git commit -m "Add some content to a"
[master ba7c349] Add some content to a
 1 file changed, 4 insertions(+)
$ git status
On branch master
Untracked files:
  (use "git add <file>...  " to include in what will
      be committed)
```

```
a~
nothing added to commit but untracked files present
     (use "git add" to track)
```

Good. But again, we have this "Untracked file" a~. This is rather annoying.

Ignoring Files We Don't Care About

Any given project will have numerous files we'd rather not track— files left over by our editor log files or created by our application.

To deal with this, Git looks into a file called .gitignore. gitignore lists files and file patterns that we want Git to ignore.

Let's create a simple .gitignore file:

Listing C.14 (⇒ vim) Ignore unnecessary files

```
$ vim .gitignore
*~
```

Save it. Now let's add .gitignore to our repo and save:

Listing C.15 (⇒ $) Add .gitignore to repository

```
$ git add .gitignore
$ git commit -m "Add .gitignore"
[master f7f5b24] Add .gitignore
 1 file changed, 1 insertion(+)
 create mode 100644 .gitignore
$ git status
On branch master
nothing to commit, working directory clean
```

 Perfect! No more pesky a~ file messing with our heads. We can also rest assured that any file ending with ~ will be dutifully ignored by Git from here on.

This is especially convenient if you add an entire directory to a repository. For instance, executing the command git add . without a .gitignore file will add every file Git encounters in the whole working directory. This may seem benign. After all, the ~ files are just backup files, who cares if they're in the repo? But this will cause problems when merging branches.

Branches

Imagine you're working on the master repository of your project and you come up with an idea you'd like to try. Git enables you to branch off commits so you don't mess up your stable master.[2]

Let's create a branch called dev:

Listing C.16   Create a branch repository

```
$ git checkout -b dev
Switched to a new branch 'dev'
```

You can now commit to dev.

You can create more banches by giving each branch a unique name. Here's how you can see all the branches you've created:

Listing C.17   List all branches

```
$ git branch -a
```

Merge Branches

If you work with other version control systems, the term checkout may be confusing. In other systems, checkout typically means to place a lock on something, preventing others from making changes.

---

[2]https://github.com/Kunena/Kunena-Forum/wiki/Create-a-new-branch-with-git-and-manage-branches

In Git, checkout merely means change the working directory to a branch. There is no locking of files in Git. Specifying the -b option with checkout creates a new branch from the current commit.

Awesome! We have a new branch. Let's make changes to file a while we're in branch b. Open up the a file and add a line:

Listing C.18 (⇒ `vim`) **Edit file a once again**

```
$ vim a
This is my file.
It contain some lines.
Of text.
That last line was not a complete sentence.
This is a new line, it fears no man.
```

Excellent. Now we save and commit:

Listing C.19 (⇒ `$`) **Commit revised file a**

```
$ git add a
$ git commit -m "Add a line that fears no man"
[dev f80773f] Add a line that fears no man
  1 file changed, 1 insertion(+)
```

Fantastic! We've added a new feature to our project. As you can see, the commit specifies that we did indeed commit to the dev branch.

Let's add a few more lines to a and then switch back to the master branch:

Listing C.20 **Add lines to file a and switch to master branch**

```
$ cat a
This is my file.
It contains some lines.
Of text.
That last line was not a complete sentence.
This is a new line, it fears no man.
$ git checkout master
```

```
Switched to branch 'master'
$ cat a
This is my file.
It contains some lines.
Of text.
That last line was not a complete sentence.
```

As you can see, all lines added to file a in dev are isolated from master.

What do you suppose happened to all lines added to file a in dev after the commit? Check it out. Hint: You won't find them.

Now let's fix a bug in file a in master:

Listing C.21 ($\Rightarrow$ `vim`) **Revise file a in master repository**

```
$ vim a
This is my file.
It containss some lines of text.
Of text.
That last line was indeed a complete sentence.
```

Save it. Now let's commit the changes:

Listing C.22 ($\Rightarrow$ `$`) **Commit revisions to file a**

```
$ git add a
$ git commit -m "Fix some typos"
[master 650b90e] Fix some typos
 1 file changed, 2 insertions(+), 3 deletions(-)
```

Great. We've determined that changes to dev are stable, so let's merge dev into master:

Listing C.23   Merge dev into master file a

```
$ git merge dev
Auto-merging a
CONFLICT (content): Merge conflict in a
Automatic merge failed; fix conflicts and then commit the result.
```

Uh oh. Conflicts! Let's explore why:

Listing C.24   Explore conflicts

```
$ cat a
This is my file.
<<<<<<< HEAD
It contains some lines of text.
That last line was indeed a complete sentence.
=======
It contain some lines.
Of text.
That last line was not a complete sentence.
This is a new line, it fears no man.
>>>>>>> dev
```

Git was unable to resolve differences in the files. So auto-merge helpfully injected these >>>>>>, ======, and <<<<<< lines to help us know which branches each change is from. We have to remove these lines manually before we can complete the merge.

Here we strike out the lines that we need to remove:

Listing C.25   (⇒ vim) Manually remove lines destined for removal

```
$ vim a
This is my file.
<<<<<<< HEAD
It contains some lines of text.
That last line was indeed a complete sentence.
=======
It contain some lines.
```

```
Of text.
That last line was not a complete sentence.
This is a new line. It fears no man.
>>>>>>> dev
```

The new file will look like this:

```
This is my file.
It contains some lines of text.
That last line was indeed a complete sentence.
This is a new line. It fears no man.
```

We mustn't forget to save and commit the changes:

```
$ git add a
$ git commit -m "Merged text changes"
[master af8eeda] Merge branch 'dev'
```

Awesome. You've now done 95 percent of what you'll ever need to do with Git. As homework you'll never regret, look into and master remote repositories such as GitHub and GitLab.

```
https://github.com/
https://about.gitlab.com/
```

Working with Remote Repositories

We say that Git is a *distributed* version control system. What does that mean?

Non-distributed version control systems depend on a central repository. Git does not. While it's quite common for projects to have a central repository,[3] the distributed nature of Git means that anyone with access can clone the central repository and have a complete local copy.

---

[3]Here's Nitrogen's: https://github.com/nitrogen

GitHub

GitHub is a popular web service for maintaining master repositories.[4]

Let's give a whirl: Create an account on github.com, then click the + icon next to your username. Now click New Repository:

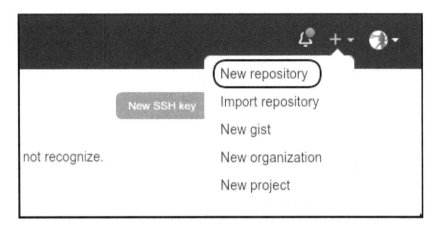

Give your repo a name and click Create Repository:

---

[4]https://github.com/

So that's it! You now have a remote repo. Before you push your work, however, you need to configure permissions. That is, you need to tell GitHub how to validate that you are you when you attempt to push changes to your master.

SSH provides a secure way to push changes.[5] But you need to generate SSH Keys and copy your private key to GitHub:

Listing C.27 Generate SSH keys

```
$ ssh-keygen -t rsa
Generating public/private rsa key pair.
...
```

Now, on GitHub, click the configuration icon on the menu bar, then click SSH Keys on the left-hand menu, and finally click Add SSH Key:

---

[5]https://www.ssh.com/ssh/

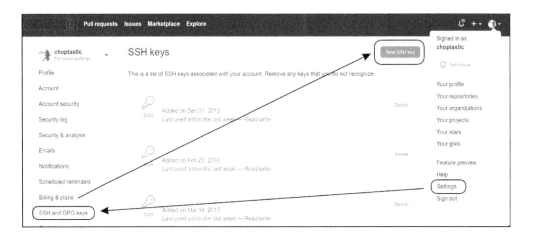

Give your key a descriptive name, like My Laptop, copy the contents of your public key file[6] into the Key field, and click Add Key:

Add an SSH Key

Title

My Laptop

Key

```
ssh-rsa
AAAAB3NzaC1yc2EadjfkjsDAHADHsfgjADFAg456454j1DwskGy9CLFcIfUewzSFhFq1fjSiBxFdw/V2h59Yq714H8SB
M0Pf0BDJueSDqAYK0A9zyteLMw0WhrV7m84erxh+6bA44uDGGqocICM86dFs2UdAgC0UzoJS2e0XVBF8Cs1sgEX
QaOiOXyTfemqTKh4xI8AUmSRIRYjwmaNqSMLtty3iQ6AGfjqIDF2/3JaKQI3OsB6VCfi0jAYOW/a2kjuTEJI231XHo1j0
7W6TWUwwL4XgUOH15FHgXfPVhYiV15UR7gqIPOYozQ1W+u0aJ8LaTTAH7uzmPzzErTk07EZIkvnoPIZJkc7CQx
SXIpy+5heP gumm@laptop
```

Add key

---

[6]By default, that file is ~/.ssh/id_rsa.pub

Pushing to and Pulling from Our Remote Repository

Now your account is set up to push to your GitHub repository:

Listing C.28   Add remote repository and push local commits

```
$ git remote add origin git@github.com:choptastic/my_project.git
$ git push origin master
Counting objects: 18, done.
Delta compression using up to 4 threads.
Compressing objects: 100% (16/16), done.
Writing objects: 100% (18/18), 1.68 KiB | 0 bytes/s,
     done.
Total 18 (delta 3), reused 0 (delta 0)
To git@github.com:choptastic/my_project.git
 * [new branch]  master -> master
```

The term origin is the default name we gave to our GitHub repo. You can connect to more than one repository so you need to keep them straight.

Not only can you push changes from your local repository to a remote repository, but you can also pull changes from that repository:

Listing C.29   Pull changes from remote repository

```
$ git pull origin master
From github.com:choptastic/my_project
 * branch          master    -> FETCH_HEAD
Already up-to-date.
```

In this case you are downloading from a remote repository and merging into a local repository. As with local merges, this can cause merge conflicts.

Forking and Cloning

Let's say there's an open source project to which you'd like to contribute.[7] You want to work on the project without pushing your changes to the official repo. In this case, you can fork the remote repository.

Let's fork Nitrogen. Note that the main Nitrogen repository is a shell that brings together a handful of Erlang applications that, in turn, become a Nitrogen deployment. The meat of Nitrogen is actually found in the nitrogen_core repository. Let's fork that.

Point your browser to:

https://github.com/nitrogen/nitrogen_core

...and click the Fork button:

You should now have a fork of the nitrogen_core repo in your account. And you'll have full push access.

Author Jesse Gumm's GitHub username is choptastic. Let's clone his newly forked nitrogen_core repository:

Listing C.30 Clone Jesse Gumm's nitrogen_core repository

```
$ git clone git@github.com:choptastic/nitrogen_core.git
```

Pull Requests

Say we've found a bug in Nitrogen and want to fix it. We've found that the #panel{} element is lacking a type signature. Let's fix it.

---

[7]You're welcome to contribute to Nitrogen, by the way.

As good Open Source practioners, we create a `topic` branch, which is just a fancy way to say we're creating a branch to fix a bug or add a feature:

Listing C.31   Create topic branch

```
$ cd nitrogen_core
$ git checkout -b panel_type_specs
Switched to a new branch 'panel_type_specs'
```

That sets up our topic branch. Fire up your editor and edit the source code for the #panel{} element.

Here's what it currently looks like:

Listing C.32   Review #panel{} element

```
$ vim src/elements/layout/element_panel.erl
-module (element_panel).
-include_lib ("wf.hrl").
-compile(export_all).
reflect() -> record_info(fields, panel).
render_element(Record) ->
    Body = [
        wf:html_encode(Record#panel.text,
            Record#panel.html_encode),
        Record#panel.body
    ],
    wf_tags:emit_tag('div', Body, [
        {id, Record#panel.html_id},
        {class, Record#panel.class},
        {title, Record#panel.title},
        {style, Record#panel.style},
        {data_fields, Record#panel.data_fields}
    ]).
```

Make the changes shown here in bold:

```erlang
-module (element_panel).
-include("wf.hrl").
-export([
    reflect/0,
    render_element/1
]).
-spec reflect() -> [atom()].
reflect() -> record_info(fields, panel).
-spec render_element(#panel{}) -> body().
render_element(Record) ->
    Body = [
        wf:html_encode(Record#panel.text,
            Record#panel.html_encode),
        Record#panel.body
    ],
    wf_tags:emit_tag('div', Body, [
        {id, Record#panel.html_id},
        {class, Record#panel.class},
        {title, Record#panel.title},
        {style, Record#panel.style},
        {data_fields, Record#panel.data_fields}
    ]).
```

We've changed -compile(export_all) to -export(...).

When writing APIs and deploying production code you always want to use explict exports.

We've also added Erlang type specs, which not only help documentation by showing what a function is supposed to accept and return but also help with debugging when you use the powerful Dialyzer tool. Dialyzer analyzes every call in the system to find type inconsistencies before they reach runtime.

Don't worry too much about what this all means. The point here is to demonstrate pull requests.

Save changes and commit:

Listing C.34 Save changes and commit

```
$ git commit -m "Add typespecs to #panel{}"
[panel_type_specs 7adc730] Add typespecs to #panel{}
 1 file changed, 9 insertions(+), 3 deletions(-)
```

Now push topic branch to GitHub:

Listing C.35 Push topic branch to GitHub

```
$ git push origin panel_type_specs
Counting objects: 36, done.
Delta compression using up to 4 threads.
Compressing objects: 100% (6/6), done.
Writing objects: 100% (6/6), 660 bytes | 0 bytes/s,

    done.
Total 6 (delta 5), reused 0 (delta 0)
To git@github.com:choptastic/nitrogen_core.git
 * [new branch]      panel_type_specs -> panel_type_specs
```

Let's check the result. Point your browser to:
github.com/nitrogen/nitrogen_core

...and click on the Insights tab on the top, then the Network tab when that opens:

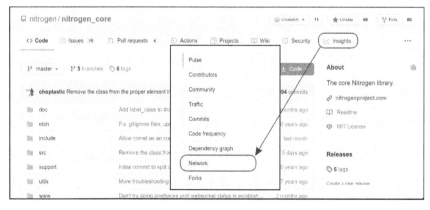

This should open up a view of all the commits and branches by all users who've forked our project and pushed their changes up to GitHub.

Network view is a very handy GitHub feature.

Here we see our branch. By hovering over it we can see how commits branch and merge with master:

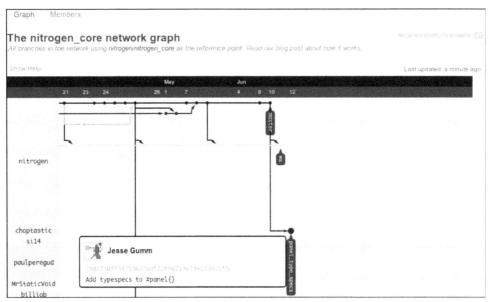

Let's issue a pull request. Click back to the Code screen, that is, the default page for the repo. Note the big blue nitrogen_core link at the top of the screen. Click on this.

Now you should see a highlighted row showing our topic branch, that is, choptastic:panel_type_specs. Click the "Compare & pull request" button:

This will bring you to a pull request page to review and initate the pull request. Fill out the pull request with as much detail as you feel is necessary. Typically, if this pull solves an open Github issue, or relates to conversation from the mailing list, it's good form to provide a link to the relevant conversation. Otherwise, explain your changes in detail. If you change an API, it's good citizenship to modify the documentation accordingly. Every project is different in this regard. Read the project CONTRIB file. Most large projects have one:

If you want to review your pull request before submitting it, scroll down the page and you'll see a `diff` of all the changes. It will look like this:

```
-module (element_panel).
--include_lib ("wf.hrl").
--compile(export_all).
+-include("wf.hrl").
+-export([
+    reflect/0,
+    render_element/1
+]).

+-spec reflect() -> [atom()].
 reflect() -> record_info(fields, panel).

+-spec render_element(Record :: #panel{}) -> body().
 render_element(Record) ->
     Body = [
         wf:html_encode(Record#panel.text, Record#panel.html_encode),
```

When you feel confident that your changes are the very best you can do, click the Create pull request button:

There you have it. You have just submitted your first pull request! If a change is simple enough, the owner will likely just merge the changes.

As a user, you'll receive an email regarding any action related to a pull request, whether comments or the owner closing, re-opening, or merging your pull request.

If you are a repository owner or have owner permission, you'll be able to act on pull requests either by closing or merging them. If the pull request can be merged by Git without conflict, you'll see a friendly green button:

If the pull request can't be cleanly merged, you'll get this message:

There are two options for completing the merge. Clicking the "use the command line" link will give you instructions on manually completing the merge.

Clicking the "Merge pull request" box is the simpler route when available. The second is to use the command line. Let's use the command line to merge our changes highlighted here in boldface:

Listing C.36   Merge changes

```
$ git checkout -b choptastic-panel_type_specs master
Switched to a new branch 'choptastic-panel_type_specs'
$ git pull git://github.com/choptastic/nitrogen_core.git panel_type_specs


remote: Counting objects: 6, done.
remote: Compressing objects: 100% (6/6), done.
remote: Total 6 (delta 0), reused 0 (delta 0)
Unpacking objects: 100% (6/6), done.
From git://github.com/choptastic/nitrogen_core
 * branch            panel_type_specs -> FETCH_HEAD
Updating 09f4301..7adc730
Fast-forward
 src/elements/layout/element_panel.erl | 12 +++++++++---
 1 file changed, 9 insertions(+), 3 deletions(-)
```

Now you need to merge those changes into `master` and push those changes off to GitHub:

Listing C.37 Push Changes to GitHub

```
$ git checkout master
Switched to branch 'master'
Your branch is up-to-date with 'origin/master'.
$ git merge choptastic-panel_type_specs
Updating 09f4301..7adc730
Fast-forward
 src/elements/layout/element_panel.erl | 12 ++++++++++---
 1 file changed, 9 insertions(+), 3 deletions(-)
$ git push origin master
```

Congratulations. You've merged your first pull request!

Eleven Git Recommendations

1. Keep commit titles short. Most projects say to keep the commit title shorter than 50 characters.

2. Keep extended commit messages under 80 characters per line. You can make your extended messages as long as necessary, but some stricter open source authors will reject commits on this basis alone. As always, read the `CONTRIB` doc for your project.

3. Keep the indentation and code style consistent with the original project. If the project uses spaces instead of tabs, make sure you're doing the same. A project maintainer will be annoyed at having to fix indentation when it's something that can be easily done by the pull request author.

4. If you accidentally commit something and realize there was a mistake in the commit message, you can modify that commit with `git commit --amend`.

5. If you need to pull a single commit from somewhere else without doing a full merge, use `git cherry-pick X` where X is the commit hash. If it's

from a remote repo, use git `fetch git://url/to/repo.git` first, then
git `cherry-pick X`.

6. Before merging potentially broken commits into master, squash them into a single working commit. You can do this with git `rebase -i X`, where X is the commit to start with. Rebasing can be relatively complex. You'll find several excellent guides online. Search for git `rebase guide`.

7. Make your git life easier with tig,[8] an ncurses-based interface for git.

8. Accidentally add a file to the index and don't actually want to commit it? Unstage that beast with git `reset HEAD <filename>`. Or use tig `status`, and press the u key (you did install tig after our recommendation, right?).

9. You can always edit your repository's configuration in the root of your project in `.git/config`. Incidentally, this `.git` directory is where the whole repository structure is kept. Feel free to spelunk.

10. If you use vim and would like to take advantage of git in the editor, Fugitive[9] is your friend.

11. Say your current commit doesn't work, but a past commit did. But you don't know which commit came first. In this case, use git `bisect`.[10] git `bisect` will do a binary search of commits and let you test each one until you discover which commit caused the bug. It's extraorinarily powerful.

---

[8]https://github.com/jonas/tig

[9]https://github.com/tpope/vim-fugitive

[10]A simple guide for git `bisect`: http://www.metaltoad.com/blog/beginners-guide-git-bisect-process-elimination

Acknowledgements

Profound thanks to Kathyrn Hargraves, Dangerous Curves, and Amy Hedrickson, TeXnology Inc., for unraveling deep mysteries of LaTeX.

And special thanks to Laurie Beckelman for ferreting out typos and clumsy construction. Any such remaining in the text are no fault of her own.

Finally, for bug reports and suggestions, thanks to: Fred Hebert, Alex Popov Jr., John Hitz, Daniel Garcia, Scott Finnie, Franklin Brauning, and @ingwinlu (on GitHub).

About the authors

Lloyd R. Prentice

Lloyd's first computer had an S-100 bus and 8K of RAM. He has designed and developed more than 100 educational and consumer software products for major publishers. Web experience includes a soup-to-nuts application to support marketing and management of world-class technical conferences. It was six months in the making and ten years under nonstop revision and unrelenting deadlines. "You haven't lived," he says, "until several hundred conference attendees—mandarins of IT—log into your URL at the same time and bring down your server." Jesse has patiently taught him much that he wishes he'd known at the time.

Lloyd is a novelist and small-press publisher. His novels include *Freein' Pancho*, *The Gospel of Ashes*, and the *AyaTakeo* manga trilogy.

Jesse Gumm

Jesse wrote his first program in QBASIC for DOS: a two-player, text-based fighting game. He's now an entrepreneur specializing in web application development. His most recent endeavor, BracketPal.com, a beach volleyball league and tournament management system (written in Nitrogen, of course), was recently acquired by SportsEngine, Inc. where he now works full-time. In open source, he's the project leader of Nitrogen and its core dependency SimpleBridge, and he has (or had) a hand in a number of other Erlang projects: qdate (date and timezone management), sync (automatic compilation), and ChicagoBoss (MVC web framework). With Lloyd's help, he's learning how to write technical content that won't put the reader to sleep. Also, if you're ever in the Milwaukee, Wisconsin area and looking for a beach volleyball partner, he's your guy.

Index

www.ingramcontent.com/pod-product-compliance
Lightning Source LLC
Chambersburg PA
CBHW080546060326
40689CB00021B/4764